mative structures are to be held responsible to injury, and a self-conscious exploratory practice is needed to
minimize the risks of arbitrary clo-
sures. For those who wish to get beyond
sloganeering in the world of education,
humane learning, and the social and
historical sciences, this book is a must.

About the Author

Abraham Edel, a distinguished American moral and social philosopher, is
research professor of philosophy at the
University of Pennsylvania. He is au-
thor of numerous books and articles,
which include: *The Theory and Practice of Philosophy*; *Ethical Judgment*;
Science and the Structure of Ethics;
Method in Ethical Theory; and *Aristotle and His Philosophy*. Transaction
has published four volumes of his work
and a festschrift in his honor.

RELATING HUMANITIES
AND SOCIAL THOUGHT

Science, Ideology, and Value Series
Abraham Edel

Analyzing Concepts in Social Science, Volume 1

Exploring Fact and Value, Volume 2

Interpreting Education, Volume 3

RELATING HUMANITIES AND SOCIAL THOUGHT

SCIENCE, IDEOLOGY, AND VALUE
VOLUME 4

ABRAHAM EDEL

Transaction Publishers
New Brunswick (U.S.A.) and London (U.K.)

10863

Copyright © 1990 by Transaction Publishers, New Brunswick,
New Jersey 08903

Library of Congress Catalog Number: 89-20351
ISBN: 0-88738-321-1
Printed in the United States of America

Library of Congress Cataloging-in-Publication Data
Edel, Abraham, 1908-
    Relating humanities and social thought / Abraham Edel.
        p.   cm.—(Science, ideology, and value ; v. 4)
    ISBN 0-88738-321-1
    1. Interdisciplinary approach to knowledge. 2. Humanities.
3. Social sciences. 4. Ethics. I. Title. II. Series: Edel,
Abraham, 1908- Science, ideology, and value ; v. 4.
H33.E3   vol. 4
300′.1 s—dc20
[001]   89-20351
                                                               CIP

Contents

Preface

The idea of a set of papers in different fields of the humanities converging on the serious general issue of the relation of disciplines grew over a long period under a variety of stimuli. Primary, of course, and always evident, was the segregation of science and the humanities in our culture. This was intensified when for a time I taught in a program of humanities for engineering students, and realized how deeply the separation had been institutionalized in education, in the attitudes of both students and many teachers. Teaching philosophy in this century was an especially good vantage point for the study of relations: in the 1930s there were very few "philosophy of . . ." courses, but by now we find everything from philosophy of law, of science, of biology, of history, of social science, of literature, to relations of philosophy and psychiatry, and philosophy and education. Meanwhile, philosophical associations dealing with many of these concerns have proliferated.

Even so, I have been impressed by the strength of an isolationist tendency in many of the sciences and humanities, the tendency to find strict theoretical borders to differentiate one's discipline from all others. This goes beyond the practical factors within the university that operate to preserve departmental separateness and autonomy as a condition for survival. The phenomena of boundaries and connections in intellectual disciplines well deserve careful study. Indeed, even in the "philosophy of . . ." inquiries, the task is often seen as simply clarifying basic ideas in those fields with philosophical refinement, and not also seeing how the knowledge gained in those fields may contribute to answering philosophical questions. The dimensions of connection in disciplines still require interdisciplinary study. This need not, however, entail a fresh general science of connections, nor a general social psychology of intellectual habits. Perhaps more fruitful at present is the careful analysis of specific cases.

A further stimulus came more recently from discussions at the University of Pennsylvania, where interdepartmental inquiries arise with a spontaneity unusual in the academy. Sociologist Ivar Berg and political scientist Henry Teune initiated an effort by a group of social scientists to reassess their disciplines. This lively interchange, involving disciplinary self–description and self–criticism over several years, was followed by a variety of more formal faculty seminars, under sponsorship of the Mellon Foundation, in which topics requiring a many–pronged approach were dealt with by groups from different departments. I am grateful for the stimulus these discussions provided.

Acknowledgments

"Theory and Practice, an Unsteady Dichotomy?" was originally published in *Philosophy, History and Social Action*, Essays in Honor of Lewis Feuer, ed. Sidney Hook, William L. O'Neill, and Roger O'Toole. Boston Studies in the Philosophy of Science, vol. 107. (Dordrecht: Kluwer Academic Publishers, 1988), 157–72. © 1988 Kluwer Academic Publishers.

"Is the Individual-Social a Misleading Dichotomy?" was originally published in *Contemporary Conceptions of Social Philosophy*, ed. S. Panou, G. Bozonis, D. Georgas, P. Trappe. (Stuttgart: Franz Steiner Verlag, 1988), 29–34.

"Elitism and Culture," written in collaboration with Elizabeth Flower, is reprinted with her kind permission. It was originally published in *The Humanist as Citizen*, ed. John Agresto and Peter Riesenberg. (National Humanities Center, 1981), 135–64. The volume was published in memory of Charles Frankel.

"Legal Positivism: a Pragmatic Analysis" was originally published in *Contemporary Conceptions of Law* (Proceedings of the 9th World Congress of the International Association for the Philosophy of Law and Social Philosophy, Basel 27/8/79–1/9/79), Pt. I. Ed. by Paul Trappe. (Wiesbaden: Franz Steiner, 1982), 77–98.

"Analytic Philosophy of Education at the Crossroads" was originally published in *Educational Theory*, Spring 1972, 131–52. Also in *Educational Judgments:* Papers in Philosophy of Education, ed. James F. Doyle (London: Routledge & Kegan Paul, 1973), 232–57.

"Anthropology and Ethics in Common Focus" was originally published in *The Journal of the Royal Anthropological Institute*, vol. 90 pt 1, 1962, 55–72. Reprinted by permission of the publisher.

Symposium on Citizenship and Education in Modern Society, sponsored by the Mershon Center, The Ohio State University, April 1980, 3–55.

''The Humanities and Public Policy—a Philosophic Perspective'' was originally published in *Small Comforts for Hard Times: Humanists on Public Policy*, ed. Michael Mooney and Florian Stuber, (New York: Columbia University Press, 1977), 335–84.

Introduction

Although the chapters in this volume span a variety of fields, they all contribute to facing the same serious intellectual problem—one increasingly pressing in our time—of the connection or relation among the disciplines that map the terrain of our intellectual life. The most notorious, of course, has been the sharp separation—sometimes even the antagonism—of the sciences and the humanities, the "two cultures" for whose reconciliation C. P. Snow pleaded. In the United States, this has meant the natural and social sciences on one side, and an array stretching from literature and philosophy to jurisprudence and the theory of art on the other. History and mathematics have led a double life: history resides predominantly with the humanities but makes an appearance when the social sciences need their temporal data; and mathematics in its purest regions consorts with logic and philosophy, but in its applied and statistical forms serves with the sciences. It is in the shade of this general problem that this book sets its task, relating the humanities and social thought, where the latter includes social science, social policy, and social practice. Some of the studies trace the influence of the social within the humanities; others start with the humanities and ask what they can do for, say, social policy.

The breadth of this kind of problem is suggested by the resistance to relation or connection found in widely different disciplines. Traditional historians take as sociological intrusion the turn from the older political history of important national events to research on what various groups among the common people were doing—women and children, craftsmen and workers generally, and intellectuals. Jurisprudence, with its traditional account of judicial decision as a strictly technical process of eliciting answers from a relatively isolated system of laws, has long been fending off views of law as an ongoing response to changing sociohistorical conditions and sociopolitical urgencies—from the pragmatism of Justice Holmes to the latest Critical Realism. Traditional literary theory, for which interpretation of the meaning of a work was largely a bounded literary problem, looks with dismay when the doors are opened to variable audience response and numerous features of interpretation that quickly generate a relativity of meaning if they do not abolish that category entirely. Traditional biography selected its figure for

notable productive work or achievement, then went to life to find what
juncture of circumstance or character precipitated the unique accomplishment. Now it was overwhelmed, not by the mass of (often trivial) detail—it
was used to that—but by the "intruding" theories (e.g., Freudian, Marxian,
and various others) that patterned the work and gave the work a life function.
Traditional aesthetic theorists had relied on a sense of aesthetic value to set off
the works of their inquiry. They were shaken when everyday objects (e.g., the
notorious Campbell soup can) were not just painted but included bodily in the
grouping that constituted a "work of art," sufficiently to meet what they
might regard as aesthetic intuitions gone wild. But some aesthetic theorists
now wonder whether the line between art and non–art has disappeared.

    Many a tale could be told of the wanderings of the different sciences of
man—psychological and social—in their endeavor during the twentieth century to establish a domain and determine their self–identity. Political science
felt on firm ground in the early part of the century, concentrating on the state
and its ways of governing (concepts of sovereignty, role of political parties,
forms of the state as it evolved, etc.). Concepts from other fields kept barging
in—notably, the psychological notion of the pursuit of power, or ethical ideas
that assigned purposes to governing. The threat of a psychological or sociological takeover was averted, and the intrusion of values rejected as contrary
to the nature of an objective science. (A compromise was to set up a separate
"policy science" which immediately tried to become very scientific.) What
really rescued political science was the post–World War II international
scene, with new nations arising, new types of struggle and a variety of forms
of governing. Nothing works so well to keep a science going as an injection of
a new range of phenomena. Sociology had comparable transformations.
Stimulated in America by social work, it nevertheless shed this aspect in
trying to become a science. It had the whole realm of associations and
institutions below the state, to study their structures and workings. But what
most overwhelmed it during the century was the multiplicity of social problems; it was kept busy with the studies that these called for. The division
between sociology and anthropology—apart from their different origins—
seems mostly now to be between the study of large societies and small
societies. Social anthropology (ethnography and ethnology) was directed to
the simpler preliterate societies in the attempt to describe their culture before
they disappeared. Its scientific advantage lay in having a manageable whole
culture to focus on. The discernment of whole–culture patterns, however,
practically called for some underlying theory of their support and transmission
from generation to generation. Hence it was an invitation to psychology and
other "outside" theories. The course of events itself shifted attention to
interaction of cultures and acculturation, in which history and sociohistorical
processes were unavoidably involved.

From the point of view of the relation of disciplines, the twentieth century story of psychology is perhaps the most revealing. The dominant behaviorism of at least the first half of the century was imperialistic, rather than worried about other's intrusion. The reality it assumed as basic was the behavior of the individual, and everything else, whether a social form or an intellectual discipline, had ultimately to be translated into some pattern of the behavior of individuals. The category of behavior was fashioned as a solution to the traditional separation of body and mind: psychology, at least for the present, was not to be pursued as a temporary path to physiology, nor, on the other hand, a trained sensitivity in introspecting, consciousness looking in upon itself. The material consisted of transactions of individuals within the visible world. Unlike the broadening that William James had given to the idea of experience, which included the vast range of qualities found in consciousness, behaviorism would not even allow a notion of purpose in its vocabulary. Think of the difficulties E. C. Tolman had in the early 1930s, in his *Purposive Behavior in Men and Animals*, in getting recognition of the cat scratching at the door as in some sense trying to get out. In the latter part of the century, of course, phenomenological psychology counterattacked against behaviorism, and the question of what categories to employ in psychology was reopened. A comparable battle was fought around Freudian psychology, where the notion of unconscious purpose ran counter to the sharp division of the bodily and the mental: the unconscious purpose seemed mental in talking of purpose, but operated causally in the way bodily mechanisms do. The sin was thus to question the body–mind dichotomy.

Twentieth-century philosophy reacted strongly to the question of relations and connections. It is not surprising in the light of the history of philosophy that it sought some form of autonomy. In older centuries, subject to theology, it had had to fight for its freedom. A bare three centuries ago, it still embraced the whole of knowledge; in Newton's day physics was "natural philosophy." In the eighteenth century Scotland of Adam Smith, moral philosophy included the whole study of human decision and action: Smith's lectures on economics, on jurisprudence, and on the moral sentiments, are all parts of a unified university course. The rapid growth of physics and technology, then the vista of biology after Darwin, established science as independent. What was philosophy to do? For a time it could think of the job of unifying disparate fields, but this soon became a technical question which scientists had better engage in themselves. Much of philosophy turned to epistemology, the inquiry into the character and methods and presuppositions of knowledge. In the twentieth century, philosophy, feeling perhaps more relieved than deprived of its universal pretensions, drew a sharp line around a more limited task: the clarification and analysis of ideas and methods. This could be undertaken in any area. Sometimes the philosopher could learn from what was going on, as in the conceptual shifts in Einsteinian physics. Sometimes the philosopher could construct a formal system, as in logic. But mostly it was the logical–linguistic analysis of ideas. How it could best be done was a matter of controversy in epistemology, where occasional philosophers still tried to show the transcendental conditions of knowledge. But others took their contexts from current uses in one or another area and analyzed them.

Having settled on this *autonomy* of their discipline, philosophers were wary of any claim that the materials and results of other disciplines played any active role in setting philosophical questions. There might be interesting matters of causality—for example, why a question was raised or how it historically developed—or of utility, say how the results of a philosophical analysis were used in education or politics. These were *external* matters, not part of philosophy proper. Perhaps the most striking instance of this outlook was the treatment of ethical theory. Proper ethical theory was taken to be metaethics, the analysis of ethical concepts; it made no moral judgments, and rested on no empirical (historical and scientific) assumptions. When in the 1970s the avalanche of practical problems overwhelmed moral philosophy and "applied ethics" spread rapidly, the philosophers had great difficulty in becoming reconciled to normative projects. The question of "relevance," the relation of theory and practice, became once again a most serious philosophical issue.

Philosophers reacted in different ways to the multiplicity of possible relations to other disciplines. Most extreme was the removal of all boundaries and the declaration that philosophy is at an end. Rorty's interesting form of this view (chap. 13) goes so far as to suggest that philosophy, like literature (seen in its contemporary theories of interpretation) is simply educative conversation. The conclusion that emerges from the papers here is less sweeping. As a slogan for a discipline it might be: autonomy, yes; isolation, no.

From a longtime historical view, the questions here considered may not seem to be a serious matter. From early on, the growing complexity of life generated division of labor, and naturally produced specialized fields and specialized expertise. People were sorted with respect to kinds of tasks, varying capacities, acquired skills. Some divisions got stabilized and consolidated. Think of castes, classes, distinctions of elite and mass, skilled and unskilled labor, and of course the massive divisions of men and women, nations and races, and languages and religions. Where accumulation of knowledge became important, priests and scribes and scholars were marked out as a group. Eventually, we came to universities and their faculties and departments. Of course in all this there were lags and readjustments. The need for readjustment has not come to an end in a perfect pattern of division. But change in the intellectual habits that perpetuate divisions is not a simple matter. The habits have been set in institutions that keep them going. Thus the separation of the sciences and the humanities is institutionalized in the educational system, as well as in the working arrangements of society. The curricula are separate; students early choose or gravitate toward one or the other as a career; the requirements of each area tend to monopolize attention; and the actual teaching of each area finds little occasion to look over the boundary at the other. Some scientists have realized that science itself is a humanistic enterprise, and some humanists that they are intimately related to social thought and social policy. But this does not change schools of education, not the entrenched habits of teachers.

It is not being suggested here that a "general theory of divisions" be developed as a new science to add confusion to the array of general theories of power or of value. Rather a fuller awareness is needed of all that goes into making a particular division, how it affects methods of working, and what opportunities of inquiry it thrusts aside. Again, it is helpful to envisage different kinds of relatedness that are possible. Eventually, too, where larger reconstruction of disciplines may be desirable, there are practical questions of change in institutional ways. Meanwhile, a first step is to liberate present disciplines for growth by attention to connections that may enlarge their insight.

What is most likely to be missed, if the foundation of a discipline's isolation is not sufficiently examined, is the effect of some basic categorial structuring of the field to begin with. The world is carved in a particular way, and attention is then directed to one side. The way in which the mind-body dichotomy operated in the case of psychology above, illustrates this well. That is only one of a large set of sharp divisions, usually dichotomies, found in the history of thought. Consider the separation of: the human and divine, temporal and eternal, body and soul (as well as body and mind), objective and subjective, intrinsic and extrinsic, absolute and relative, pure and applied, theoretical and practical, fact and value, work and leisure, elite and mass, and so on. Each starts out as a carving of the real world or of experience and proceeds to build up a different way of dealing with each side—often a basic methodology for investigation, or a set of separate disciplines, or a fixation of different attitudes—and channels investigation and action along the lines so established. It is rarely realized that such structuring is itself a program for inquiry or for testing in experience rather than antecedent truths to be taken for granted. Usually the division is set up by looking at clear areas of difference in experience, and only when they are entrenched do we begin to discover all the difficult problems at their borders.

This happens over and over again. For example, in Western religious theory, the sharp separation of the divine and the human is tempered at the outset by man being made in the image of God; later by the concept of a God–man (with technical debates about the moment at which divinity departed from Christ on the Cross); and in many a later religious movement throughout the centuries by different conceptions of the inscrutability of God's will. In the separation of body and mind, the obvious Cartesian dualism with its division of the physical world and the domain of consciousness reigns for some three centuries over the work of psychologists . The sharp contrast of the rational and the empirical—first entrenched in Western philosophy in the contrast of mathematical (deductive) reasoning and (inductive) observation—feeds the general philosophical battles of Rationalism and Empiricism, and carries through into twentieth century debates over the analytic–synthetic distinction. And in ethics, the distinction between intrinsic and extrinsic is so much taken for granted that the debate gets centered instead on what "intrinsic value" really means. More broadly, the grandiose segregation of fact and value for a long period ruled the relations of science and ethics. This is better seen as a program than as an established truth, and one that becomes increasingly difficult to carry out in actual cases, or to use in other than a contextual way, for local special purposes. The general recommendation for dealing with basic divisions or dichotomies is that they are fundamentally misleading when taken absolutely, and so should be judged for their utility in particular contexts. They can be very useful at times, and very misleading at other times.

Once liberated from coercive structuring, inquiry is freer to look for connections the particular problem may call for—for example, particular purposes operative within a scientific investigation or factual assumptions in accepting a particular humanistic value. The next step, in following on some interdisciplinary relation, is to recognize the variety of connectedness and not to ask for more than the subject will bear at that point. The mildest kind of connection occurs when disciplines contribute each in its own way to a project for which their knowledge is relevant. Thus in preparing food relief after World War II, apart from what agricultural and economic knowledge and food-processing techniques were invoked, anthropologists were asked to determine what kinds of food would be compatible with the traditional food habits of particular peoples. (Incidentally, this was said to be the beginning of "culture–at–a–distance" studies, which produced valuable anthropological writings.) A somewhat closer relation of disciplines comes when the knowledge or products of the one begin to influence the procedures of the other. Such influences may be of a widely different sort. For example, it may be a structure in the one providing a model in the other—as historically, organic models from biology are reinterpreted for the relation of classes in the body politic; or an atomic theory from physics is distilled into a "mechanistic model" for the psychology of sensation and perception. Or again, the influence may lie in one discipline providing instrumentation for improved work in the other—for example, electronic devices for medical research and treatment. Sometimes one discipline's connection with another may set up tensions, as sociological and psychological study of juvenile delinquency affects and may find itself at odds with traditional juristic assumptions. A much more intimate relation of disciplines arises where one discipline finds that it needs the knowledge of the other in order to formulate or establish its own theory. These are serious cases, often treated logically in the language of "reduction" of the terms and laws of one field to the terms and laws of another—the very language itself reeking of conquest. But the situation is real enough. There is an item in Watson's *The Double Helix*, the story of the basic discovery of the genetic process, in which he was checked for a while because he used a chemistry text that was not up–to–date; the discovery moved on once this was corrected. This kind of interdisiplinary relation has long been understood. In wholesale form of the relation of sciences it generated the traditional Laplacean determinism which envisaged every future event predictable from a full knowledge of position and momentum of the elementary particles, and so a universal physics. What stood in the way of this dreamed conquest was the basic metaphysical dichotomy of body and mind, noted earlier. Physics made inroads on the mental field by way of the physiology of the experiences of vision and sound, and in our time through the subtle phenomena of the energy of the nervous system. By that time, however, the complexities of knowledge had proved more troublesome to that dream than the lingering of the body–mind dichotomy.

The present studies are ordered by the contribution they make to our understanding of connections and relations. The first group (chaps. 1–4) samples fundamental divisions of one kind or another relevant to the remaining studies. Each criticizes a dichotomy that leads us astray when it is absolutized, entrenched, hardened in the institutional division of ideas, people, activities, outlooks. Each is found to have an inner complexity, with elements helpful in some contexts, not in others, and therefore is best to be regarded as an intellectual instrument for contextual use, not a fundamental carving of natural or social reality. The dichotomies here dealt with are the methodological contrast of science and the humanities, the bifurcation of theory and practice, the persistent categorizing as individual or social, and separating of the elite from the mass.

The second group, and bulk, of the papers (chaps. 5–13) deals with problems that arise in different disciplines within the humanities. When Congress set up the National Endowment for the Humanities, it included in its list "the study of philosophy, history, literature, language, linguistics, jurisprudence, comparative religion, ethics, and archaeology; also the history, theory and criticism of the arts and those aspects of the social sciences concerned with values." All the papers included in this volume would accordingly find a niche in the humanities, except education. We may suspect that Congress left it out because the immediate interest was funding work in these fields, and education was already taken care of under the Executive division. (In any case, philosophy of education would be admitted). The studies in this part were not, for the most part, directed toward ascertaining the values of connectedness or relation of other disciplines. They were concerned with issues in their specific field, and it was the needs of their inquiry that led them to one or another way of relating.

The study of positivism and pragmatism in legal theory (chap. 5) is initially a comparison of two philosophical methodologies. When they are seen actually at work, it becomes clear that one is isolating law, the other putting it into the mainstream of sociohistorical problems and human means of regulating and dealing with them. The required legal studies, ignored under the one and carried out under the other, show the importance of the connections.

The paper in educational philosophy (chap. 6) starts with a critique of a philosophical approach that claims to be purely analytic, without empirical or valuational assumptions; it challenges that claim and looks for the unrecognized assumptions. When found in specific cases, they turn out to be powerful determinants of the direction in which educational answers are to be sought and even the meanings of educational ideas to be understood. Relations to the knowledge sources and experiential sources of these assumptions become unavoidable.

The four papers in moral philosophy (chaps. 7–10) are explicit in their concern with relation of disciplines. The first two grow out of a previous book that tried a joint philosophical–anthropological exploration of morality (May Edel and Abraham Edel, *Anthropology and Ethics*, 1959). It was stimulated by the fact that philosophical attempts to define the moral or to give the mark of the moral were too thin and too variable among philosophers themselves, while anthropological and sociological references to morality were culturally rich but unrefined. Chapter 7 reports the study and urges a common focus. Chapter 8 goes beyond moralities to ethical theories and applies the joint anthropological-philosophical approach on the theoretical level. The following paper (chap. 9), responding to the question whether ethics is a science— that is, whether it lies on one or another side of a dividing road—finds that the dividing road gets very thin as we look for it, and there are many pathways in all directions. Thus the question is altered. The last of the group (chap. 10) tries out the contributions of history in a fresh way: it lines up the succession of Anglo–American ethical theories in the twentieth century and finds that central features of the theories can thereby be more clearly understood (e.g., the shift from an emotive theory of ethics to a rights theory).

The study in aesthetics (chap. 11) starts with the fact that the idea of *form*, a philosophic construction, has had wide use in the arts. It seeks to understand the idea, particularly its operation in painting and architecture, by comparing the story of its philosophic construction with the variety of its aesthetic uses—for example in the relation of form to material, form to function, form as a guiding idea. The result is clarifying for both the scope and the limits of the idea.

The study of biography (chap. 12) starts from current controversies as this branch of literature veers between the ''superpowers'' of history and science. This issue is clarified and to some degree transcended by recognizing the effects of major philosophical shifts in the conception of what is a person.

That the search for connections needs not lead to the abolition of boundaries is the lesson of the last study in this part, the critique of Rorty's view of philosophy. Rorty, so far from isolating philosophy, is ready to abolish it; it has no distinctive character as compared to literature, and all we have is *conversation* that is *educative*. (In short, he has pursued relations so far as to abolish boundaries.) The critique suggests that this conclusion is a consequence of the isolation of philosophy itself—particularly epistemology—which therefore dealt with the general character of method but missed the significant role of specific results or parts of knowledge in developing philosophical problems and ideas. (No general methodological considerations can substitute for the role that the discovery that light has a finite velocity played in generating new epistemological problems, or the role of the discovery of germs played in change of moral ideas.)

The last group of papers (chaps. 14–17) shows some serious effects of the division of theory and practice, elite and mass, individual and social. Two of the studies (chaps. 14 and 15) arise from the work of the State Humanities Councils, state committees on the humanities set up in the original Congressional legislation founding the National Endowment for the Humanities. Whereas the Endowment deals with research and institutions concerned with humanities, the state committees, operating independently, are to work out ways of relating to grass roots concerns, and thus to spread acquaintance with and appreciation of the humanities. Broadly, it is a continuing effort in the extension of scope and application of the humanities. In due course it was attacked as using scarce resources to put culture to work, when the money had better be given to scholarship in the humanities itself (the old value scale of the theory–practice dichotomy) and as a futile populism that watered down a culture only genuinely appreciated by a scholarly elite (the elite–mass dichotomy at work again). Some of the arguments in this controversy are to be found in chapter 4, above.

Experience in work of the state committees often impinged on discipline lines. Projects that were dominantly sociological could not be funded; they belonged under applied social science and were thus under the Science endowment. But projects that dealt with values in sociological materials could be admitted, because values are a humanistic matter. On the other hand, projects that were primarily artistic did not fit; they should go to the National Endowment for the Arts. But reflection on art was aesthetics, which was part of philosophy, which was in the humanities. So money could be granted for a critical audience discussion held for an hour after a play, but not to help production of the play. Again, with relation to practice, a project to enlighten an issue of policy—say, a matter of racial discrimination or equality for women—could be supported if dominantly reflective inquiry, not if dominantly agitational.

Chapter 14 examines the lessons of ten years' work of the state of committees, and considers the problems that have been raised about their theoretical bases. Chapter 15 examines briefly a controversy about how best to use professional humanists in the actual programs of the projects. Here too, practice quickly seeks the aid of theory.

The study of the educational requirements of citizenship (chap. 16) was not intended to be the display of interweaving of disciplines, of the crossing and recrossing of lines that are actually found in the resulting product. Its aim was simply the practical one of determining the appropriate education of democratic citizenship today. That the analysis of the question led to matters of history, of political theory, of sociology and psychology and ethics, and issued in proposed revision of basic categories, shows the complexity of contemporary practical social problems, even on their ideational side.

The last of the studies (chap. 17) is the only one that set itself the full task of rendering more precisely the relations of the humanities and social policy, working through a wide range of specific problem areas of contemporary importance. The stage for this study was set by a conference of more than two years at Columbia University on the humanities and public policy. The paper had the task of integrating the ideas that had emerged and providing a philosophical perspective.

If the kinds of studies here presented are taken as representative of the need for greater attention to relations and connections, for the more persistent development of interdisciplinary relations, there is no danger, either in the sciences or the humanities, of a focus on connections becoming coercive, nor for disciplines to fear for their integrity in reaching out. Disciplines have good reason for their independence in that they are trying out distinctive concepts and methods in special areas of interesting and important problems. But this does not warrant a not uncommon feeling that a discipline is a competitor in a free market of ideas, in which the best can win. Such a spirit is occasionally seen even in technical scientific areas. People almost felt like cheering at the spectacle of the chemists upstaging the physicists in producing fusion in the kitchen instead of with a billion dollar apparatus—of course, it's in the limbo, but it would have made a nice American scenario. Such an approach would look upon pressing for relations as almost the analogue of a corporate takeover. But of course the whole analogy to the free market is misdirected. The disciplines we are here concerned with are all taken to be engaged on a common enterprise of *advancing knowledge, understanding and apprecia- tion.* (There are real dangers to the open community of science and culture in the secrecy imposed in defense research and in corporate agreements with universities, as well as in the extreme privatization of copyright of ideas.) If a political-economic analogy is sought, perhaps more appropriate would be the coming Common Market of the European countries, in which countries are not abolished, but passports are not demanded in free crossings.

The essential point for disciplines is to understand their own ultimate basis. They are not endowed with natural rights by metaphysical categories and dichotomies. They are a functional division of labor, justified by their fruits, with loose borders set by intellectual habits that correspond to older services and have become institutionalized. They are accordingly practices hard to change, particularly if they have become ossified. An openness to relations and connections is one way of learning how far borders are satisfactory or how far change is needed.

1

Comparative Modes of Inquiry:
The Sciences and the Humanities

The separation of the "two cultures" is usually argued in terms of the disparity of their methodology. One is calculated to produce the impersonal objective observer of the ways of nature and man, the other an impassioned participant, whether through feeling or imagination. The "objective observer," looking at the historical succession of arguments, may be tempted to comment that what is going on here is preserving a contrast at all costs. In the end we are left simply with the institutionalization of the contrast in education and in professional habits of thought.

I recall a TV discussion shortly after the publication of C. P. Snow's *The Two Cultures and the Scientific Revolution*. Physicist Rabi said to theologian Niebuhr that the scientist was culturally better off than the humanist because he could learn about what was going on in poetry and literature over the breakfast table from his wife; no such luck for the humanist about science. We need not dwell on what Rabi's remark reflected about the position of women and the presumed leisurely wifely role, as well as the assumption that the scientist is male. Our business is the legitimacy of the dichotomy in the modes of inquiry in science and the humanities. I do not recall Niebuhr questioning that.

My concern is the desperate attempts that are made to set off science and the humanities by invoking all sorts of dichotomies as basic support. I want to examine some of these dichotomies and suggest an alternative approach to the kinship of the fields.

1

Preliminary Considerations

Since William James and pragmatism, one thing seems clear: that a person orders his world, in perception as well as in thought; that there are always alternative possible orders and that the use or selection of one rather than another reflects the purposes at work in the context. This holds from the simplest act of identification to the elaborate patterning of a discipline, or classification of groups of disciplines. The trouble is that the classifications made usefully for some purposes become institutionalized, set roles and prohibitions and impose constraints which are inimical for other contexts and other purposes. But even an initial classification does not guarantee constancy. They have unforeseen as well as foreseen consequences.

No simple picture is to be found whether we look at the allegedly staid formation of the natural sciences, the shifts and realignments of our social sciences or the grouping of numerous disciplines under the label of the humanities. The natural science chart of the nineteenth century has been crisscrossed by hyphenated sciences (like biophysics and biochemistry) and the matings are prolific in offspring. The social sciences have been fissioning and fusing in a disorderly way, breaking up on the use of a technique or a dispute about concern with values versus computers, or even as a result of a power struggle in academe. Or a world war comes along and forces physical and social scientists to work (successfully) in teams on very specific projects; and lo—the policy sciences are born, or at least we all become inter-disciplinarians. What are called the humanities today bear some resemblance to what is left of the liberal arts when some deserting disciplines are abstracted. They began to get together in the early part of the century when the emerging social science turned to the natural science model. This happened more in America than in Europe where all human studies (*Geisteswissenschaften*) were regarded as studies of the spirit as contrasted with studies of nature. The congregating of the humanities was thus a reaction to the alignment of the social sciences with the natural sciences. When the federal government eventually listed the humanities in a solemn congressional act (1965) they stayed together out of protective self-interest (and discovered new intellectual interests). We may then properly think of their unity with political overtones as the *third force* (alongside of science and art), or, if you will, the third intellectual world demanding parity with and transfer of resources from the entrenched worlds.

Not all disciplines were wholly assigned to, or fitted comfortably into, the now established divisions. History is found in both the humanities and the social sciences, and has not fissioned into two separate kinds of history to be shipped in different directions. Mathematics has obvious quarters in science and, since the rise of statistics and probability, in social science. But from time immemorial and into the present, pure mathematics has had a claim (though not in the congressional list) to a place, occasionally a throne, in the humanities, whether it be conceived as spinning an intellectual web or tracing pure universal truth. Philosophy too, in virtue of its analytic mission, while placed in the humanities in virtue of its activity, can enter anywhere in virtue of what it chooses to analyze. Hence it has a roving commission.

The story of the organization of the disciplines can be read in the history of nineteenth and twentieth century philosophy: a metaphysical account of emerging levels—physical, biological, psychological, social, spiritual. In effect, they were transforming discipline distinctions of the time into eternal dichotomies and trichotomies. They overlooked the process by which disciplines become established, and strongly institutionalized, to generate vested interests, which are reflected in consciousness and become solidified to the point of ossification. They push aside the restructuring which may be required by the advance of knowledge in unexpected directions.

Merely to focus today on mode of inquiry will not do. Let us, however, face it initially in these terms and see where we are driven. Now the humanities are reflective disciplines, not to be equated with the creation of poetry and drama and painting and the rest; the humanities are second–order disciplines studying a great variety of primary fields. If by mode of inquiry we have in mind general method, the humanities certainly engage in hypothesis, deduction, observation, verification, and the rest of that intellectual paraphernalia. (What would our doctoral theses in the humanities be without this?)

Does "the scientific mode of inquiry" bring to mind formalism and abstruse mathematics, the equipment of deductive chains and the formidable array of statistics? There is formalism in linguistics, not to speak of philosophy; there is topology in aesthetic analysis of paintings; there is the romance of measurement in historical revelation of medieval architecture (as in the plan of St. Gallen); there is growing use of quantitative methods (for example, Anthony Kenny's attempt to measure stylistic and linguistic features to date the order of Aristotle's ethical writings). Should we say this is the use of science in the humanities, as if we were borrowing tools that properly belong elsewhere? Why should mathematics, that glorious product of the imagination, be allocated to one dimension of the mind's work? Would we do that in the case of observation? T. H. Huxley complained that students coming into medicine do not really know how to *look*. Henry James says practically the same for writers dealing with interpersonal relations. Shall we say that psychoanalysis in dissecting a feeling is using humanistic methods while a Galileo in breaking up a motion into its vectors is using scientific method? Our conceptual tools in such judgments are far too crude. And as for mathematics, itself, the humanists might redefine it as the music of precision. It does not predict; it does not experiment by preparing observations; and it does not do all the respectable things a science has to do if it follows the etiquette books about science. But neither for that matter do a great many of the sciences: evolutionary biology scarcely tries to predict, and economic science does not succeed.

On the other side of our comparison, *significance* has often been taken to be the hallmark of the humanistic. What has usually been meant is insight into the human being, human potentials and aspirations. If, however, this be limited to a methodological category, it spreads out over all disciplines. An historical characterization of an item, for example, may enlighten whether it be in Shakespearean studies or in paleontology. When Muriel Bradbrook explains that the phrase "Cry havoc" in Mark Antony's speech scene in *Julius Caesar* is precisely the term that kings use in giving their troops permission to sack a conquered city, it throws a flood of light on everything from Antony's strategy in the political-military situation precipitated by Caesar's assassination, to the techniques of rhetoric so masterfully exhibited in the speech that Shakespeare bestows on him. But we get precisely the same kind of illumination when we are told that this stone is a fossil, or when that small bone grows with imaginative skill into a dinosaur.

Partisans of basic methodological difference in scientific and humanistic inquiry have to face this serious difficulty: for every methodologically differentiating feature proposed, you will find one of the sciences and one of the humanities that share it, and one of the sciences and one of the humanities that lack it. If you reply that there are boll weevils and gypsy moths in any classification, you are simply following through on dogmatic assumption of basic general difference. The center of gravity in the problem really lies elsewhere—in the assumptions that underlie the usual comparison of modes of inquiry. These are assumptions about nature and mind, about the purpose of inquiry, about scientific law and individuality, about pure theory and practical application, about the nature of fact and value. In short, they are assumptions cast in ready–made dichotomies. We have therefore to deal with some of these, or kindred ones.

Some Presuppositions

Some of the underlying dichotomies that have kept science and the humanities apart have been slowly evaporating, under the heat of scientific progress, refinement of methods, and philosophical analysis. For example, that science deals with what is *objective* and humanities with what is *subjective* reflects the old Cartesian dualism of matter and spirit. But this has never worked out in methodological practice for any discipline. Adam Smith considered moral man and economic man in a single university course. We are the ones who put them in different reading lists—*The Theory of the Moral Sentiments* in a humanistic philosophy course and *The Wealth of Nations* in an economic science course. And as for subjectivity, Smith was careful to point out that sympathy—the root phenomenon of his moral science—could not be grasped in any particular case simply by looking within our feeling or by straight empathetic response to another; we had to know the conditions and causes and situations under which and in which the other's suffering arose and the objects with which it was concerned. And this is objective enough. It may be reasonable in our present academic world to separate the two Smiths for the purpose of grant applications, but not for understanding what is going on.

An accompanying dichotomy, less metaphysically obtrusive, is that of *quantity/quality*. But this too really rested on the assumption that matter was regular, quantifiable, simple (shall we say dead?) enough to be subject to law, whereas spirit was complex and variable, free and living, and not subject to measurement. Tying in as it did with all the other presuppositions, this dichotomy was perhaps the most serious and persistent in supporting the contrast of scientific and humanistic method. It became outdated in practice with the rise and classification of psychology and the social sciences as sciences, for its terms would have disqualified any such studies of man and his conduct. Its most effective retirement came from a logical recasting of the idea of quantity itself. Measurement, particularly once it was extended by the work of statistics, came to be understood as the search for order; it did not require a metaphysical notion of quantity. There were different kinds and strengths of order, and the proliferation of types offered variety of conceptual instruments for all kinds of inquiries. A statistical genius, like Paul Lazarsfeld, could provide a way of ordering anything—even what the statistician would call randomness, and the humanist, I suspect, chaos.

A quite different dichotomy often invoked was that of the individual and the universal. Science, with its sweeping laws, is set upon universality. The humanities—history typically, as well as art in its construction and so the humanities in their reflection on art—are concerned with the individual. To deal with the universal one has to pursue the abstract, the analytic, the recurrent; to cope with the individual one needs the synthetic, the concrete; one grasps the unique and empathizes with the particular. This dichotomy acquired on the way a technical designation; the distinction was drawn between the *nomothetic* or law-seeking disciplines, and the *ideographic* or individual–describing, almost portrait-painting, disciplines. But once again this formidable conceptual apparatus fails to correspond with what the sciences and the humanities do. Physics has given us sweeping laws, but astronomic history and geology go after the careers of individual systems. Clinical psychology was ideographic enough in its concern with the individual to describe its work as "global," that is, dealing with the individual as a whole, despite the aid it got from statistical projections. And recent refinement of the elements handled by computer show growing rapprochement, as if the break-up of the individual into enough elements can now help in the more systematic description of the whole individual. On the other side, from the humanities, if we cling to the dichotomy, what shall we do with the history and theory of abstract art—from impressionism (recall Verlaine's urging that we pursue not the color but the nuance) to the recent presentation of pure chromatics? Some see it as getting closer and closer to the unique, away from standard essences. But for others it is getting purer specimens and so extracting purer essences. It is not surprising that even social scientists are occasionally uncomfortable with the particular/universal dichotomy and try to fashion concepts that will bypass it—for example, patterns, ideal types, systems. Perhaps we should conclude that some of our sweeping dichotomies are not adequate for the complexity of the materials we deal with in both science and the humanities.

We may consider finally the most powerful and perhaps the most confused of our traditional dichotomies: science, it is said (in a chorus from Bergson to Roszak) is of instrumental value and deals with the practical; humanities is focused on intrinsic value. The one is directed to control, the other to appreciation. This combines two distinct dualities: theory and practice, knowledge and appreciation.

Unfortunately for such a thesis, both these dichotomies are found within science and within the humanities, and cannot therefore be used to distinguish the fields and their methods. Science from ancient times on makes the familiar distinction between pure science and technology, and it was never seen more forcefully as a value problem than by Archimedes. Plutarch (in *The Life of Marcellus*) tells us that Archimedes, in spite of his many and great inventions, refused to write about technology, spurning it as a matter of profit and utility. Instead, he lost himself in mathematical contemplation, in appreciation of its beauty and grandeur and precision. Faced with the dichotomy of instrumentality and intrinsic value, Archimedes would clearly have put pure science among the humanities. Think again of the dilemma of T. H. Huxley when, in his "Science and Culture," he argues for including science in education—and that in the Britain of not much more than a century ago. The entrenched humanistic classicists would have education bring clarity to the great ideals of life. Huxley agrees with the aim but maintains that the study of science does it as well as the study of the classics. At the same time he is faced by the practical men who are not convinced that teaching science will have sufficiently practical results. (That question at least has by now been settled.)

Today, the inner relations among science and technology are still like the outer relations of the humanities and science: basic research gets justified by the technological applications it sooner or later generates, and in one way or another is subsidized by government or industry. But the scientists themselves will find intrinsic values in their work, and treat its practical consequences as a matter of good fortune if it does not operate to overwhelm their genuine interests. Now the internal relations of the humanities would seem to be heading toward the same balance but in a reverse direction. Having traditionally stressed their nonpractical character to bring out the intrinsic value of their pursuit, humanists are now engaged in exhibiting the practical fruits that the humanities can bring in enlightening public policy, in clarifying values and directions. In fact, the humanities have always borne the practical responsibility for the moral organization and the quality of life. What else is Job up to? Or Antigone, who strikingly came to life in the drama of the French resistance in World War II? Or current revolts against cost–benefit analysis in the name of human dignity? Or the battle of the utopias and the dystopias in modern literature? And so a more sensible concept of the practical sees the humanities as highly practical.

We come then to what used to be called the $64 question, if I may quote preinflationary prices—that of intrinsic value. If it is pressed strictly, perhaps all knowledge, scientific and humanistic, is put into jeopardy. This is not a new problem. Already in the first century A.D. Seneca writes a long letter on Liberal and Vocational Studies (Epistle 88). First he dismisses money-making; studies to that end may be an apprenticeship, but they are not our real work. That is the pursuit of wisdom. He goes unsparingly through humanistic research. He condemns theses that plot Ulysses' travels: don't ask where he strayed but how you can prevent yourself from going astray. The musician teaches the harmony of the treble and the bass, but Seneca wants to bring his soul into harmony and not have his purposes out of tune. And as for learning calculation, what point is there in knowing how to parcel out a piece of land if I know not how to share it with my brother? Liberal arts may prepare for virtue but do not bestow it. Clearly, Seneca has identified intrinsic value with virtue, and all the humanities are in danger of moralistic reduction—they are instrumental. This puts human learning at the mercy of a theory of morality. One thinks of Augustine, fearing to enjoy the music of prayer, lest it lead him away from the focus of his spirit on deity. Of course curiosity, the foundation of knowledge, shares the same fate as music. And what may sound exalted in the passion of an Augustine, sounds menacing when voiced by the Moral Majority.

The theoretical point is obvious enough. Behind every conception of intrinsic value lies some theory of value, and ultimately this is a function of a theory of human life, the world in which it exists and can perhaps flourish, its knowledge and its possible aims. Apart from this background, intrinsic value can simply mean those values that directly attract or stir human beings, those values that engage their energies and heighten their interests. And here there is no basis of distinction between the pastures of science and those of the humanities.

An Alternative Hypothesis

Do these considerations erase the well-established distinction of the sciences and the humanities, as an historical error based on the unfortunate dichotomies of the past that in turn rested on earlier stages of knowledge and earlier ideas now due for demise? By no means. Distinctions are important and necessary, but they are geared to context and purpose. Distinctions are made to clarify, but too often they stay to tyrannize. What I am suggesting rather is the overall continuity of human inquiry. Imagination, values and purposes, evidence, responsible tracing of relations, general ideas, particularity, and the rest, belong to all inquiry. There are divisions of labor and different emphases. In the varied disciplines that constitute the humanities, purposes and values are overt; in the sciences in our age they are more standardized and submerged. (Only a Poincaré or an Einstein would dare to include beauty among the criteria for an acceptable hypothesis.) In the humanities the exercise of the imagination is in the forefront and constantly obvious; in the sciences it is most evident in bold leaps on the theoretical frontier. In the humanities, the rigorous search for evidence is often relaxed; in the sciences it is on its best behavior. But no inquiry is exempt from questions about its purposes, justification of its specific methods, problems of evidence, understanding of its context and consequences in human life, and so on.

There are three coordinates along which any inquiry can be plotted: knowledge, purpose or value, practicality. We could ask of any inquiry: what is the information it relies on, what are its assumptions about our world; what is it aiming at; what are its criteria of judgment; what will it enable us to do? These are not cut off from one another: if we plotted the knowledge of knowledge it would include our purposes in seeking to know and the practicality or degree of control that knowledge brings. Similarly for the other two. For many reasons which the humanistic field of the history and sociology and philosophy of science is only now beginning to uncover, the sciences in their growth narrowed their own self–image. At some points it was to protect themselves, at a later point when science became a multibillion dollar enterprise, to avoid responsibilities. At any rate, instead of seeing themselves as, so to speak, science–in–context, they blotted out all such background in their self–portrait and left only the narrow focus. And so they retreated from any reckoning with context questions of the character of their supporting civilization, their implications for the direction of development of society, their impact on other institutions, the nature of the technologies in which they were applied, and all the rest, and answered all questions about these by affirming that their motivations were pure and disinterested. The resulting disaster is epitomized in Webster's definition of "disinterested"; Webster equates it with "uninterested" rather than the attitude of mind requisite for sober and judicious decision. If Webster is right about the usage, it speaks volumes for the state of our humanities as well as the state of science. But to go on with the story: given the narrow self–model which many scientists are now trying to correct, the social sciences in some countries also narrowed down their scope, even though they were dealing with human beings. Sometimes it was to secure the status and prestige of science, but sometimes, on the other hand, to protect themselves as they began to tackle touchy social problems. In the latter, they were in effect repeating the early history of the natural sciences. The humanities in their consolidation as a third force have tended to react by stressing their value character as a defining mark. Thus they sell themselves short, for one of the most stimulating elements in their long history has been the high degree of precision, evidence, and ingenuity that is found in everything from history to jurisprudence to linguistics and literary studies. In the same way, they sell themselves short when they refuse to recognize their practical role in human life. All three fields—the physical and natural sciences, the social sciences, and the humanities—will be led increasingly to realize that they are all cut from the same cloth, that the themes of knowledge, human purpose, and value, practice and control, run through them all, often without a break, and that we must recover in spirit the unity and integrity of the mind that older times were able to have under conditions of limited knowledge, even though we necessarily require greater division of labor.

This paper was written for the second annual meeting of the American Association for the Advancement of the Humanities, held in Washington, D.C., October 31, 1981.

2

Theory and Practice:
An Unsteady Dichotomy?

Any scholar or scientist who turns to consider the broader relations of his or her work is usually confronted with a repertoire of distinctions to shield the work from possible invasion. The product (of art, of literature, of theory) is declared complete in itself; application is a separate matter. Or, never mind what led you into the work and gave you ideas to follow up; that is a causal or psychological matter, external to the nature and validity of the product. Or, to look for the functions of the work, or the uses it may serve, has little to do with the work itself—heaven only knows in how many different ways people will use it. Perhaps all of these and many more are encapsulated in the venerable dichotomy of theory and practice.

The pecking order within the roster of science and humanities often establishes a social value reckoning. Examples are pure science and applied science, science and technology, social science and social work, medical research and medical practice, moral truths and solving moral problems, stage theatre and street theatre (or even a propaganda play). In general it is the marked cleavage between contemplation and craft, thinking and doing.

When, however, one looks with care into the many uses and contexts of the fundamental distinction between theory and practice, the constructed complexity becomes evident. This study explores the construction that has gone into the dichotomy, and so is able to distinguish its uses and abuses.

The distinction between theory and practice is so familiar, so hardened, that we scarcely bother to analyze it, and rarely if ever think of possible replacements for it. After all, numerous and obvious distinctions feed it: thinking and doing, planning and carrying out, understanding and performing, and so on. Attention has centered rather on the general *relation* of theory and practice: whether theory is independent or in any way dependent on practice, whether pure theory can develop on its own, whether theory can guide practice or whether practice requires its own skill or intuitions, whether in reality theory reflects practice. In brief, the tradition assumes the characters of the drama and wants to go directly to the plot.

This chapter approaches the problem of theory and practice in another way and accordingly asks different questions. It puts aside the older concern with the ''purity'' of theory for which the vital question was whether there was or was not a relation between theory and practice. It asks instead what kinds of relations may be possible, to what extent and under what conditions they are present, and in what contexts each kind may be useful. It is led to ask whether these notions have not themselves been fashioned for specific purposes under specific conditions. In pursuing this agenda the paper considers: familiar debates on the relation of theory and practice; theory and practice as themselves constructions; sample historical alternatives; types of relation (the heart of the inquiry); how theory and practice were related in twentieth-century educational philosophy (a case study from practice, illustrating the practical importance of the way in which theory-practice relations are theoretically construed); and concluding reflections.

Familiar Debates

Some advocate the separateness of theory and practice and take it to follow from their distinct natures. As activity theory is the thinking, and practice is the doing; the one lies in the realm of mind and the other in that of body. If we look to the object at which the activity is directed, then theory as intellectual formulation is distinct from practice as the product or application. (Ohm's law is a formula, not an electric circuit.) Others hold that theory and practice are correlatives, that operationally the meaning of a theory or concept is to be found in its practical or observational consequences; that the meaning of a social institution is to be found in the way it works out in practice. Still others argue normatively that whether or not they can be separated, they ought not to be; that new lines of inquiry, conceptual refinement and correction, in a word the growth of knowledge, depend on the interplay between theory and practical problems.

Matters are made much more complex by the ways in which theory and practice are relativized. Thus we could arrange a continuum in which what is practice or application with respect to what precedes may be theory with respect to what follows it. For example, consider: mathematics, physics, engineering, architecture, actual construction (literally digging); or in another field, physiology, medicine, theory of therapy, actual curing or operating. Of course how we treat such cases depends on the context, that is on the kinds of activities people are engaged in at a given time under given conditions.

Such general arguments, with occasional favorable illustrations thrown in, are by now boring. It is much more interesting to go to the blossoming studies of the history of science and technology. Nevertheless, the history of the general debate does reveal some things.

The Constructional Character of Theory and Practice

To think of an idea as a construct (or construction) is to regard it as fashioned to serve a purpose in inquiry. It does not involve a commitment to conventionalism or to subjectivism. The history of the general debates indicated shows that *theory* and *practice* are themselves theory–laden, and when we unpack underlying theory (including any surplus) we can see what prompts the sharp separation or the greater closeness. Thus the dichotomy is sharp when coupled with a metaphysics that instates a mind–body dualism or with an economic theory that differentiates intellectual or skilled production and unskilled labor, brain and brawn. On the other hand, the distinctness of theory and practice tends to fade under the influence of a naturalistic psychology which stresses a controlling cognitive function (explicit and implicit) in virtually all behavior beyond sheer physical movement. Purposive doing in general implicates thinking where the overt behavior is construed or felt as a means to something beyond itself. Finally, theory and practice are firmly wedded under the influence of an epistemology in which ideas are seen as plans of action and knowledge is for the sake of action. Even on a less pragmatic epistemology, thinking in experimental science involves a reference to doing.

Perhaps we could also bring to bear on the consideration of theory and practice what can be learned from the history of dichotomies in Western thought. They usually enter on the scene with confidence, proclaiming their analytical necessity or metaphysical truth. Sooner or later phenomena appear in the middle ground which raise doubt about their sharpness. Eventually they are revealed as programs, and not always very successful programs at that. The hardened dichotomies are then turned into contextual distinctions, useful in some cases, misleading in others. It is experience that refuses their absolute partitioning and that determines their relative utility. Such has been the story of body and soul, human and divine, body and mind, sensation and thought, sensation and feeling, is and ought, fact and value, and innumerable others. Why should it not be the story of theory and practice?

Historical Alternatives

The twofold division into theory and practice is by no means the only possibility. Indeed it was not the first on the scene. In Aristotle's philosophy the concept of theory was narrower (*theōria* limited to a grasping of eternal truth), and instead of practice there were two notions—*praxis* or action and *poiēsis* or making. These are distinguished by whether the end or goal lies in the act itself (as taking a ride) or in a product separate from the activity (as in making a bridle). Now Aristotle's trichotomy obviously stands out as a conceptual construction. We can see what went into it. One strand was the belief in a dichotomy between the necessary and the contingent, itself identified with one between the eternal and the changing. Hence theory is concerned with what cannot be otherwise. And into the division between *praxis* and *poiēsis* there is incorporated at least the social distinction between the craftsman or producer who makes things and the leisured class who enjoy their use.

The constructional character of Aristotle's distinctions is further made manifest by the modifications insisted on in Puritan theology. Aristotle's view of *theōria* is condemned precisely for its assumption of an eternal world that has always existed, a pagan belief. Since God created the world, what we are learning in theory is the scheme of God's production; *theōria* thus becomes incorporated into a universal *poiēsis*![1]

There is no reason to think that our current distinctions are less constructed, shaped by philosophical assumptions and traditional cultural attitudes. Certainly the dualism of mind and body is transparent in the dichotomy of theory and practice, and the social dichotomy of leisure and work is as much associated with it as with the Aristotelian distinction of *praxis* and *poiēsis*. It is interesting to note that *praxis* is now coming to take its turn at getting to the top. If Aristotle had at the pinnacle his conception of theory, and the Puritans their conception of making as creation, contemporary humanistic Marxism is attempting to fashion the concept of praxis to embrace human free activity in which theory is fruitful and production itself satisfying.[2]

Types of Relation

There are many possible kinds of relations between theory and practice. If we pursue them in detail, it is not mapping for mapping's sake, but in the hope that their varieties may suggest fresh ways in which theory may furnish guides to practice and the influence of practice on theory be more fully understood. When we think of theory as the activity of people theorizing and practice as their doing, the relations that come to mind are ways in which, as a matter of psychology and history, the one has influenced the other in either direction. These are largely the genetic relations that Feuer has studied in broad scope.[3] When we think of theory as the body of knowledge gathered and systematized, and practice as the formulation of its application, then the relations that come to mind are likely to be logical, methodological, and instrumental.

This latter set of relations—the logical, methodological, and instrumental—require more detailed examination to see the factors that determine their utility. These factors will, of course, depend on how good the theory is and how rich the practice is. On the side of the theory, the important factor is the state of knowledge. It may run from the highly axiomatized and highly systematized down to the roughly empirical. A possible ambiguity in the term "theory" needs to be noted here. The notion of theory has considerable stretch. Strict use would distinguish a theory from a scientific law; it would be some higher–level set of relations which unified laws. But in a broader use theory comes to include all established universal knowledge, and the theory of a subject would include the empirical generalizations as well, if they were not simply rule–of–thumb. But the borders of usage are shady. A discipline begins to use the term when it has worked out a schema for future theory, or else it has concepts refined in terms of which theories will be stated, or it has theories on the loose but none established, or it has bodies of data rapidly accumulating and the hope of theory is in the air. Soon every field has its theory, which is scarcely more than reflective inquiry or where practice will go for what help it might get to light its way. We are not called on here to approve or disapprove, but simply to note the breadth of usage. If we wished to exercise greater caution, we would speak in some domains of theory–surrogates, in others of theory–hopes, in still others of mere hypotheses.

On the side of practice, two factors important for determining the kind of relations readily emerge on inspection. One is *the purposive pattern* of the participants, or the established purposes of the institution or enterprise in which the practice is involved. Thus the practice of medicine has purposes of curing, adding to medical knowledge and making a living, while the practice of farming has the making of a living in addition to growing food, so that on occasion grain or coffee is burned in order to support prices. (In that instance the impact of economic theory on farming practice is enough to reverse the usual practice.) The purposive pattern of a practice may be one of established common aims or even of intense value conflicts. Now a second factor on the side of practice that is important for determining the kind of relations between theory and practice is more complicated than the purposive patterns. For any practice it is not enough to bring in some theory to be sure that it can be used. Particular conditions have to prevail or else the theory is irrelevant. It is no use bringing the advanced farming knowledge of the green revolution to a country that has no way of getting fertilizer, or advanced medical knowledge for complicated tests and surgery to a situation that has no relevant facilities or equipment. In the practice of teaching, the best theoretical knowledge of methods is of no avail if the class does not know the language of instruction or is hungry or is hostile. For brevity's sake we may call this factor on the side of practice the *situational conditions*.

Now if we put together the three factors—*the state of knowledge* in the case of theory and the *purposive pattern* and *situational conditions* in the case of practice—we have to ask what variations within them make possible what kinds of relations between theory and practice. In the state of theoretical knowledge, focus is on the degree of development of the relevant science and its specific methods of inquiry. Behind this, of course, lies the character of the actual phenomena involved: whether the particular subject matter happens to be simple and fairly uniform, stable like the motion of the planets, or a complex and volatile one like the weather, or even worse, like the stock market or much of human behavior. Putting it abstractly, the extent to which we have systematic knowledge depends on both the advanced state of the science and on the stability and manageable complexity of the phenomena. The domain of the practice is a fresh area of phenomena and how stable it is depends in part on the extent of harmony within the purposive pattern, in part of the stability of situational conditions.

Inner conflict is not unusual in many of our professional practices. For example, the traditional medical aims of curing and advancing knowledge sometimes involve the doctor in a trade–off, and the modern journalist sometimes has to choose between his obligation to report the news and the loss of advertising revenue. In education, the devastating impact of the conflict between academic objectives and job preparation is a familiar source of difficulties. As for situational conditions, all fields were thoroughly shaken in the last few decades by the political and technological changes after the Second World War; even had theoretical knowledge remained unchanged, its impact and relation to practice would have been radically altered. Finally, since the three factors vary in a relatively independent way, the character of each of them may, in a given case, affect the kind of relations possible between theory and practice.

The kinds of possible relations are patterned on the variety found in science (where it is well worked out in the practice of prediction), in means-end action (which is a practice of goal achievement), and in reflective experience generally. It thus moves from logical relations to methodological and to instrumental relations and then to a kind of craft or skilled insight. Whether we have here a continuum corresponding to diminishing degree of orderliness and increasing complexity in the phenomena or utterly different capacities in the human makeup, is a controversial issue.

From the sciences we borrow the idea of relations that are either deductive or inductive. In the first place there are conclusions for practice deduced from statements of theory in that ordinary sense of deduction in which the occurrence of the eclipse at a given time is deduced from the laws of planetary motion and the positions and velocities of the relevant bodies. Engineering makes such deductions constantly in the course of its applications. The usual assumption has been that human affairs have too much variability (whether from "free will" or from complexity) for such relations; they do not provide laws of sufficient strictness and regularity to be scientifically serviceable. Strangely enough, in matters of social practice, regularity may be secured through different means—by social fiat or determination. Large scale institutions may be assigned a strictness of procedure so that conclusions and calculations may be made with a precision at least analogous to engineering deductions. Thus in an area in which all other features but a specified number could be ignored—for example, specific insurance policies—the "laws" set up by the contractual relations that serve as the "theory" can be programmed and when situational conditions are entered after inspection the payments can be revealed ("deduced") by computer. This type of relation is then worth keeping open as a possibility because larger areas of human affairs may come to be thus handled mechanically as a matter of social policy—for example, if a "negative income tax" or a guaranteed annual wage were enacted. In human affairs, human fiat might thus create an order stricter than natural tendencies would manifest.

Inductive–experimental relations are familiar enough where prediction is involved. If theory–practice relations were so conceived, the practice would not be merely an application but testing whether the theory works or whether there is some hidden flaw or missing variable or sometimes whether the analysis of conditions of application has been wrong or incomplete; in any case, the theory–practice relation is here assimilated to the hypothesis experiment relation. A mass innoculation program, primarily a practical application of a theory and not intended as just an experiment, occasionally shows this character.

Where the sense of theory is weaker, or the complexity of phenomena very great, the best that can be done is construe the relation so as to have theory furnishing a set of methods or instruments for assisting practice, but not pointing to a specific result. Different analogies are helpful. Some theories are like charts or roadmaps; they guide explorations but do not warn of obstacles or disruptive factors or improbable occurrences. Some theories are simply theory–schemas; they are useful as instruments in that they tell the kinds of dimensions or components to look for in analyzing a situation, but not necessarily where to find them or how to put them together. In the social sciences, what is often called a theory of society turns out to be an analysis of just such factors. To divide the society in one way rather than another will provide a more systematic picture.

Finally, there is something which does not at first sight seem to be associated with theory at all, but appears to be a substitute for it. This is a kind of intuitive judgment or insight, not in the sense of beholding a self–evident truth, but rather grasping that something fits. It is the scientist's insight that a formula may fit the data or a curve is the one which will do the job, or a theory will unify materials. Perhaps there is only a difference of degree between this and the way in which an experienced sailor senses a coming storm or an experienced politician the first signs of a political rumble or an experienced teacher grasps where a lesson will take hold. The question here is whether these phenomena should be seen as embedded theory being translated into practice, or whether they express a distinct human capacity. They are often invoked in the claim that practice is an art, rather than akin to the family of theoretic science, but it is better to recognize a continuity with the other relations of theory and practice.

The kinds of relations given here are perhaps more than enough, expanded to suggest that when a distinction between theory and practice of the relative sort is emphasized it gives the freest rein to the different ways that theory can respond to the varying conditions and needs of practice. The variety of relations of theory to practice provides modes of guidance that should not be wasted. It is equally important to clear channels for getting what feedback there may be from the experience practice may have in the guidance of theory. Finally, there may be other cultural experiments that dispense with the whole theory–practice construction, and they are worth working out, but they would involve a major epistemological recasting, for they would have to carry out systematizations across our present theory–practice lines.

Relating Theory and Practice in Twentieth Century Educational Philosophy

Twentieth-century philosophy of education has treated rather cavalierly its own problem of relating theory (i.e., philosophy) and practice (i.e., educational practice). Unfortunately, the matter was debated about a categorical presence or absence of a relation. For example, it used to be said, when metaphysics and epistemology were seen as a set of conflicting "isms", that a Platonic metaphysics meant an authoritarian classroom; a Lockean epistemology entailed an insistence on memorization, rote learning and the use of rewards; or that a Kantian ethics promoted rigidity and a pragmatism of the Deweyan kind, individual initiative. The objection was of course offered that the Platonist could be more Socratic than authoritarian, the Lockean's burden of homework could cause the pupil to catch fire in the concentration of his effort, the Kantian could stimulate moral insight and strengthen moral fibre, and Deweyan flexibility might turn into opportunism. Not only could the same philosophical theory be associated with different educational practices, but different philosophical theories with the same practice. Educational philosophers jumped to the conclusion that there was no determinate relation between theory and practice, precisely because they were assuming that it had to be of a single kind. Actually they should have gone on to examine the cases more minutely, to find out at what point the theory operates and how it produces what effect.

The challenge took the form of denying that philosophical theories have had any relation to educational practice, although philosophical discipline might be effective insofar as it increases sensitivity or sharpens intuition. For example, some time ago a sheriff in Texas advertised for a deputy, announcing that he would give preference to someone trained in ancient Greek philosophy; he explained that he had found such students to be better at analyzing situations sensitively. It would scarcely do to say that the deputy would be *applying* or *practicing* Heraclitean philosophy if he kept an eye on changing conditions in the town, or Platonic philosophy if he acted on the assumption that all criminals have a fixed nature. His contact with these philosophies and his struggles with their arguments would have quickened his spirit; his actions proceed from a quickened insight, not a theoretical learning, any more than the politician's strategies come from the study of political theory rather than accumulated experience.

Approaches such as these create an atmosphere of cleavage between theory and practice. One form it takes in the philosophy of education is to divide knowledge sharply into the theoretical and the practical, with the educational consequence that learning is sent in two different directions. In this manner, Gilbert Ryle distinguishes *knowing-that* and *knowing-how*.[4] The latter, as practical learning, comes through experience or in apprenticeship in which the experience of others is taken over. The former, as theoretical learning, comes through verbal instruction. Ryle's dichotomy set a direction which was richly mined in contemporary educational philosophy, but steered toward multiplying different modes of learning. Criticisms of it simply bid higher by making more distinctions, for example between *knowing–how* and *knowing–how–to* and differentiating other kinds of knowing which invoked still further human capacities, for example aesthetic, and so other modes of learning. Now on our strategy, instead of multiplying types of learning, we should look to the different conditions under which learning takes place, those factors we explored in studying the various kinds of relations. Thus the atmosphere of sharp cleavage is dispelled and continuities in learning may be restored. The absolute types should not have been created at the very beginning: Ryle's *knowing–how* has not that sharp a distinction from *knowing–that* as his selected illustrations suggest. It may look that way when we think of learning to ride a bicycle, but not when we think of learning to pilot a plane; of knowing how to win an election under simpler conditions, but not under contemporary conditions of large-scale organization; of sea-faring in olden days, but not for computerized space–travel. In short, we have not here absolute differences in kind, but relative differences in degree.[5] Apprenticeship is not a cognitive mystery, even though it is a very complex matter. Many tasks have been sufficiently unravelled not only to become matters of instruction but even to be mechanized so that a robot can do them. Others have been sufficiently understood so that they can be improved by instruction and the handicapped enabled to do them in normal fashion. Some are not yet fully fathomed, so familiar as reading a page of a book. Differences in conditions support differences in the relations of available knowledge and possible educational practice.

If this general outline of the relations of theory and practice is fruitful, the philosophy of education will not antecedently limit its direction of development by some fixed formula of their relations. Analysis of specific context of practice will be required to determine what is possible in what areas and in what ways at what times and where emphasis should fall.

Concluding Reflections

There remains the (less than gnawing) worry whether we have succumbed to our present dichotomy, instead of rejecting it, by exploring its inner relations. Perhaps we would do better by reverting to a trichotomy, in Aristotelian fashion, or else by overcoming (dissolving, transcending, over-riding) the dichotomy in some way that makes a unity out of its components. These possibilities—tinkering with our present dichotomy in one way or another, and unifying its two sides in one way or another—merit at least brief exploration.

The theory–practice dichotomy was set up earlier as including in theory the systematic knowledge available for the particular field of consideration, and in practice the purposive pattern and situational conditions invoked in the application of the theory. Now the simplest alternative if we are to preserve a dichotomy might be to include the purposive pattern in theory, leaving the situational conditions in practice. This is a ready model for human action and planning: all action involves on the one side some cognitive and value equipment (presuppositions, established habits and directions of effort), and on the other side the field conditions under which they are being exercised. Should this seem to threaten the purity of theory, we might set up a trichotomy instead, with theory in its abstract form as the first party, theory interpreted for action as the second, and application as the third. (Compare a pure geometry rendered abstract in Hilbertian fashion, such a geometry interpreted for a Euclidean space, and thirdly carpentry or surveying.)

A more complex alternative would be to assemble all the knowledge invoked on both sides of our original dichotomy and regard it as theory. Clearly there is considerable knowledge embedded in a purposive pattern and in the description of the situational conditions. The result might be rather hard on practice: all the sciences, laws, classified types, universals on the theory side, leaving nothing but bare existence or movement on the practice side. This brings us back to the crude dichotomy of all that is cognitive, all the thinking, on one side and the mere fact of spatio–temporal doing on the other. It may remind us of the Platonic treatment of universals as the real, monopolizing all account of sorts and kinds, with existence as simply the convergent reflection of a group of universals in some shadowy matrix. Or in a more even–handed way we could repeat with Kant that percepts without concepts are blind and concepts without percepts are empty.

Attempts to overcome the dichotomy in some unity of theory and practice take different shape in different philosophies. Some go in for transcendence in an ultimate unity of mystical experience; others trace the interaction of cognition and movement in human activity, or again the mutual involvement of the practical and the theoretical.

Of the efforts at unity by transcendence, the ancient neo–Platonic is the supreme example. It develops the Platonic duality noted above. Practice (in the sense of what goes on in the material world) is reduced to a bare resistance to the rational–theoretical. The full analysis of any productive process is found in the rationality it embodies. (Plotinus may yet come to be installed as a patron saint of an automatized and computerized production in which thinking and planning are all that really counts and the rest follows as a matter of course!) But—to complete the story—a dualism remains within theory itself, for it takes for granted the distinction between the knower and the known. This is what is ultimately transcended in the mystical–religious experience, which is itself indescribable.

More earthy attempts at finding the unity of theory and practice focus on human action. A commonplace instance is the perfection of a skill so that the *temporal* distance between cognition and movement is minimized. Take, for example, driving an automobile. The better the driver, the more rapidly the cognition involved in perception of the surrounding conditions, together with all the knowledge embodied in the theoretical interpretation of signs, signals, warnings, judgments of speed, knowledge of the habits of pedestrians and other drivers are translated into movements of the driver's wheel. In short, habit operating intelligently, is the unifier of theory and practice. Where, however, in a more elaborate operation theory takes the form of complex intellectual activity expressing a pattern of ideas while the practice is some construction of art presumably embodying those ideas, then the unity of theory and practice has to be found in the way the theory functions with respect to the practice. This brings us back to the path we dismissed in beginning the discussion of different types of relations—the psychological and social modes in which the theory operates. A familiar distinction here is whether it operates in realistic guidance or in ideological justification. (The theory of such relations is itself well developed in the twentieth-century analyses of ideology.) It is, of course, the closeness of real guidance that constitutes the stronger unity. Nevertheless, the quality of the guidance and the quality of the product may itself be a factor in the judgment of the unity achieved. For example, a writer discussing Wagner's own theories in relation to his music may say: "Wagner varied the philosophical, aesthetic and political theories he proclaimed in his writings entirely for the sake of his musical dramas, which in the last analysis were the only thing that truly possessed him. The works are the key to the writings, not vice versa."[6] Or an architectural critic may complain that in the past "The critic and historian, quite properly, came after the creative act, with a particular knowledge and insight, to probe meanings and processes, discern norms and standards, evaluate the work of art, and relate it to the larger setting of time and place," but now the critic gets in ahead and expounds aesthetic standards to evaluate before the work is done.[7] Doubtless it is the fact that the writer does not approve of the outcomes of such influence that affects the judgment about the shift in the critic's mode of functioning. Such examples, which one comes on in all sorts of different fields, show how important has become today's relation of theory and practice and the assessment of the theoretician's role. In questions of public policy and political action it becomes particularly crucial. Whereas in the 'old days' the theoretician proposed an ideal that might be approached over the ages, so that some testing went on in the steps toward its achievement, nowadays the distance between theory and practice has diminished so that instead of ideals we have instant political programs. To some extent this is doubtless due to the rapid development of instruments of communication and agitation, as well as of course to the multiplication of serious social problems.

Such considerations suggest that perhaps the critique of the dichotomy of theory and practice is simpler than it appears in the many directions in which we may struggle with it. The very attempt to explicate each side of the dichotomy carries us into the other. No establishment of theory is possible without experimental practice and no guidance of practice is possible without some theory or theory-surrogates. How particular divisions are patterned is itself an experimental matter geared to the particular contexts and problems which that division is to serve. Every division has its limitations and its costs and is on constant trial to earn its keep.

In general, the distinction of theory and practice comes from the division of labor that gave rise to specialized bodies of knowledge, pursued with increasing independence, from the ancient Egyptian priestly studies of earth and heavens to predict the flooding of the Nile to contemporary separation of basic research in all fields from even research directed to technological application. It is not a distinction without social and intellectual costs: its history is replete with the privileges and snobbery of class and status, and with the illusions that have masqueraded under the slogan of the neutrality of science (invoking another dichotomy, that of fact and value).[8] The democratic attempt to diminish the costs by broader education, greater appreciation of science, and even increased participation in some ways in scientific ventures, points a direction for effort but scarcely amounts to overcoming the distinction. In sum, the present basis of the distinction in its most serious use is the social context of a relatively independent accumulation of systematic knowledge. Overcoming the distinction in this respect is logically possible: doubtless there was a time of largely self–sufficient practice in the form of rudimentary craft production in which the ordinary experience of Everyman was adequate for the daily round as practiced. And in the twentieth-century context it would seem that Mao's cultural revolution in China was in great measure prompted by the fear of the relation of specialized knowledge and a class monopoly of power. It looks as if, however, in the context of our contemporary world as it is likely to be for an indefinite time, the problem both for knowledge and action will remain the quality of relations between theory and practice rather than the dissolution of any distinction.

Under these conditions we may rest content with realizing the contextual rather than the absolute character of the division of theory and practice, with the vista of the many types of possible relations, and with establishing a practice that, when it has to face a division in some inquiry, will always look, in a normative stance, for the most suitable mode of relation in the materials and purposes provided by the context. Appreciating the instrumental character of the distinction, we can also be sensitive to the search for fresh modes of relation, if those at hand are not adequate or satisfactory. While such an outcome may not satisfy the metaphysical inclinations so often at the base of traditional dichotomies, it provides a fruitful replacement for a barren dilemma.

The paper was written for a festschrift honoring Lewis Feuer.

Notes

1. Thus what is regarded by us as science that contemplates would be really from God's point of view art that produces. Such continuity is found, for example, in the teaching of William Ames, a seventeenth–century Puritan philosopher working in the spirit of Ramus. His views were influential in early Massachusetts controversies against the Aristotelian philosophy.

2. See, for example, Mihailo Marković, From *Affluence to Praxis, Philosophy and Social Criticism* (Ann Arbor: University of Michigan Press, 1974).
3. Cf. Abraham Edel, *Method in Ethical Theory* (Indianapolis: Bobbs-Merrill, 1963), chap. 11 (Genetic Inquiry and Truth Determination). Pages 273–79 examine critically Feuer's attempt to establish a basis in genetic inquiry for determining truth or adequacy of philosophic ideas.
4. See Gilbert Ryle, *The Concept of Mind* (London: Hutchinson's University Library, 1949).
5. Ryle was attempting to get rid of the mind–body dualism in the theory of knowledge but the outcome of his way of doing it was to substitute a theory–practice dualism. For a fuller critique of this whole episode in educational theory, see chap. 6.
6. Joseph Kerman, "Wagner and Wagnerism" in *The New York Review of Books* XXX, 20 (Dec. 22, 1983), p. 27. Kerman is here quoting Carl Dalhaus, from *The New Grove Wagner* by John Deathridge and Carl Dalhaus (Norton, 1984).
7. Ada Louise Huxtable, "After Modern Architecture" in *The New York Review of Books* XXX, 19 (Dec. 8, 1983), p. 29. She declares that "The influences passing between print and practice are subtle and insidious, and the relationship grows increasingly incestuous."
8. For analysis of the fact–value dichotomy in its various aspects, see Abraham Edel, *Exploring Fact and Value* (Science, Ideology, and Value, Vol. 2). (New Brunswick, U.S.A. and London: Transaction Books, 1980), The appendix (338–363) outlines the sociological history of the dichotomy.

3

Is the Individual-Social
a Misleading Dichotomy?

No categorial divide has ruled the thinking by people in the last three centuries so completely as that between the individual and the social. Yet it was never an even–handed division of areas or tasks or values. Its purpose stood out frankly, to subjugate the social or communal to the individual or collection of individuals. This can be read everywhere: in accounts of the origin of institutions (the social contract of individuals coming together), in the classification of virtues (not by common needs but as either self–regarding or other–regarding), in ethical theories whose triumph lay in adding individual pleasures to achieve a maximum, in an economic theory that shifted the core from productive social labor to individual buying and selling in the market.

This study surveys the recent crumbling of this categorial divide, and tries to find a proper place in which the distinction can engage in honest specific labor.

The contrast of individual and social is a familiar—too familiar—dichotomy, and one on which people take sides in both theory and practice. *Individual* has, of course, been the favorite over the last three centuries, but in our time *social* is coming on apace. In many fields it has made inroads on the philosophy of individualism: many philosophers and social scientists who have been committed to an extreme individualistic model in their work—whether trying to build a common world out of private sensations or a common well-being out of individual preferences—are beginning to be attracted in one subtle form or another to the social. On the other hand, many who have made extensive use of the category of the social find it too general to do the real work of social and moral analysis, and are driven to break it up or experiment with more refined substitutes for the generic social and individual. This paper explores each of these broad tendencies, as well as the practical impact of the contemporary turn.

Part 1

Admittedly, individualism has been entrenched in the disciplines that deal with human affairs—politics, economics, morality. The normal and unquestioned mode of theorizing has been to start from the individual and his/her desires and preferences (usually *his*, since men held political power, controlled the family finances, and laid down the moral law) and show how the operations of human nature in individuals produced macroscopic results. This was the way in which Bentham built a social morality out of the calculations of individual pleasures and pains, Adam Smith a market economy out of choices of individuals in buying and selling, and contemporary political sociologists have been showing how social policy is generated in democracy from the polled preferences of voter samples. Twentieth-century ethics has been permeated by this individualism which runs through most of the schools, no matter how they are opposed. Emotivism starts with individuals expressing their feelings and attempting to influence others; existentialism with the decisional predicaments of the individual; ordinary language analytic ethics often with the individual prescribing or evaluating and in Kantian fashion legislating for all; Rawls with individuals under a veil of ignorance being led by rational calculations of the unknown to formulate universal principles of justice; human rights theory unveiling the inherent rights of individuals (while quarreling over what they are); and naturalistic ethics from Perry at the beginning of the twentieth century to Pepper at the mid–century starting with individual interests and purposes and building up corporate interests. To see the signs of the reappearance of the social in so vast a field, a few samples are all that we can offer here. They come from the trend of disciplines and significant papers of individual theorists.

Among the disciplines, linguistics has steadily and unavoidably been oriented to the social. A language is a social formation, though its study may be through informed native speakers. The prominence of the linguistic in contemporary philosophy would mean that the social would eventually be brought to attention. However, the discipline that seems most to have made inroads on theoretical individualism, almost to the point of restoring an organic model, is ecology. Here the perspective of looking at the whole, tracing the interactions, and seeing the individual event in its widest systematic relations, was forced on investigators by the inability, otherwise, to understand the individual. "An ecological perspective" becomes almost equivalent to a total systemic perspective. And the rapid growth of communications with the development of a global economy has begun to force movement in that direction for the social sciences. Eventually, psychology, the most stubbornly individualistic of the human sciences, may itself take a larger step in that direction. The present crisis in the social sciences seems to be largely an uncertainty what to put in the place of the inadequate individualism.

In ethics, the signs of a shift are particularly interesting. As long as an individualistic model prevailed in the major ethical conceptions, the social was limited to the content. The right was the individual universalizing; or the good man was motivated by the social interest. An early indication that the social was penetrating the formal structure of ethics came with the use of the notion of "practices"—for example, in Rawls' well-known "Two Concepts of Rules." Thus promising was not just an individual act whose justification had to be sought outside of itself (whether through intuition or utilitarian reckoning); it was a practice (akin to an institution), and what could be evaluated was this social practice, but given its existence the obligation to keep a promise was internal to promising. In a similar vein, Philippa Foot[1] attacked the view that approval and disapproval were merely sentiments within the individual, and compared them instead (though individual acts) to voting, which is a socially structured and regulated act. On such approaches, the Kantian ethics, itself so influential in the whole of contemporary moral individualism, would be seen at its key point not as the individual testing the inner morality of his action by universalizing his maxim, but as the individual asking himself whether he is ready to live with an institution along the lines of his decision.

Perhaps the clearest example can be seen in comparing rights theory and decision theory today. Rights theory has not moved significantly to look for the rights of groups; it deals with the natural rights or human rights of individuals. Yet occasional historical pronouncements might have led it in this direction. For example, when Richard Price included among natural rights of men the right of Englishmen to cashier their government (in his sermon that so enraged Edmund Burke), he could not have meant it distributively, but only for Englishmen collectively. By contrast, questions of group preferences and of group rationality, even of group agency, have clearly surfaced in the debates of decision theorists. In a paper on "Conflict and Social Agency," Isaac Levi discusses such questions as whether we should attribute rationality to social groups, whether groups can be regarded as agents, whether social agents can be selfish or directed toward other social agents, whether judgments of social agency are affected by the fact that they may be directed to individual interests, and so on. The underlying perspective which makes such inquiry possible is stated as follows:

> When we focus on characterizations of social groups in terms of their beliefs, goals, choices, and other such propositional attitudes, we are no more concerned with the underlying mechanisms than we are when we use such characterizations of human agents or, for that matter, of automata. Perhaps differences in the "hard-

ware'' should make a difference in the view we take of the principles of rational preference, belief, valuation, and choice; but, unless a decisive case is advanced that this should be so, it seems sensible to seek an account of rational choice, belief, preference, and valuation which is indifferent to whether the agent is human or not and, if not, whether it is automaton, animal, angelic, or social.[2]

Levi recognizes that to speak of groups as agents may offend ontological sensibilities. His argument lies partly in suggesting phenomena of already existent scientific usage (e.g., families qualifying as consumers in the economic theory of consumer demand, corporations often qualified in the law and business firms making decisions) and partly in suggesting how use of such group formulations may help resolve some of the technical problems in the exploration of rational decision, such as those raised in Arrow's treatment of the way in which social choice is related to individual values. Levi is led by his argument into questioning the common assumption that ''rational agents should have resolved all conflicts when fixing on a decision, so that they can claim that the option chosen is for the best, all things considered.''[3] This means not only decision under risk, but decision where one cannot assert probabilities of consequences and so evaluate alternative options in terms of expected utility free of any conflict.

The move of isolating the social group properties from the underlying mechanisms is by now a familiar one. It is what Frege and Russell and others did in isolating logic from psychological considerations and treating it purely formally. This revolt against psychologism, so widespread in the early part of the century, paid off in logical developments, though some may regard it as postponing relations which have later to be dealt with in applying the formalisms. In our day, the same move has been made to advance the theory of artificial intelligence: intelligence, first characterized by human thinking, is formally analyzed and then its properties sought wherever they can be found, automata as well as humans. There seems to be some payoff in this move, at least promising enough to pursue it. Levi is here suggesting the same procedure for the properties of preference and agency; separated from the individual they can be tried out for the group. It is an experiment to be justified by its theoretical fruits.

Part 2

We turn now to those who, in spite of a marked preference for the category of the social, nevertheless begin to express reservations about its broad or generic use. Dewey is a good example. In Dewey and Tufts' *Ethics* of 1932, Dewey wrote in a chapter, ''Morals and Social Problems,'' concerning the conflict of individual and social:

We shall accordingly substitute the consideration of definite conflicts, at particular times and places, for a general opposition between social and individual. Neither "social" nor "individual," in general, has any fixed meaning. All morality (including immorality) is both individual and social:—individual in its immediate inception and execution, in the desires, choices, dispositions from which conduct proceeds; social in its occasions, material, and consequences.[4]

This was by no means an off–the–cuff dismissal. For about a quarter of a century, since the first edition of the *Ethics* (1908), Dewey had grappled with the question of individualism and the role of the social. In the first edition, individualism marks the moral progress of civilization. Later, however, Dewey treats individualism as a particular historical phenomenon emerging under the specific historical conditions of the seventeenth century on, and having specific consequences in human life. Such an unseating of the category of the individual was bound to be followed sooner or later by a comparable unseating of the category of the social. For the individual and the ideal of individualism Dewey substituted (in his *Individualism Old and New*, 1930) the ideal of *individuality* as a socially cultivated character with its virtues of initiative, intelligence, originality productive of diversity, and so on. For the generic social he substituted the variety of specific groups with their special interests within definite historical contexts.

Now it might be said that the shift from the social to the variety of groups is not particularly significant, for "social" is simply all along a general name for social groups. Who—apart from organic theories of society mystically viewed literally as an organism—has ever held to a social–in–itself? Such an objection forgets that a point becomes trivial and commonplace only when its intellectual revolution is over. The shift embodies a new way of looking at what previously had to be said in terms of the isolated individual and the general social. In the old way a theory of instincts could be offered to explain human behavior; as against this it could be argued that the social enters into the very formation of the individual. (Dewey wrote that all psychology is either biological or social, not individual.) Similarly, as against the individualistic formulation of the moral problem as egoism versus altruism, Dewey could pit the social formulation that the issue was neither, but rather the kind of social institutions that developed what kind of character. In the old way, deviance was an individual revolt against the social pattern; but it could cogently be argued that it was rather an incipient social pattern itself. (Recall the New Yorker cartoon of the 1960s: an advertisement reading "Lessons in non-conformity, Wednesdays at 8:00 p.m. Do not be late.")

I am suggesting that the broad reference to the social sufficed as long as the chief problem was to reject special explanatory accounts of behavior or decision in terms of the individual. But with the rejection of the general individual–social contrast as a way of formulating theoretical and practical issues, more specific group categories would have to be worked out in different areas of life. Thus, in politics Dewey (in his *The Public and Its Problems*, 1927) proposed that the distinction of public and private be substituted for that of social and individual. (A public grows up when lines of conduct have wide consequences affecting sizeable numbers and a common organization ensues.) Similarly, the problem of the scope of the moral community is not dealt with effectively in the simple terms of individual respect for the other; both for understanding action and for moral decision we are concerned with family and kin, class and nation, regional or ideological blocs, and the like.

To deal with specific groupings in given historical stretches is not the only way in which the category of the social has been altered. It can also be narrowed by division. A good illustration is the rise of the concept of the *interpersonal*, set off against the social. Familiar roots are George Herbert Mead's account of the growth of the mind in the direct interactions of person with person; Harry Stack Sullivan's interpersonal approach to psychiatry as against Freud's focus on intra–individual processes; and Martin Buber's use of the categories of encounter and dialogue as against subjectivity and group formations. (Dialogue has itself become a hardy, almost imperialistic category.) The interpersonal has thus broken off from the social, restricting the latter to the organized, the rule governed, usually the impersonal. Such a shift has had implications for both morals and politics, as well as for psychology, psychiatry, and education.

Part 3

The approach I have been following in the previous sections—through the career of the category of the social in a diversity of fields and disciplines—allows for cumulative experience and some generalization based on the convergence of results. This need not, however, belie a more abstract and overall mode of inquiry. But that would itself be seen as the formal creation of alternative models, to replace, for example, the individual and the social on which we have concentrated. It would be philosophical arrogance to assume that the latter two exhaust the field. For example, few models have been tried out that are sub-individual and would, in the traditional formulation, raise doubts about the solid reality of the individual. (Such models would repeat for the biological the kind of dissolution of the individual that Hume's treatment of impressions brought for the mind.) Enthusiastic sociobiologists today sometimes talk in that way; I came somewhere across the assurance that the genes don't care whether they are in a giraffe or an assistant professor, for they are only interested in their expansive multiplication. Perhaps some Aristotelian sociobiologist will find substantive human reality to lie in the *gene pool* from which forms and diversities emerge. I do not myself believe that sub–individual models at present look very promising and that we will find ourselves worrying whether a gene pool is a *universitas* with corporate identity or a *societas* with distinct members. But the experimental attitude with respect to the field of interacting persons and the kinds of categories that can open up its most fruitful study is another matter and one of vital importance. Perhaps we need categories that will do for the interacting group what field conceptions did for the study of electricity, or what feed–back conceptions do for the operations of a cybernetic complex, or what Dewey and Bentley tried to do by substituting *transaction* for *interaction*—not to speak of the more massive reorientation of categories that the contemporary attention to process has brought in a broader field. It is probably in such directions that the present frontier of the study of the social is most likely to expand, not in the repetition of past controversies over individual versus social.

An important practical consequence of this experimental perspective is that we need no longer envisage a monolithic conflict between societal systems defined in terms of the individual and those defined in terms of the social. There are, of course, real differences between different societies in the major goals they support, in the scope of benefits and burdens they bring to different groups, in the virtues and liberties they promote, in the effectiveness of their projects, in the quality of life they achieve, in the degree of justice they bring to submerged groups. But if there is any clear lesson from the last half century it is that moral judgment and social policy cannot be routed wholesale through what are essentially ideological structures. It requires very specific reference to specific values and goods, rights and responsibilities, and indeed to human hopes and fears.

The paper was read at the 12th World Congress of the International Association for Philosophy of Law and Social Philosophy in Athens in 1985.

Notes

1. Philippa Foot, "Approval and Disapproval," in *Law, Morality, and Society, Essays in Honour of H.L.A. Hart*, ed. P.M.S. Hacker and J. Raz (Oxford: Clarendon Press, 1977), 229–46.
2. *The Journal of Philosophy*, May 1982, 234.
3. Ibid., 239.
4. John Dewey and James H. Tufts, *Ethics*, rev. ed. (New York: Henry Holt & Company, 1932), 363.

4

Elitism and Culture

This study, in collaboration with Elizabeth Flower, was prompted by the growing suspicion that the use currently made of the issue of "elitism versus populism" represented fundamentally the survival of the aristocratic outlook when it had finally acquiesced in the existence of a democratic society. It hardened into a fighting slogan the commonplace fact that differences of expertise and skill exist, and made it into a social classification by fusing it with the common idea that merit deserves some reward. Tracing historical roots and development and observing mode of functioning yielded a quite different picture of the human phenomena forged by the dichotomy into a weapon.

The analysis of such concepts as liberalism and conservatism, virtue, culture, and civilization that shape our perception of social reality and its problems is no easy task. Not only their present use is significant, but also their history, the context in which they arose, their interrelations with other ideas, the functions they served, and the consequences they encouraged. Often their history will leave, perhaps unnoticed, a mark on the present that carries a distinct coloring and affects their utility.

Such a concept is that of *the elite*. It has a historical career; it enters into historical events as participant. We are tempted to hold it responsible for benefits bestowed as well as havoc created. It cannot be evaluated in general terms, for it may have different consequences in different fields, and these consequences may seriously affect policy. Perhaps its continued use distorts our perceptions and blocks fresh and more creative approaches. We are led to wonder whether the concept of the elite has outlived its usefulness. Our strategy here is, first, to look at some aspects of the historical career of elitism, and, second, to review a recent situation in which it cantankerously exploded on the American cultural–political scene (which assures that it is not a dead issue). Thereafter we scan appeals to the elite in politics, education, and culture and offer a conclusion.

The basic distinction in elitism is between *elite* and *mass*. Elitism is an outlook (including a theory) that takes this distinction to be fundamental in understanding society and culture and in guiding social policy. It takes the elite to be the source of knowledge and culture, the guardian of quality, the preserver of standards, and the proper locus of leadership and authority. Populism is often regarded as the contrary or opposing outlook, believing vitality to lie in the mass. Populism would hold that policy should be directed to removing the shackles of tradition and authority that have bound it and that where a choice is necessary, resources should be directed to the education and liberation of the masses.

In earlier times the elite were an established aristocracy; the masses had no share in their activities. The lines were visible. Power and glory, as well as accomplishment, lay on one side. (Historians still have problems finding out what went on across the line.) The division was justified by theories of all sorts—theological and metaphysical, biological and social. Plato gave elitism a strong start with an underlying theory of human nature in which he saw the human psyche as composed of appetite (the dragon), will or spirit (the lion), and reason (the human). Appetite is demanding; lacking in self–control, it requires continual repression by reason with the aid of spirit. Assuming that reason is strong only in the few, Plato makes the central social task to be the need for restraint of the masses by the elite.

So blunt a theme admits of many variations in the history of aristocracy and elitism. Burke renews it for the modern world in the thesis that tradition is central to restraint, that respect and veneration for the traditional are essential bonds not to be lightly loosened, that if there are natural rights the most important is the right of the people to be protected against themselves, that it is better to retain any privilege, however arbitrary, than to precipitate the spirit of revolt against all privilege. In the nineteenth century, democratic advances in politics and democratic programs for education were opposed as diminishing respect for authority and opening the door to the passions of the populace. Even such a liberal as John Stuart Mill feared (in his *On Liberty*) that individuality was being swamped by popular conformity, while conservatives raised the slogan of liberty versus equality, suggesting the premise that the masses cannot achieve equality without ruining the liberties that support quality and culture.

In the early part of our century, the self–styled elite among our college youth could be reassured about their superiority by reading H.L. Mencken's column in the *American Mercury*, in which he jibed at the American "boob-oisie" and depicted its antics. Or they could turn, in the academic world, to the humanism of Irving Babbitt and find democracy accused of lacking standards and engaged in "the irresponsible quest of thrills."[1] Babbitt analyzed the psyche more genially than did Plato or Burke; not simply the aggressive and the predatory but the sympathetic and the humanitarian could work havoc. The humanitarian goes astray, for example, by seeing in the college "a means not so much for the thorough training of the few as of uplift for the many."[2] Only an inner discipline (of which apparently few were capable) could maintain civilization. In the grim struggles of the 1930s under the shadow of fascism, there was despair about the impasse of democracy, even in the United States. The idea of government by the people was repeatedly attacked as leading to chaos. "Government by the consent of the governed" was interpreted as at most the right of the people to elect their rulers, not to participate in governmental decision making.

The advance of democratic ideas from the seventeenth century on had been slow, and from the beginning it was attacked as "leveling." When, however, political democracy became fairly widespread in the Western world, the concept of the elite could not survive by identification with aristocracy. It began to lose its immediate descriptive validity as a concentrated and isolated elite was dissipated. The opposition to leveling had then to move from an outside criticism of democracy as a whole to an inside advocacy of policy within an established democratic framework. The elitist response was not to abandon the distinction of elite and mass, but democratically to open the elite to the best of the multitude. When all come to wear the same clothes and use the same language and even have a higher education (although the beginnings of mass higher education are not yet half a century behind us in the industrially advanced countries), it may be difficult to spot who are the elite. Aristotle had said that nature intended some for slavery and that if nature had not mistakenly given some slaves the appearance of natural masters we could tell at a glance which were which. Moderns have sometimes thought that if we could peer into the minds and hearts (and genes?) of men and women, we would know who was destined for accomplishment. In the absence of such an easy way, meritocracy is invoked: keep the doors open and let success make the choice.

Admittedly, such a democratic conception of an elite tends to yield a dispersed elite. But it firmly saves the concept. Indeed, by becoming democratized, elitism seems almost to purify itself of any concern but excellence. The once sinister distinction between elite and mass seems now a truism and harmless. It simply asserts that there are in every field some who are abler, and they usually go farther. Everybody, it may be said, plays baseball, but only a few make the teams and fewer yet are stars. They are the elite. Many people go in for acting, but only a few make it; they become the elite. In every field some are *chosen* (the root idea of "elite"—the elect). Culturally, the elite write the successful books, get the top jobs, edit the successful journals, are wooed by the aspiring young, and so on. Even after the spread of higher education, the total productive group in all disciplines—those who produce as distinct even from those who perpetuate—is relatively small. A Shakespeare, a Newton, an Einstein, a Freud, a Mozart, are scarcely of the rank and file.

Comfortably ensconced within democracy, then, the concept was untroubled as long as the meritocratic idea went unchallenged. The world of the elite has perhaps to acquiesce in some dilution of culture as the multitude are encouraged to enter that world. This, however, simply reinforces a distinction between the higher culture of the few and the popular culture of the many. But with the populist "revolt of the masses" under the banner of the equalitarian ideal, the elitist sees a real threat emerging in the challenge to the standards of excellence. As the elitist sees it, the belief that "vox populi vox dei" has been spreading from politics to culture. Standards of excellence are being rejected as expressing the aristocratic values of the establishment, and the emptiness that results is being filled by any populist wind that blows. The taste of the populace, anything that "turns them on," becomes the test of quality. Elitism is thus confronted by populism in one or another theoretical form, and the antagonism between quality and equality comes out in the open. The question is now far removed from aristocracy. In politics, elitism conceives the contemporary task to be in control of the demos within the democratic framework; in education, to select from the many those who are most able; in culture—regarded as itself an elitist concept—to foster the creative few.

To have pushed such issues into the center of democratic attention is the triumph of the democratized concept of the elite, for the dichotomy of the elite and the mass is perpetuated in the very formulations. Even populism counterattacks with the same distinction. Yet there is a far different possibility—that the dichotomy as it has historically emerged is now outworn, that the issues packed away in the concepts should now be separated and analyzed in different terms and the dichotomy itself abandoned. This is the thesis we wish to explore.

The power of a categorial dichotomy is not to be underestimated. The history of thought is strewn with dichotomies in terms of which questions were formulated, theoretical energies riveted, and answers constrained. Take, for example, the twentieth-century's obsession with the cleavage between fact and value. This involved desperate attempts to parcel out phenomena, linguistic forms, activities, disciplines. It isolated science from ethics and insulated ethics, thereby supporting a science without responsibility and an ethics cut off from the growing resources of science. Decades passed until the realization grew—it has not yet been fully grasped—that the presumed absolute dichotomy is a relative distinction, useful in some contexts, irrelevant in others where other distinctions are more fruitful, and where to cast inquiry in this presumed absolute only creates intellectual havoc.[3] Similar problems can be found in the history of absolute dichotomies of matter and mind, body and soul, human and divine, objective and subjective, sense and intellect, cognitive and affective, and countless others.

Has the dichotomy of elite and mass now run its course? Will democratizing the distinction rescue it, or do our problems require some other mode of organizing the study of social and cultural differences?

Before we enter on the several fields, let us examine the contrast of elitism and populism at work in a public controversy that recently swept the journalistic reportage of culture.[4] Here, for example, are some headlines, largely from the Arts and Leisure section of the Sunday *New York Times* from 1977 to 1979: "Funding Culture, High and Low, and Calling it all Art" (16 October 1977); "Elitism, In the Arts, Is Good" (5 February 1978); " 'Elitism' in Arts and Humanities Units Is Debated" (27 April 1978); "A Populist Shift in Federal Cultural Support" (13 May 1979). The issue erupted when President Jimmy Carter considered fresh appointments to head the National Endowment for the Humanities (NEH) and the National Endowment for the Arts (NEA). Senator Claiborne Pell had criticized NEH for leaning to esoteric projects instead of reaching out to the length and breadth of the country; he called it a pale shadow in comparison to its sister arts establishment, which "generated more momentum" at the "grass roots." NEH was said to have an elitist image, and the taint of elitism seems to have been fatal to some candidates. NEH was also said to be serving a narrow academic constituency instead of a broader popular constituency. These criticisms—pursuit of the esoteric, elitism, narrow academic constituency—were usually packaged as if they were one or aspects of one defect. When Joseph Duffey was nominated to head NEH, *The Chronicle of Higher Education* had a story headed, "The Humanist Endowment: Elitist or Populist? Carter's Nominee as chairman says agency can be both."

It may be said that the exigency of headlining drives to sharp contrasts. Yet the stories themselves show that this was indeed the structuring of the issues. We find questions like "Are we really prepared to sacrifice quality for numbers?" Elitism in culture and the arts is also equated with "the influence of acknowledged achievement of a high order." Among other strong statements we find: "Intellectual activity, of which the arts is one manifestation, is and always has been elitist. Demagogues and yahoos do not like this; they would like to drag us down to their own level." "On its highest level the appreciation of art is as elitist as the creation of art. Those listening to a Beethoven symphony, content merely to let the music wash over them, are operating at a very low level." "Elitism of the intellect should be a term of praise rather than disparagement." One participant in the debate was reported as offering a history of elitism defined as "concern for the best" and as contrasting Matthew Arnold's idea of a democratic culture with that of the minority culture of the highly educated advocated by T.S. Eliot. Another put to Senator Pell the contrast of Athens (which produced Plato, Aristotle, Socrates, Aeschylus, Sophocles, Euripides, Aristophanes, Thucydides) and Sparta (which produced military heroes) and asked whether money for the arts and humanities should go equally to both. Senator Pell said it should, for in that way the arts and humanities might be stimulated in the city that lacked them. Populist policies were taken to be putting support for education in place of support for creation, and concentrating on making the humanities comprehensible and useful to the wider public. They were described as arranging "a marriage between popular access and professional excellence." There was fear that the attempt to navigate the treacherous waters between elitism and populism might yield a flabby populism.

The question is whether the formulation of issues in terms of elitism and populism had really tapped the problems that had to be faced, or whether it distorted the argument over real differences of policy. Perhaps the first task is to unpack the bundle of issues about the pursuit of the esoteric, outreach to a broader constituency, and the concept of elitism.

The matter of the esoteric may be disposed of briefly. A problem is esoteric if it can be understood only by a professional in–group, but not by a wider out–group. But the esoteric is relative to time and place. Einstein's theory of relativity was esoteric only at first when just half a dozen people were said to understand his mathematics. Whether in art or science or humanities, what is esoteric in one age may become in the future a prevalent style, unifying theory, or dominant theme. Hence it is not wisdom to avoid investing in the esoteric. Indeed, there is no general problem of the esoteric. There is no point in praising a project or condemning it because it is esoteric. Every esoteric project has to be judged on its own as a separate question. Thus to be esoteric is not necessarily a permanent feature but a changing historical feature. The scholar with an esoteric interest need not be elitist, for elitism deals with a quite different dimension.

The core of elitism, as the statements quoted suggest, is not the values, the excellencies desired, but the conviction that the few are the bearers of such values and that the people at large cannot participate in or create these values and perhaps not even adequately appreciate them. Elitism reflects thus a kind of club spirit or small–establishment spirit. It is not a matter of extent of outreach, but of quality. An outreach to the length and breadth of the country could still remain elitist in spirit. For example, an arts endowment could conceivably offer the objective of "every American child a painter," but if it attempted to do so by furnishing paint-by-number sets it would be an elitist outreach, keeping people inert. The question would be what kind of momentum was generated. Aesthetic feeling cultivates fine shades; it does not simply arouse gross (e.g., aggressive) emotions. Humanistic dialogue engenders deliberative discussion, not simply ideological rhetoric. Elitism takes many different forms in a democratic context. It can be found, for example, in the tendency to talk down to an audience and to render it inert rather than participatory. There is also that strange permissive elitism in which the mere quantity of talk engendered is taken to be the measure of participation, for the attitude to people is paternalistic. In any case it is important not to look for elitism in the wrong place. Elitism is not identical with supporting esoteric projects, and it is not to be identified with supporting the academic. Neglecting the nonacademic often reflects a straight struggle of different interests for support where there are limited resources, just as within education itself graduate and undergraduate and adult divisions vie for greater shares of limited funds. In the case we have examined, there was clearly the fear that wider support of cultural education would be at the expense of cultural creativity through established institutions; sometimes the elitist tone seemed simply added for good measure.

The issue of constituencies to be served by NEH and NEA—or for that matter, by the National Science Foundation—was a wider one than (as one press account put it) the bid of other colleges, junior colleges, labor, ethnic groups, other cultural institutions, against the eastern academic establishment. It was not surprising that the more established academic community got more of the fellowship grants where support for original research was the point involved, for the simple reason that they had more opportunity to store talent for that kind of research. The wider question was what other kinds of educational and cultural objectives should be carried out by the use of public funds and through what other kinds of institutions—museums, labor unions, local groups, informal community organizations, TV and radio, and so on. The language of constituencies concentrated on the fact of different pressure groups, but ignored that of meeting different needs that were neglected or of using different methods that might prove efficacious for the desired objectives.

The central formulation of the problems involved could therefore be carried out only by facing directly the specific tasks required in advancing science, art, humanities. These tasks are of three sorts, just as in the case of education or, for that matter, health. One is advancing original creation: research, investigation, and production of an original work, by the professionally equipped. The second is imparting knowledge, communicating learning, and offering occasions for appreciation, whether through lectures or performances or other methods, and as widely as possible. The third is developing skills and encouraging participation and practicing, whether in laboratory and scientific experiment, humanistic and scholarly inquiry and writing, artistic production and composition and performance. There will, of course, be some overlapping. Essentially these are the basic functional differences, and all are obviously necessary in an ongoing progressing society over the generations. The question for any foundation or endowment, the difficult choice given limited resources, concerns distribution and emphasis among objectives.

In an obvious logical sense of "priority," original creation is prior, for if it did not take place there would be nothing to spread educationally and nothing to practice or participate in. There are also other kinds of priority. For example, experience has shown that a wide supporting and understanding public is necessary in a causal sense to stimulate creation and prevent its systematic thwarting and sidetracking. In an understanding, supportive atmosphere, eager spirits among the young turn to the field in greater numbers, audiences exhibit keener taste, and criticism can penetrate to deeper questions of structure and technique rather than be limited to impressions and gross affective responses of consumers. The story of science as well as of art offers evidence. Even when science began to bring large practical benefits in its technological applications, support long was limited to immediate practical gains rather than to underlying basic research. Moreover, the public attitude to the scientist as an elite mystery worker was a ready concomitant of the attitude to the field as esoteric. Both the overconfidence of scientists and technologists in facing the ecological and social consequences of their work and the readiness of a public to turn on science with a revived irrationalism reflect the isolation of science from the citizen and the lack of a general public understanding of science itself. Science education and science journalism and everything from attractive exhibits to mathematical games play a serious part in building a responsible, scientifically minded culture. So, too, in the arts it is not merely that a culture in which men burst into song is one in which opera is more likely to flourish, but that it is more likely to be sensitively appreciative of differences in the quality of singing. The same audience that Aristophanes lampooned hooted an actor from the stage, the story goes, for a subtle mispronunciation. The Spartans, on the contrary, regarded taciturnity as a virtue. Perhaps a National Endowment for Hellenic Art, in ancient times, would not have gone astray if it had invested part of its funds in encouraging ordinary Spartans to talk, for the love of talk is the first step to distinguishing good from sloppy talk.

Tocqueville is often quoted for the view that democracy has a leveling effect on culture, that low culture drives out high culture. It is well to recall that John Stuart Mill, in his long and careful review of *Democracy in America*, argued that commercialism, not democracy, was a cause of such phenomena and that although America was much more advanced in commercialism, Britain in his day was already beginning to show the same effects. Mill's thesis well merits consideration today when we hear tirades against popular low culture, particularly in the light of what is going on in television and in book publishing, where the desire for huge immediate profits is hemming in the "high."

In sum, of the three tasks—supporting creation, educating for wider under-standing and appreciation, and encouraging experimental practice—to con-centrate only on the first is like watering the stronger plants without attending to the soil in which they grow and ignoring the struggling shoots. It may be added that without support for the third task as well as the second, the older models of creation are likely to become tyrannical. Ample evidence of this can be found in the history of successive revolutions in modern painting as well as in the difficulties encountered by research in the humanities that goes counter to prevailing schools.

Such considerations justify public support for all three tasks, not merely the first, but do not provide a formula for partitioning support. The fact is that there is no formula. Decisions have to be made not by rule, but by careful analysis in context of circumstances and prospects. Consider the parallel of an educational system in a developing country. Shall it invest its limited re-sources in a primary school system that raises the educational level of the whole population, though in a rudimentary way, or shall it select the most promising to create an advanced core of highly educated professionals by sending them to advanced educational systems in other countries? Surely the answer depends on the economy, whether the professionals are now abso-lutely necessary for the productive well–being of the country, whether they will return when educated or enter the stream of a ''brain drain'' to more comfortable modes of life elsewhere, what mixture of objectives is possible, what are the longer–run aims of the country for development, and numerous other relevant considerations. Not least might be whether absence of educa-tion at the lower level at home might retard health and production and industrial advance and whether supporting a select core might create a middle class isolated from the people and likely to pursue its own advantage. The weighing of complex possibilities is a central and familiar feature of policy decision.

The situation in the controversy we have been exploring is parallel. It might be worth comparing the science and art and humanities endowments with respect to the three tasks distinguished. In scientific fields there have been fewer complaints because scientific research is the recognized prime objec-tive; nevertheless, greater attention has been paid in recent years to advancing public science education and encouraging entry into scientific work. In the arts, although part of the resources went to fellowships for artists and compos-ers and some to encourage Americans to engage in artistic production, not merely to appreciate artistic performances, the focus on the second task was probably the secret of popularity, for it made performance much more wide-spread. The humanities endowment traditionally gave a considerable part of its resources for scholarly fellowships, doing for humanistic research what the science endowment did for scientific research. With regard to the second task it was in a different position from the arts endowment, for this area of educational work is traditionally part of the curriculum of the high schools and liberal arts colleges, whereas performance in the arts has much less place in the educational curriculum. The humanities endowment thus played more a stimulating role, for example, on fresh methods (such as newspaper courses), TV programs on special topics reaching a wide audience, programs for senior citizens, and so on. In its state–based public programs it tried linking the second and third objectives, encouraging the cooperation of the academic and the nonacademic in consideration of public policy. The underlying assumption here was not merely that academic humanists had something to offer for consideration of public policy but that the public experience would enhance their view of their own fields and their understanding of the full scope of their work.

Whatever the values of particular experiments and programs, there seems little place, in evaluating them or deciding whether to adopt or abandon them, for the concept of elitism and its general dispute with populism. Its only effect would be to foreclose experiment by an assurance that all experiment is bound to fail. To regard such assurance as the lesson of past experience would be naive, for the past was an aristocratic world, the world of an elitist establishment, or restricted education and restricted participation. The development of democratic political forms was faced with the same arguments, the same assurances, the same forebodings, the same neglect of critical points and revolutionary changes in human life and social institutions. Of course, there is no antecedent guarantee of success, but this calls all the more for experiment, not for fixed apprehension of failure.

Let us now look at the part that the concept of the elite has played in matters of leadership—in politics and political theory.

Politics is a natural home for elitist concepts. As long as aristocracy in one or another form prevailed, the ruling group was clearly set off from the mass, and it monopolized the power, the glory, the benefits, and the culture. The long rise of democratic forms appeared to fragment the power, scatter the glory, hand around the benefits. Culture, however, remained concentrated in the educated classes, and here the question was who had access to education and what kind.

Elitist political theory in the twentieth century rejects the appearances. It sees the liberal hope of a shifting pluralistic pattern of power as vain, and it turns against the Marxian dynamics of proletarian revolution with its dream of universal liberation. It is best seen in the modern Machiavellian tradition that speaks in the name of realism: whatever the formal description of government, it is said, every society has a ruling group and the masses follow. Revolution in the name of the masses is deceptive; it only means that a new ruling group takes over. Vilfredo Pareto underscores the irrational relations of the mass to the rulers, with its affective responses to charisma. Robert

Michels studies the oligarchic processes in democratic society and indeed in socialist movements and formulates his iron law of oligarchy. Gaetano Mosca bluntly redefines democracy as a ruling class open from below. James Burnham looks about for the emerging new class and pinpoints the technical group that is taking hold in the managerial revolution.[5] All this occurred in the first four decades of the twentieth century when the dream of a spreading universal democracy began to be overshadowed by world war, the rise of communism, the emergence of fascism and nazism, and the consequent general feeling that democracy was in retreat and at an impasse.

The elitist stance not only invaded political analysis and redefined democracy, but it also staked out a commanding position in the philosophical analysis of social concepts. It extended far beyond the Machiavellians; for example, Bertrand Russell at one point even hoped that power might play the scientific role in social science that energy played in physics.[6] He, however, sought to mute power, whereas the others took the power concentrations to be unavoidable. Yet the attempt to recast political science as the science of the distribution of power had a distinctive character. It was not simply pointing to the importance of pressure and pressure groups as a political phenomenon and urging that ideals be examined in the concrete context of their political functioning, as A.F. Bentley had done in his classic *Process of Government* (1908). Its tone can be seen in the title of Harold D. Lasswell's *Politics: Who Gets What, When, How* (1936) and his initial formulation of politics as the study of influence and the influential: "The influential are those who get the most of what there is to get. Available values may be classified as *deference, income, safety*. Those who get the most are *elite*; the rest are mass."[7] The distinctive character of this view, although evident, is hard to pinpoint: it is not just realism, and it need not be cynicism. Let us try to track it down.

Such power theories present the appearance of neutrality and a generality that could avoid commitment to any one type of ruling class. They realistically formulate laws of the location of power and the rise and circulation of elites. They usually see the important values of a society concentrated in the elite, and they resist any conception of a society without an elite. For example, Lasswell and Abraham Kaplan, in *Power and Society* (1950), probably the most analytically sophisticated of the studies of power, say, "If political equality were defined so as to exclude the existence of an elite, the concept would be vacuous."[8] In such a perspective, the analytic stance of power theory with its concept of the elite clearly is that of the ruling group, not the ruled. Every topic is formulated in terms of the struggle for the maintenance of power of the elite. Goals of the rulers are telescoped into power maintenance and power expansion, and their psychic expression is prestige and the claim of greater reward in values received. The aims and ideals of the ruled enter only as they provide firm or insecure bases for the maintenance and aggrandizement of power. Such a stance suggests that the distinctive character of the approach lies in its self–limitation: it can see nothing as important except what impinges on the power effort and registers on the power barometer. In short, it not merely studies elites but is an elitist outlook. It accepts the implicit presuppositions of the view that the mass is irrational, that it does not count in scientific study except insofar as it affects the power struggles. The borderline between counting for purposes of scientific description and prediction and counting in a value reckoning often becomes very thin.

What are the distorting consequences of such an elitism in political theory? For one, the aims and ideals of the ruled are robbed of authenticity in this way of understanding the needs, conflicts, and directions of striving of the mass of people of the society. Ideals, particularly, are seen as bases for manipulation rather than as the articulation of needs. The approach need not be undemocratic, but its interpretation of democracy as simply a ruling class open from below and coopting the ablest is at most the meritocratic version of democracy noted earlier. By tacitly assuming the disparaging view of the mass and focusing solely on elites, the approach has no tolerance for concepts of democratic leadership, for any forms of participatory democracy, or even for a condition of widespread checks and balances through devices that ensure a broader public deliberation and more persistent popular initiative in determining policies. Its analysis of leadership focuses on the measure of authority preserved or charisma exercised, on the skill in building up and organizing mass support, on the propaganda that is likely to take hold, and so on. Experiments in the democratic world today range from forcing publicity through sunshine laws and legislating by popular initiative to giving workers representation on boards of industrial corporations. There is no guarantee that such experiments will work, but they are not to be written off in advance as sure failures and not worth trying. Our major institutions up to this point have been so overwhelmingly authoritarian that any democratic experiment is hardly likely to get a fair try in the sense that all the variables are under control. The elitist approach would thus incline us to let such experiments go by default.

It might be objected that power theory in the sense described had its day in the midcentury and that political science has since moved away in many other directions. That is perhaps the case for the academic discipline, but it remains in much of practice—obviously in questions of international relations—and markedly in our present political culture. Political life as reflected in the media shows it clearly. Polls are constantly being taken, not about the merits of current measures to advance public well–being and resolve pressing problems of meeting needs, but about how these measures affect the standing of the president (or would–be–presidents) in the eyes of the public. News broadcasts raise at every point the question whether a president's specific action will help or hinder his reelection. The net effect of this elitist mode of analysis is to reinforce the power struggle in motivation as well as understanding. In its theoretical as well as its practical impact, it imposes the ghost of the older aristocratic society as the categories of thought and action in a world that has been thoroughly transformed and is seeking to develop its own categories.

Although elitism in politics operates today largely in a framework of an accepted democratic outlook, attached to either a presumed picture of underlying realities or to the need for a special kind of leadership, an older elitism still marks the practice and outlook of education. The great advances since World War II in educational opportunity in Europe and America remain within a meritocratic framework of opening the doors to the best, even in servicing professional and industrial needs. Some attempts have been made to replace tracking with mainstreaming and to replace separate schools for the elite and the mass with comprehensive schools. The manner of grading and testing, which tends to turn schooling into the fashioning of an elite by the way it shapes student motivation and teacher attitudes, has also come under growing suspicion. The functional distinction between liberal and technical or vocational education is still often assimilated to a distinction of higher or lower status. The equalitarian ideal that would invite every student to partake of whatever education he or she can master, needs, or is interested in has only begun to be implemented. In the successive liberation movements of Blacks, women, the aged, the handicapped, children, and other groups, the demand for open education of quality has spread throughout the whole community, bringing in larger and larger masses of people. The pressure on services and resources has been great and confusion of aims and methods rampant. In the resulting complex social conflicts, the same fears we noted earlier have found frequent expression: the dilution of standards, the loss of excellence, and the threat of a populism that rejects traditional quality as the ideological bias of an establishment. A few remarks on the issues of quality, popular capacity, and attitude to differences may therefore be pertinent.

It is a common mistake to assume that students or people generally lack a sense of quality or excellence and that it is imparted to them with great difficulty. Children engage in all sorts of physical activity—they run and fight, play ball and skate, and as they grow older drive cars or repair machines. The role of learning and of practice in acquiring skill is no mystery to them in at least one or another domain. In the commercialism of our culture, they rapidly distinguish the shoddy from the well constructed—in tools, clothes, equipment. General attitudes to sport have almost a religious character with detailed attention to ritual and to correctness in performance. The vicarious enjoyment, even worship, of excellence belies the lack of an idea of quality; indeed, the idea is usually accompanied with the understanding of the part played by disciplined practice and hard work in achievement. The educational problem is thus not to impart a sense of excellence where one is lacking, but to direct that sense to additional worthwhile cultural pursuits.

Concerning popular capacity, the dispute is old and persistent. As against elitist assumptions of mass incapacity, critics of contemporary education (often explicitly populist) assign its failures to inadequate resources, outworn methods, entrenched bias against the new entrants to learning, social conditions that incapacitate, and so on. Nearly everyone has some capacity for learning. Did not a person learn to walk, to talk, to distinguish the real from the fantasy about him, to form relations with other people, to work in one field or another? If ways were found so that a Helen Keller could learn to communicate in spite of her disabilities, surely ways can be found to develop in anyone the tools and skills for entry into the community of knowledge and culture. Assumptions of incapacity only hinder the effort. Neither the matter nor the manner of learning need necessarily be that of present schooling, nor need it be glued to the aristocratic elements in the cultural tradition. The capacity to learn is not absent; the challenge is that obstacles bar its expression. The situation requires a rich overall social effort that is focused on people and their needs; for clearing the way to exercise what capacities and interests they have; for developing ways of teaching in the generic sense of helping others learn; and for all this on a far larger scale than the traditional schooling with its preset design. If it shares the optimism of the eighteenth–century Enlightenment and refuses to accept the disillusion of the last century, it can at least point to gains and educational progress. How far the ideal can carry us is for the future to determine; novel experiment should not be barred by the prejudices of elitism.

But surely, it will be said, there are acknowledged differences in ability. Genius is a fact of experience, not an elitist myth. The question is whether this constitutes an unbridgeable chasm or whether there is continuity in human capacities. In his essay "On Genius," John Stuart Mill saw "the act of *knowing* anything not directly within the cognizance of our sensing (provided we really *know* it and do not take it upon trust) as truly an exertion of genius, though of a less *degree* of genius, as if the thing had never been known by anyone else."[9] His point is that to know something for the first time is a novel discovery even if others have known it before, and that others have not known it previously is adventitious. The same active thought is involved, though the degree in the genius who makes the first discovery may be greater. The educational task is therefore to encourage activity of thought.

All sorts of differences exist among human beings without becoming the basis for distinct social groups or for privileged and underprivileged classes. How, then, should the fact of differences be regarded in education? Some parents, for example, object to their children being classified as "gifted children," not because they are displeased at learning of their high abilities, but because they do not want them set apart from their fellows as a special group. The recognition of their abilities has revealed that these children can advance in certain kinds of work with greater rapidity and that their performance will have a higher quality. To see them as having opportunities for advanced work along certain lines, whether or not it may involve some work in separate groups, even with an extra sense of commitment, is one thing; to make them an elite group by name and type of school life is quite another. A realistic attitude to differences focuses on performance and quality, on serving needs and interests. Students with an ability for advanced work should have the opportunity for it. Students with greater athletic ability are, through the institution of school teams, given the opportunity of special coaching. Students with special psychological problems are given the opportunity of psychological counseling, others of remedial work. All of these can be seen under the same rubric as efforts in different ways to serve needs and advance quality. If we track them in different ways because of possible future careers, then we are allowing a vocational orientation to enter into early schooling—an approach quite inconsistent with the usual educational objection to vocationalism as permeating even higher education.

The ideals we are projecting may be called utopian because competition and the desire for success are natural tendencies that slide over easily into admiration of the successful, hero and heroine worship, and rank ordering of people. It is true that the present structure of schooling helps to entrench these tendencies, particularly if they are tied together. Let us take each separately. Whatever the controversy about economic competition, it is surely agreed that aggressive competitiveness is destructive of rich interpersonal relations and of a sense of community. The more pervasive it is in some areas of activity, the greater the need for muting it in education and for developing cooperative and supportive relations. In the case of hero worship, doubtless role models play a part in the development of the person, but hero worship that emancipates by emphasis on the quality of the achievement has to be distinguished from hero worship that enslaves—as in familiar cult phenomena. Indeed, moral respect for persons dissolves when persons are identified with their successes. The social issue is how to preserve a general concern for quality and performance without forming elites.

It was, we think, the French utopian Saint–Simon who, under the enthusiastic view that changing social conditions could change human beings for the better, envisioned a France of thirty million people *each* of whom was not merely a Newton but also a Shakespeare. Doubtless he underestimated what makes a Newton and a Shakespeare, but one could have a worse dream for culture.

What captures first attention in considering this notion is its universality. Again, nothing less is dreamed of than each person being a Newton and a Shakespeare, not simply an entire people capable of fully understanding and appreciating Newton and Shakespeare, or all youth having the opportunity to work in a laboratory and to write plays. Extent, maximum achievement, opportunity—these are identifiable components in the ideal of equality projected from the experience during the French Revolution of the magnitude of possible change, the upsetting of entrenched ways, the hope of the future. There is, however, a further aspect that may have escaped notice: the dream embraces both Newton and Shakespeare in a common concept of cultural achievement. Looking back from Saint–Simon's time this is commonplace. But by our time, with the growth of science and the isolation of the humanities, Newton and Shakespeare live in different worlds.

When science was natural philosophy it was part of the culture of a well–educated person. It furnished an organized conception of the world of nature in which human beings were set. By the latter part of the nineteenth century, however, an adversary relation had arisen between science and the older literary or classical culture. There is no simple explanation for the cleavage. (In the twentieth century, a growing technology shifted the popular view of science away from its philosophical import to its practical role.) Perhaps the confrontation of science with religion that came with the Darwinian revolution provoked an antagonism of the scientific and the classical–humanist culture which was linked with the religious view of man. Thomas Huxley's formulation in his lecture on "Science and Culture" (1880) is suggestive: he does not question Matthew Arnold's view that a criticism of life in the light of the best ideal is fundamental to culture; what he questions is that literature alone provides the material for such criticism. He argues that science can serve equally or even more as a source of understanding. By the middle of the twentieth century the antagonism had not been healed. If C.P. Snow's popular contrast of the "two cultures" elevated science to the status of a separate culture, it still lamented the separation. The last few decades have witnessed many efforts to recast the image of the scientist from that of practical controller of nature and human nature to that of an imaginative and sensitive explorer of the cosmos, engaged in an enterprise that falls fully into the spirit of the humanities. Many studies in the history of science and of thought show that Newton is rightly coupled with Shakespeare in a comprehensive view of culture.

The import of this history for our consideration of elitism is considerable. Elitism in culture today focuses on a narrow concept that equates culture with a traditional segment of the arts and the humanities. To exclude the scientific outlook and the awareness of what the progress of science has brought to the understanding and possibilities of man–in–the–world is to suggest entrenched and partisan rigidities in the concept of culture itself. Such narrowness has been noted in the history of the arts and the humanities—for example, in the successive broadening of what is aesthetically acceptable in music and painting. It is not implausible that in the contemporary world we are at a turning point in which we are almost overwhelmed with new possibilities and new directions. Fresh arts are springing up with the emergence of new technologies; older arts are being altered in significant dimensions. There are doubtless many attempts to make distinctions of primacy or to allege cultural superiority within all these: for example, of writing a drama over its theatrical production, of theatrical over film production, of film over television production. Such elitist claims are wearing thin. If we have not yet reached the limit urged by some philosophers, at which the aesthetic is regarded as a possible dimension of almost all experience rather than as tied to a specific content, we have moved very far in that direction in the current state of the arts.

The notion of "culture" packs many value attitudes with its theory. The narrow view that has been controlling in the humanities ties it to very specific ideals: culture is the property of highly civilized people who—to take Werner Jaeger's account—have consciously pursued the ideal of perfection, a creation of the classic Greek mind.[10] In contrast, the concepts that prevail in the social sciences are more inclusive.[11] The anthropological notion stemming from Edward B. Tylor's *Primitive Culture* (1871) refers to the capabilities and habits, the entire social tradition, acquired by man as a member of society. A more limited account, used by some anthropologists and sociologists, identifies culture with the symbolic aspects as distinct from social structure. It is not that these latter definitions are value–free while the humanistic is value–laden and honorific. At stake simply are different and opposed values. The social science view is that primitive societies have cultures, not only advanced or "highly civilized" societies. This recognizes that a complex, ordered way of interacting with nature and fellowman is a genuine social accomplishment, whatever the differences. This is but a step short of urging respect for all cultures, as Franz Boas and Ruth Benedict did in the anthropological battles against Nazi theories of racial superiority in the twentieth century. The social science definitions thus turn out to embed democratic values.

In breaking with elitist concepts of culture, it is important not to lose any vital impulse they contained, particularly the insistence on quality and disciplined excellence and the emphasis on the tie to the past in which the past is assimilated in present efforts. In such general form, however, these are pertinent to any area of craft or inquiry. They are not the marks of selection for a group. Of course, not every purpose, every activity, every enterprise upon which people expend energies becomes thereby an art, or every reflection upon it a part of the humanities, just as not every questioning of nature becomes thereby a science. The old descriptions, the old borders, the old restrictions, are going. What constitutes an art, what the humanities are about, what makes an inquiry scientific, are questions currently controversial. The controversy is itself the scene of older conceptions stretched to the breaking point by technological, social, cultural, and intellectual change. We should make no attempt here to resolve this intellectual ferment of our age by too ready dogmas. What we insist on rather is that the old formulation in terms of elite and mass in the understanding of culture is outworn.

Elitism, even in the democratized form, fails to address realistically the social issues in connection with which it is invoked. We need to turn now more directly to the issues themselves. These centrally include the cultivation of quality and standards, the need for discipline and self–mastery, the role of tradition and innovation, the place of individual differences in the social scheme, the extent of access and participation, and the range of abilities.

The ideal of quality and the pursuit of excellence are intrinsic parts of effort and achievement. A rich society or a genuine community depends on the pervasive cultivation of this ideal throughout the population. It pertains to varied endeavors—production and daily chores as well as art and science, leisure as well as work, appreciation as well as creation. Quality in the appropriate sense is not necessarily tied to prestige, grading, or reward, or other such fumbling devices to ensure it. Although we may not yet know how, surely the problem is one of the quiet development of the sense of personal worth and dignity and the growth of aspiration. In all this there is the need to cultivate self–discipline and self–mastery, hard work and the mastery of technique, which are constitutive of any art, any practice, any inquiry. Such features do not gain by being refracted through the prism of elitism versus populism.

Tradition and innovation seem, however, more directly related to elitism with its veneration of the past and populism with its embrace of change. But to force a commitment to the past or to the future misses the mark. The tradition that policy must reckon with is not simple piety (in Santayana's definition as loyalty to the sources of our being), or the use of past materials as the stones of an ancient castle might be reused, or even the obviously important preservation of well–tried values. Similarly, the innovation to be reckoned with is not sheer love of change for its own sake, or simple dissatisfaction with the old, or even the perennial hope of something better. What is critical, rather, is the attitude toward both past and future. It is, of course, a lesson of experience that more advances come from assimilating and then transcending the past than from always starting afresh. Appreciation of the past involves an understanding of the problems and their contexts as well as their efforts at solution and answers; but it is also an effort to elicit criticisms and rules of critique with which to face the present. Critique also involves alternatives and faces toward possible futures, toward experiment and innovation that will meet continually changing situations. How much change in fact is advisable does not depend on attitudes alone. It depends on existent structures and the pace of change.

The range of human differences has often been a bone of contention between elitism and populism. In the former, selected differences in leader-ship, in intellectual and artistic and athletic ability, in occupations, in wealth and family background, are exploited to generate pecking orders and to mold elites out of those who self-consciously share the differences, and to monopolize prestige and acquire social benefits. Populism, in contrast, emphasizing the similarities of people, appeals to the democratic ideal of equality and moves to strike down the benefits of differences. The realistic problem, as we have seen in discussing education, is to recognize differences and share their benefits and problems. We must not lose the kinship generated by shared specific interests or the communality of professionalism and of occupation. Nor should we lose the sense of common purpose in our human identity. We need not lose either if we come to view differences as task–centered rather than person–segregating.

One of the consequences of this last would be to break down old and hardened classifications of labor along elitist lines—the contrast of head and hand, of liberal and servile. An automated technology has removed the material bases that earlier perhaps encouraged such divisions. The divisions linger on, determining job specification and roles and, by isolating initiative and authority, engender passivity and obedience. Clearly, this involves a radical change of attitudes that now appear entrenched—witness the familiar intellectual hierarchies of university departments (theoretical mathematics and physics in contrast to applied and either of these in contrast to language teaching) or the fine status lines drawn throughout the medical professions. Doubtless some occupations will always be more desired and some better paid, in virtue of the character of the work and the risks involved, and some, like the military, necessitated under given conditions. This seems a curious base for creating an elite, insofar as all useful labor merits respect. The argument for not turning differences in kinds of work into cultural deference is part and parcel of the respect for persons that belongs in any genuinely healthy society.

Most of the above involve changes of attitude and outlook. There are already signs that we are moving in such directions. On the other hand, access and the opportunities for participation in culture are more open to institutional intervention. Indeed, that, too, is the direction in which we have been moving. The common democratic outlook about the need for universal literacy and education and the surge to higher education in the last quarter of a century have broken many barriers to access. And there is no doubt that the complex character of our technology and society requires higher general levels of education and even broader participation. Where the elitist wants the breadth to secure rise of talent, the populist stresses raising the general basic level. Putting aside for the moment differing estimates of popular capacities and where responsibility for past failures should be assigned, the serious problem is how to allocate limited resources, for example, whether to gifted children or to basic literacy. As we have seen, however, these are problems whose solutions are not much advanced by invoking the general slogans of elitism and populism. They involve a weighing of the specific needs and conditions of the society at the time.

Finally, there is the question of the range of abilities and the possibility of increasing participation in the life of society and culture by larger and larger segments of the population without sacrificing standards or excellence. We have seen the elitist's dim view of human nature pitted against the populist's romantic faith in the people. The former view operates to block experiment, whereas the latter usually underestimates the difficulties. Many changes, however, have taken place in our understanding of human nature and capacities under the impact of psychological investigation and the advance of the social sciences. However inconclusive and controversial the specific results may be, they are enough to show us that the essence of human nature is not to be captured in those broad, age–old generalizations. At least in some important way human abilities at any time are functions of the material and social conditions (including aspirations) and institutions of the society in which they live. If the borderlines in the great heredity-environment controversy are unclear, and if even the formulations of the controversy are being challenged (notwithstanding the recent claims of sociobiology), then experiment or exploratory practice is certainly called for by our democratic commitments. Our understanding also of leadership, of authority, and of the roles they play in social conflict has been immeasurably increased by twentieth–century experience of a variety of social forms and changes.

Whether understanding in confronting these issues can be harnessed to meet the novel conditions that now face us, is, of course, an open question. The future is always chancy and the immediate future doubly so. We need not only understanding but will. At least we ought not to be hampered by conceptual tools that are inadequate to even understanding. As Charles Frankel pointed out in his *The Case for Modern Man*, "We need to have some sense of the crucial variables in our present situation, the handles that will allow us to deal with the clusters of problems together. . . . Clearly, the way to begin is to try to find out just where the outlook on history with which most of us grew up has misled us."[12] We believe that the deep elitist presuppositions of our culture have been one such source.

The paper was written for a volume in honor of Charles Frankel.

Notes

1. Irving Babbitt, *Democracy and Leadership* (Boston: Houghton Mifflin, 1924), 242. Cf. 5: "This book in particular is devoted to the most unpopular of all tasks—a defence of the veto power."
2. Irving Babbitt, *Literature and the American College: Essays in Defense of the Humanities* (Boston: Houghton Mifflin, 1908), 78.
3. This lesson is a particular contribution of the pragmatic approach. Cf. Elizabeth Flower and Murray G. Murphey, *A History of Philosophy in America* (New York: Putnam's, 1977), chaps. on James, Dewey, and C.I. Lewis.

4. In exploring this situation we draw on an earlier brief examination of it at the time it was taking place. See Abraham Edel, ''Elitism and the Esoteric in the Humanities Endowment,'' *The Public News*, The Public Committee for the Humanities in Pennsylvania, No. 1 (Fall 1977), 5–6.
5. For a revealing, if overenthusiastic, study of this tradition in the twentieth century, see James Burnham, *The Machiavellians: Defenders of Freedom* (New York: John Day, 1943). The specific works mentioned are Vilfredo Pareto, *The Mind and Society* (New York: Dover, 1963; original Italian publication 1916); Robert Michels, *Political Parties: A Sociological Study of the Oligarchic Tendencies of Modern Democracy* (New York: Dover, 1959; first English translation 1916); Gaetano Mosca, *The Ruling Class* (New York: McGraw-Hill, 1939; original Italian publication 1895, enlarged edition 1923); James Burnham, *The Managerial Revolution* (Bloomington: Indiana University Press, 1960; first published 1941).
6. Bertrand Russell, *Power: A New Social Analysis* (New York: Norton, 1938).
7. Harold Lasswell, *Politics: Who Gets What, When, How* (New York: Meridan, 1958; first published 1936), 13.
8. Harold D. Lasswell and Abraham Kaplan, *Power and Society: A Framework for Political Inquiry* (New Haven: Yale University Press, 1950). For a critique of this work, see Abraham Edel, *Analyzing Concepts in Social Science* (New Brunswick, N.J.: Transaction Publishers, 1979), chap. 7.
9. John Stuart Mill, ''On Genius,'' in *Mill's Essays on Literature and Society*, ed. J.B. Schneewind (New York: Collier Books, 1965), 89.
10. Werner Jaeger, *Paideia: The Ideals of Greek Culture* (New York: Oxford University Press, 1945), 1:xvii. Jaeger maintains that culture is properly so conceived and is unique: ''We are accustomed to use the word culture, not to describe the ideal which only the Hellenocentric world possesses, but in a much more trivial and general sense, to denote something inherent in every nation of the world, even the most primitive. We use it for the entire complex of all the ways and expressions of life which characterize any one nation. Thus the word has sunk to mean a simple anthropological concept, not a concept of value, a consciously pursued *ideal*. In this vague analogical sense it is permissible to talk of Chinese, Indian, Babylonian, Jewish or Egyptian culture, although none of these nations has a word or an ideal which corresponds to real culture.''
11. The social science uses are included in Alfred L. Kroeber and Clyde Kluckhohn's comprehensive survey, *Culture: A Critical Review of Concepts and Definitions* (Cambridge, Mass.: Peabody Museum of American Archaeology and Ethnology, Harvard University, 1952). Their comment on the humanistic usages is of interest: ''The Arnold–Powys–Jaeger concept of culture is not only ethnocentric, often avowedly Hellenocentric; it is absolutistic. It knows perfection, or at least what is most perfect in human achievement, and resolutely directs its 'obligatory' gaze thereto, disdainful of what is 'lower'. The anthropological attitude is relativistic, in that in place of beginning with an inherited hierarchy of values, it assumes that every society through its culture seeks and in some measure finds values. . . . Incidentally, we believe that when the ultra–montane among the humanists renounce the claim that their subject matter is superior or privileged, and adopt the more catholic and humble human attitude—that from that day the humanities will cease being on the defensive in the modern world'' (32).
12. Charles Frankel, *The Case for Modern Man* (New York: Harper and Brothers, 1956), 45–46.

5

Legal Positivism: A Pragmatic Reanalysis

Among the theories of jurisprudence, legal positivism and legal pragmatism constitute a clear contrast of isolationism and connection. Positivism makes an independent realm of law, almost capable of scientific formulation. It expels the ethical as outside judgment. The law remains as a system of rules, so far as possible logically organized, with the basic ones authorized by the legal sovereign. Legal pragmatism sees the law rather as a social instrument within a changing context of sociohistorical problems, to address which requires both varied knowledge and clarification of purposes.

In the United States during the 1980s, lively controversies, including two widely publicized Congressional hearings (on the Iran–contra affair and on the nomination of Robert Bork for the Supreme Court), rekindled the perennial issues of the relations of legislative and executive, legislative and judicial, executive and judicial, and thrust into prominence conflicts over the theory of judicial interpretation, judicial activism, and the like. Reanalysis of the nature of law thus acquires added practicality.

Analytical jurisprudence consists on the one hand in a way of analyzing legal concepts and the structure of legal phenomena, on the other in an attempt to construct a theory of the nature of law or what law is. In its theory it is usually identified with legal positivism, which also has its characteristic way of analysis. Today the two are often run together, in a tradition that is taken to extend from Austin to Kelsen to Hart. (From here on I shall use the label of legal positivism.) Its basic theory (schema, paradigm, model— perhaps simply *perspective* as literally a way of looking at the law) is usually formulated as that law is an independent (self–enclosed) system of norms or prescriptions or rules. Its method is generally characterized as conceptual-linguistic analysis; sometimes emphasis falls on formalistic construction that logical positivism aspired to, sometimes on the more informalist procedures of ordinary-language analysis. In either case there is the underlying positivist trichotomy of fact, value, logic, or (in terms of types of inquiry) science, ethics, philosophical analysis. Indeed, when critics of legal positivism occasionally launch omnibus attacks on "analysis," defenders are likely to counter-charge that they are being asked to abandon philosophy for sociology and ethics.

A reanalysis today has to deal with the impact of philosophical changes in the last half century—I venture to say philosophical progress—upon the way of looking at law that legal positivism staked out. I attempt here three things. First I sample in outline a few trouble spots within the theory, much like Kuhn's picture of a paradigm beset by anomalies. Significantly, these soft spots, which the theory in the past was able to smooth over, are now generating alternative models or directly challenging methodological presuppositions. Second, I suggest that changes in the theory of method have substantially altered our picture: there is no single "analytic method" of which legal positivism acted as custodian; there are numerous analytic modes of which legal positivism has employed two that are not wholly comfortable together. Analytic modes do not justify "schools" and legal philosophy should be free to use at different points whichever are more effective. I suggest that for a general perspective on law a pragmatic mode—in a special sense to be explained below—is more effective; hence the title of this paper. This leads us, third, to reconsider the positivistic trichotomy and a reconsideration of the place that legal positivism has given to value (relations to ethics), change (relations to social investigation), system (relations to the conception of a science). Here I suggest that a pragmatic analysis undercuts the sharp distinctions and makes them contextual. Particularly with respect to system, I speculate on the changed view of law if juristic theory looks upon it as an amalgam of crafts rather than as the subject matter of a traditional science.

Part I

The three trouble spots concern the interpretation of international law, the manner of coping with indeterminateness in the law, and formalism. They thus sample an area of the law, a pervasive problem throughout the law, and a specific emphasis in juristic theory.

International Law

The status of international law offers a problem for the theory since there is no sovereign to do the coercing or generate basic authority. Acquiescence rides on a tenuous balance of forces: custom, agreement, hope of gain, fear of attack, etc. Austin regarded international law as simply positive international morality, the term "law" being extended by analogy, as when we speak of laws of honor. A century later the picture is changed, whether because the concept of sovereignty is crumbling or because the impact of international affairs in national life is now overwhelming. Kelsen recognizes the possibility of international law as a system insofar as a basic norm is accepted. Hart, seeing no a priori need for primary rules to have a unity (a basic rule or a rule of recognition, he says, is not a necessity but a luxury found in advanced social systems,)[1] is ready to acknowledge what primary international rules are accepted as a primitive stage of legal development. On different grounds, therefore—whether the idea of a dominant coercive world power, a hoped for acceptance of an international system, or the rudimentary growth of a plurality of primary rules—international law may be envisaged as becoming more like law as we know it in its national (or municipal) form.

What if, on the other hand, the reverse turned out to be true, that instead of international law growing up to be like national law the intensity of modern problems would make national law more like present international law, both with respect to degree of conflict and use of mediation and compromise rather than effective legal decision? Legal positivism would simply say that law is still the sort of system found in national law but it is breaking down under social stress. Nevertheless, other interpretations are possible. For example, Gidon Gottlieb[2] proposes that we construct two distinct concepts of law, applicable under different existing types of power relations—the usual model for vertical or hierarchical relations between unequal centers of power (as in the national states) and the non-hierarchical or horizontal between equal centers of power (which characterizes the international situation). He traces the features of each model of law, and suggests that the second is beginning to fit portions of the law within nations—parts of domestic constitutional law, civil rights and labor law—in short, legal fields dealing with power groups and political organizations rather than with individuals' rights and interests. This is not construed as a reduction of law to politics. In short, neither model of law is entitled to preempt the title of law.

Interestingly, Hart brushes by this problem when he mentions how the law enforcement provisions of the UN Charter have been paralyzed by the veto in the ideological conflicts of the great powers. He says, "The reply, sometimes made, that the law-enforcement provisions of municipal law *might* also be paralysed by a general strike is scarcely convincing; for in our comparison between municipal law and international law we are concerned with what exists in fact, and here the facts are undeniably different."[3] But his speculative possibility stays within the limits of the hierarchically organized threat of a general strike. In the interval between the publication of his book and Gottlieb's paper (1961 and 1969), history, at least on the American scene, exhibited non-hierarchical ways of curbing legality: the civil rights movement and the strife of the inner cities, growing strength of municipal employee unions and their use of the strike, and popular resistance to the Vietnam War.

In short, the type of law embodied in international law is not so easily to be thrust aside as not law, or as a primitive stage of law. If so, some reconstruction is now required in the traditional positivist model.

Indeterminateness

Law as a system of rules can stand some indeterminateness, but it depends on the character and extent of that phenomenon. Legal positivism keeps it in check by acknowledging a place for judicial discretion. Sometimes discretion is interpreted as a legal resort to cover gaps in the law; then it is a case of rule vs. discretion, and a legal system can tolerate a moderate amount of such indeterminateness. Sometimes, however, discretion is viewed as the creative aspect of all judicial process, operative within legal rules; in that case the degree of constraint exercised by rules would be the crucial point for restricting indeterminateness. Many interesting controversies concern the limits of discretion, whether rules or social policies ultimately govern the form it takes, etc. Moreover, all areas of law can be scanned to see how far they offer opportunities for individuals or groups to determine what the law will then be required to support. For example, the law of contract can be interpreted as the rules under which individuals may engage in private legislation within limited spheres and create rights and obligations with respect to one another. A systematic study of gaps, limits, permissions to legislate, permissions to create law, the kinds of legal concepts that open the way to such processes, would thus be part of the fuller program of legal positivism. At least it would generate no paradoxes.

On the other hand, there appear to be more radical phenomena of indeterminateness within the law which militate against the view that it is a system of norms or rules. Mortimer and Sanford Kadish, combing legal processes in this vein, call attention to such phenomena in their provocatively titled book, *Discretion to Disobey*. They start with the jury in criminal law and its departure from the judge's instructions which it has an obligation to follow, and the absolute way in which its verdict of innocence is final. They find this not to be delegated discretion, nor usurpation, but a distinctive type of legitimated interposition in which the jury exercises a liberty it has (not a right) in the system. With an eye on the history of American law as well as the variety of interpretations of the phenomenon, they conclude that this institutionalized unaccountability serves as a functioning instrument for achieving ends of the legal system. It is an inner conflict which helps the law to accommodate change, arising typically where the prescribed role of the jury (or generally, the official) conflicts with prescribed means. (Rule departures in role "offer, suitably hedged, fair gambles for answering social needs that might otherwise go unanswered, where those needs are measured by the ends for which the role was initially instituted."[4]) The phenomenon, once located, is studied for police, prosecutor, judge, even president; and in the kindred but varied form of legitimated disobedience for citizens (where they bet on the norm being invalid, or appeal to the lesser evil in action, or call for justifiable nonenforcement of the law).

The Kadish analytic thesis is that the accepted phenomenon of legal departures from legal rules is incompatible with a rule–of–law model which would at best regard it as an element of inefficiency in the law's operation. They see the legal positivist theory as a rationalistic–bureaucratic model fashioned from the producer's perspective, and call instead for including principles of acceptance of the law as part of the legal system. Finally, they outline an alternative model of checks and balances; it applies to law just as its counterpart furnished in the political theory of the *Federalist Papers* applies to politics. Recipients of the law as well as its producers thus have some authority to determine legal obligations, and indeterminateness is part of the system's response to social change, complexity, and indeterminacy of social objectives.

Formalism

Ever since Holmes said that the life of the law is experience, not logic, it has been customary to level the charge of excessive formalism at analytical approaches to the law. This is initially plausible only with respect to that segment of legal positivism that entertained hopes of fashioning a large–scale logical system for prescriptions or norms that might rival the organizing power of propositional logic. It also, however, depicts on a broad canvas the problem of the relation of the formal and the material.

When the charge of excessive formalism came from the outside, the criticism could readily be ignored or rejected as a lack of appreciation of the importance of logical analysis. But what happens when the challenge arises in the inner shrine of the logic of norms and prescriptions, where formalism is taken most seriously, when the point of the challenge is what we are to make of the notion of inconsistent prescriptions, and when the challenge comes from a philosopher who has himself contributed richly to the development of deontic logic? Are inconsistent prescriptions ones that cannot be prescribed together or cannot both be obeyed since they order opposite behavior? Von Wright sets out to pinpoint the answer. He offers the illustration of a man ordered to close the window when it is open and open it when it is closed. This he calls a pair of "Sisyphus–orders," cruel but possible. Again, a man could be ordered by two different authorities to do opposite things; this is a conflict of wills, not a logical contradiction. Finally, he asks, why is it a logical contradiction for the same authority to command and prohibit the same act? If this is possible, do no commands (or norms) ever contradict one another? Von Wright comments, "I wish I could make my readers see the serious nature of this problem. (It is much more serious than any of the technicalities of deontic logic.) It is serious because, if no two norms can logically contradict one another, then there can be no logic of norms either."[5] And, we may add, if that is so, there can be no system of norms, and what happens to legal positivism?

Von Wright's own answer is to relate the contradiction to some conception of the unity and coherence of a will. Contradiction in this realm becomes possible because people seek some degree of stability and order, and we value coherence because of our psychological makeup. He puts it in terms of the nonformal conditions for the occurrence of norms and commands; a man who commands is in effect trying to get things done, and to command opposing things usually does not get things done. The significance of his answer lies in its sending us from the formal to the material in order to solve the problems generated by the formal.

Alf Ross comes to the rescue of the analytic theory.[6] He distinguishes: a norm directing the judge to punish the act and its complement, which is possible but unreasonable, for it means that a person getting into a certain situation is to be punished whether he does the act or refrains from it; a norm directing the person to do the opposites, which is impossible of fulfillment; a norm permitting and prohibiting the same act, which is directively pure nonsense. Underlying his criticism, however, is a basic objection to a psychological interpretation of deontic logic. He takes it to be concerned with logical postulates defining directive speech, quite as much as there exists an indicative logic defining indicative speech. We may wonder, however, whether Ross is not just postponing the problem which will come in the application of his system in determining what "directive" really consists in. He runs the risk that his logic will not be rich enough for application if he postponed the complexities. By contrast, Von Wright wants to carry the problems through in advance. Thus he seeks to establish first a logic of change and then a logic of action, so that he can then pursue a logic of norms.

Unlike our previous examples, this has not issued in an alternative model. It shows rather that the separation of the formal and the material, when pursued far enough, itself generates internal problems that reopen the issue of the separation. The topic of method is thus moved into central focus.

Part 2

Turning to method, we question the monolithic character of analysis by considering different modes and what goes into them, offer an outline of pragmatic analysis, and compare the two analytic modes that are operative in traditional legal positivism.

Modes of Analysis

The common identification of legal positivism with analytical jurisprudence assumes first a monolithic and distinctive kind of philosophical analysis that employs only logical ideas or at most utilizes neutral lessons about language and its clarification. It assumes second, that analytical jurisprudence carries out such analysis for law and separates it sharply from the sociological–causal and the normative–ethical.

This monolithic thesis has been increasingly criticized in contemporary philosophy. One line of criticism is that the history of method exhibits many analytic modes, distinguished by specific nonformal demands or presuppositions which have to be elicited from the operations of the mode.[7] Logic and lessons about the use of language and rudimentary demands of clarity are common to them all, but beyond that they are distinguished by nonformal demands that may even reach out into epistemological theories and metaphysical outlooks. This can be illustrated from the original prototype of analysis, the Socratic. Socrates first demands consistency, and then insists on an answer to a "What is . . . ?" question in general or non-extensional terms. When he goes beyond this to clarity, he imposes a specific form for the ultimate result of the analysis, namely that is be a general statement of the essential. Thus he criticizes Euthyphro for defining "piety" as what is pleasing to the gods, and wants instead an account of the essential features of piety, that is, a rational account which would contain reasons justifying the gods' pleasure. A more sophisticated Euthyphro, say Justice Holmes defining law in terms of the decisions of the courts, might have argued that not all concepts are of one type, that there does not have to be a single or unified rational basis for the tastes of the Olympian hierarchy, or an Austinian sovereign, or the decisions of the courts. In the rough–and–tumble of both Homer and history, it is nearer the mark to say that we do not punish an act because it is a crime, but by calling some act a crime we mean that it is the sort which for a multitude of varying reasons will get punished; similarly we do not protect a person's relation to something because it is property, but we mean by its being property that for a variety of reasons (many of them historical) it gets protected. There can be definitions that answer to procedures and historical accumulations, not merely to essences. Indeed, Kelsen might very well be asked why he assumes that there must be central general features of legal systems, or even Hart why he is entitled to occasional remarks about the essential features of a legal system. May not the notion of law itself be looser and more historical?

Through such differences about modes of analysis (and there are many modes), special assumptions are brought into the theory of law and incorporated in an answer. The positivist theses of this sort are well–known. They lie in the pre–assumed trichotomy of the logical, the empirical, and the valuational. The philosophical status of these assumptions is not wholly clear.

Positivism advanced them as a correct epistemological or methodological analysis. I have argued elsewhere[8] that they are to be construed as *programs*, that their acceptance or rejection depends on whether they can really be carried out and on how fruitfully they deal with fields like science, ethics, law, etc., as well as on the strength of their own presuppositions that rest on the cumulative knowledge of the various fields. The present philosophical tide is running against the sharp trichotomy. To sort out the theoretical and the analytic from the observational and the empirical has proved more difficult in both theory and practice than in general proclamation. The division between fact and value seems to shift, depending on the way terms function in processes of describing or evaluating (and these processes are not themselves wholly independent). Indeed the cut between fact and value is as relative to context as that between theory and observation. And comparable problems have arisen in the separation of logical and valuational—for example, in the alleged separateness of metaethics from normative ethics. The suspicion is even strong that the trichotomy reflects a psychological separation of thinking, sensing, and feeling, in a manner that few respectable contemporary psychologists would support. Under these circumstances, why should not an alternative program be considered, one that expects continuities and relative differentiations in purposive contexts? At least the philosophy of law should become aware of how far any particular form of positivist legal theory embodies the trichotomy and how our perspective on law would have to be modified if an alternative program were tried out.

Pragmatic Analysis

The alternative program to be tried out is the use of pragmatic analysis. Clearly "pragmatic" has to be rescued from its Nixonian sense of opportunism and from many comparable European misunderstandings. My use of it here is modest; as an analytic mode it is compatible not only with a general pragmatism but also with various forms of materialism, idealism, naturalism. There are certain features first brought out most thoroughly in pragmatic analysis which seem particularly appropriate for a general view of law. This does not mean that other analytic modes—e.g., phenomenological, hermeneutic, historical-dialectic, positivist—may not be singularly profitable for different domains and different enterprises, or for special concerns in different parts of law.[9]

By pragmatic analysis I have in mind the lessons of William James's treatment of perception, concepts, categories, and human activity in the process of knowledge; and of John Dewey's institutional, sociohistorical and activist treatment of ethics and social philosophy with its emphasis on the evaluation of consequences. We cut into the stream of experience in many ways in the light of interests and purposes; we frame concepts of things and processes, and construct a world in the interests of stability and predictability. But the objects are constantly coming into experience in new ways; every experience may add fresh aspects and invite recategorization. Value is thus operative throughout; it is the selective organization of experience; and it constantly takes fresh forms. Value is separated from fact in particular contexts, and the distinction functions for certain purposes in certain types of situations; it is not a general one and it does not designate a set of distinct materials or fields or types of being. Nor, as traditional empiricism claimed, are there pure elementary facts. The units that an inductive empiricism works with, the objects that present certain frequencies for generalization and judgments of probability, are themselves already constructed by fastening on some rather than other likenesses and differences (there are no isolated Humean impressions), and reconstruction by cumulative experience is always possible. To this analysis of individual experience, Dewey adds the socially functional character of all human institutions (despite our tendency to construe them in individualist–contractualist terms). The recognition of change and the increasing rate of change leads to posing questions about institutional problems in relation to the specific historical character of human life, rather than in terms of universal features or permanent natures. And the outcome of such an analysis may be a clarification of directions for reconstruction in change, both social and conceptual.

Such pragmatic analysis is in serious conflict with both the Kantian (which operates to some extent in Kelsen) and with the view of analysis as an independent self–enclosed process. It questions the basic sharp distinction between formal and material, form and matter. Form is not a distinct set of categories or schemata independently established. It is simply those material components which have been elevated into a position of leadership in the theoretical or practical enterprise by virtue of their ability to organize the material, an ability which has constantly to be proved. The distinction between material and formal is itself contextual as well as functional.

That the pragmatic mode of analysis is particularly fitted for a general view of law will be tested shortly by seeing what it leads to in the themes of value, change, and system. It may also furnish an effective mode for analyzing particular problem areas in legal theory. For example, it brings to the analysis of judicial decision the recognition that legal cases come with an already theory–laden character. They are not bare facts or givens; they have been selectively constituted. If we take a broader view of legal phenomena as conflicts between individuals and groups, the functional role of law is obvious.

Analytic Modes in Legal Positivism

It is well recognized that the twentieth-century analytic revolution went through two phases. The first was positivist. Its way of analyzing demands a high degree of formalization, and embodies the trichotomy we have examined. The second phase was known as ordinary language analysis or Oxford analysis. It is informalist in spirit, and relishes a plurality of distinct contexts of use; it looks for almost a different logic for every concept, related to its own contexts; it criticizes general sweeping concepts as technical and prefers minute analyses of different shades; it even puts aside constructs of sense–data as a definitive account of the empirical in favor of distinctions of describing, telling, reporting, etc. One would not have expected a general account of law, perhaps not even a general concept of law, so much as the exploration of different perspectives conveyed by usage in a multitude of situations. Operating almost on a Common Law model in its treatment of concepts, it is more historically oriented than the positivist mode of analysis. Much of the added sophistication in Hart's treatment of traditional questions comes from his replacing an outright question with sets of considerations for different ways of formulating and different directions in answering.

Common to the two modes was the strong linguistic orientation, which is probably the chief reason why they have remained linked. The significant point for the theory of law is that there was little in the ordinary language mode that compelled it to adhere to the positivist trichotomy. It could readily have crossed from a study of linguistic contexts to one of social-functional contexts and unified the two. It could even more readily, in the light of its pluralism, have broken down the unified treatment of value and so contextualized the value–fact distinction. Indeed, it did in effect substitute contextual distinctions of practice and theory for general discussion of value and fact. Unlike pragmatic analysis it lacked the activist attitude which focused on tendencies to change and the functionalist critique of directions of change. It faced rather the past, the forms that had been established as working ways in ordinary experience. (Positivism, however, with its concentration on technical languages could take a frank constructionist attitude.) In many respects the ordinary language mode can be seen as a half–hearted linguistic pragmatism, enmeshed in its heritage of the positivist trichotomy. In descriptive–analytic theory of law it captures well the sense of the past in the present, but not the sense of control of the future in the present.

Part 3

We turn now to the pragmatic reanalysis of the nonformal conditions in the method of legal positivism, that is, to the (by now) familiar trichotomy. This is done in the order of value, change, and system.

Value

The place of values in the legal system is a complex one. Legal positivism, with its separation of value and fact or the *ought* and the *is* (two formulations not always sufficiently distinguished), is particularly attentive to drawing the line between law and morals. In some contexts law stands out as factual with morals as normative, but in others—since law is itself described as a system of norms and rules—legal norms are distinguished from moral norms. It is not here a contrast with what is or exists, since the system of morality exists as much as the system of law, but rather of distinguishing two *oughts*, the legal and the moral, and of determining whether legal norms implicate moral norms. To plot the appearance of moral terms such as ''ought'' is thus of little help, when there are non–moral oughts as well as moral oughts. In the Hart-Fuller debate on the separation of law and morals[10] there is even talk of immoral moralities. And there is always the possibility of shifting standpoint to reformulate a non–moral problem as a moral issue. For example, the most extreme legal positivist view of law as a self–enclosed system of norms that are not necessarily (although some may be coincidentally) moral may be translated into an ethical issue about the duties associated with the role of officials; it is the duty of the judge to decide according to legal norms even when moral promptings incline him otherwise. (A Catholic judge in the United States has the duty of granting a divorce under legally satisfied conditions.)

Pragmatic reanalysis of the value issue would begin with the idea that value in the broad sense of purposive selection considered earlier operates through-out. The analytic task is not to debate whether values (either as purposes or as moral items) are inside or outside the legal system, but to carry out a systematic search for where in the structure and processes of law value–variables are hidden or built in, where settled values operate unnoticed, where values have to be selected to determine a result. Such a search is a retail, not a wholesale matter. The following are a few samples of the variety of contexts in which such a search may be carried on.

The traditional context, in which positivism engaged natural law theories, was the metaphysical one, the belief in an inherent natural or purposive order whose teleological operation permeated law as it permeated every human field. The secular (positivist, naturalist, materialist) substitution was human interests and needs, some variable, other invariant. Bentham assumes an invariant hedonistic motivation which would characterize legal institutions as it would all conduct. Hart offers certain contingent features of man's nature and situation which, given survival as an aim, constitute reasons why law and morals should include a specific content; this is his minimum content of natural law.

An epistemological context is the background view of human action in-volved in different legal theories. Some hold action or conduct to involve intention or purpose, while others (since positivism is occasionally attracted toward behaviorism) think in terms of behavior. Both philosophical theories of mind and scientific schools of psychology thus affect the answer whether purposes are constitutive within the law or outside causes of the law. Bentham broke down action into small units of behavior—for example, the analysis of an assassination could be narrowed down to pressing a finger—and he translated dispositions into sets of acts and trends in acts. Contemporary legal positivism would seem to follow contemporary analytic views of action as intentional, not just behavioral. Alf Ross, while maintaining the fact-value dichotomy, insists that a behavioral account of the judge is inadequate and that interpretation of the judge's ideology (value–system) is required. Hart calls for the inner view as well as the outer. Obviously then we can count on the law being redolent with purposes. The question becomes where they operate and what they are permitted to do.

A directly functional context for the legal system as a whole used to be common in analyses of "the ends of law." Lists of ends began with keeping the peace and providing security. Bentham gave economic reasons why the law need not devote itself to subsistence and abundance, and social reasons why security should be preferred to equality. Specific forms of security appeared, for example Demogue's distinction between static security which aimed at securing possessions, and dynamic security which aimed at securing rapidity of transactions. Whether such discussions of the ends of law would be construed as finding a basic place for the ethical within the legal would depend on the interpretation of ethics itself. If ethics is concerned with the good life for human beings, a natural view of law would be one like Roscoe Pound's engineering conception or Dewey's instrumental interpretation. The analytic task would be to discover where and how and how effectively the functions were carried out in a particular legal system. Some social aims and ethical aims belong within the legal system even if sociological explanations and other ethical evaluations fall outside. On the other hand, contemporary legal positivism has largely inherited a narrower (Kantian) view of the scope of morality, limiting it to the inner motivations, or else it has taken an emotivist interpretation in which ethics concerns the subjective feelings and their expression. On the whole, then, purpose is moved into the context of explaining behavior or giving its causes, falling beyond the scope of the analytic description of the legal system. Some purposes then appear as necessary causal conditions of the existence of a legal system. Specific purposes, of course, are found within the content of specific laws and decisions. To some degree at least, discussion of the ends of law fall victim to the positivist insulation of logical–analytical meaning from psychological–social causation.

Another context, definitely within the legal system, is the appearance of such notions as justice. How far this central ingredient carries ethics into law depends on its own interpretation. If it is given largely a procedural cast, the entryway for the ethical is narrow. But if justice is magnified into basic human equality and respect for persons and principled action, then much of the law is imbued with ethics.

A major context concerns the central operations of the legal system, particularly the process of judicial decision. Here different moves are found in the positivist tradition to limit the ethical within the legal. The legal realist gambit, from John Chipman Gray on, was to insist on the distinction between law and the sources of law. If law consists of the rules that the judges or the court lay down, social needs and ethical values may be among the sources to which the judge goes. Even more, legislation is distinguished from law, for it is simply a standard source of law. This was a broad traditional move in any case, for legislation is obviously the home of different social interests and purposes and moral beliefs. Kelsen, however, sees no difference in principle between the legislative and the judicial, only in degree; there is legal creation all along the line. Why then not recognize the pervasive presence of values? They are, of course, present, but in the content and the causes, not in the law as such, that is, not in the formal features that mark the legal system. The latter, in Kelsen's view, are concerned with the power to generate norms, which is passed along from the original source. But even this source, the ground norm, the acceptance of the postulate which generates the powers of legal officials, is only dubiously seen as valuational; it is the object of commitment.

Hart would appear to offer a compromise. Having distinguished the core of settled meaning for words and a penumbra of the debatable, he can say that laws are incurably incomplete and that social aims may enter into the decision of penumbral cases. Yet this should not preclude settled values underlying settled meanings.

So strong is the extrusion of value from the formal account of law in legal positivism that Ronald Dworkin sees himself as breaking with the positivist model when he insists that principles and policies play a part in judicial decision, not merely rules, and so are part of the system.[11] Policies are utilitarian standards, while principles refer to justice or fairness or some other moral aspect. (Basic rights can enter by this route.) Thus the ethical is clearly brought within the legal process, with both the wider and the narrower ethical tradition represented. Almost as if to suggest that the doors of the self–enclosed legal system have not been totally opened, Dworkin defuses the idea of discretion by insisting that the principles established within the system have an authority that constrains decision. His departure from the positivist treatment of values is thus not a departure from other elements in legal positivism.

It should perhaps be added that the very discussion of the judicial process and the assigned role and directives to the judge themselves constitute a context in which different values and ethical judgments about how to deal with social change are reflected.[12]

The most controversial context has been that of evaluation of the law. This is where the full force of the fact–value dichotomy has found expression: if ethical judgment is not kept outside, how will we be able to talk of unjust laws? We need not review here the debate about whether it is more clarifying to criticize law or to reject some evil prescriptions and procedures which are duly lodged in the law as not really law. Hart concludes that the complex and varied problems of moral response to the law "cannot be solved by a refusal, made once and for all, to recognize evil laws as valid for any purpose."[13] But the same could be said for the problems of social response to needs and changes: they cannot be solved once-and-for-all by acknowledging all evil laws to be valid for some purpose. The consideration of once-and-for-all solutions is out of line with the differentiation of issues in informalist (ordinary language analysis) as contrasted with formal positivist method. It might be better to recognize that this meta-theoretical decision is itself on the border where the penumbra of the term "law" is involved; decision may very well depend on the particular historical situation and whether the forces for anarchy or those for tyranny were more threatening. In any case, it would be a mistake to think that the separation of law and ethics is required to ensure the possibility of ethical evaluation of law. *Further* evaluation of any material is always possible, even of the existent state of morality itself. The fact–value dichotomy can be read as the exaggeration of a context in which their separation is fruitful because the need for further evaluation is central in that context.[14]

Change

In its attitudes to change, legal positivism reflects nineteenth century liberal assumptions. Change can take place when structures are developing in the early history of civilization, but it becomes a change of content, not structure in a developed civilization, unless there are basic upheavals or revolutions. Thus change will be recognized in the early history of law. It is quite proper to have Maine describe how the concept of contract became generalized in the convergence of several separate roots; or to note in the history of law how the concept of embezzlement was invented when certain kinds of misappropriation could not be captured under the existing concepts late in the eighteenth century. Revolutions that play havoc with the law are important for Kelsen because there is a change in the ground norm; Hart is concerned with the attitudes to be taken to the laws of the Nazi period in the judicial processes of the subsequent period. The normal situation envisaged in the perspective seems to be one in which change is properly domesticated, and takes place without upsetting the continuity.

Of course the legal system allows for change in content. This happens through legislation directly, the legislators being authorized within the legal system to make changes. It happens also by the gradual reinterpretation of the courts. Kelsen's view of the law directly allows for change; it is not a static system in which the norms are derived from the basic norm by intellectual operations, but a dynamic system in which a power to create norms is vested in a certain authority by the basic norm and this power is legally handed on within constraints. Hart includes rules of change as one of three types of secondary rules.

Today, change is rapid; technological and social changes are the order of the day, and radical institutional change is near normal. Its scope is international, but its effects are national too. How can the traditional positivist perspective accommodate vast changes that are not limited to revolutions but happen with almost perpetual revolutionary effect? There is often in the standard legal views a resistance to the experimental rise of new concepts which begin to make changes in the settled concepts. For example, the concept of privacy is taking new shape in American law. A legal writer[15] can trace its course in legal decisions: where it is ambiguous, how it brings many scattered things within its scope, what finer shades are overlooked or expressed, etc. But he tends to see it as creating a logical mess in the system of law. A pragmatic analysis would see it rather as a juristic experiment to help solve in a more systematic way problems in our society of electronic eavesdropping, control over one's own body in sex and marriage, safeguarding the individual against pressures that intrude from an excessive commercialism. It would look to see what this rising concept was doing that was needed but not satisfied by the older concepts of liberty and trespass. (In this sense the U.S. Supreme Court decision on abortion was a bold experiment.)

To go even further, why should not the very concept of law undergo change? Perhaps the concept should have changed when the shift came from monarchy to democracy. It was not merely a case of the Austinian notion of command proving too crude, but perhaps the dispersing of the phenomenon of sovereignty. And why should not massive changes in content be reflected in changes of both structure and concept—although the social and intellectual changes may go on at different rates? The state as an institution certainly has undergone changes with its turn from a policeman state to a social service state. Of course, Kelsen subsumes the state itself under the legal system because its officials are acting legally only when they conform to the legal norms. But there is a strange contortion in the conceptual way he accommodates the new administrative and social service functions to his scheme. Hägerström points this out in his review of Kelsen's *Allgemeine Staatslehre* in 1925:[16] "A legal prescript is held to be primarily an ideal rule of coercion. Therefore only those acts are primarily to be ascribed to the state which are an application of such rules, whereby this application itself can produce new coercive law. It is therefore clear that the so-called administration is not a genuine act of the state, if it does not have the character of an application of existing rules of coercion. It merely involves such action of the 'state-organs' as shall enable them to avoid being subject to legal coercion themselves. If, e.g., 'the state' through its 'organs' builds hospitals, runs railways, etc., this is not a primary act of the state, but only the 'behaviour in avoidance of coercion' of the active individuals in question." (With a more benign view of the social service and a less benign view of coercion, this distinction could almost coincide with the Marxian distinction of state action and administration as used in its theory of the withering away of the state.) Hägerström[17] calls attention to political problems in the background, the theory of a constitutional monarchy in which the monarch alone gives force to the laws while the consent of parliament is just a necessary condition, and sets Kelsen's view of the primacy of the constitution in the context of these controversies.

A clear case of specific change in the concept of law due to the rise of social service functions of the state in American law is the rise of administrative law in the 1930s.[18] Its acceptance as a kind of law came in response to new needs, new dangers, and new social responsibilities; whatever its precise analysis, the outcome suggests that change cannot be limited to content or to isolated legal concepts. Of course it might be replied that Kelsen is interested in defining the *general* character of law, the generic features of legal systems and so is not touched by such specific changes. This carries our inquiry into the heart of the question, the idea of system itself.

In general it looks as though the pace of change is breaking through the legal positivist compartmentalization of the strictly legal and the sociological, and the philosophical defenses of that compartmentalization are wearing thin. Take a striking example from Hart's discussion of the relation of natural facts and legal content, in presenting his minimum content of natural law. He recognizes the natural fact of the approximate equality of men and the further fact that if a system of forbearance (of the aggressive and the predatory) is established there will always be some who try to break it for their own advantage. These are allowed to justify going from merely moral to legal controls. This is seen as a *rational* connection of the natural and the legal. But the discoveries of psychology and sociology that certain psychological or economic conditions are necessary for the establishment of a system of law is treated as purely *causal*. "Connections of this sort between natural conditions and systems of rules are not mediated by *reasons*; for they do not relate the existence of certain rules to the conscious aims or purpose of those whose rules they are. Being fed in infancy in a certain way may well be shown to be a necessary condition or even a *cause* of a population developing or maintaining a moral or a legal code, but it is not a *reason* for their doing so."[19] Such a line of argument from the abstract distinction of rational and causal inquiries neglects the fact that what is discovered as a cause of the legal system makes us aware of a danger to the system if the causal conditions are neglected and thus furnishes a good reason for incorporating an insistence on the conditions in the law. There is no difference in principle between learning about the factual equality of men and the economic conditions necessary for stability in law, except that the one was earlier. Hart is thus allowing his distinction of the rule–guided rational behavior and the causal connection to bar the study of their interrelation and the way in which advancing knowledge and the realization of changing conditions turns an awareness of causes into a recognition of good reasons. Here the positivist compartmentalization survives to hamper the fuller view of legal development.

System

In legal positivism the idea of a legal system is that of a set of rules (as in a game) unified in a given way. It is not, as Kelsen's distinction between the static and the dynamic shows, the older purely logical notion of a rational deductive system. Two questions remain: why the focus on rules when there are other vital phenomena in the law as well and if a focus on rules, what exactly provides the unity of the system, or in what way do rules constitute a system?

In older style such questions were approached by asking for the nature of law. With the positivist abandonment of teleology and the resulting uncertain status of the idea of the nature of a thing, questioning shifted to "What is law?" or the demand for a definition. Kelsen is still working in this vein; he is looking for the most general features of legal systems. Hart has profited from the last half century's loosening of the theory of definition. He examines others' definitions to see what considerations prompted them to move in different directions; he rests on clear instances of legal systems, and aims at an improved analysis to answer persistent questions and cope with uncertain or penumbral cases (as whether international law is law). The crux of his analysis therefore lies in the focus of the persistent questions. He selects three: how law differs from the coercive gunman situation; how law differs from morality; and what are rules—how they exist and operate.[20] His inquiry is thus posed from the beginning as an account of the law in terms of rules that are differentiated from coercive orders on the one hand and moral prescriptions on the other.

It is important to realize that there are alternative focusings among legal phenomena. For example, the legal realists, even though rules play a large part in their exposition, focus on the process of decision. Law is a particular method of deciding conflicts in society in an organized way. We have seen how in Gray's analysis statutes are (like customs and moral beliefs) a source of law, not law themselves. It is true that for Gray[21] the law still consists of rules, but they are the rules that the court accepts and the significant fact is that the court has the last word. This, as has often been pointed out, may make sense from the standpoint of the lawyer who is trying to predict what the court will decide, in advising his client, or from the standpoint of the law professor who want a system of the law, but it makes less sense from that of the judge who is surely not trying to predict his own decision. By concentrating on decision as the vital focus, it was only a step for others, such as Jerome Frank,[22] to regard Gray's rules as simply sources of law themselves, not law as such; even the lawyer in the heat of battle is trying to fashion rather than predict the decision, and the complexity and conflict of rules adds to the importance of guiding selection for the case. At this point, where it seemed that the law would be reduced to a heap of cases and not be a system at all, philosophers began to battle about metaphysical nominalism vs. realism.

This historical episode underlines the importance of selection of focus in fashioning a theory of law. The same was seen where acceptance as a central phenomenon was added to coercion or prescription as the ruler's perspective. Furthermore, why should the general fact of acceptance loom as more significant than the variety of grounds of acceptance? As the state adds the functions of social services, much of the machinery is instrumental to purposes that are welcomed. The law seems then to have a dual character, just as medicine originally centering on curing the ill finds itself involved in the whole field of public health and its maintenance. As the proportion of tasks changes, so the conception of the field and its work changes, although it is quite possible that the two sides will fall apart and a much reduced medicine go back to the narrower limits. So too, crime and the King's Peace once occupied the center of the legal stage and was proportionately overwhelmed by the regulation that civil law brought. And today, with computerization and no-fault procedures and vast areas of administrative law, will there be a choice between service law whose central focus will be instrumentality for agreed-on ends and conflict law for dealing with disputes? Ethical theory has a comparable duality, with emotivism focusing on ultimate disagreement, while others focus on the ways in which an area of agreement could be cooperatively broadened by developing practices and institutions.

In the light of the variety of perspectives, should we expect the law to constitute a system? In the earlier positivist formulations the model of a science is strong; even though the phenomena are norms or rules there is a discoverable order and the science must be intellectually protected against reductionism. Kelsen, as we have noted, stringently narrows the phenomena to norms relating officials, and takes the unity of the system to lie in the ground–norm which generates the law–making authority. Hart's approach at the foundation is thoroughly empirical. He rejects the "obstinate search for unity and system where these desirable elements are not in fact to be found."[23] He differentiates a system from a mere set of rules; a legal system exists where primary rules of obligation which function as standards in rule-guided behavior are united with secondary rules that confer powers. The secondary are rules of recognition, which alleviate uncertainty about the location of authority; of change, which fix the ability to alter rules; and of adjudication, which meet the dangers of inefficiency by establishing ways of settling disputes.

Legal positivist theory in this contemporary form furnishes a way of looking at the law. What it sees is the existent situation with its officialdom, its legislature and its courts, all engaged in the production of rules. The theory traces the workings and analyzes operational concepts. It is a narrowed–down perspective which looks at its material in isolation both from outside evaluation and underlying sociohistorical causes. This is manageable if the institution is sufficiently stable; outside evaluations have then no immediate urgency and underlying causal conditions are not changing too rapidly. The theory rides on the attitude that history will carry through slow changes and legal theory will analyze the phenomena after the fact. There is no forward–looking or activist component in the theoretical attitudes of a positivist as contrasted with a pragmatic mode of analysis. The positivist assumptions that insulated the field of analysis were originally developed in their twentieth-century form in relation to physical science. Legal positivism incorporates this heritage and operates as if it has an independent legal realm to analyze in a scientific spirit. Norms or rules as the output of the legal system, extracted by analytic inquiry, might almost be compared to scientific laws extracted by scientific inquiry from the operations of nature. That they are rules for guidance seems almost to be an application of the legal system (like applied science) or else a conditioning purpose in having a system. This comparison fits the positivist mode more than it does the informalist mode, since the latter does distinguish the context of practice sharply from that of theory, and law like morals is taken to fall into the domain of the practical; thus the function of guidance seems more integral to its notion of rules. But it would be a matter of serious and detailed inquiry to decide how far the hangover of the positivist approach still permeates the attitude of the later mode to the nature of legal theory.

Recent work by historians and philosophers of science is, however, beginning to suggest other ways of looking at the relation of science, technology and the crafts, as contrasted with the tidied-up versions that have constituted our standard portraits of science. Would we get a quite different approach to the law if we saw it as an amalgam of a set of crafts developing over a historical period? How would it affect our view of the role of coercion and the character of rules, and the insulation of the law?

There is no need to go into the idea and structure of a craft. It obviously is purposive, instrumental, involves skill and tradition, works on the environment, and yields a product. In earlier stages, when the whole process is in the hands of the craftsman, he makes or at least controls the making of his instruments. Changes come with the rise of technology. Technology is frequently characterized as applied science, but this is looking at it from the side of science as theory—as science getting practical. If we look at it from the side of practice, what happens is rather that crafts are altered and repatterned through the use of instruments and mechanical, electrical and biological devices. The preparation of instruments shifts from the operating craftsman to the machine designer, and new crafts grow out of old ones as new instrumentation opens up fresh possibilities. But at the same time standardization of instruments and their use over different crafts renders the production or performance more mechanical. (In time a few of the artisans become designers; many are reduced to factory hands.) Finally, as for science, it develops as a craft with a tradition and expertise of its own. What we think of as applied science is still for the most part various crafts or their successors drawing on the resources of the new scientific discoveries to solve their own problems. Only occasionally has a science itself begun to produce science—based industries. Some areas become professionalized as a wide base of general or theoretical knowledge is required among their resources.[24]

If we bring this approach to the law, then as we trace its historical growth we see a multiplicity of crafts—the rhetorician, the politician, the administrator, the lawyer, sometimes the notary and the barrister—and can trace their operations, the instruments and skills they fashion and hand on, the typical tasks and purposes that come within their scope. Any unity comes from the interrelation of tasks and results, all looked at from the standpoint of the craftsman. If we insist on a general characterization of their tasks, they are perhaps better seen as *persuasion* rather than as rule production or steering coercion. Persuasion is a widespread way of human beings attempting to control behavior, and such control is the admitted objective of many institutions, the law included.

Coercion and rule production fall into place as instruments. After all, the work of coercion in the law is only partly to be exercised on malefactors; by far the greater part of its work is admittedly to generate apprehension, furnish persuasive motivation and establish habits of acceptance. The consolidation of coercive power in the unified system of law that follows the rise of national states, with police and armies, is the generalization of an instrument, analogous to the centralization of the production of energy for industrial purposes. It may be a necessary condition for modern legal systems as energy is a necessary condition for industrial production (shoe factories, for example) but it would not be fruitful to define industry as the independent science of using high-technology energy for production, even when energy crises rock the whole social foundations. The more accurate picture is that shoemaking resorted to electrical power to get mass production of shoes, once the generalized instrument was available.

Rules (simpliciter) in law are instruments for forming standards by use of generalization. They guide in action, but they do not accomplish this alone. In operation they are enmeshed in a complex of intention, motivation and consequential relations without which a rule has no sense. (This is manifest in the use of rules and the problem of interpretation in judicial decision.) Even the presentation of a rule as answer to the question ''What is the law on this matter?'' does not imply that law consists of rules; it is a shorthand to direct the questioner to the complex, so that he can use the lessons of past experience to guide his present decision. Of course crafts themselves have rules for their work that traditionally are handed on from one generation to another to transmit knowledge and experience and guide operations. Some of these may also become rules of law as the specific legal crafts come to be given official place. Again, just as coercion became a generalized instrument with the growth of the state, so rule making became a generalized instrument with the invention of legislative bodies. Their task cannot, however, be properly described as producing rules, but as trying to get definite jobs done in their societies through the use of rules. The legislative craft in many places had a serious effect on the judicial craft, which was concerned with disputes and their decision. The traditional controversy about the relation of statute law and judicial law shows how careful we have to be to distinguish mode of operation of rules in different contexts rather than bundle them into a characterization of law.

Fresh instruments may come from changes and inventions in society. Theoretical fields have sometimes furnished generalized instruments—for example, a formalized logic, or recently computers which may be expected to bring large changes where legal crafts are used for service functions.

The rise and exercise of crafts is a sociocultural matter and is affected by broader cultural traditions. Jerome Hall has reminded us[25] that in Japan and other oriental countries there is a traditional reliance on mediation and the attitude that it is shameful to resort to law, and it is not surprising, as Maine had already observed, law was assimilated to custom rather than to commands. For the Western tradition we could do worse than start a study of the craft approach to law with Aristotle's *Rhetoric*.[26]

Looking at the law in terms of the career of constituent crafts and their instruments should give us a fairer picture of what actually happened in the history of law and its changes. It should have greater explanatory power in understanding how and why, as for example other instruments became available, areas of content are moved out of the law, or how as social problems become serious, attempts are made to use the crafts of the law more extensively in hitherto untouched fields, and whether such attempts have promise. Again, by cutting the phenomena in a wholly different way, the approach undercuts the separation of value from law. Crafts are resorted to for purposes, whether to get a pair of shoes or win support (by persuasion) in a project or to open up definite opportunities. The very idea of a craft therefore implicates purposes and the efforts of people to achieve some goods. Further, the state of a craft and its instruments and resources are rooted in the sociohistorical processes and conditions of the society. Hence the examination of legal processes and techniques, so conceived and formulated, will be tied closely to the understanding of the changes that are taking place in society and the role that legal operations can play in social change and furthering social aims. Without sinking into either morals or sociology, legal theory could reflect an institution–in–society rather than an institution–in–itself.

Let me summarize what I have been trying to do and what conclusions are suggested about philosophical perspectives on law. We saw that the trouble spots in legal positivism were beginning to generate alternative models and that important formulations in other fields were beginning to cast a new light on its hardened theses. The monopolistic grip of analytic method was challenged, partly because it covered two somewhat discrepant analytic modes, partly by the variety of other modes. A pragmatic type of analysis was recommended for the most general view of law because it provides the clearest sense of variety, changeability, and self–corrective learning in human experience. A pragmatic theory of law was not implied, unless *theōria* be taken in the Greek sense of contemplation or a way of looking at. It was more an invitation to look in fresh and many ways. Instead, the pragmatic reanalysis of legal positivism raises sharply the meta–theoretical question of what we expect of a theory of law.

If, following the suggestion concerning a craft approach to law, we begin to look on all sides and relations of the enterprise, processes as well as forms, acceptance as well as prescription, persuasion as well as coercion, and if we take a functional and contextual view of formal elements, then the different theories may no longer come before us as proposed correct accounts of what the law really is. They are ways of looking, relative to certain methods and spurred by certain contextual interests. Some are better than others for particular purposes. Legal positivism, we have seen, gives a narrow view positing certain conditions. Contemporary natural law theory with its method trimmed down from classical metaphysics shows by its persistence in current forms how vigorous is the ethical aspect of legal phenomena. The general stream of Marxian historical approaches shows how internal to legal understanding is the sociohistorical understanding and the interrelation of the causal and the normative.

I am not here proposing an integration of perspectives just because each may carry a bit of truth. To see the whole is to see the variety and at the same time the limitations and exaggerations of each focus. Pragmatic analysis is desirable precisely because it opens up rather than closes our viewing. The question is then what we should do with all the perspectives if we proceeded under this stimulus to multiply them rather than to repress all but one. The simplest answer is that as the variety of models is worked out, each carefully elaborated and furnished with a study of the conditions under which it would be applicable, they could all become available as tools, not as conflicting schools. They could be used in varied theoretical and practical context, whether descriptive, causal–explanatory or evaluative. It may be that in given cultures and legal systems one model reads better certain parts of the law, while another other parts; or again, the legal phenomena in one society might better be described with, say, a checks-and-balances model, those in another with a bureaucratic–authority model. Legal positivism, we saw, might admirably fit the narrow view of a stable system, or regions of the law in which a sharp distinction of the existent and the ethical is particularly pertinent. But in other regions, such as criminal law, the place of the ethical and the causal may be an immediate one relevant to daily operations. Differences in the applicability of a model may even become relevant to very specific questions: for example, the dispute in American law whether in cases of delinquency of minors legal considerations should determine decisions of guilt while sociological considerations should enter into punishment, as against having sociological considerations enter into decisions of guilt themselves. In such questions, large and small, the models could be put to work.

In general, the ultimate matrix of legal theory is the totality of social experience and reflection upon it. The life of the law is not logic, nor an abstract way of looking at the law. But it is not experience either. It is the reflection on experience in the effort to guide further experience. No model should become so entrenched as to hamper this process.

The study was presented at the 9th World Congress of the International Association for Philosophy of Law and Social Philosophy, held in Basel, Switzerland in 1979, as one of the initial formal papers devoted to different conceptions of law.

Notes

1. H.L.A. Hart, *The Concept of Law* (Oxford: Clarendon Press, 1961), 229.
2. Gidon Gottlieb, "The Nature of International Law: Toward a Second Concept of Law" in Richard Falk and Cyril Black, *The Future of the International Order* (Princeton: Princeton University Press, 1969) 4, chap 9. See also his "Is Law Dead?" in *Revolution and the Rule of Law*, ed. Edward Kent (Englewood Cliffs, N.J.: Prentice-Hall, Spectrum Book, 1971), 77–91. Particularly good illustrations of the noncoercive (cooperative and compromise) operations of international law are to be found in Oscar Schachter, *Sharing the World's Resources* (New York: Columbia University Press, 1977).
3. Hart, *op. cit.*, 227–28.
4. Mortimer R. Kadish and Sanford H. Kadish, *Discretion to Disobey*, A Study of Lawful Departures from Legal Rules (Stanford, California: Stanford University Press, 1973), 32–33.

5. G.H. von Wright, *Norm and Action*, A Logical Enquiry (London: Routledge & Kegan Paul, 1963), 146–47.
6. Alf Ross, *Directives and Norms* (London: Routledge & Kegan Paul, 1968), 172–81.
7. Cf. Abraham Edel, *Analyzing Concepts in Social Science*, Science, Ideology, and Value, Vol. I (New Brunswick, New Jersey: Transaction Publishers, 1979), 1–41 ("Modes of Analysis: A Philosophic Overview").
8. Abraham Edel, "Toward an Analytic Method for Dealing with Moral Change", *The Journal of Value Inquiry* 12, no. 2 (Spring 1978): 81–99.
9. For example, in analyzing the concept of justice, a phenomenological approach may be most useful in providing an account of a burning sense of injustice. Accounts of justice too often limit themselves to analyzing the principle of distribution and its grounds.
10. H.L.A. Hart, "Positivism and the Separation of Law and Morals", *Harvard Law Review* 71, no. 4, (Feb. 1958): 593–629; Lon L. Fuller, "Positivism and Fidelity to Law—A Reply to Professor Hart", ibid., pp. 630–72.
11. R.M. Dworkin, "Is Law a System of Rules?" in *The Philosophy of Law*, ed. R.M. Dworkin (London: Oxford University Press, 1977).
12. Cf. Abraham Edel, "On Locating Values in Judicial Inference" in Edel, op. cit. 1979, 333–42. See also, Julius Cohen, "The Political Element in Legal Theory: A Look at Kelsen's Pure Theory", *The Yale Law Journal* 88, No. 1, Nov. 1978, 1–38.
13. Hart, op. cit. 1961, 206–7.
14. A fundamental move in entrenching the absolute fact–value distinction is to be found in G.E. Moore's treatment of the open–question argument (*Principia Ethica*, Cambridge: Cambridge University Press, 1903). This pointed out that for any definition of "good" by natural or metaphysical content, it was always possible to ask of the content thus specified whether it itself was good. This move was interpreted as giving value a non-factual status. All it establishes, however, is the perpetual right of further evaluation for anything. For fuller studies of the dichotomy, see Abraham Edel, *Exploring Fact and Value*, Science, Ideology, and Value, vol. 2 (New Brunswick, New Jersey: Transaction Publishers, 1980).
15. E.g., Louis Henkin, "Privacy and Autonomy under the Constitution", *Columbia Law Review* 74 (1974): 1410–33. For a judicious weighing of advantages and disadvantages, see Paul A. Freund, "Privacy: One Concept or Many" in *Privacy, Nomos* 13, ed. J.R. Pennock and J.W. Chapman (New York: Atherton Press, 1971) 182–98.
16. Axel Hägerström, *Inquiries into the Nature of Law and Morals* (Uppsala: Almqvist & Wiksells, 1953), 289.
17. Ibid, 293–95.
18. Cf. James M. Landis, *The Administrative Process* (New Haven and London: Yale University Press, 1938), especially chap. 4.
19. Hart, op. cit. 1961, 189–90.
20. Ibid., chap. 1.
21. J.C. Gray, *The Nature and Sources of the Law* (New York; Macmillan, sec. ed. 1930).
22. Jerome Frank, *Law and the Modern Mind* (New York: Tudor Publishing Co., 1935).
23. Hart, op. cit. 1961, 230.
24. I am indebted to Professor Hunter Dupree of Brown University for very clarifying discussion of the relation of craft, instrumentation and technology. Cf. his "The

Role of Technology in Society and the Need for Historical Perspective'', *Technology and Culture* 10, 4 (Oct. 1969), 529–34.

25. Jerome Hall, ''Religion, Law and Ethics—A Call for Dialogue,'' *The Hastings Law Journal* 29 (July 1978): 1259. The reference to Maine is to his *Early History of Institutions*. Lecture 12 (1875).

26. Aristotle's *Rhetoric* can fruitfully be read as a curriculum for legal studies. It distinguishes fundamental contexts of persuasion, each of which generates different concepts: regarding the future, in effect the legislative context, arguing about what is advantageous (good); concerning the past, the justificatory context, in effect the judicial, arguing about what is just; concerning the present, ceremonial contexts concerning what is praiseworthy (noble)—in a broader contemporary extension, what is acceptable or justifiable present practice. He deals with the techniques for different modes of persuasion (including tricks of the trade), psychological bases and ethical evaluations. The close relation of the purposive, the factual, and the ethical, and the integration of concepts with contexts and purposes, are akin to the pragmatic mode. This is not surprising in the light of the functional character of his use of the final cause.

6

Analytic Philosophy of Education
at the Crossroads

This study is a critique of the paradigm of analytic philosophy of education, which long dominated the second half of the twentieth century and is still entrenched in philosophic habits. It attempts to show that analysis in education, so far from being a purely logical–linguistic process, has hidden empirical assumptions and value presuppositions in its operation, so that a richer notion of analysis involves fashioning educational ideas in more direct relation to human knowledge and human purposes.

On the American scene, there was a sharp change in the philosophy of education that was manifest at least by the late 1950s. It consisted in a shift from what was to a great extent either a Deweyan–centered outlook (whether in acceptance or attack), or an outlook identified in terms of one or another large-scale philosophical system, to a new–broom analytical model. In part it was tied to some effort of rapprochement between academic and educational philosophy, bringing to the latter the mood that was in the ascendant in the former.

The sort of analytic philosophy that proved attractive was not the formalistic positivist type, but the British ordinary–language type. After all, education did not and does not operate with refined or high–powered symbolic systems; it is still itself an ordinary–language activity. Yet the turn to analytic philosophy of education of this type[1] was in one sense surprising at that time. For it was after World War II, the world was in ferment, colonialism was breaking down, Africa and Asia emerging into the modern world, a massive upsurge imminent of the oppressed and disadvantaged everywhere including the United States, a demand in sight for the extension of educational opportunity as well as for some share in political power. Traditional institutions in all areas of life were questioned, if not actually already crumbling. One might have expected to find in American educational philosophy at least an echo of the demands for social reconstruction as an educational obligation that had been loudly advanced by philosophers of education in the depression decade of the 1930s. A revolutionary educational philosophy might have seemed much more plausible than a cool analytic one. But perhaps the fuller social picture itself makes the intellectual outcome understandable. America was in the throes of a revived capitalist ideology, corresponding to its dominance after World War II. There were calls for the restoration of the status quo in the global cold war. Neo–conservative ideologies in an atmosphere of McCarthyite repression made a virtue of obscurantism and equated intellectualism with near–subversion. Dominant educational groups had themselves called for gearing American education to the objectives of the Cold War. Although with the Russian launching of Sputnik I, the upgrading of the intellect was demanded as a crash program for American education, this meant chiefly producing scientists and engineers. Perhaps the demand for neutral analysis was itself as revolutionary a step as the philosophical intellect could venture under these conditions! It may be recalled that in academic philosophy, political and social philosophy were at very low ebb; the brightest spirits went into the logic of the social sciences instead.

Now it is generally evident that the analytic approach has in the past fifteen years turned into a "school," with all the philosophical disadvantages of hardening lines of division, attack and counterattack familiar in the conflict (as contrasted with the dialogue) of philosophical schools. This would be less significant if the attacks on the analytic philosophy were just rear guard actions by older entrenched philosophical tendencies, or by philosophical romantic importations. In fact, however, they come increasingly, in the philosophy of education, from the younger people who are concerned with the problems of actual teaching in a period of intense social transformation, and see little relevant guidance coming from philosophy of education in its analytic shape. I was particularly struck by these complaints and the polarization they involved, at a recent conference on "New Directions in Philosophy of Education" held April–May 1970 at the Ontario Institute for Studies in Education.[2] One of the younger critics put it this way: "I come from the trenches of teaching to the Pentagon of Philosophy, and am dismayed to find the generals playing chess."

Now of course philosophers of education are not generals, and they have no inclination to give orders to teachers; indeed, value–neutrality is a major tenet in the analytic creed. But the discontent expressed in the metaphoric quip is not so easily thrust aside. For even practitioners in analytic educational philosophy have begun to raise the question whether it is adequately fulfilling its promise. In this sense, what is currently called analytic philosophy of education may be thought of as standing at the crossroads. What is at issue is precisely its potential in the philosophical contribution to education. The aim of the present paper is to diagnose the situation and to suggest what is required to enhance its contribution.

The Theoretical Diagnosis

A central difficulty in analytic philosophy of education seems to me to reflect a soft spot in the analytic theory generally—how to judge what is a correct or adequate analysis. Insofar as the analysis is linguistic analysis, one would expect it to issue either in an empirical–linguistic outcome or in a phenomenological resolution—in both of which the decision of adequacy would be a factual issue—or in some pragmatic–evaluative judgment determined by the purposes of the specific inquiry. Instead, we find a costly hesitation. In part, as early participants in the British analytic movement will say, the question did not arise. They had wandered into new pastures and were too busy culling the uses; there were enough to go round, and if anyone stopped short, he could usually be brought to continue by a counterinstance. Where would it end? It might never end.

But this was a symptom. The basic diagnosis lies deeper. Analytic method was given a certain cast by the dogmas it inherited from logical positivism. There was the sharp separation of philosophical analysis from empirical inquiry, the sharp separation of the analytic from the normative, and the sharp separation of the analytic from genetic–causal accounts. (Left on its own in this way, analysis was robbed of all vital criteria for decision; hence the symptom fixed on above.) Now all these sharp separations were essential to positivism. And they made a certain sense, for positivist analysis was concerned with building large formal systems. System–building can go on by itself in some degrees, without asking what factual structure it might apply to, or what purposes it might further, or what socio–cultural forces begot it. Analysis here can call its own tune without being brought to account till it is finished. The risk it runs is having a beautiful elaborate formal system that serves no purpose after it is built! But ordinary language analysis cannot defer payment in this way. It is analyzing linguistic uses that are thoroughly embedded in particular contexts. It has to face promptly nonformal conditions which are material in character, and the context when fully explored is inherently purposive—not only in the general purposes of language, but in the specific goings-on that give meaning to the uses. It is not surprising that the more J. L. Austin explores the uses of words, the more he is led to abandon the great dichotomies—to see illocutionary elements in the idea of truth and to reject the broad fact-value dichotomy.[3] Indeed, all the dogmas would have been rejected in analytic philosophy if the notion of context had been taken with full seriousness and if linguistic change had been as well–tilled a field as linguistic pattern.

If such a diagnosis is correct, the remedy would seem to lie in a fuller integration of the empirical, the normative, and the contextual (especially the sociocultural) *within* the analytic method. This is the major point of the present analysis. I shall try to show by selected case study from analytic philosophy of education that there is a growing loss of faith in analysis as a separate self–sufficient process, but that a remedy is being sought only by *adding* empirical, genetic, or normative elements. The key to an adequate remedy lies in the demonstration that these are not elements to be added to a separately performed analysis but play an internal part in the analytic products themselves. Hence integration, not just addition, is the cure.

The Unhappy Analytic Consciousness

The first step in presenting my thesis is to see the form taken by the loss of faith in the powers of the analytic method. I have not carried out a study of the field from this point of view, and am relying largely on impressions which others may not share. Let met take, as a good example of what I have in mind, a recent paper by Professor Jonas F. Soltis of Teachers College, Columbia University, himself an avowed analytic philosopher of education, entitled "Analysis and Anomalies in Philosophy of Education."[4] Professor Soltis sets his account in the framework of Thomas Kuhn's theory of scientific revolution.[5] Soltis traces the rise of the analytic paradigm in educational philosophy, how it displaces or sweeps into oblivion traditional questions and approaches, how it achieves dominance, and then how it develops its own anomalies. He explores two such anomalies. One is internal to the analytic paradigm itself "in that careful, cumulative, and persistent use of analytic techniques to clarify the concept of learning has brought with it disturbing results which run counter to the expectations of those who believe in the power of the paradigm to make clear, precise, and distinct 'fuzzy' categories." The second anomaly is external: "previous educational questions concerning values and social issues persist as major philosophical problems in education, but seem to be resistant to the strategies of analysis."

Whether these anomalies—or the situation as a whole—fits Kuhn's pattern is not my present concern. The second anomaly seems to amount simply to the fact that having expunged values from analysis as such—"One can ask for clarification of the idea of equality of opportunity, but he cannot ask if the schools *should* provide for equality of opportunity"—it remains frightfully difficult to prevent them from creeping in sideways. Soltis illustrates from Professor R. S. Peters's varying attempts to locate the *worthwhile* within the analysis of "education." Soltis takes Peters in effect to be asking and answering general ethical questions which the analytic paradigm would disallow. This question—whether "worthwhile" should be included or omitted from the analysis of "education" seems to me to raise problems chiefly for the reason I indicated at the outset, that there is no well–defined procedure for deciding which of competing analyses is more adequate. I shall look at Peters's treatment more explicitly later.

The first anomaly is the more formidable one. It concerns the distinction into types of learning that was the outcome of analytic grappling which began with Ryle's distinction between *knowing that* and *knowing how*. Voicing no dissatisfaction with the analytic job that developed the distinction and turned it from kinds of knowing to kinds of learning, Soltis offers it as a matter of fairly general consensus that there are at least four types: learning *that*, which is propositional; learning *how to*, which furnishes procedures or skills; learning *to*, whose outcome is dispositions, propensities or tendencies; and states of attainment via learning, such as appreciation and understanding. (One can, he illustrates, learn a poem but fail to appreciate it.) I should like to stress that Soltis's dissatisfaction arises not from the analysis but from the state of affairs we are left with when the analysis is finished. I need not go into his several reasons for dissatisfaction; more important is why he regards the outcome as an anomaly. The anomaly is that analytic procedures intended to produce distinctions end up with distinctions that do not distinguish. He illustrates with the way in which the very conditions of propositional knowledge involve procedures (*how* to pattern data to constitute a proof), and attainments (appreciation or understanding). He reinforces this with reference to Scheffler's detailed analysis in *Conditions of Knowledge*.

I have given this brief sketch of Professor Soltis's points to show the character of the unhappy analytic consciousness. As an analyst in the philosophy of education, Soltis simply wonders whether his methods have done jobs that get anywhere. He conjectures that what may be needed is "to try to find more acceptable answers or different ways to ask the questions. . . ." He toys with an appeal to a philosophical–empirical study of genetic epistemology for the first anomaly, and a kind of hybrid "analytic–pragmatic" paradigm for the second. In short, he wants to stop shutting out the empirical and the evaluative in the name of a "normal" paradigm of analysis.

If Soltis' account is at all typical of the dissatisfactions with the analytic method among analysts, then there is obviously a reaching out for what the method has kept beyond bounds. But it is not a thoroughgoing reconstruction of the method—simply an adding of the empirical and the evaluative to the analytical. I have suggested in the proposed remedy that this is not enough. I think I can suggest the line of integration needed if we go over the groundwork in the examples Soltis has given, and ask how the analyses themselves took place. I focus first on the distinction between the kinds of knowledge.

The Strange Career of "Knowing That"
and "Knowing How": A Closer Look

The relation between analysis and philosophy of education in the examples given illustrates the one–way sovereign stance: educational philosophy is the handmaiden of philosophy; philosophy furnishes the analytic products; and philosophy of education digs them up, brings them to teaching and structures learning and teaching. But what do these analytic products represent? As they come from ordinary language, they represent collective accumulated ordinary experience. Here lies the assumption that learning and teaching fall into the ordinary middle–sized domain. They are not like physics, which has had to dip to the micro–domain and fashion its own language; or mathematics which, as Ryle said of formal logic, had to drill ordinary words to behave in strange ways. Now there is much to be said for this whole approach. At best it might presuppose a view parallel to the effort in one stage of positivism (e.g. Neurath) to give physical–object sentences a primacy (over other forms like sense data, for example) as the protocol sentences of science; and to turn micro-constructs into instruments of macro–description. This would show the continuity of science and ordinary experience.

But education, after all, represents a large domain of experience in its own right. Can we impose on it the framework of our ordinary language categories? Even if they fit because it is a domain of ordinary experience, why should they be derived from analysis of ordinary uses elsewhere, rather than from its own experience? And why cannot its own experience be used to correct and revise run–of–the–mill ordinary language, precisely because education too, is happening in the common ordinary life? Analytic philosophy and analytic philosophy of education have scarcely begun to explore the assumptions inherent in their partnership.

The division into types of learning we have looked at above, as an analytic product, started in Gilbert Ryle's well–known separation of *knowing–how* from *knowing–that*, in his *The Concept of Mind*[6]. Ryle was primarily attacking the intellectualist language as set in the dualist philosophy—the intellectualist legend that doing something is first to do a bit of theory and then to do a bit of practice. Actually, it seems to me, Ryle was waging a battle in a series of strategically superb stages. One step is to distinguish knowing how from knowing that—in short to rescue practice from the intellectualist grip. Paradoxically, this may enshrine the separation in types of knowledge, itself a residual dualism. The next step is to give primacy to the practical: efficient practice precedes the theory of it, and even the competence to apply theory must be present first. Understanding too is a part of knowing how—the knowledge it requires is simply some degree of competence in performances of that kind. When doing has thus been safely ensconced in primacy and has had most of the book to show its capacities, the final attack on the enemy is launched. Chapter 9 is, in effect, a massive reduction of theorizing to the activity of teaching: "Having a theory involves being able to deliver lessons or refresher-lessons in it." Unfortunately, some teaching is like a spectator sport, rather than participant athletics. Ryle says: "Had arithmetic and chess been brought into the curriculum before geometry and formal logic, theorizing work might have been likened to the execution of calculations and gambits instead of to the struggle for a bench from which the blackboard can be clearly seen. We might have formed the habit of talking of inference in the vocabulary of the football field instead of in that of the grandstand, and we should have thought of the rules of logic rather as licenses to make inferences than as licenses to concur in them."

There is a great deal in all of this that is of interest to education. It reminds one of the case method in legal education. It is suggestive of the questions long debated in educational theory about the best ways of learning specific subject matters—whether by relation to practical activities and cultural interests, or in a pure symbolic manipulation. It suggest also the psychological–educational inquiries in rote learning and insight learning. It suggests again, the issues in the history of science teaching—how far success is achieved, and at what stages of schooling, by exposition of formulas and systems of laws, by student participation in experiments, by retracing the history of science in careful studies of problems and the way they were solved. No doubt, it will suggest many other educational problems as well. But the last thing I think it should have suggested is the distinction of knowing into a set of types certified by ordinary language and amplified by appeal to linguistic counterinstances.

Even when this became the setting of the problem in analytic philosophy of education, and progress was made, it seems to me to have come from letting the lessons of educational experience break in—even if only surreptitiously—upon the analytic process. Let me illustrate this briefly from one of the very able articles that made a contribution to the development of the topic of modes of knowing—Professor Jane Martin's "On the Reduction of 'Knowing That' to 'Knowing How'."[7]

Martin, after expounding Ryle's basic distinction, considers an attempt by Hartland-Swann to reduce "knowing that" to "knowing how." This, she says, rests on regarding "know" as a dispositional term; thus to know that is to know how to answer questions about the material involved. Martin objects that even if such a reduction is carried out, the newly expanded category of "knowing how" requires a distinction within itself based on the fact that two very different sorts of dispositions are involved. Suppose, she says, Jones witnessed the murder of Y. Jones accordingly knows that X murdered Y and knows how to answer the question "Who murdered Y?". But such a capacity is essentially different from Jones knowing how to swim or to speak French. Martin suggests a feature to explain this "intuitively obvious" essential difference. It is that the one set of capacities had to be learned *through practice*; learning to answer the question about the murder didn't require practice.

Martin goes on to considerable discussion of alleged counterinstances and ends with a distinction of several types of "knowing how." One implies the capacity has been learned through practice, and a second does not. My interest is not in the types, but in questioning why she introduced the distinction between what is learned by practice and what is not, as intuitively essential. There are, after all, so many distinctions that might compete for essentiallity between knowing how to answer questions and knowing how to swim. For example, one involves talking, the other does not; but this may be ruled out because she coupled "knowing French" with swimming. Why isn't the division made between acts that involve communication and acts that one can do alone? Thus knowing French goes with knowing how to answer questions, as against swimming. I need not labor the point, nor raise diffi- culties about the fact that the child learns to answer questions by practice in human communication, though he need not practice each answer; nor again that he can learn one activity without practice if he knows another activity (e.g., to run a motor boat if he can run a car). Surely what is happening is that it is intuitively essential to Martin the educator to consider the difference between what requires practice and what does not because that is a vital lesson from the experience of learning and teaching. Here Martin the analyst profits from Martin the educator, and the analytic products are steered precisely along those distinctions that are important to educational experience. Martin is less applying analytic distinctions than setting them up to be useful to what the lessons of educational experience have shown important.[8] And I'm in- clined to think that this is precisely the way in which analytic products come about. There must always be some purposive context that calls the tune.

Let me give another example of the way in which Professor Martin's sensitive combination of her double role is philosophically profitable. In a paper on "Basic Actions and Education,"[9] she examines the controversy over the idea of a basic action in the currently fashionable theory of action. She starts out to see how the theory that has been built up about basic actions may help the theory of learning, and she reckons with the analytic works of Vesey and Melden and Danto on this question. But gradually Martin the educator begins to call the tune. The distinction between doings to which a person attends and devotes effort and those doings to which he does not attend and does not direct effort—that is, the educationally relevant distinction—takes over. Not only is the idea of a basic action relativized (or rather, contex- tualized), but the normative question for education is raised—"whether we want whatever it is that a person is learning how to do to be learned as a basic action or not.'' In the progress of the investigation from this point of view she has been led to question the analytic distinction of bodily movements and actions, to find a halfway house in some phenomena and to wonder whether the whole framework is not shaky.

Note the implications of such a study. It calls for a two-way interaction of educational problems and experience and analytic process and products. It does show the operation of the educational purpose in the type of analytic product that emerges. But it does not simply make action theory dance to the educational tune. For action theory is a meeting place of other interests as well—legal and moral, for example—and so the analyst in considering action should be listening to many tunes, and his products, when tried out in any *one* field, in effect are bringing models from other fields. The analytic philosopher could be the integrator of wide areas of human thought and effort, if he kept open his sensitivity to them instead of isolating his craft in a misguided conception of analytic autonomy. (He might also be the inventor of new models and new distinctions to be tried out in specific areas.)

Now what would a full–scale investigation of the distinction between knowing that and knowing how involve? Let me suggest a few lines of inquiry for the philosopher of education, concerning (i) the sociohistorical stage of development of education as an institution, (ii) the underlying psychology of human action as it affects educational theory, (iii) the kind of linguistic-philosophic inquiry that may be relevant.

(i) To what extent has the distinction of knowing that and knowing how been written large in educational institutional development? I think, for example, of the difference between academic and vocational high schools—say, New York in the 1930s. One was directed to the kind of learning that got one college entrance, the other to having skills that might get one a job. This is surely knowing that and knowing how, roughened and magnified. Of course one could point out that many of those in colleges ended up in professional work (engineering, teaching, etc.) that gave one a know–how; and the vocational schools thoroughly impoverished the preparation of their pupils in knowing how, because they had dilapidated old–fashioned machin-ery discarded from manufacturing. And in any case there were no jobs in the 1930s, till we moved from a depression economy to a war economy that needed skills. I leave it to the philosophers of education—especially those who may have had teaching experience in these schools—to expound the evils that the separation gave rise to. Impressionistically, I recall the repeated demands and arguments for a comprehensive high school on the ground that the separation impoverished both. Similarly, I recall the writings in vocational psychology that worked hard to show how intelligence enters into skilled labor and urged intellectually minded students not to scorn those areas as against the then overcrowded professions. Maybe the distinction between knowing that and knowing how draws the line at the wrong point. It might be drawn instead between enlightened action (professional and skilled labor) and unenlightened action. (But this might be socially temporary, for unskilled labor is being automatized anyhow.) Think of how much Marx inveighed against the massive social dichotomy of brain and brawn as an exploitative set up.

The fact is that the more complex production becomes the more the integration proceeds. I recall in the early 1940s, when the Board of Regents of New York State proposed a set of institutes for post–high school education which would combine technical and liberal education in something like what is now the partially technical community college, opinion in the labor movement was at first very suspicious of the proposal. There were fears that on the one hand it might bring a free flow of nonunionized cheap labor into the market (memories of depression and unemployment were still strong) and on the other hand that it was shortchanging the workers who wanted an education. In Rylean language they might have said: if you want to know that, go to a liberal arts college; if you want to know how, join the union as an apprentice. To meet the situation a gathering of top labor leaders was addressed by the State Commissioner of Education. I recall the skillful way in which he explained how the growth of complexity and the rapidity of technical change was making a basic education in science more and more necessary for actual work—down to the care and running of a diesel engine. In a way, it was parallel to the situation that had prompted Robert Hutchins, as dean of the Yale Law School in the earlier 1930s, to demand basic education in the law school: the New Deal was sweeping away old laws so rapidly that a law student who studied in the old way would graduate with a knowledge no longer relevant to the laws on the books. But whereas Hutchins went off to a basics in terms of a classical conception of mind and man, the breakdown of the liberal–vocational distinction called for an integration in which in the long run the dichotomy of enlightened and unenlightened action would become the central one. That such movements have advanced in the contemporary world is evident in the increased role of basic research in relation to productive effort. In the long run, it is the whole dichotomy of theory and practice that is being brought under scrutiny.

All this, you may be tempted to say, is interesting reminiscence. But has it anything more than the association of ideas to do with Ryle's distinction? I think it has. It suggests that Ryle's dichotomy, like all dichotomies, is attuned to particular phenomena that give it relevance, whereas in an extended view its severe limitations may become evident. It holds for a limited domain of ordinary activity in which there is sufficient actual (that is, practical) separation of thinking and doing to keep the distinction relatively useful. Look at Ryle's examples of know-how: we ride bicycles and play chess and talk

French. We do not operate control stations at London airport or break codes or build translation machines. If the distinction of knowing-that and knowing–how remains in the more complex situation, it is only the survival of the distinction between planning and carrying out plans, or it is an invocation of the ''intuitive'' element in synthesis or diagnosis or skill. I am not proposing to reduce action to thought as Plotinus reduced production to reason, so that even the creation of the world was an overflow of reason! I am rather suggesting that what has been called knowing-how is a very gross phenomenon, perhaps insufficiently understood, which will not support very precise categorical distinctions. I would not dream of denying that there is some distinction in some contexts, just as I would not obliterate the difference between studying the nature of love and falling in love.

In short, the examination of the institutional embodiments of comparable dichotomies, in their social context and historical relations, suggests that the Rylean distinction holds only within the limited domain in which an apprenticeship system is possible. As a distinction of types of knowledge it is parasitical on the distinction between abstract form and existent instance, planning and carrying out plans, studying and feeling, and a number of others. The educators should then start at the other end and study where apprenticeship learning is possible—not merely the plumber's apprentice, but also the politician's apprentice and the doctor's internship. To make the dichotomy an initial hardened distinction analytically certifiable and coercive on education may be just as much an ideology as Michael Oakeshott's attack on reason in politics in his conservative defense of an aristocracy brought up to rule.[10]

Please note I am not assuming that I have the answer to this type of inquiry I am suggesting into the institutional–historical dimensions of the dichotomy. The inquiry has still to be carried out.

(ii) A second line of inquiry would look to the underlying psychology of human action. I can indicate this briefly by reference. Ryle's distinction is involved, as we saw, in rejecting a dualistic theory of mind. But may it not, in spite of itself, enshrine a dualistic cut between the sensory–cognitive and the motor? At least a very famous reconstruction of the reflex arc concept long ago[11] suggested that the separation of stimulus and response, or of stimulus, central process, and response, retained the older dualisms that were ostensibly rejected. If, as Dewey argued, the stimulus at any point already is different in the light of the previous response which has changed its meaning, and the present response is an effort of reconstruction in the coordination of the total situation, can the dichotomy be much larger than between habit smoothly functioning and habit that involves reflection? It is interesting to note that in his *Human Nature and Conduct*,[12] precisely after he has attacked the isolated ethereal view of knowledge, and even gone so far as to say ''concrete habits do all the perceiving, recognizing, imagining, recalling, judging, conceiving and reasoning that is done,'' he rejects *knowing how* as knowledge. We may, he says, be said to know how by means of our habits; but this is knowledge only by courtesy. ''Or, if we choose to call it knowledge—and no one has the right to issue an ukase to the contrary—then other things also called knowledge, knowledge *of* and *about* things, knowledge *that* things are thus and so, knowledge that involves reflection and conscious appreciation, remains of a different sort, unaccounted for and undescribed.'' And significantly in presenting the account of the difference—that the more efficient a habit is the more unconsciously it operates, while ''a hitch in its workings occasions emotion and provokes thought''—he goes back to the central picture of the basic thesis of the old article on the reflex arc.[13] I cannot pursue this further here, but it suggests that no dichotomy of the Rylean type be admitted as more than a rough ordinary relative distinction—that is, be made the basis of educational theory—unless it makes clear its psychology of the sensory-motor relations.

(iii) It is also clear that the linguistic inquiry involved in the analysis is too limited, in at least several respects.

(a) Its range of expressions involving ''know'' that can generate proposed distinctions is too narrow. I need not recapitulate the further distinctions that have developed, as indicated in Soltis's paper discussed above. There are wholly different paths. Aristotle distinguished between knowing–that and knowing–why. His ''that'' was differently cut—limited to the isolated fact as against the explanatory reason. Philosophy of science has developed the whole notion of the relative distinction between description and explanation, or between a descriptive account and a systematic account. This is, of course, highly relevant to educational ideas of explaining and understanding. Again, the difference between ''knowing John'' and ''Knowing about John'' or ''knowing the job'' and ''knowing about the job'' might support the sort of distinction Russell made at one time between *knowledge by acquaintance* and *knowledge by description*,[14] in which the former involved immediacy of presentation. But it might also support a quite different distinction such as William James made[15] between *knowledge of acquaintance* and *knowledge-about*, in which the extent of the knowledge is contrasted (mere acquaintance vs. the inner nature of the things). James also adds that I cannot impart acquaintance with things as I can knowledge about them. But fundamentally he is thinking of the contrast of the relatively simple thought with the articulate and explicit. It is interesting to note the contemporary reversal in ordinary use. To be acquainted with something is almost ''really'' to know it, while to know about it may be just what we got from hearsay (or book reviews instead of reading the book). But perhaps the significant differences may lie in what is known. Thus there are tremendous differences between ''knowing

John'' and ''knowing arithmetic'' or ''knowing the town,'' in none of which any preposition or conjunctive adverb intervenes. While a Bergson might elaborate a distinction between *outer* and *inner* knowledge (scientific vs. metaphysical),[16] a Martin Buber would make the cut between persons and things—*thou–knowledge* and *it–knowledge*.[17] And what educator in these days of alienation and bureaucratic manipulation would dare deny the significance of this distinction for educational work!

(b) The linguistic inquiry has not focused sharply enough on whether the cutting line is drawn through ''know'' (by distinguishing meanings), or through the difference of preposition and conjunctive adverb or through the type of object. It has thus not been sufficiently aware of the relativity of cuts and the options involved. Thus in the Biblical formulation, when David knows Bathsheba and when he knows the strength of his enemies, it is the different sense of ''know'' that bears the burden of distinction (carnal, informational or experiential). When we know how, how to, about, where, etc., the line of difference is drawn by the preposition or conjunctive adverb attached to the ''know.'' When the object takes over the work of distinction, it cannot be a wholly linguistic inquiry. We must have in mind some set of object types. An interesting example is to be found in Professor R.S. Peters's recent suggestion[18] that the knowledge of what is good is different from either ''knowing how'' or ''knowing that,'' since, as Socrates and Plato argued, it is intimately connected with caring about something. If we develop this suggestion, it would seem that to ''know the fact,'' ''know the job,'' and ''know the good,'' would be distinguished by category words such as FACT, TASK, VALUE. Perhaps to ''know what's up'' or ''know what's going on'' might add EXPLANATION.

(c) A third shortcoming would be insufficient attention to perspective. Most of the types of knowledge are looked at as attained states of a person. Educationally, they are thus either what the teacher has and is offering to the pupil, or they are what the pupil has when learning is complete. The transition from types of knowledge to types of learning is thus not an automatic one, and the types of learning as a process may be quite different from the types of end products in learning. Types of learning may furnish some of the ideals for the end product. But in some cases the end may supervene on very different procedures. Learning may depend in part on the tone of voice of the teacher or the demanding or accepting atmosphere of the classroom, neither of which is reflected in the product. Nor is it possible to regard every feature in learning as itself embodying a further end to be learned. For while there is what Gregory Bateson has called ''deutero–learning''—the child learns in the same situation permissiveness as well as reading—whether permissiveness is to be subsequently redressed is a separate question. The process may be rationalized in the way in which a reading-readiness program concentrates on the separate skills and conditions that when put together will be requisite for reading. But rationalization may not be wholly complete, and means and ends not always congruent.

In general, knowledge is the teacher perspective—he has it. Learning is the underdog view. A shift in emphasis from teaching to learning today is a social shift, quite comparable to the pressure for participation in politics. (It is suggestive too, that responsibility for the pupil's not learning seems to be shifting from the pupil to the teacher.) J. S. Mill says in his essay "On Genius"[19] that the end of education is not to teach but to fit the mind for learning under its own consciousness and observation; that we have occasion for these powers under varying circumstances for which no routine or rule of thumb can possibly make provision. For educational purposes the linguistic analysis might better be directed to the uses of "learn," and in the educational situation directly, not by new hardened distinctions between "learning with," "learning from," "learning by"! The approach from learning would certainly take better account of the situation in higher education where the teacher Socratizes, or where a discussion is begun in a field in which a teacher does not know the outcome, but is bringing analytical skill and educational experience to a seminar in which all, himself included, may learn.

How Then Does One Decide Which Analysis Is Correct?
How Peters II Corrects Peters I

I have tried to show the genuine complexity involved in the analysis of "knowing that" and "knowing how," and to suggest the way in which empirical and scientific considerations and historical stages of social life and human and educational purposes play an integral part in the very process of analysis. They are not simply added at the end. I would now like to return to the soft spot in analytic method mentioned as the central symptom at the outset, and see how an analysis may be judged for its adequacy. For this purpose I focus on Professor Peters's recent rich paper on "Education and the Educated Man,"[20] in which he revises his previous analysis of "education." I want to spot the way in which the revision takes place and why the resulting analysis is regarded as more adequate than the earlier. I should point out that I am not concerned with psychological or other causes in Peters—his shift is not like the old appeal from Philip drunk to Philip sober—but to the content of his analysis. And I choose it because Peters's general position seems here to be like Soltis's above—ready to go beyond analysis after the analysis is finished, but not apparently ready to admit that the beyond operates within the analysis.

Peters's earlier analysis of "education" as developed in *Ethics and Education*[21] included: (1) the transmission of worthwhile activities to those who become committed to them, (2) some knowledge and understanding and cognitive perspective which is not inert, and (3) the exclusion of some procedures as lacking wittingness and voluntariness on the part of the learner. This conception was criticized by some as being normative and laying down values of knowledge as against passivity. But in the familiar analytic fashion it could be said that the values were packed way in linguistic uses of "education." The analyst need not advocate them any more than in, say, the analysis of the meaning of "law and order" in a familiar current use he need approve of the streak of violence he will find embedded.

In the paper now under consideration Peters is troubled by counterexamples, especially by use of "education" for societies (his example is Spartan education), where the second condition of the three is not satisfied. He considers proposals to make the value condition (1) the sole one; thus any society could fill in its values for its educational system. And, on the other hand, he considers making the cognitive condition (2) the only one. He decides against both, and offers instead the distinction between "education" and "the educated man." His older definition, in effect, had viewed education as the family of processes which contribute to the outcome of an educated man. By breaking the connection between the processes and the outcome, he is able to accommodate the deviant uses of "education." It also helps resolve arguments concerning the first definition that had centered on Peters's contention that we could not speak of the "aims" of education; since education was initiation into worthwhile activities, it already had all the aims it needed. Now with the separation of concepts, one could speak of aims with respect to education, but not with respect to the educated man.

This is a very bare outline. The full analysis involves constant resort to uses, to what would simplify and what would complicate the picture of uses, to counteruses and objections. Now the question I want to consider in greater detail is what makes Peters's revised analysis better than his original analysis. What does he himself have to say, whether directly or in asides, on the question?

The chief passage treating this is on pp. 12, 13. Peters tells us that in his previous analysis he had always assumed the connection between "education" and the development of an educated man. (Even where other people did not have this more differentiated conceptual structure, it was important to make the distinction.) "But perhaps I did not appreciate how widespread the older use of 'education' is in which there is no such tight connection between various processes of bringing up and rearing and the development of an educated man. It may well be that many people still use the word 'education' to cover not only any process of instruction, training, etc. that goes on in schools but also less formalized child–rearing practices such as toilet–training, getting children to be clean and tidy, and to speak with a nice accent."

Actually, considerable historical examination of changing usage is associated with this confession. There has been an etymological digression in which we were told that the Latin "educare" was once used for rearing plants and animals as well as children; and the English word in the seventeenth century covered animals, birds, and, in the nineteenth century, silkworms. The use of "education" for "Spartan education," in which there is training without close connection with knowledge and understanding, is put into such a category. In addition, there was a precursor ideal to the present educated man in the pre-nineteenth century notion of the cultivated person, who was the product of elaborate training and instruction. It was only with the coming of industrialism and the greater importance of knowledge and the development of schools that the association of knowledge with instruction became close. "So close has this association become that it is now possible for some people, who do not value anything to do with books or theory, to say that they do not value education."

In short, Peters's old definition represented the outcome of a historical trend not quite completed, and breaking the connection between "education" and "the educated man" helps focus on the relation of the different elements and understand the surviving uses that were puzzling.

I do not see why, to ensure the greater clarification, it is necessary to carry out a redefinition. The break in connection could be seen by showing that the earlier definition had such–and–such separate components related in such-and-such a way, presupposing such–and–such empirical connections; the historical–genetic reflections and reflections on people's values that enter the process could then be put into an explanatory preamble. Thus in the familiar example of the way in which "conducting electricity" gets put into the definition of "copper," it is seen how copper was identified and defined before we knew anything about electricity and how the growth of the empirical connection and the increase of theory leads from turning what was an empirical generalization into a material leading principle, and formally when the theory becomes extensive and the feature involved significant enough, into part of the definition. In Peters's account the burden of clarification is borne by his historical–genetic–valuational account of the ways in which and grounds on which the usage changed. To put the results of such an account into the reanalysis and change the definition thus reflects some ground of decision on Peters's part, and it is this I am trying to locate. It is not easy, so I shall probe in a few different ways.

First, though he seems to think of his second definition as more adequate than the first, he is not claiming, in the older analytic style, to be giving the "correct use." It is, in the distinction Ryle made between "use" and "usage,"[22] rather the usage that is involved—the actual incidence of employment of the term.

Secondly, Peters seems to feel he has to accommodate all the counterexamples, but not in a uniform way. There are analogical uses, secondary uses, bypaths, and so on. Some uses, significantly, have died out. Now in such accommodation there is considerable constructive activity on the part of the analyst. A use that is analogous or secondary is so only relative to a definitional use accepted as primary. If we reversed their roles, the other would be secondary. Peters's struggles with "Spartan education" illustrate this. Drop the knowledge condition for "education" and the secondary use becomes an instance of the primary use. In fact, this stubborn example plays a large part in Peters's separation of education and the educated man. But if there is a constructive activity on the part of the analyst, there is some meta–analytical decision involved.

Thirdly, the resort to historical explanation of counterexamples is not itself decisive of what will be done with the outcome. For example, there is the counterexample to including a value condition in "education" that lies in many people regarding being educated as a bad state; people, they say, are better off without it. Peters identifies them as simple, hardheaded, practical men. Presumably, they are the relics of an earlier form of life suspicious of contemporary civilization. Their judgment that education is bad is a moral judgment directed on the values embedded in the definition. If the definition had no embedded values or left a value–variable to be filled in by each group use, then they could not say that education is bad; they could only say that education is misdirected in contemporary society or has to be tolerated for some of its instrumental effects. Having seen all this surely does not foreclose Peters's options. He could still have gone either way—to keep his old definition or to shift, as he does, to his new account. Neither would rob the simple practical men of their right of value criticism; they would have to express it in one case as a condemnation of education, in the other as a condemnation of modern life. If anything, the latter would be clearer—and that is a consequence of sticking to Peters's first definition. So there are gains and losses in clarity whichever way we go. Why rob Peters to pay Paul? Simply give an explanatory preamble and choose your path on *conscious and significant grounds*.

What then are significant grounds? Peters seems to be abandoning, as I suggested earlier, his old definition (let me call it E_1) which represents the outcome of a historical trend which has not quite been reached, for a definition (E_2) of two terms which leaves an empirical relation between their material content. So far as I can tell from the considerations I have given, it is because E_2 better reflects the current state of usage. But if his historical analysis is correct, this current state is not likely to last. The forces of industrialism, the importance of knowledge, and the use of formal schooling, are likely to become more effective. Some indeterminate time from now, an analyst with the same perspective as Peters in his revision may come to Peters's old definition as his answer! The present counterexamples may die and be neglected by him as Peters thrust aside "education" for training of animals. If a present analytic answer represents an intellectual investment, doesn't the analyst want to be secured at least about the stability of the linguistic situation? Suppose it is likely to change in a decade? In a year? In a week? Tomorrow? Does it make no difference to him? Actually it does. In his rating of counteruses, he may sift dying uses, no longer vital, analogous uses that were once on an older outlook thought continuous, and so on. Having used historical grounds for explaining minor corrections in present use, he might as well expand his historical judgments as a basis for distinguishing more significant from less significant uses. And having seen this integral role of historical factors in the fashioning of his analytical product he might as well recognize the purposive and valuational components that operate both in history and in their own right in the analytic process.

Along these lines, Peters's first definition may be reconstrued as follows: begin with a preamble, giving the kind of historical information Peters invokes in the paper about industrialism and the growing stress on knowledge. Estimate the extent and strength of the trends and analyze the vital conflicts as they effect the lives of man—for example, the forces of corporatism that make them passive organization men and the pressure of problems that require active participation and inventiveness. Add the kinds of ethical considerations Peters holds to about worthwhile activities—as explicit ethical views. Add the picture of the current state of linguistic usage and the historical and value roots, and what coalescence and what fissions are taking place. Then, propose the definition as expressive of historical–valuational–linguistic grounds, showing how far it represents trends or resistance to trends, possible solution to problems, and so on. Why not then tie together, as Peters's former definition did, worthwhileness and knowledge and creative activity in one bundle, setting a goal for our social and educational development in the conditions of the contemporary world, genuinely fitting at our present stage of knowledge and social development? How timorous by comparison is a definition attuned to the condemnations of relics of an earlier society, or permissions to speak of "Spartan education" in an anthropologically neutral way, which anthropologists don't need from philosophers anyhow to carry on their profession! Whatever clarity there is in the second definition about corrections could have been achieved in a richer type of analysis of the first definition.

I hope in this appeal from Peters II to Peters I, I shall not have both Peters set against me. Let me by way of caution add a linguistic ground for my position. If we examine fully the contexts in which "education" is employed in the modern world, I think it becomes clear that it is often a policy–setting word, or an institution–shaping word. In this respect it is like "freedom" or "morality." Even terms like "science" or "family" carry this aspect, though in subtler shades. To include or exclude grandparents in the definition of "the family" is to take a stand on the institutional shaping, and to make obligations either an inner matter or an outside matter in a fashion quite parallel to what Peters has argued about education. So too the terms "education" and "educational activities" function in discourse that determines policy in the schools. Think of the long history of controversy over extension of the curriculum in the United States, in which additions were popularly branded as not education but simply "fads and frills." For in the system in which the concepts are involved—I need scarcely remind philosophers, at this stage, that concepts do not stand alone—if an activity is not educational, it does not belong in the schools. You can expect a teacher to keep class records because it is part of the educational job, but you cannot expect him or her to sweep the floor and tend the stove, as in the old one–room school house; that is custodial labor. Soon too keeping records may be certified as "clerical" and come under another jurisdiction. With the growing use of paraprofessionals, we may expect more rather than fewer distinctions. Major questions of policy are likely to be settled under the definition of "educational activity," as major questions of the American way of life have been settled under the analysis of "due process." To take one example, Peters in his *Ethics and Education* points out that the question may significantly be raised whether teaching belongs in a university. In the United States, the more likely question arising is whether research belongs in the college. Both require for their understanding long historical–valuational explanation. But the solution is rather likely to take the form of what educational contribution the faculty's engaging in research makes in the college—as against having separate research institutes. If we recognize the policy-determining and institution-shaping function of discourse about "education" and "educational activity," it becomes necessary to track down the components that shape the outcome and the values embedded therein.

An afterthought: this should not be construed as an appeal for a persuasive use of analysis. I have no objection to this being frankly done in its own terms. For example, I might urge the old use of "education" to cover plants, on the ground that it might suggest a good botany class in the early elementary school, in which children could be teacher apprentices, and the plants be pupils (perhaps on a Buberite approach). But to see my argument in this light is to misunderstand and misrepresent it. Peters, in adding a reflection on the limitation and point of analysis, paraphrases Wittgenstein: "conceptual analysis leaves everything as it is." That is, the ethical and social decisions are separate and after the analysis is completed. I have been arguing that they are integral to the analysis at the point of choice throughout, together with the empirical and scientific considerations and historical considerations.

Concluding Notes

I have tried to show the following. There is dissatisfaction in the philosophy of education with the current form of the analytic approach. Some of the analysts are themselves unhappy, professors as well as students. The source of the trouble lies in a weakness in current analytic method itself, which purports to exclude empirical and valuational and sociohistorical components. These cannot be added successfully after the analysis is over—this yields an unsatisfactory halfway house. Such components play a role in the analysis itself, surreptitious if not recognized; they determine in part the shape of analytic products. If you ask what analysis looks like when this is recognized and these components integrated, I am tempted by the way Richard Robinson, in his book, *Definition*,[23] characterized one type as "any process, whether verbal or otherwise, by which any individual, whether God or angel or man or beast, brings any individual, whether himself or another, to know the meaning of any elementary symbol. . . ." Let me say then that analysis is any way which God or angel or man or beast can devise to make clearer the conceptual instruments one is using, and the processes of using them in specific materials, and to dig out the presuppositions in the questions asked, and the problems and purposes involved, so as to be able to refine and improve them in the light of the stage reached by mankind in its total development of life and society.

I do not mean in such a definition to disparage linguistic sophistication, but to put language in its human relations. When words are dynamite, it is because of what human beings and their milieu are like at the time. When Peters says casually that a non-value use of "education" would be treating it, "as indeed it is sometimes called, the 'knowledge industry'," I cannot help remembering the explosion set off in California by Clark Kerr's reference to the "knowledge industry" in his *The Uses of the University*.[24] To the Berkeley students, the comparison of knowledge production today to the railroad industry in the nineteenth century and its role in American development, meant accepting the purposes of the establishment and the alienation of students!

If there is doubt and controversy about "education" today, it is because the concept of education, like most traditional concepts, is itself cracking. Uses are altering and new concepts are in the making because human history and institutions and social life and values are at a point of extremely rapid change with the potentials of great creation or great destruction. If philosophical analysis is to be helpful to education today, it must be the sort that is responsive to the problems of education in this rapidly changing world, that will realize the constructive task of fashioning intellectual instruments for dealing with these problems. It cannot limit itself to current uses and even to current problems within education, for the relations of this institutional complex to the whole of the social milieu are being transformed. Education as we have known it as an institution may be breaking up and being realigned in myriad ways. It is no longer clear that *any* domain will keep the shape and isolated problems and isolated concepts that it has had. A constructive philosophical analysis will not sit passively by waiting for something to consolidate either institutional or linguistic form to be retrospectively dissected. Both the owl of Minerva, and whatever glottal deities there may be, have work to do before the dusk. Philosophy of education today has to use whatever resources it can muster to clarify and cope with the way in which the major problems of men today are impinging on the present state of educational policies, programs and institutions. Formidable as this task sounds, it can be quite concrete and quite philosophical even though the philosopher will not usually be able to go it alone. But the fact is that in no field of policy or practice today can any professional go it alone without distorting the results.

Such a philosophical analysis in education which involves cooperation with empirical and scientific studies, with historical analysis of development, and with systematic analysis of trends and possibilities, may indeed seem overwhelming. But what other path is possible for a philosophy which can respect its work and win the respect of its students? It may withdraw from the field, of course, finding it too complex, as Plato withdrew from physics, finding nature too Heraclitean—and then proceeded to fashion physical myths! It may, instead, content itself with constructing general schemata, indicating in detail the kinds of blanks that will be filled by empirical knowledge, and the kind by value determinations. This at lease will have the virtue of noting what is needed, instead of making a virtue of ignoring it. But if it gives up both retreat and the hope of all–comprehensive schemes, it may find a host of problems in the actual contexts of today's education which the philosopher can tackle in cooperation with other professionals—the scientists, the historians, the experienced educators—without pretending to more than his philosophical skills.

Such problems may take different shape. One is, for example, the problem of *consistency*—surely a philosophical specialty. Every educational establishment has programs set in objectives and traditional ways of running itself. There are always, and especially in a complex changing society, inconsistencies between different objectives, different programs and policies, different ways of running the school, and among those several categories as well. There are for example, contradictions between democratic objectives and bureaucratic modes of organization, as well as authoritarian discipline; between equalitarian aspirations and textbook materials and teacher attitudes to disadvantaged and minority groups; between cooperative objectives and competitive methods; and so on. The general search for consistency of educational functioning is certainly an area in which analytical and logical skills should enable the philosopher of education to initiate and explore, even if he will need sociological and psychological support in tracing the unintended consequences of policies, programs and procedures.

Another area of problems concerns the "external" relations of education to the rest of society. Current demands for community control and current charges from the student left that the universities are instruments of the establishment, show vividly the pressing need for an understanding of educational institutions in the light of the total analysis of the society, rather than simply in terms of a limited set of traditional objectives as the "essence" of education. Philosophy has worked a great deal on the logic of the relation of parts and wholes, philosophy of history and society on the concept of institutions and the relation of goals, rules and practices to underlying social aims, conflicts and conditions. Both phenomenological and analytical skills are needed to recast our very way of looking at the schools to see them in the diversity of perspectives that constitute the contemporary community and to prepare the ground for vital normative judgments that reflect the total historical situation of our age.

Another type of philosophical skill is to discern the reach of a principle over diverse subject matter. When it becomes a pressing necessity in the contemporary world that an objective be given a central place in education, such philosophical aptitudes have a special responsibility. Thus it is agreed that the schools should play an important part in education for peace. The perfunctory educational tendency would be to add a peace course or at best even a peace department. A philosophical analysis would be required to see the reach of peace education throughout the whole curriculum—what elements in teaching of geography, language, history, economics and so on, what attitudes in teaching and administration, what traditional modes of thought and feeling, and presuppositions about human nature, had built-in war and violence proclivities. The philosophical analyst cannot alone answer either the descriptive or the normative questions but he is sophisticated enough to realize that the answers depend to a marked degree on the kinds of questions asked and the scope of the issues attended to. What I have said about education for peace here holds in even a more complicated way for recent controversies over the place of Black, Puerto Rican, Mexican–American, or in general third–world studies. I have not seen—though I may have missed—serious contributions to the *analysis* of such issues in the philosophy of education.

In general, with so much of education today ripe for major reconstruction, philosophy is in the best position to raise the question concretely—though not always to give the answers—about hardened categories and modes of organization of studies on all levels of the schools. I have suggested above that discussions of types of knowledge may be a pale reflection of such problems and issues. To bring such discussion into relation with the underlying problems is not to dismiss it but to call for its fuller consideration directly and consciously. To take an example of shifting categories from higher education, think of the experiments over the last few decades in combined courses—unified social science courses, contemporary civilization courses, humanities courses, and so on. In these there have been theoretical justifications in terms of inherent unity, simplicity and convenience, least common denominator acquaintance, etc. Given all the work that philosophy has done on the division of knowledge into fields and the relative character of the joints in the fabric of knowledge, and how different schemes of the sciences and fields of knowledge have been hardened into schemes of levels of reality, it seems incredible that philosophy of education has not pressed for reform, at least imparting the lesson of contextual relevance to basic categories and divisions in the structuring of education.

Obviously the listing of philosophical tasks could go on endlessly. I conclude with a comment on the notion of *relevance*, so frequently invoked by students today in educational controversy. Too often, it seems to me, it is analytically disparaged as a vague slogan term, and the philosophical analysis is directed to proving its ambiguity. That it is contextually differentiated is clear enough. Sometimes it indicates instrumental importance, sometimes the general sense of "meaningful" in which the older philosophers debated whether life had a meaning, and sometimes it refers to pertinence in solving basic social problems. But it also most of the time refers to pertinence in *understanding* what is going on in a full philosophical sense. I cannot see how the philosophy of education could fail to find both the use and misuse of the notion to be other than the symptom of a growing questioning in education and the occasion for encouraging critical discussion and cultivating insight. An analytical philosophy of education could take hold of this situation in the comprehensive questioning of all life and its organization in that same spirit in which philosophy generally and perenially praises its origins in the Socratic quest.

The paper was written for a working conference sponsored by the American Council for Philosophical Studies, held in St. Louis in 1971.

Notes

1. In this paper I am dealing primarily with the one type of analysis, because it is predominant in contemporary philosophy of education. There is, of course, a great deal of analytic work to which my diagnosis may apply only in part.
2. It was the picture of the state of the field emerging in this conference that stimulated the reflections of this paper.
3. J.L. Austin, *How to Do Things with Words*, ed. J. O. Urmson (New York: Oxford University Press, 1965), Lecture 11, esp. 141 ff. Cf. his remarks on the true/false fetish and the value/fact fetish, 150.

4. Professor Soltis's paper was presented to the conference on "New Directions in Philosophy of Education," held at the Ontario Institute for Studies in Education (OISE), April 30–May 2, 1970.
5. Thomas S. Kuhn, *The Structure of Scientific Revolutions*, (Chicago: University of Chicago Press, 1962).
6. Gilbert Ryle, *The Concept of Mind*, (London: Hutchinson's University Library, 1949).
7. Jane Roland Martin, "On the Reduction of 'knowing that' to 'knowing how'," in *Language and Concepts in Education*, ed. B.O. Smith & R.H. Ennis (Chicago: Rand NcNally Co., 1961), 59–71. This paper was included by the editors as an example of educationally relevant analysis that exhibits a kinship to the work of Oxford analysis.
8. Professor Martin may not realize the extent of this penetration of educational experience into the analytic work. In the last part of the paper, she examines implications for teaching and learning on the assumption that "One test for the utility of our classification lies in its relevance to education," as if it had been independently established.
9. Presented at the OISE Conference; see note 4.
10. Michael Oakeshott, "Rationalism in Politics," in *Rationalism in Politics and Other Essays*, (New York: Basic Books, 1962).
11. John Dewey, "The Reflex Arc Concept in Psychology," *The Psychological Review*, (July 1896) pp. 357–70. Reprinted in *John Dewey: Philosophy, Psychology and Social Practice*, ed. Ratner (New York: Capricorn Books, 1963).
12. John Dewey, *Human Nature and Conduct* (New York: The Modern Library, 1930), 177–78.
13. *Ibid.*, 179–80.
14. Bertrand Russell, "Knowledge by Acquaintance and Knowledge by Description," in *Mysticism and Logic* (New York: W. W. Norton and Co., 1929).
15. William James, *The Principles of Psychology* (New York: Henry Holt & Co., 1890), vol. I, 221f.
16. Henry Bergson, *An Introduction to Metaphysics*, trans. T. E. Hulme (New York: Liberal Arts Press, 1949).
17. Martin Buber, *I and Thou*, trans. Ronald Gregor Smith (Edinburgh: T. & T. Clark, 1937).
18. R.S. Peters, "Education and the Educated Man," *The Philosophy of Education Society of Great Britain, Proceedings of the Annual Conference*, vol. 4, 8.
19. J.S. Mill, "On Genius," in *Mill's Essays on Literature and Society*, ed. by Schneewind (New York: Collier Books, 1965), 101.
20. See note 18.
21. R.S. Peters, *Ethics and Education*, (London: Allen & Unwin, 1966), Chap. 1.
22. Gilbert Ryle, "Ordinary Language," *The Philosophical Review*, LXII (1953), 167–86.
23. Richard Robinson, *Definition*, (Oxford: Clarendon Press, 1954), 27. The reference is to "word–thing definition."
24. Clark Kerr, *The Uses of the University*, (New York: Harper Torchbooks, 1966).

7

Anthropology and Ethics in Common Focus

This lecture was the outcome of a study (in 1960) of the way in which British anthropologists dealt with morality in field work and theoretical writings. It was a continuation of the attempt to develop a fruitful relation of anthropology and ethics. I immersed myself in the writings of the leading British anthropologists and went on to hold discussions with a number of them who varied in their mode of treatment. For example, one included morality largely in the context of religion, another parcelled it among kinship and economics, a third aligned it with the discussion of motivation, a fourth with cultural symbols. This lecture, given to the Royal Anthropological Institute in the spring of 1960, thus had the chracter of dialogue with British anthropology.

In *Anthropology and Ethics*, a cooperative experiment designed to bring anthropology and philosophical ethics into common focus on the study of morality, Dr. May Edel and I (Edel & Edel 1959) proposed a concept of morality which had a number of unusual features. In the first place, it was oriented towards cultural description; it looked for the kind of conception which one might use if one were asked to draw a moral map of the globe, as one might be asked to draw a linguistic or a religious map. Such a descriptive orientation is taken for granted by the anthropologist, but is likely to startle the philosopher who thinks of morality in terms of moral judgment. Moreover, whether the philosopher's approach is analytic or normative, it is usually not carried on in relation to the social sciences and the study of culture; such materials enter only as furnishing information on means or else providing areas of illustration and application. In the second place, we treated morality as a relatively independent dimension of culture. Such independence is likely to be taken for granted by the philosopher, who is used to insisting on the "autonomy" of morals. But it is likely to meet with anthropological

105

resistance, since the anthropological treatment of morality is more often enmeshed in one or another of the areas of social and cultural description, or dispersed over several. In the third place, we fashioned a generalized concept of morality, much broader than the informal set of indices that are usually found in anthropological field research, and the sharply etched though competing conceptions that are found in formal ethics.

Since this conception of morality and its investigation runs counter to some of the established habits in both disciplines, it requires justification to both, if they are to be induced to cooperate—but in different respects. To the anthropologist, it is the independence focus that requires consideration; to the philosopher, it is the extent of the empirical descriptive stress. I should like, therefore, to address myself to these two topics, and thereafter to add a few comments on the appropriateness of our proposed conception, as a scientific construct useful for both descriptive and theoretical purposes. I need scarcely add that in setting so wide a task I can do justice neither to the detailed analysis that philosophy increasingly rightly demands, nor to the specificity in which lies the great strength of anthropological investigation. Today I rest content with groping for the larger vision which reformulates our questions.

Part 1

Suppose one picks up the little volume of B.B.C. lectures entitled *The Institutions of Primitive Society* (Evans–Pritchard *et al.* 1956). One finds a treatment of economic and familial and political institutions, and in addition, lectures on Religion, Aesthetics, Law, Mind, Modes of Thought. Where is Morality? Is it tucked away somewhere within, or just omitted? There are, it is true, occasional remarks about values at the base of economic choices (Ibid., p. 23), the way in which aesthetic values reflect ethical standards of artists and patrons (Ibid., pp. 37–8), some values that appear in legal process (Ibid., pp. 48–9), the moral authority in language (Ibid. p. 83). There are even searchlight glimpses of how a morality might function—"the recognition of a moral order which would allow the society as a whole to enjoy peace, and go about its business" (Gluckman, p. 73); or how in turn a social system may produce an excessive burden of moral decision for the individual (Fortes, p. 89); or a view of law and morals as means of social control over inborn impulses (Ibid., p. 94). Morality, in short, is taken for granted, in the sense that one can invoke it or refer to it at will; but it is not explained, depicted, or analyzed. It scarcely seems to be among the institutions of society.

But after all, it can be said, the B.B.C. lectures are popular and limited by time. Something had to be left out. What do we find, then, when we look to *Notes and Queries on Anthropology* (1951), which is a professional training guide for field workers? Where here do we find suggestions for the study of morality?

Notes and Queries gives us only a few leads. Occasionally we find moralistic terms, such as "socially recognized ties", "duties and obligations", but their meaning and mode of identification tend rather to be taken for granted. Most reference to moral content is of an ostensive or denotative type: for example, rules of hospitality, of politeness, propriety and respect, in social life; observation of action in cases of homicide, incest, adultery, etc., in describing law and justice; and procedures of praise, blame, ridicule, ostracism, etc., in reference to sanctions. We are told that "careful investigation of the different forms of sanctions should be made noting the basis on which they rest—beliefs, moral precepts, actual institutions" (Ibid., p. 145), but there seems to be no specific guide to what kinds of precepts are identifiable as moral precepts. Perhaps the clearest references to morality come in the section on the ideology of production, where it is recognized that moral values play a part in determining the efficiency of individual labour (p. 163). But here, as in the chapter on rituals and belief, where it is stated that supernatural sanctions are nearly always to be found for moral values, it seems to be assumed that moral values have been separately identified and mapped. But nowhere is this task carried out. The index, incidentally, contains no listing of "end", "ethics", "goals", "morality", "virtues", or "vices".

I do not want to belabor in pedestrian tabulation this almost studied avoidance of the problem of morality, what it is, what identifying marks are to be sought for it, and how to go about mapping it. Nor am I suggesting that the absence of theoretical recognition of morality means the absence of materials on morality in the field reports. There is a great deal to be found, but most often in the dispersed form which *Notes and Queries* might lead us to expect. But equally important, there is a great deal not to be found—many questions that are not even asked.

How are we to explain this lack of a well articulated concept to serve as guide to enquiry? Three preliminary answers suggest themselves. One is that it is assumed that we all know what morality is and no explicit account need be given. If this is so, it is an unsatisfactory state of affairs. It runs the risk of ethnocentrism in our working conception of morality—for example, looking everywhere for pangs of conscience as a mark of the moral. Explicitness has been sought in mapping equally "obvious" fields—legal or religious. Why not in the case of the moral?

A second path of explanation is to stress the practical difficulties in locating the moral. Morality is so abstractly ideational. There are no moral institutions or moral products to lay hold of, no priests or quasi–courts, or pictures and books. Perhaps we are still in the stage indicated by *Notes and Queries* when it says: "The first rule in all investigations is to advance from the concrete and tangible to the abstract. Social events must be recorded as they happen. Accounts of how natives "think" or "feel" are of little value without information as to how they actually behave in concrete situations" (p. 37). I do not want to argue here the question whether morality is largely a matter of thought and feeling or how far in a Deweyan vein the moral situation is to be construed as one of the conflict of habits necessitating decision. But even thoughts and feelings have to be tackled in the long run, if the culture is to be understood. And interestingly enough, when John Ladd, a philosopher, worked among the Navaho specifically on questions of moral discourse, his major informant expressed to Kluckhohn (Ladd 1957, p. xiv) a genuine delight that here at last he was being asked really important questions! (But, of course, he was a sophisticated informant, and practically sent Kluckhohn grade reports on the different anthropological workers who kept coming to consult him.)

A third possible explanation is that there is some theoretical difficulty in the concept of the moral itself. It may, after all, be a residual or again a miscellaneous class of sanctions or motivations. Perhaps we only really discover a moral sanction by stripping off what is not definitely religious, or legal, or fear of violent action, and seeing that something is left moving people. Obviously, however, once this is located, we should want to pursue deliberately the identification of such motives. Even the miscellaneous invites itemization and the breaking up of the problem. But this third line of explanation does raise the possibility that in principle little more can be done anthropologically in the delineation of the moral than has so far been done practically. It is therefore important to probe for the implicit conceptions of the nature, scope, role, and relations of morality in the work of anthropologists, and to differentiate what may be different assumptions influencing the operation of research and the formulation of results. Let me try to do so, for brevity's sake, in the form of a set of reassurances that anthropologists might be tempted to offer the enquiring philosopher.

Reassurance 1.

Anthropologist: Look here, old fellow, why are you making such a fuss over morality? Perhaps we don't put it in blazing headlines. But you're a scholar, you ought to be used to reading whole books and not complaining about chapter headings. You'll find plenty about morals in any anthropological report about religion. And it will call it morality, too. For example, when Evans-Pritchard in his *Nuer Religion* (1956, p. 181) reports that the Nuer say that were a man's nakedness often seen by his wife's parents his children might go blind, he adds, "We may surmise that the convention is felt by Nuer to have also a moral significance from the violent indignation I have witnessed in female relatives of wives at exposure by husbands in their presence although they were not their mother–in– law and the exposures were entirely accidental." The moral is here implicitly tied to what one feels indignant about when it is violated, as distinct from what would have harmful consequences as a result of religious violation. Isn't that enough for you? You could even call it an operational definition, or a pointer- reading if you go in for that kind of language.

Philosopher: Thanks, and I'm glad to have it underlined, but after all, my interest isn't intellectual housekeeping, but to see how far the understanding of morality can be furthered by anthropology. It isn't enough to rely on a few pointer–readings, especially when they are merely utilized in passing, rather than culled out for comparative consideration. What is this indignation? Is there not a moral indignation different from an ordinary indignation? Do we have to go to psychology to understand it or can we rely on ordinary introspection? If the latter, isn't there a danger, when we look in, of seeing the mirror reflection of our own culture in our emotional reactions? In general, what we need is a formulation of the moral so that even the relation of the religious and the moral would be an empirical comparative issue. Thus the claim, if it were made, that in a given society morals are wholly merged with religion, would have the status of an *empirical* proposition, and would require an understanding of what has not been differentiated, just as in the claim that there might be no differentiated political institutions in a given society. But as I understand it, you are not saying that there is no fuller account of morality because it hasn't been differentiated in the societies you deal with, since you are showing me an occasional differentiating mark.

Reassurance 2.

Anthropologist: But really, aren't you asking for the impossible? To give the kind of systematic account you seem to want of morality would regard it as an institution. But morality is rather a kind of pervasive spirit between people. When we say a man is glad, do you want us to tie it down to some part of his body? We'll tell you which people dance when they're glad, and which hug one another, and which simply sit and smile, but don't ask us what we mean by "glad" or an itemized list of modes of recognition. Morality is like that. Some anthropologists have said as much. For example, Redfield (1953, pp. 20–1) talks of the moral order as a bond, and denies that it is a category of culture.

Philosopher: No, that won't quite do. Even if morality is a kind of spirit, you have to have a clear account of it in some terms or other, or you'll get into comparative trouble. For example, Redfield talks of the moral order as giving way to the technical order in which utility relations between individuals become more central. Yet why should the technical order not be regarded as a type of morality, though a different one from the previous type? It will have its own characteristic virtues and obligations though the latter may be regarded as issuing from individual will or consent. A Benthamite morality is still a morality. If we don't clarify the concept we may be smuggling in subtle valuations of our own tradition.

Reassurance 3.

Anthropologist: You're barking up the wrong tree completely. The reason you don't see the anthropological treatment as explicit is because you expect to find it somewhere. But really, it's everywhere. So don't worry, we're expounding the morality of a society in all our descriptions of its institutions. The very idea of a determinate social order is that of structural lines embodying what people regard as *important*. To have a kin system is to mark out patterns of preferred and prohibited marriage, and so a moral rule about incest; to have an ownership system is already to have implicit norms of distribution and "social justice"; and so on.[1]

Philosopher: No, this generous gift troubles me. Pervasiveness should be a separable issue, and an empirical one. The religious may be pervasive in one society without being indistinguishable from what it pervades; so too the political. Why not the moral? Nor is the reference to importance clear enough. Things are important in different ways—as fundamental unavoidable means, as requiring considerable energy and attention, as intrinsically worthwhile ends, and so on. What kind of important things are moral?

Anthropologist: But surely you do not expect the anthropologist to point to a domain of particular moral phenomena? On this anthropologists and philosophers must be agreed. For example, Raymond Firth (1951, p. 184) says: "We commonly speak of exchange as an economic action, or worship as a religious action. There is no corresponding category of moral actions *per se*. Morality refers to the qualities rather than to the substance of actions." Similarly, in a recent paper before the Aristotelian Society, Peter Winch claimed that it wouldn't make sense to say you'd spent three hours doing morality—unless you meant working at moral philosophy.

Philosopher: Somehow I do not find these assumptions convincing. If I spend three hours deciding what is my duty in a particularly trying situation, why is this not as much a moral phenomenon of a very concrete and active sort as spending three hours bargaining over a house is an economic phenomenon? There are many distinctively moral phenomena to be found in that vast mass of data that is constituted by our desires and aspirations, commitments and appraisal activities.[2] And as to what is substance and what is quality, metaphysical controversies can arise in economic examples as well as in moral ones. My desire to have a home may equally well be the substance of the economic situation.

Reassurance 4.

Anthropologist: Well, you know, we British anthropologists are keen on social organization and social structure, and so naturally we put morality there. And that's where it really belongs. You'll find it in Chapter VI of Firth's *Elements of Social Organization* under the title "Moral Standards and Social Organization". And you might note the publication date—1951—the same as *Notes and Queries*, sixth edition, which seems to have upset you so much.

Philosopher: If morality is not going to be given an independent treatment, perhaps social organization is its best home. It helps convey some lessons: that morality is basically a social not a pure–individual phenomenon—not a lone mind scrutinizing or expressing its feelings as so many philosophical theories seem to locate it—that it has all sorts of causal and functional relations, that it is basically a regulative mechanism. And Firth's conceptual experiments with its location seem to be a conscious effort to decide where it best belongs. The chapter you referred to comes perhaps closest to focusing on it directly. In his Marett lecture (1953) on "The Study of Values by Social Anthropologists" it is the wider value–presuppositions of institutions that are central; the study of values is taken to help us understand the meaning of action. *Social Change in*

Tikopia (1959), however, presents its moral references in the framework of an operative concept of social control.

Anthropologist: Well, what objection do you have to this? Doesn't it answer your conceptual quandaries?

Philosopher: It may be the correct answer to some of the major factual questions, but is it the best methodological policy? For example, the question of the structure of ideals doesn't fall comfortably in this, and has to be shipped off to another chapter. I suppose the fundamental objection to letting morality be cut loose would be that we might lose sight of its intimate relations to social structure and its functional roles. But there is the opposite danger in merging the morality concept with social control concepts. There are whole facets of the problem which will have greater difficulty in coming to light. There are psychological studies—even in depth—of the kinds of feelings and emotions involved, as well as of the structure of conscience, the kinds of orientations which a culture provides for its members, as Hallowell (1955) has so fruitfully probed them, or the degree of extension of the self, as Marian Smith (1952) has suggested. There are all the analytic questions raised about moral concepts by philosophers, which point to the comparative linguistic study of terms and modes of moral discourse; about moral reasoning, which point to the comparative study of modes of justification; as well as all the questions about virtues and vices and moral ideals which get lost when they are merged in a social structure chapter or even in a chapter on personality.[3]

Even the obviously appropriate treatment of sanctions in a social structure framework will not yield an understanding of the moral without going considerably beyond the initial confines. For example, ridicule is obviously an effective sanction to support a rule in many places. But is it a moral sanction? (We may compare the way in which police force constitutes a sanction for some moral rules but is not usually considered a moral sanction.) If we recognize that ridicule sometimes is a moral sanction and sometimes is not, we are driven beyond the overt social relations to questions about the way it is felt by agent and recipient. For example, is it moral where it rests on some inner sense of shame or sense of estrangement from one's fellows? This would lead us to a psychological core for the meaning of moral. An alternative would be to construe ridicule as a moral sanction simply where it is an expression of public disapproval.[4] There are serious issues involved in these alternatives, and they are not likely to be faced if the treatment of morality is limited to social structure. But what is more, even the treatment of the role of morality within social structure gains in richness by a fuller independent study of morality itself. If we do not probe into the roots and effects of ridicule, we cannot get a clear picture of the kinds of social structures in which ridicule can and those in which it cannot be an effective mechanism. Similarly, an independent comparative study of ideals and virtue–sets can sharpen immeasurably the social and historical research into the functioning of utopian and realistic ideals in social movements or the place of virtue-sets in supporting specific social systems. The most general question of the extent to which the moral is merged with other aspects of social and cultural life itself acquires empirical meaning when the moral is independently identified and clarified. And beyond all these, lie the configurational properties of moralities for which we can look when the various parts of a morality are gathered together, but which we cannot even ask about when we see morality only in a particular compartment. I shall want to come back to this later on.

I do not mean to minimize the methodological issues involved—both technical problems of discovery and theoretical problems of interrelations within a society. There have, of course, been many claims that understanding in human matters is of the society as a whole, that the extraction of themes or the breaking up into elements, even into institutions, is artificial. But I take it that the use of constructs in scientific work needs no defence by this time; it is rather a question of which constructs are best for a given field. This holistic approach never seems to trouble anthropologists in dealing with law or religion; but it does get invoked for morality. Maybe Durkheim was describing tendencies in anthropological theory as well as phenomena among peoples when he put the "sacred" into the core of morality! It should not mean too sacred to analyse. If morality has such a special character it is certainly time to spot it more explicitly and delineate it more clearly. If it is not special among institutions it ought also to be explicated.

Actually, there is a deeper logical problem involved. Several claims would have to be distinguished. One is that moral concepts have no *meaning* without the social content reference. Another is that though they have independent meaning, no instances are found without *functional* relations to social organization institutions. A third is that there are social *causes* for moral concepts arising and remaining or changing. And so on. But in such a case, no *general* answer is required. For example, the very meaning of "adultery" involves some reference to a marriage system, and it is probable that "justice" may turn out to be literally unintelligible without some reference to distribution systems; any account in terms of "giving each his due" or through an idea of equality may be only a temporary detour. On the other hand, a concept like sympathy may have an invariant transcultural meaning, though the incidence and contexts of sympathy in a society may be causally dependent on social conditions. How then can we tell in advance that *some* phases of morality are not best regarded as a function of other aspects of culture, such as mode of child–training, kinship relations, standardized personality type, specific accumulated historical traditions, and so on, if we do not set it as an initially empirical enquiry with some independent concepts? I do not think any theory of the functions of morality has anything to lose from the attempt to map morality in a systematically independent way. Its claims will rather be brought to the test of empirical investigation than be embodied in implicit definitions.

Reassurance 5.

Anthropologist: Well, if what you really want is the right to explore in many uncharted regions—psychological as well as social—if we British anthropologists are moving too slowly for you, the Americans have surely gone ahead with jet propulsion. Maybe your search for a proper concept of morals can find its goal in all the value studies and all the materials on personality and culture. There's enough on thoughts and feelings and attitudes there to meet your most grasping demands for more modes of enquiry.

Philosopher: You put it almost as if my choice were starving in England or drowning in America. I don't think either is the case. Or, to shift the metaphor, I'm not interested in general hunting rights; it *is* open territory. I'm interested in the logic of a working concept. Now take a value concept like Clyde Kluckhohn's (1951, p. 395): "A value is a conception, explicit or implicit, distinctive of an individual or characteristic of a group, of the desirable which influences the selection from available modes, means, and ends of action.'' (He adds that it is not merely a preference but felt or considered to be justified.) Once such concepts were presented, there was almost a frontier settlement quality to the way in which people rushed into new studies in all directions. It was almost as if permission had been given to enter a forbidden domain. Many of the studies traced themes in familiar areas—value patterns in law, family life, mythology, acculturation situations. But some plunged ahead into the sensitive exploration of unchartered areas—orientations to life, attitudes to time, the relations of man and nature, to knowledge, to feeling. Transition to such themes in American anthropological studies was no doubt easier because of a prior more receptive attitude to the impact of psychology and personality studies.

Now morality is somewhere in that domain as well as in the social structure field. But I don't think it settles our conceptual problem for a very simple reason. I do not believe that the concept of value is as simple as it sounds. Before the social sciences appropriated it, it had a whole history in philosophy, where with even wider scope it threw into a single basket everything from economics to aesthetics, as well as religious and moral ''values''. And so, unless it is merely a tag-word for the basket—comparable to ''skill'' or ''power'' in other enquiries—it also has to justify itself by some theory of the unity of such diverse phenomena. In some writers it is a psychological unity of a single Eros running through everything; in others a unity in the biological source of impulse or appetite, with all sorts of historical-evolutionary proliferation; in still others, it is a unity of spirit as such in its distinctive difference from the organic-material (Cf. Edel 1953; Krikorian & Edel 1959, Introduction to part iv). The history of the general value concept in philosophy does not make it likely that its social science analogue will produce a theoretically unified value concept. Whether the unity that the new value studies seek is to be in terms of biological needs, psychological constants, social structure relationships, cultural pattern-ings, sociohistorical developments, is not prejudged by use of the concept. And so we cannot tell precisely where morality will fall within such a value framework. At present the growth of value studies leaves us simply with enlarged vistas and greater freedom of enquiry.

So much for the reassurances. I am not reassured. But I do see a pattern emerging from their very diversity. Each is stressing some particular feature of morality. One tells us that the moral is a matter whose violation arouses strong feeling; another that it permeates life like a spirit, which we can translate as saying that moral considerations may arise in any context; a third that it deals with what is important; a fourth that its major context is the regulation of human relations; and a fifth that it is among the objects of value or preference in human life, that it has an independent attraction. It looks as if all these features are relevant when so interpreted. But I hope that their very diversity shows the necessity for focusing in a clear and systematic way on the study of morality as a relatively independent dimension both in conceptual analysis and in descriptive investigation.

Part 2

Can we suggest to philosophy the penetrating role of empirical materials in ethical theory as we have suggested to anthropology the need for independent enquiry into the meaning and forms of existence of the moral? In some respects this is a more difficult task, because the professional attention to methodological problems has often meant a hardening of the methods employed.

In the old days, the recognized ritual of enquiry in philosophical ethics was a critique of the major schools. Outstanding hypotheses about the nature of morality were embodied in Utilitarianism, Kantianism, Eudaemonism, and the rest. Each made assertions or rested on assertions about the nature of man and his world, human problems and the human predicament. Each had its description of the moral consciousness and its analysis of moral concepts. Ethical enquiry in its survey of these schools asked which was basically true or more adequate or acceptable, and in what respects: was it true that all men pursued pleasure in all that they did, was the utilitarian analysis of obligation sufficiently refined, did the good (among moral concepts) presuppose the right or the right presuppose the good? And so on. In any case, there were, at least in the background, factual assertions about men and their ways.

Contemporary ethics—and British philosophy, as is well known, is out front in this respect—casts its enquiry in the linguistic mode. Questions about the nature of morality or the meaning of moral are interpreted as questions about the analysis of the language of morals. This is a specialized type of enquiry taken to characterize uniquely the philosophical enterprise, quite independent of scientific empirical investigation or causal investigation. To undertake a general critique of this position would here be too vast a task.[5] Perhaps the best way to argue for the view that answers to questions of ethical theory require data from the psychological and social sciences would be to work through in outline a particular example.

Let me then take an illustration which will cut across both older formulations and contemporary ones. And in all fairness, let it be a hard case. Kant is the father of contemporary theories of the "autonomy" of morals—mistakenly construed, I am maintaining, as the lonely isolation of ethics. Take then his famous declaration at the outset of his *Fundamental Principles of the Metaphysics of Ethics*: "It is impossible to conceive of anything anywhere in the world or even anywhere out of it that can without qualification be called good, except a Good Will." Let us more modestly construe it as "only a good will is good without qualification". How can we decide whether this is true? Or first, rather, what does it mean? If we do not take at its face value the Kantian claim for synthetic *a priori* propositions, there are two quite different approaches to this proposition. One of these follows an empirical path, the other goes by way of problems of conceptual relations and linguistic analysis.

The first one today is quite unorthodox. We look for the kinds of tests Kant is offering implicitly or explicitly for "a good will" and for "good without qualification". He makes it amply clear that a good will is one that is ready to act in terms of his universalization test—to ask whether the maxim on which it acts could consistently be willed as a universal law. But it is not so easy to see what is his mark of "good without qualification"—unless he means simply good in every context for all possible interpretations of "good". But there is much in his work which would lead us to interpret "good without qualification" as the unqualified object of moral respect; for Kant takes this feeling of moral respect to be the central constituent of the moral consciousness, and to be every man's common possession. The plain man need not wait for the philosopher to tell him what is his duty. But what is this feeling of respect itself? We know that Kant hangs a great deal on it, that in his more psychological probing he carefully distinguishes it from fear of consequences, or self–love (Kant 1930, e.g. pp. 135 seq., 185 seq.), that in the long run it becomes the slender thread leading him to the postulates of God, Freedom of the Will, and Immortality. But despite its importance, this feeling of respect is a psychological missing link in Kant's doctrine, and when it is tracked down we have to say with that most careful student of ethical notions, John Laird (1935, p. 105) that "what Kant called 'respect' for the moral law is a ghost from Sinai, a crepuscular thing that sins against the natural light. Therefore consistent Kantians must either bring divinity into their ethics, not as a consequence but as part of the analytic of their fundamental conceptions, or else retire to purely terrene ramparts".

Now what has all this Kantian discussion to do with anthropology and the other sciences of man? If we follow this avenue of analysis and succeed in a psychological identification of this feeling, we are led to the question whether action on a principle of universalization is really the sole object of our moral respect. Is law its object always and in everyone? But whose inner life has this feeling–structure? Is it the people of Koenigsberg, or all mankind, or every conceivable rational creature whether on earth or—Kant's specualiton—even on Saturn? Kant of course thought in terms of all conceivable rational creatures. But was it not Marx who remarked that every Prussian carries his gendarme within his breast? Would a cultural product of other areas have the same structure? Freud (1950, p. 103) tells the story of the sign concerning high–tension electric installations: in Italy it says simply, "Who touches will die". In Germany it says, "To touch the wires is most strictly forbidden, because of danger to life". In America, we might add, we should probably find simply: "Danger: Exposed Wire". Piaget, in his *The Moral Judgment of the Child* (1932, chap. 1, especially pp. 95 seq.) treats the question whether moral feeling attaches to law or to persons as an observational–experimental problem of psychology. He traces its career as such and from his own studies of rule-formation in children suggests that there are two separate respect attitudes involved—an authority type directed to law stemming from cross–generation contexts, and a person-oriented type arising among children in the same generation level. He is even led to speculate on what this latter "democratic'' consciousness would be like if a generation of children were brought up without elders. Piaget's conclusions too may indeed be culture–bound. It is not so simple a question, if we think of the role of peer group pressures in strengthening conformist tendencies and the fear of being ''out of line''. And for that matter, Kant himself fashioned his categorical imperative as involving respect for law chiefly in its first formulation. In its famous second formulation, the so–called human imperative, it calls for respect of persons as ends, not to be treated as means alone. But whatever be the correct answers, I invite you to compare for yourselves the clarity of the issue as a psychological–social–science research problem with the obscurity of the attempted deduction of the second formulation from the first in the reams of Kantian scholarship.

The line of thought I am suggesting for ethics has, however, a more general scope. It calls for the application of an anthropological–comparative spirit. Kant's is only one theory of obligation. The Utilitarians have another and the moral sentiment theorists still another. And these are but a small part. Suppose we read Kant and J. S. Mill and Adam Smith, not for the moment as theorists, but to extract from each account the type of moral consciousness which it is depicting. We read them as informants,[6] and what do we find? The Kantian conscience is a law–court conscience; his actual description of conscience in the *Critique of Practical Reason* is that of an inner tribunal in which we judge ourselves according to law. The Millian conscience is a feeling of overweighing importance, where importance involves a sense of massive instrumentality for general welfare. The Smithian conscience is perhaps the most attractive, for it consists, as his analysis of duty shows, of a pyramiding of spontaneous sympathetic reactions in a variety of relationships. I have not time to probe for Hobbesist and Stoic, Platonist and Hegelian conscience. But surely it is clear that the question which of the theories is correct becomes on this line of analysis: what are the alternative patternings of obligation-feelings, what configurations of personality do they fit into; how far is any one either universal, or more likely to be unavoidable in the conditions of human life and development; and which is more desirable in so far as it is possible.

Here we have a clear combination of psychological-anthropological descriptive and explanatory enquiry with philosophical analysis and evaluation. It involves the kind of considerations that Ruth Benedict (1946) raises in comparing Japanese ethics and traditional Western ethics with respect to the role of guilt and shame; or Margaret Mead (1940) raises in comparing the early educational procedures of different cultures; or Erich Fromm (1947) considers in the psycho–analytical tradition when he differentiates the authoritarian and the humanistic conscience; and so on. I am not *reducing* the philosopher's theories to such an account, but suggesting that *within* the theories you find background assumptions of the *universality* or *greater naturalness* and *ineradicability* or even the *desirability* of one or another pattern, and that questions of the truth or adequacy of the theories come in part to rest on the correctness or incorrectness of these assumptions. Hence a basic component in the evaluation of ethical theories is to be found in the answer to such matter–of–fact questions about what men are like and what constitutes their human makeup and how invariant or inherent it is, and what are its explanatory bases. And these are psychological and anthropological questions.

The older ethical theorists saw this clearly, although they were prone to assume universality naïvely. They knew that when they talked of obligation they were engaged in descriptive and explanatory tasks as well as conceptual–analytic tasks, although much of their thinking was one–sidedly oriented to the supernaturalist–naturalist controversy. Butler knew that his critique of Hobbes's egoism would stand or fall by whether he distinguished accurately the components in human nature as well as analyzed masterfully the concept of human nature itself, and whether it would as a matter of fact turn out to be true once these analyses were complete, that the verdicts of self–love and conscience would coincide. And T. H. Green saw perfectly the relevance of causal enquiry for moral phenomena when he warned that unless the sense of obligation was understood as transcendent it would be seen as simply a more complicated pattern built out of fear reactions. He stood in the shadow of the Darwinian naturalization of man, and Darwin said that there was nothing awe–inspiring about remorse—it was to repentance simply as agony was to pain. But of course, Darwin, like Adam Smith, took sympathy to be the central moral fact, and he sought an evolutionary account of its stabilization in society.

My point is not merely that the older philosophers dealt with these factual questions, but that they saw them as supremely relevant to their ethical theories. And what I have traced about obligation, I should equally well want to trace about intrinsic good and the assumption of the universal or predominant orientation of human desires; about ideals and the factual intermeshings of human aspirations; about virtues and vices and the need for insight into psychological and social relations, often in order to understand their very meaning; about the methodological soundness of interpreting abstract values as asserted invariant elements in diverse human social orders; and so on.

Let us now look at the second approach to understanding the Kantian dictum. It brings us closer to the ways of the contemporary philosophers. The proposition that only the good will is good without qualification, on this view, has nothing to do with moral sentiments psychologically and culturally analysed; it is rather a proposition about the logic of ethical judgment and expression. This is an autonomous discipline, and in effect what Kant is showing is that universalizability is part of the very meaning of ''moral'', that to regard anything as obligatory is to imply that there are reasons for it of a universal form, so that anyone else without differentiating reasons would be bound by the same obligation. Kant himself, of course, insisted on the nonempirical character of his ethical results.

As long as such a logic of ethics was considered to provide an analysis of some absolute structure of mind, or the inherent structure of practical reason, its status remained a mystery or a metaphysical bias. But contemporary philosophizing in the linguistic mode can have no such pretensions. In so far as it is analyzing moral terms in ordinary English, it cannot claim that its results must hold for all possible languages. If one can unearth the feature of universalizability from ordinary English use of "ought" by showing that one who rejects it thereby is led into logical paradoxes with respect to acceptable uses—and I do not assume here that this can or cannot be shown—one has established at best that the Kantian universal element is part of the built-in meaning of "moral" or "ought" in English. If you do not find it in ordinary Navaho or ordinary Assyrian, it does not mean that they had no moral conceptions. This is familiar anthropological history in the extension of the concept of "religion", and it is likely to be repeated in the history of contemporary ethics when it develops a genuinely comparative perspective. In some ethical theories of the linguistic philosophers it is masked by a respect for language as the accumulated wisdom of the ages—a kind of common law model applied to language, reminiscent of Blackstone and Burke in its emotional overtones, or else by beliefs in perennial or universal elements, or universal traits in modern languages. But all these are not part of the procedure of linguistic analysis—they are propositions of a factual sort *about* languages, and they are thus historical or anthropological or comparative linguistic generalizations.

In spite of its frequent claim to be a nonempirical philosophical method, linguistic philosophy seems to me, in its internal problems, to be in many respects analogous to anthropology—it is a kind of anthropology of the mind filtered through speech. John Austin (1956–7, pp. 7 seq.) used the phrase "linguistic phenomenology" in describing its nature; but the social character of language analysis makes the pure–experience reference of phenomenology, while suggestive, perhaps less pertinent. Linguistic analysis has its standard cases and its aberrant cases, its structured rules that have to be uncovered. It is particularistic, wishing to see each use in its own context, and fragmentarian in being suspicious of general unities. My chief complaint would be, especially in ethics, that it does not carry this anthropological spirit far enough. It moved from talking about the *meaning* of words to talking about their *uses*. I think it is going from uses to a recognition of *functions* performed in given contexts. But it does not treat these contexts in their full sociocultural richness. For example, in ethics, linguistic philosophy reacted against the view that moral statements were merely emotive, and went on an exuberant hunt for other uses, proudly exhibiting its finds in the issues of *Mind*. By the time that Nowell-Smith's *Ethics* appeared, he could list (Nowell-Smith 1954, p. 98) as some uses for value–words "to express tastes and preferences, to express decisions and choices, to criticize, grade, and evaluate, to advise, admonish, warn, persuade and dissuade, to praise, encourage and reprove, to promulgate and draw attention to rules; and doubtless for other purposes also". Those are all very concrete activities. Why not extend the scope of ethical enquiry to see how these activities are carried on in given societies, how widespread is grading in the life of a people, how frequent and effective advising and whether it is sought or resented, and in what human relationships it takes place, the foci and limits of praise, and so on? Thus moral expression, understood in terms of contextual functions, would become related to typical institutions and processes of the society, imperative uses to structures of authority and obedience, advisory uses to structures embodying guidance, leadership and suasion in the particular forms of the given society, and so on. The logical analysis of the language would thus provide clues to the relationships and built–in values of the morality (cf. Edel & Edel 1959, 125 seq.).

But there is another phase of the subject not to be omitted. Claims of neutral analysis often obscure this. The analyst may be quite neutral in mapping the use of ordinary English, but this does not make what he discovers a neutral subject matter. And he is usually led to take some stand, indirectly if not directly, on the aims or values or purposes embedded in that subject matter. For example, he may *accept* the ordinary usage for theoretical purposes, or he may *reconstruct* his theoretical language; in either case he is reckoning with the embedded values. He may reach the same result by deciding that one or another aspect of the meaning of "moral" is *primary*. Look back, for example, to Kantian universality. Whether you discover it in linguistic analysis of modern English or in sociological analysis of modern society, is there much doubt that it reflects, from the eighteenth century on, in its very sweep, the growing economic, social and cultural one-world tendency? The issue is not merely one of causation but of built–in values in modes of thought and modes of expression. Our very ethical concepts have a history and a social content, and there is no reason why we should not become conscious of the human aims that get built into them. And so, if after discovering universalizability in our linguistic use of "moral" we leave it unchanged, we are tacitly sharing a moral scheme in addition to analyzing it.

I have dwelt perhaps sufficiently on the way in which questions of ethical theory whether empirically or conceptually or linguistically approached involve matter–of–fact assumptions that require certification by the sciences of man; and suggested more briefly that even formal ethical ideas contain built–in values related to the state of human life of the age. The conclusion that would follow from this is that self–conscious ethical theorizing today, whether considering the meaning of "moral" or specifying fundamental properties and methods of morality, has to pay careful attention to factual assumptions of one or another kind that it is unavoidably making, as well as to purposes implicit in its constructions.[7] The former when laid bare become responsible to scientific knowledge in so far as it is available; the latter become open to normative criticism and refinement. And in so far as anthropology can furnish wide comparative materials on moralities by more systematic investigation, it can contribute markedly to the relevant scientific knowledge.

Part 3

I turn finally to the concept of morality which we elaborated in *Anthropology and Ethics*, considered as a scientific construct for theoretical analysis and descriptive research. It is clear that anthropology has not furnished a systematic concept. It is perhaps not equally clear that philosophy has not furnished a systematic concept that can serve the anthropological purpose of descriptive investigation. Philosophy has many concepts, tied to different theoretical approaches. Some today talk of morals in terms of the apprehension of phenomenological qualities of fitness or requiredness. Some begin with distinctively ethical terms. Some prefer distinctive ethical uses of terms, such as to express certain emotions, or to decide, to commend, or persuade or subscribe. Some delimit a set of behaviorally or phenomenally described activities or states, such as being pleased by, or interested in, or approving of, or desiring for its own sake, or reflectively appraising, or ascribing obligations, recognizing claims, evaluating, and so on. The very wealth of candidates prevents us from committing ourselves antecedently to any one of them. From a descriptive point of view they provide us with a set of varying phenomena on the linguistic, psychological, phenomenological, interpersonal, and social level. We may suspect that in the long run any choice among them will rest not on initial presuppositions but on the results of empirical study of these kinds of phenomena and their interrelations in human life. But the study itself requires a guiding concept of what a morality is. What form, then, shall it take at the outset?

I indicated at the beginning that the concept of morality we proposed was descriptively oriented, that it was a generalized concept, and that it treated morality as relatively independent. It is possible now, in the light of our analyses in the preceding parts, to sketch the justification of these features.

The descriptive orientation is, of course, required for an anthropological comparative investigation. To show that it is a desirable orientation from the point of view of ethical theorizing is a large and difficult question. Its obvious advantages are that it would furnish a more or less demarcated domain of phenomena to which propositions about morality would refer, where verifying observations for factual assertions relevant to ethics could be identified and the assertions put to the test. The fuller justification of this orientation, however, could come only from taking stubborn issues in theoretical ethics and showing in detail how they can be reanalysed, paradoxes minimized, and familiar controversies at an impasse give way to specific tasks (cf. Edel 1963, chap. 10 for a sampling of such analysis). The analysis of the Kantian example above can serve as one illustration.

Our decision to fashion a generalized concept was guided by both anthropological and philosophical considerations. Three conditions may be set down for a contemporary descriptive concept of morality. (1) It must avoid ethnocentrism, that is, it must not choose such initial marks of the moral as would rule out in advance materials that might make a bid for inclusion. The policy to be followed is: better too much at first than too little. For example, we cannot say that it must deal with concepts of right and wrong, since it may turn out in some peoples to deal with what is safe and dangerous, or what is folk and un–folk. (2) The very marks of the moral must allow of the widest variety of possible cultural specialization. If one of the marks, for example, is a kind of individual feeling correlated with transgression, it must be so formulated as not to prejudge that it be a remorse type or a shame type, but must allow in advance for varied cultural patterning as a theoretic possibility. (3) It must make possible its own refinement as the systematic data on moralities are accumulated, as comparative empirical generalizations grow, or as established knowledge from other disciplines (e.g., psychology) casts light on the moral materials. The aim is, of course, eventual embodiment, within the marks, of knowledge that is acquired about moralities: for example, if there should turn out to be invariant feeling–responses to transgression, or if all injunctions turn out to be addressed directly or indirectly to the problem of interpersonal aggression (as Freud seemed to think), or if the social functions of moralities prove to be limited to a specific set of control aims. In short, we expect eventual revision in the concept of morality just as there has been revision in the concepts of religion and of law in anthropological investigation. But this is *after* comparative investigation.

A concept of morality satisfying these conditions could embrace all the phenomena pointed to by varying philosophical approaches and provide a field in which these approaches themselves could be put to the test. Accordingly, in *Anthropology and Ethics*, the generalized concept was explicated through an inventory of constituents. The constituents were partly types of content, and partly features of the way the content is organized in the life and consciousness of a people. A morality is thus taken to contain: selected rules enjoining or forbidding (e.g., a set of commandments); character traits cultivated or avoided (virtues and vices); patterns of goals and means (ideals and instrumental values); a bounding concept of the moral community and a set of qualifications for a responsible person; a more or less distinctive selection of linguistic terms and rules for moral discourse; some patterns of systematization; some selected modes of justification; some selection from the range of human feelings which in complex ways is tied into the regulative procedures; and, involved in all of these, some specific existential perspective or view of man, his equipment, his place in nature, the human condition and predicament.

Such an approach uncovered many clues for understanding the integrated pattern of a morality, both the kinds of configurations to be looked for and the interrelations of morality with other phases of human life. It also pointed to ways in which each of the constituents might be sharpened in further research. Take, for example, a configurational feature like stringency in a morality. Comparatively, we found it could appear in: specific obligation–content where many acts are ruled in or ruled out; virtues, where firm adherence to rule is made the mark of appropriate character; ideals, where peace of mind in doing one's duty is a dominating goal; organization of moral discourse, where morality is cast in absolute rules rather than probability judgments; systematization, where deductive certainty is the garb that morality takes; sanctions, where punishment is heavy for simple violation; moral feelings, where the weight of guilt finds no ready expiation. Thus the identification of the one modality in a multitude of expressions made it possible to push further questions about causal and functional relations—where stringency is to be attributed to a traditional personality type, where to social pressures and continuing tensions, and so on. It seemed to us, therefore, that the generalized concept "paid off" rapidly in opening up more clearly areas for investigation.

As for the feature of relative independence for morality, I have in part argued for this by showing that the reassurances on behalf of a specific institutional location or on behalf of a dispersed concept of morality are inadequate. In part, of course, the proposed construct has to justify itself by how it works out in anthropological and philosophical enquiry. One of its special advantages is that it prevents morality from being narrowly construed in terms of some initial hypothesis about its nature, causes and functions—as has happened so often in wholesale social theories. The stress on independence makes the search for antecedent data a primary goal. Hypotheses about what morality can be correlated with stand out separately, instead of being built into initial definitions. Independently establishing the data thus serves the methodological role of widening the range of evidence for social theories. There is, however, a further kind of justification for the stress on independence which comes from seeing that it is not an arbitrary feature or simply a happy thought—though one would not want to belittle happy thoughts—but in some sense emerges from the development of the field and is addressed to the growth of problems in it. This can be shown in the analysis of philosophical and sociological trends on the question of independence itself. Let me suggest how it appears, in brief outline.

In philosophical ethics, as is generally known, most ethical theories for the greater part of Western philosophy were bound to a particular view of existence. Ancient theories were teleological; they tried to read off men's morals from an account of the purposive nature of man. Religious philosophies also were teleological, with divinity prescribing the human purposes. Where scientific trends grew, they sought to outline how men's strivings and obligations followed from their constitution and the laws governing their constitution. Only from Kant's time onwards do we find explicit attempts at securing the complete independence of ethics. In Kant, its "autonomy" means dismissing empirical considerations. In typical twentieth–century forms—for example, Nicolai Hartmann's *Ethics* or G. E. Moore's *Principia Ethica*—it is primarily an argument for the independence of ethical judgment from theological, metaphysical, and scientific, in brief any existential pictures of the world and its necessities. It is a revolt from bondage in ethical decision. Whatever the extreme concepts it employs, whether a realm of pure values in Hartmann or the familiar naturalistic fallacy accusation in Moore, when all the philosophical arguing is over and done with, its human import seems to me to have been a stress on the frontier–like quality of moral decision, to enable the free or extricated self to face the world in the light of demands acknowledged as its own. Perhaps the exaggerated autonomy of those theories constituted—as I believe the stress on the prescriptive in ethical theory today still does—a reaction to lulling determinisms and creeping conformities. It is, no doubt, the expression of a now traditional liberalism with its emancipation of the individual, faced in turn with overwhelming problems that seem to submerge the individual. And if it still has the self–exaltation of Russell's older free man's worship, it does in its substance correspond to a pervasive need for critical and responsible individual thought and action.

This active evaluative process is certainly one phase of moral choice; but the ties of the evaluating self to the rest of the world constitute a complementary phase. A full ethical theory has to find a place for the scientific study of the self, its growth, and its determinants, rather than take pendular swings between an all–encompassing determinism and an isolating absolute freedom. To study morality as relatively independent gives us the best opportunity to see it in its evaluative processes and in its causal relations.

Now compare the ideational development of autonomy in ethical theory with the picture of historical differentiation that Morris Ginsberg (1956, especially pp. 20 seq.) gives for morality—the growth of a distinctively moral attitude and the separation of the moral from the religious and the legal. He relates it to the growth of secularization and the widening of the area of individual free choice, and regards it as one of the distinctive attributes of modern morality.

Such a sociological account suggests that there are definite phenomena and definite needs to which the development of morality as a relatively independent concept is addressed. This would constitute part of the justification for such an independent treatment. But there would also be required an appraisal of the philosophical and scientific consequences of the employment of the concept. Along both these lines we would have to ask such questions as the following: is there in fact an increasing level of decision phenomena with qualities of its own, stemming from the complexity of modern life and its specialized agencies for regulation and solution of specific problems? Are moral phenomena, whether in individual or in social life, *becoming* literally more differentiated today in the same way as political forms did at one point in the past, or tool making has in economic processes? How far will a differentiated concept make oversharp distinctions in consciousness and be likely to obscure connections to realistic social processes? Will the concept prove useful only for modern differentiated moralities? Or will it encourage a search in the moralities of primitive societies for points of individual moral decision? Can it be that attentiveness to morality as embedded in social control sees less of the role of the individual in relation to others, or of the social creativity in selectively adapting to changing conditions, than it does of the pressures of conformity fashioning the individual, more of the equilibrium tendencies in a society than of the erosion and sometimes sharp overthrow of older patterns? Will conceptual differentiation of the moral make sharper the very notion that older societies were less differentiated in their morality?

These are provocative speculations that a philosopher can raise, though he may have no ready answers. But concerning the criteria for evaluating a proposed construct there need be little dispute. We ask how far it will help make our concepts clearer, how far we will be able to ask more fruitful questions and open up more extensive areas of research, how far it will help us answer or reformulate the theoretical questions already on the scene. And in all these respects, the independent study of morality whether anthropologically or philosophically approached, is in great need of development.

This lecture was delivered to the Royal Anthropological Institute on 9 June, 1960. The writer is gratefully indebted to the National Science Foundation of the United States for a grant to work on the relation of science and ethics, during the tenure of which this and other studies were carried out.

Notes

1. In his Marett Lecture, speaking of values rather than morality alone, and the way in which they are often left untouched, Raymond Firth (1953, p. 148) says: "Such abstentions may be due to a conviction that since values are basic to and inherent

in all social action, they are best dealt with indirectly, and discussed in terms of their content, without specific reference. It is perhaps for this reason that contributors to a recent British series of broadcast talks on the values of primitive society discussed beliefs, behaviour, organization, institutions, modes of thought as much as they did values as such,''

2. I have elsewhere (Edel 1961, sec. 17) suggested classifying these as aspiration–phenomena, binding-authority phenomena, and appreciation–phenomena, as a first step in restoring the concept of moral phenomena and moral experience to our theoretical work.
3. For some of the scope that the enquiry in these areas gains when focused on morality directly, see Brandt (1954) and Ladd (1957); also Edel & Edel (1959, chaps. 10–12).
4. For a fuller treatment of this problem of sanctions, see Edel & Edel (1959, chap. 13).
5. The relation of methods in ethical enquiry is the subject of Edel (1963). For an analysis of analysis, see chap. 5.
6. I owe this description of what I am doing to a suggestion in conversation with the late Robert Redfield.
7. I have dealt in some detail with the former of these by analyzing the way in which scientific results enter into ethical theory (Edel 1961).

References

Austin, J. L. "A Plea for Excuses." *Aristotelian Society Proceedings* (1956–7): 7 seq.
Benedict, Ruth. *The Crysanthemum and the Sword*. (Boston: Houghton Mifflin, 1946).
Brandt, R. B. *Hopi Ethics* (Chicago: University of Chicago Press, 1954).
Edel, Abraham. "Concept of Value in Contemporary Philosophical Value Theory." *Philosophy of Science* 20, (1953). 198–207.
Edel, Abraham. "Science and the Structure of Ethics." In *International Encyclopedia of Unified Science*, vol. 2, no. 3. Chicago: University of Chicago Press, 1961.
Edel, Abraham. *Method in Ethical Theory*. (Indianapolis: Bobbs-Merrill Co., 1963).
Edel, May & Abraham Edel. *Anthropology and Ethics*. (Springfield, Illinois: Charles C. Thomas, 1959).
Evans-Pritchard, E. E. *Nuer Religion* (Oxford: Clarendon Press, 1956).
Evans-Pritchard, E. E. et al. *The Institutions of Primitive Society*. (Oxford: Basil Blackwell, 1956).
Firth, Raymond. *Elements of Social Organization*. (London: Watts, 1951).
Firth, Raymond. "The Study of Values by Social Anthropologists." *Man* (1953): 231.
Firth, Raymond. *Social Change in Tikopia*. (London: Allen & Unwin, 1959).
Freud, Sigmund. *The Question of Lay Analysis*. (New York: Norton, 1950).
Fromm, Erich. *Man for Himself*. (New York: Rinehart and Co., 1947).
Ginsberg, Morris. *Reason and Experience in Ethics* (Auguste Comte Memorial Trust Lecture, no. 2). Oxford, 1956.
Hallowell, A. I. *Culture and Experience*. (Philadelphia: University of Pennsylvania Press, 1955).
Kant, Immanuel. *Lectures on Ethics*. (London: Methuen, 1930).
Kluckhohn, Clyde et al. "Values and Value-Orientation in the Theory of Action." In *Toward A General Theory of Action*, ed. Talcott Parsons & E. A. Shils. (Cambridge, Mass: Harvard University Press, 1951).

Krikorian, Y. H. & Edel, Abraham. *Contemporary Philosophic Problems*. (New York: Macmillan, 1959).

Ladd, John. *The Structure of a Moral Code*. (Cambridge, Mass: Harvard University Press, 1957).

Laird, John. *An Enquiry into Moral Notions*. London: Allen & Unwin, 1935).

Mead, Margaret. "Social Change and Cultural Surrogates," *J. Educ. Sociol.*, 14: (1940): 92–109.

Notes and Queries 1951 (ed. 6). R. Anthrop. Inst., London.

Nowell-Smith, P. H. *Ethics*. (Harmondsworth: Penguin, 1954).

Piaget, Jean. *The Moral Judgment of the Child*. (Glencoe, Ill., Free Press, 1932).

Redfield, Robert. *The Primitive World and its Transformations*. (Ithaca, New York: Cornell University Press, 1953).

Smith, Marian W. "Different Cultural Concepts of Past, Present, and Future: A Study of Ego Extension." *Psychiatry* 15 (1952): 395–400.

8

The Confrontation of Anthropology and Ethics

This paper, written with May Edel, appeared in 1963 in an issue of The Monist devoted specially to papers on the topic of Ethics and Anthropology. The cultural variety of moral patterns, to our understanding of which anthropology had contributed, was by this time widely accepted. Many philosophers, however, were holding out for the autonomy of ethical theory, as distinct from the moral code or pattern. As a purely analytic philosophical discipline, they argued, ethical theory could furnish definitive answers that would govern the structure of morality— answers about the meaning of "good", "obligation", and so forth. The paper carried through for ethical theories the same kind of analysis that the preceding paper offers for morality, showing how ethical theories also are grounded in the social contexts and knowledge and purposes and problems of a people. It points, therefore, to a different way of doing ethical theory.

The confrontation of anthropology and ethics has not been a peaceful one. Entrenched attitudes, hardened lines, frequent anxieties about trespass have tended to prevail. Philosophers may allow anthropology, like any other science, to putter about in the external investigation of causes and conditions of morality, perhaps even to play an ancillary role in the practical decisions of normative ethics, but they are prone to rule it out as an interloper in the reflective analysis of theoretical ethics. We should like to suggest that anthropology has a contribution to make, through both its content and its method, in the latter domain; and paradoxically, that it is through the light it throws on theoretical ethics that anthropology makes its profoundest contribution to normative ethics.

Part 1

The first dramatic impact of anthropology on ethics was the realization that just as there are differences in all other aspects of behavior, from motor habits to ways of socializing babies or the structure of group authority, so too there are differences in the actual *content* of different peoples' moralities, in goals and ideals, in character traits selected for approval and disapproval, in rules and specific codes. The range of reactions to this discovery has included:

Holier than thou: They're wrong and we're right.
Eclectic flower–gathering: Let's be sexually uninhibited, like the Samoans, generous like the Crow, cooperative and nonaggressive like the Pueblo.
Cosmic dejection: So morality is just another illusion.
Leap to freedom: No morality is therefore binding. We're free to do what we like.
Happy functionalism: Every morality fits the culture of its people. Thus every morality is right for its own people.
Universal tolerance: You have no right to criticize other people's morality.
Private possession: Our morality is at least our own. Let's love it.
Optimistic confidence: The difference must be on the surface only. Beneath it all there must be common insights, goals and needs.

All of these are like enthymemes, whose missing premises—whether of value, fact, definition, metaphysics—would be the most interesting and possibly surprising parts of their analysis.[1] Let us look at one of these views, the thesis of *the moral unity of mankind*, in the light of modern anthropological knowledge of man and his works. What becomes of the assumption that man as one species should be expected to have one set of underlying goals, feel ennobled by the same virtues, acknowledge the same set of duties? Can we cut through the divergent cultural expressions of morality to find this view meaningful?

Some anthropologists have tried to pinpoint a few principles on which there is wide human consensus: there are always mating regulations, in–group aggression must be kept within some limits, babies must be cared for. These are so general that they are more nearly universal principles of social organization than statements about moral agreements. They say nothing about whether whipping children punitively is permissible or cruel, whether wives may be lent to visiting strangers, about whom one may marry or kill.[2] If such varied expressions of common social necessities are to be considered moral agreements at all, they are so at only a most attenuated level. And the areas of even such minimal agreement are very limited, leaving us with large blocks of fundamental differences in major evaluations and commitments. So, for example, approving the pursuit of sensual pleasures as the major good in life involves a quite different moral stance from eschewing it in favor of glory or wealth or the salvation of one's soul. It implies different virtues and rules, and a very different evaluation of the meaning of life and man's role.

A more promising approach to unity might seem to be the search for common meanings and motives underlying different specific moral rules. Unfortunately, proposed techniques for winnowing out moral kernel from contextual chaff have not proved very fruitful in eliminating, though they may perhaps somewhat diminish the "diversity of morals." Differences in knowledge and preferential weighting may be acknowledged; one may sometimes separate common ends from divergent means, see the effects of counterconditioning or diverting pressures, and take account of varying situations obscuring common meanings.[3] But basic differences do not seem to dissolve away. So, for example, we might agree that a scalp trophy—even a human head—is just a culturally variant symbol for the "same" bravery we honor with a combat stripe (though the parallel is a little dimmed if we discover such honors may be bought, or gained in ambuscade). On the other hand, what is proved by noting that a commitment to community solidarity and well being underlies ritual murder? This may indicate a common respect for community well being, but it hardly demonstrates a common view of the value of human life.

What is to become of such hard differences? An occasional moral unitarian has sought refuge in the intuitionist concept of "moral blindness" or the "discovery of preexistent truths" in the advance of civilization. But such notions tend to be question-begging; they present no indices for differentiating true from cloudy vision, nor for separating preexistent truths from actual changes in moral values. What then can we do? It is at this point that anthropology suggests a reexamination of the very issues before us: let us understand the differences rather than deny them. Anthropology can study the range of their variations, their functional and causal interconnections with the social matrices in which they are embedded, the common or divergent roles they play in human society. This, if it is fruitful, leads to an understanding of common grounds for morality, if not to common moral agreements. It suggests the reformulation of the moral unity thesis as a thesis of underlying *psychological unity* or *social–needs unity*, or points to patterns of *historical convergence*.

This reformulation may supplant rather than salvage the thesis, but it provides a powerful tool for normative probing. For indeed, without such understanding of the meaning and grounds of morality in human living, uniformities themselves tell us little. They may be accidents of history or evolutionary hangovers rather than perennial and necessary truths. May not some of our common modern beliefs, though shared with much of the rest of mankind, already be obsolescent? From the standpoint of our descendants, incinerating our enemies may appear as barbarous as eating them, and our failure to solve the problem of distributing our surplus productivity for the benefit of all mankind as wicked as public hangings on Tyburn Tree. If the aim in looking for agreements be to reach a consensus for solving problems of the modern world, and to avoid its exacerbated conflicts, it seems unlikely that looking for what man once held to will be as important as creative thinking in the context of the present—creative thinking which needs for its tools as much understanding of moral processes, of the role of morality, and of moral change, as we can gain by the richest possible comparative study.

Philosophy reaches a similar conclusion by a different path—analyzing the logical conditions for normative judgment. For it has made clear that neither differences in moral attitudes and beliefs, nor their uniformity, can establish anything about their desirability or correctness. Any theoretical proof of the "correctness" of moral ideas requires criteria of correctness, a definite concept of the moral, including moral reasoning and justification.

The scene of confrontation thus shifts to the basic category of the moral itself. Traditional ethics in analyzing its normative uses thinks in terms of a single meaning for "moral". In fact, however, there is the widest disagreement in contemporary ethical theory about what the primary characteristics of the moral are.[4] What if, instead of assuming that these differences represent difficulties in analysis which will eventually yield to conceptual clarification, we ask anthropology to try on the moral category the same type of inquiry it has carried out on moral content? Would the fate of the moral unity thesis be repeated for what we may call the *constancy of the moral category*?

Part 2

To the anthropologist the lack of a sharp definition of "moral" presents both a dilemma and an advantage. There are no sharply defined criteria by which to delimit the search for cross-culturally comparable phenomena, but there is a more open, and perhaps a fruitfully less ethnocentrically constricted area of inquiry.

Clearly, if all societies have rules of appropriate behaviors, approvals and disapprovals about courses of conduct, responsibilities whose fulfillment is expected, virtues cultivated or admired, some structural features and processes by which these are organized and utilized would seem to be everywhere required. Words expressive of condemnation or approval, of obligation or preference, like "right" and "wrong", "good", "evil", "tabu", or like such second-order terms in our language as "mature", "ill-judged", "worthy", "contemptible" might be expected to occur. So would sentences of command, comment, or exhortation, feelings of delight, disgust, and abhorrence, disappointment, fear, shame and the like, together with various kinds of external sanctions. And since man is presumably ever curious, and if not always rational then at least rationalizing, some ways of talking about the reasons for the rules, some symbolic or reasoned framework in which the moral codes make sense would appear to be likely in any society. All these constitute an appropriate field for inquiry into the structure of its morality.

When we scan the range of data available we find that some such elements are usually to be discerned, though often enmeshed in some special area of cultural description or dispersed among accounts of different institutions.[5] One can find positive moral bonds and negative moral sanctions, contexts of moral discourse whether for individual decision, teaching, advice, community punitive action, or just scandal, and many interesting discussions of moral justification. These yield terms and principles, patterns of obligations and ideals, affective meanings and cognitive views. We can thus set up common structural categories for study. But this does not guarantee uniform cross–cultural contents for them.[6] Even if common categories of morality do prove to be structurally present everywhere, they may point to a common functional role for morality or a common logic of analysis, rather than any common quality of the moral "category" itself, unless such unity is empirically discovered.

No first look at the anthropological data suggests such a simple outcome. We find moral terms ranging in stringency from "absolutely tabu" to "this is virtuous" (meaning that ideally good men do it this way, but there is no expectation that most men will be ideally good). We find moral statements that are advisory rather than imperative, ones that state, "People don't do this," rather than "Don't" directed at the individual, weighing-of-consequences and considering-the-circumstances rather than absolute formulations, even interrogative ones (reminiscent of our own "what shall it profit a man . . ."). Moral maxims may be richly developed and sharply delineated for teaching and argument, or scarcely formulated at all except as breaches call forth social action or comment—a kind of end point minimum, perhaps, of applying the term "moral structure" at all. Similarly we find justifications of rules of conduct that range from community or family goodwill and security, personal safety against supernatural threats or neighbors' envy, the dictates of gods or the ancestors, to what is almost equivalent to our own "man's fulfillment of his duty to God"—"this is the way to maintain the harmony of the universe, which only man and gods working together can achieve."

As for what many would consider the core of the problem, the *meaning* of "right", "obligation" or "good"—we cannot pretend to have worked with a sensitive phenomenologically tuned camera to probe the inner *feeling* of prescriptiveness, but it clearly has different quality at some levels to the individual whose code requires a weighing of consequences than to one whose rules are absolute, rigid, inner voices of command; for those whose rules have a quality of "all men at all times must" and those whose rules are situational,

pertaining not to behaviors as *such* but to their contexts. There are differences
in the sanctions, positive and negative, written into or accompanying different
moralities, in the extent to which they are ego–syntonic and deeply internalized, or externally imposed and situationally interpreted. Feelings of
shame, guilt, sin, pride, fear of penalty or ridicule color reactions differently
in different societies, and thus affect the very meaning of "basic right and
wrong," moral awareness, and conscience. As for the *good*, the sought–after
and valued—happiness, or self-fulfillment, universal harmony, or any other
basic goal—how these shape up cross–culturally is even less adequately
analyzed. We know something of the difference in content of goals but very
little of how these are written into justifications, and therefore of cross–
cultural views of the relation of the right and the good. The inklings we can
glean suggest that human satisfactions rather than duty fulfillment is the *point*
of moral regulation, and its justification, in at least some of the cultures of the
world, whose further study would help us understand more fully how wide the
gamut of possibilities really is.

But the anthropologist need not stop at the sheer discovery of differences
within structural features. He will also want to know whether these variations
are independent or interconnected, and how they are related, separately, or in
discovered patterns of covariance, with moral content. Are there particular
kinds of moral-rule formulations, imperative, perhaps, or advisory, that go
with particular kinds of conscience, or principles of justification? Are moral
systems based on positive sanctions, or on patterns of ideal goals, different in
their ways of posing questions for decision by the individual, or in the
phenomenological "bindingness" of obligations? Are there any systematic
relations between the content of a morality—its emphasis on warlike virtues
or community coordination or competitive individual aggrandisement—and
the kinds of justifications it will employ such as ethnic pride, love and
harmony, or paths of duty set down by the ancestors or the gods? Do such
proposed dichotomies as shame and guilt or situational vs. universalistic,
serve as typologies pointing to patterns of difference in other areas of moral
structure? Are there modalities such as degrees of stringency or flexibility,
which color many aspects of a moral structure—sanctions, justifications,
types of injunctions and modes of inculcation and decision—or can various
features of a moral structure be different in such qualitative ways? What are
the roots of any observed covariance? Are they causal–functional, historical,
or in some sense logical? Are they patterned within the moral structure itself,
or tied to other aspects of culture? Some possible interrelationships between
specific features of morality and psychological or social structure variables
have been pointed to in the anthropological literature, though not very
systematically—for example, the relation of conscience to the nuclear family,
or the role of envy and witchcraft as moral sanctions in some types of social
systems. Such questions can be broadened into inquiries into interrela-

tionships with more complex patterns of moral structure once these are delineated.

In *Anthropology and Ethics* we suggested a technique for describing moral configurations of whole cultures by plotting their profiles with respect to as many aspects, categories and modalities of structure as can be discerned—relative development of shame or pride, guilt and sin; rule or situation-oriented structuring of moral discourse; role of authority figures or personal analysis in decision-making; pervasive stringency or leniency, and so on. This can be done for Indian pueblos, Melanesian villages, Periclean Athens, mediaeval manors—or Oxford or Cambridge intellectuals. This yields an abstract level of description of moral systems and provides a basis for their comparison at many levels, especially through the discovery of repetitive syndromes and patterns of covariance, and the clustering of sharp contrasts.

So, for example, the moral structure pointed to by Max Weber in his delineation of Puritan morality, which includes such features as strictness of conscience, individual responsibility, imperative rule formulation, divine sanctions, and in its content a strict emphasis upon work and duty as against sex and pleasure, has been found to be most interestingly paralleled in the Yurok of California and the Manus of the Admiralty Islands in the Pacific.[7] Both have strict and rigidly internalized moral rules, which are also strongly sanctioned in the religious ideology, but which are justified in terms of individual rather than community goals. And here too there is an emphasis upon work, scrupulous attention to wealth–getting and debt–repayment, and eschewing the pleasures of the flesh, as distracting, and sinful. (The Yurok are not against all sex indulgence, but certainly believe in keeping it in its place, which means carefully isolated from anything remotely related to the serious work–and–wealth goals of living—even to the extent of requiring that married couples never have sexual relations in a dwelling–house, for shell money is stored there.)

The congruence here is obviously extremely provocative, especially since such a pattern is by no means usual in the primitive world. Its significance is sharpened by the presence of some impressive candidates for causal or functional explanation. For in both Manus and Yurok systems, vertical mobility is possible, replacing an older, more fixed hierarchical status system; and in both, vertical mobility is achieved through wealth manipulation. (Shades of the emergent bourgeoisie!) In addition, there is the interesting suggestion that it is the character-structure concomitants of the moral structure that lend it its unity. Erikson[8] has noted the compulsive rigidity of the Yurok, and their markedly anal symbolism, and much of the Manus data suggests that they fit the same pattern.

Pursuing this theme further, the anthropologist would examine other wealth manipulating vertical mobility societies to develop hypotheses about their rather different moral configurations. He could also compare the rule–

oriented, stringent, strongly internalized morality of Pueblo Indian culture, with its social control emphasis, to see how much it differs in structure as well as content from achievement–oriented individual systems. Such comparisons would be productive of hypotheses to be studied more systematically on a wider and more controlled scale. Questions of culture history and evolutionary emergence could also be explored: for example, do structural styles remain constant as content changes? Are moral structures and ideologies always dependent variables, yielding in the process of technological and social change? Or do they sometimes influence its direction or at least affect its timetable?

What implications would such anthropological inquiry into morality have for normative and theoretical ethics?

In the variegated field of normative ethics, stretching from simple deciding of particular duties or desirabilities to selection of ideals and self–commitments, its implications are manifold. Anthropological data generally help us assess means, consequences, costs, functional relations. Specific anthropological study of morality would go further. In giving us tools for understanding our own moral patterns in comparison with alternatives, and all in relation to wider cultural patterns and dynamics, it would furnish the intellectual lever for conceiving changes in our own morality and for affecting such reconstruction. It would give us a better grasp of coherence in our morality and its inner conflicts and discrepancies, and a sounder reckoning of what is possible. For example, if we could learn how a morality structured in terms of "good", oriented to fulfillment and love rather than restriction and duty, might be tied to particular educational procedures and social organizations, we could better assess the desirability of such a morality and judge whether it could be achieved in a world-society, and what kind of closely knit but nonhostile subunits within it might be essential in its moral operation. In general, there would be a shift in our way of looking at our morality, getting beyond fragment of rule or edict to wider relations and purposes. Appreciation of alternative configuration would put our own morality on probation, "Know thy culture" becoming an essential ingredient in the traditional moral injunction, "Know thyself."

The effect on theoretical ethics is more systematic. It emerges sharply in the changes taking place in the use of the term "moral". It is a common current realization that shifts in rules of discourse may betoken changes in basic conceptual frameworks. While the moral unity thesis was unquestioned and the categorical constancy thesis not even rendered explicit, "moral" was used in a singular or monistic way: there was one morality as there was one truth, whether the context was descriptive or normative. When anthropological data exhibited different patterns of moral content, the descriptive use became plural—the world had many moralities. This remained tolerable because it was associated with a monistic normative use which assumed that the plural referred to moral beliefs or attitudes but only the singular to moral truth or justified attitudes. But the deeper anthropological study of moral structures and profiles, by undermining the categorial constancy thesis in its exhibition of varieties in moral structures themselves, makes possible a conscious shift to a more adequate general conceptualization for the field.

It is very important, however, not to misunderstand what is being proposed. We do not deny that there may be moral unities and categorial constancies in our field. The degree of unity to be found in moral content and moral structure, the levels on which unities may appear, become questions of evidence. No absolute pluralism is enshrined, no arbitrary relativism, no a priori indeterminism. But there is a shift in the burden of proof together with the shift in the rules of discourse. What then is the conceptual transformation?

Instead of an assumed single morality of mankind with large indeterminate elements within it, and indeterminate modes of reducing and eliminating variant components, we propose accepting the language of many moralities, which has gradually crept into the literature, just as one speaks of many languages or many religions or many legal systems. The status of the moral unity thesis, if it is maintained, becomes that of a synthetic proposition about the specified range of moralities: e.g., that there are universal component elements, or psychological or social need or historical problem bases reflected in all moralities, or a particular unifying pattern in their evolution. Or else the unity thesis becomes a unifying moral program, justified within a particular morality with given content, or involving a convergent basis of emerging consensus.

Similarly, instead of the assumption of constancy of the moral category, there would be the language of many moral structures, each shaping up in its own configuration. This would focus attention on the role that structural elements play in the operation and relations of the morality. Theses about the unity of structure would be synthetic generalizations or else normative programs, in a way quite parallel to the revised unity theses about moralities.

What would be the impact of this conceptual reconstruction on ethical theorizing? Primarily, it would provide a way of viewing or understanding ethical theories and their tasks, trying to see more explicitly what theorizing is doing, to understand its functioning and appreciate the purposes underlying its different forms. It would not supplant theorizing by something that was not theorizing. To learn lessons *about* theory is not to supplant theory, but to make it more self–consciously efficacious, to sharpen its criteria for what would constitute correct answers to its problems.

Part 3

What would the suggested shift in conceptualization accomplish in the philosophical operations of ethical theory? Would it take sides in disputes of informalist and formalist, of cognitivist and noncognitivist, or add another "school" to complicate the scene? We think not. It would rather suggest a perspective within each current controversy which would show where to look for criteria of solution.

Suppose we introduce the concept of the *anthropological transcription of an ethical theory* as a report of what the theory tells us—whether explicitly stated, implicitly assumed, presupposed in the kinds of arguments used, contextually implied, expressed so as to be clear to an informed onlooker, or in any other ways philosophical analysis can sort and dissect—about how the nature of man and his predicament are envisaged, to what problems the theory is addressed, and the underlying modalities and structural components it embodies. We expect to find in every ethical theory presuppositions about the tasks of ethics, the character of moral experience, what constitutes evidence for moral judgment, and all the other *theoretical counterparts* of the moral structure. This provides a unified framework for studying theory variants, not an assured categorial unity. We cannot, prior to the transcription, assume a unity even in the questions to which different ethical theorists are addressing themselves. But just as we found a synthetic unity meaningful for moral content and structure, so we can inquire whether unities are discoverable on the theoretical level—e.g., that there is a role always played by ethical theories, imposing a fixed form; or a developmental pattern in a changing historical role; or perhaps a normative unity about the desirable shape or role of ethical theory in the light of shared objectives.

Take, for example, an anthropological transcription of Aristotle and Kant. Aristotle starts the job for us, by stating his teleological presupposition that all men strive for one ultimate good. Kant is less obliging, and we have to dig out his assumption of the unity of moral experience for all men. Such factual propositions have, of course, conceivable alternatives. Men's goals may be basically varied, and moral experience may represent a heterogeneous class of feeling–cognition clusters unified by mode of functioning in the moral structure rather than by any common quality or use of the same feeling in the human repertoire. Evaluation of such factual presuppositions requires cross–cultural evidence.[9]

The transcription would have to elicit also whether Aristotle and Kant tell us about the same moral structure. Probably they do not: their ethical–theory profiles fall too far apart. Aristotle's theory is essentially good–oriented, teleologically grounded; Kant's is ought–oriented, rational–lawful in character. The one is ancient Apollonian Greek, the other is modern puritanical north German. Nor can we assume that they are (normatively) recommending the same structure: Aristotle's is local with a strong hierarchical cast; Kant's is universal with a strong individual will–act cast. (Modern philosophers ignore such confrontation of different moral structures either by treating the question as one of the history of philosophy, or by fashioning a broad eclecticism). The anthropological transcription reveals both the structure each philosopher is delineating and how he is refining it into a model for preservation or reconstruction.

One would examine contemporary ethical theories in the same way. For example, the emotive theory of ethics, in Stevenson's version[10], thinks of itself as a neutral analysis of ethical language whose correctness is to be judged on purely analytic criteria. An anthropological transcription shows how it begins by selecting a very limited set of phenomena for fashioning its theoretical ideas—the dyadic interpersonal relation of disagreement in a context in which each party seeks to bring the other around to his side. We immediately ask for conceivable alternatives—why not select, instead, the situation of many people working toward a unified goal, and trying to fashion adequate working rules for its achievement or to revise older rules under changing conditions? Since emotivism develops a dominant model from its selected typical situation; it has made a theoretical choice of wide ramifications. The transcription can then read off its factual presupposition that the most important, pervasive, troublesome question of disagreement is what in fact morality is directed toward, that this problem permeates the use of moral terms, the giving of moral reasons, and all the other constituents of moral structure. We are thus enabled to raise the evaluative question whether this assumption is a true one. Does it refer to our time or all times, our culture or all cultures? We can then judge how far it is true of the modern world.

We need not, however, stop here. We can track down the same assumption in a quite different theoretical profile—Dewey's—more explicitly expressed as the flux of changing problems. This leads Dewey to define the moral situation as one involving hesitation between alternative paths and to spurn as secondary the situation in which a man knows what he ought to do but is tempted not to do it.[11] But why are the resulting theoretical profiles in Dewey and Stevenson so different? As we continue the transcription the reason emerges. Dewey does not have the man stand alone; he is in a group culture equipped with habits of cooperative decision pushing forward from core centers of our culture into more chaotic areas. Stevenson sees each man alone recognizing his own desires and approvals and having no other resource but to engage in a diversity of emotive pressures on the other party. It was a deep cultural insight on Margaret MacDonald's part to compare emotivism to an extreme protestantism with one man missionary sects.[12] Note how differently the evaluation of emotivism is now approached. We see now in what sort of a world and what sort of culture it would make sense to focus on the disagreement aspect in an ethical theory, to use the disagreement situation as a paradigm in constructing an ethical language, to abandon as hopeless the attempt to furnish a deductive or inductive methodology for ethics. But the evaluation would have to decide whether in fact this is the human predicament or a special situation of a particular cultural tradition; it would have to make similar decisions about how the shared purpose of securing a wider agreement can be achieved. (At this point, it may be noted, the current sharp distinction between theoretical ethics and normative ethics wears thin.)

Anthropological transcription of theorizing in the informalist-linguistic mode yields comparable insights. This realm concentrates largely on the conceptual organization of moral experience in relation to justification patterns. Its generic emphasis on the prescriptive character of moral terms reflects initially the particular imperative way in which our culture has tended to organize moral expressions. The informalist attempt to articulate and preserve this prescriptive priority is found to be directed to normative problems of our time. For example, Hare's universal prescriptivism[13] may be transcribed—when we track down the reasons he gives for regarding prescriptive meaning as primary—as saying that in our troubled world we need a sharpened sense of responsibility which attentiveness to choice will furnish but which a descriptive interpretation will dull, and hence let us see ourselves as constantly renewing subscription to our principles rather than just applying them.

On the other hand, the pervasive search for patterns of good reasons[14] is providing an anthropological corrective to the emotivist rejection of validity in ethics by tracing in detail the actual fragmentary patterns of justification in the existent moral structure as reflected in English. Yet often this position implies that we have no choice about the resultant patterns, presumably because they are enshrined in the language! Such an assumption suggests the familiar malady of cultural "blinders". For alternative patterns can be read not merely from different cultural forms in justification in different cultures, but even from the history of Western ethical theory. No assumptions about the nature of ordinary language—and least of all a view of language as articulating social practices—can supplant the normative issue of which kind of an organizational structure is most desirable for a morality in given conditions of culture and history. The linguistic formulation simply shows admirably what has crystallized in a given area for a given period. It is a strange reversal when an anthropological perspective is required to recall philosophy to its truly normative tasks!

We shall forego similar excursions into other ethical approaches, whether of a cognitivist or a formalistic type. These are usually less intent on denying—although they may not bother to explore—their cross–cultural factual presuppositions or that specific tasks are implicit in their criteria of value and comparative value. Thus a humanistic naturalism or a humanistic idealism is readily seen to assume the uniformity of phenomena of pleasure-pain or desire or pursuit of ideals, as well as (more dubiously) the universal aim of maximization in goal-achievement, and so forth. Phenomenological and existentialist ethics can be easily transcribed to show assumptions of constancy of the phenomenological field or of features of the human predicament, as well as of the tasks of facing reality or reconciling oneself implicit in criteria of "authenticity"; the anthropological transcription would, for example, raise clearly the issue whether they are mistaking the shambles of our social order for the cosmic predicament of man. Formalistic approaches, now flowering in the development of deontic logics for ethical theory, are clearly working out *possible* conceptual and organizational structures whose interpretation on application would pinpoint field assumptions and criteria of successful application. We see no difficulty in making a transcription so as to face directly their factual and normative (often called "pragmatic") assumptions.

By exhibiting ethical theories as proposed structures for moralities, our conceptual reconstruction breaks the deadlock in theoretical ethics at precisely the point where it has reached an impasse. For it focuses on the factual presuppositions built into ethical theories and on normative components entering at theoretical choice–points. Thus it enables ethical theory to refine its criteria of "correctness" and to bring ethical theories to the bar of responsible judgment. Ethical theorizing is thus brought back from its self-imposed isolation and seen as the sensitive frontier–probing by which philosophers endeavor to refine and reconstruct the moral structure of their culture in response to the basic problems of their time and to articulate their hopes and dreams about the life that men may lead. Such restoration carries no deterministic overbinding. It does not substitute scientific assertion for the integrity of moral choice, nor diminish the freedom or far-ranging importance of philosophical analysis. It shows rather how the carrying on of each of these distinctive human enterprises is dependent on the materials furnished by the other two.

Notes

1. For fuller analysis of themes entering into ethical relativity, cf. A. Edel, *Ethical Judgment: the Use of Science in Ethics* (Glencoe, Ill.: The Free Press, 1955), ch. 1.
2. For a fuller treatment of this theme, see M. Edel and A. Edel, *Anthropology and Ethics* (Springfield, Ill.: Charles C Thomas, 1959), chs. 3–7.
3. Cf. Morris Ginsberg, "On the Diversity of Morals" in *On the Diversity of Morals*, Essays in Sociology and Social Philosophy, vol. 1 (New York: The Macmillan Company, 1957); also, Karl Duncker, "Ethical Relativity? (An Inquiry into the Psychology of Ethics)", *Mind*, new series, 48 (Jan. 1939).
4. Cf. A. Edel, *Method in Ethical Theory* (New York: Bobbs Merrill Co., 1963), 178ff.
5. See Chap. 7.
6. Cf. Clyde Kluckhohn, "Universal Categories of Culture," in *Anthropology Today*, ed. A. Kroeber (Chicago: University of Chicago Press, 1953).

7. Walter Goldschmidt, "Ethics and the structure of society; An ethnological contribution to the sociology of knowledge," *American Anthropologist*, 53 (1951). Cf. also Margaret Mead, *Growing up in New Guinea* (New York: Mentor, 1953).
8. Erik H. Erikson, *Childhood and Society* (New York: W. W. Norton and Company, 1950), ch. 4.
9. Compare, for example, R. B. Brandt's attempt in his *Hopi Ethics* (Chicago: University of Chicago Press, 1954) to show the similarity of Hopi moral experience to ours.
10. Charles L. Stevenson, *Ethics and Language* (New Haven: Yale University Press, 1944).
11. Dewey and Tufts, *Ethics* rev. ed. (New York: Henry Holt & Co. 1932), ch. 10.
12. "Ethics and the Ceremonial Use of Language" in *Philosophical Analysis*, ed. Max Black (Ithaca, N.Y.: Cornell University Press, 1950), 220.
13. R. M. Hare, *The Language of Morals* (Oxford: Clarendon Press, 1952), and *Freedom and Reason* (Oxford: Clarendon Press, 1963).
14. S. E. Toulmin, *An Examination of the Place of Reason in Ethics* (Cambridge: Cambridge University Press, 1953), Kurt Baier, *The Moral Point of View* (Ithaca, N.Y.: Cornell University Press, 1958); Paul Taylor, *Normative Discourse* (Englewood Cliffs, N.J.: Prentice-Hall Inc., 1961).

9

Ethics—A Modest Science?

At the annual meeting of the American Association for the Advancement of Science (San Francisco, January 3–8, 1980) a symposium had been arranged to consider whether ethics was sufficiently scientific to establish a section of the Association devoted to it. This paper, presented on that occasion, recanvassed the meaning of "science," and the sharpness of lines drawn between science and non-science. It examines the wide–ranging complexity of being a science and the degree of "scientificality" in carrying out the tasks of ethics. The question itself ends far different from the way in which it began.

Traditional views place science and ethics at opposite poles among human disciplines. Science is objective, theoretical, concerned with describing and explaining the facts or what is, dealing with means; ethics is subjective, practical, prescriptive, concerned with values and what ought to be, focused on choice and decision, and dealing with ends (particularly ultimate ends). Science thus is value free, and so scientists make ethical decisions as citizens, not as scientists. And ethics, not leaning on science, must rest either on faith or on individual taste and intuition or else on group preference and tradition.

That the question whether ethics is a science is being raised now suggests that something has happened to these old dichotomies, that some kind of intellectual rapprochement is being negotiated. It is not hard to discern the practical background for this move. The traditional iron curtain between science and ethics served definite social functions. It insulated science from social responsibility, in earlier stages protecting it against charges of religious and moral subversion and in more recent times relieving it of responsibility for social effects. And it isolated established moral and social values from the currents of change. But both of these functions have been made obsolete by the twentieth–century changes of industrialization and urbanization, by the technological reshaping of life, the effects of war and revolution, demands for democratization and equality. It is difficult to spell out a value–free science in the midst of nuclear problems, recombinant genetics, and experiments with human subjects, or even simply where public investment of several billions is needed for supporting scientific research; scientists may claim that the responsibility is not theirs alone, but this is far different from not being responsible. And it is too late to isolate moral and social values when the established patterns already are profoundly altered; it becomes important to understand specific moral change, not merely the forms of moral discourse. The contemporary turn to problems of biomedical ethics, environmental ethics, the ethics of technology, etc., shows the penetration of largely new problems as well as the reshaping of the old ones. What has not been attended to sufficiently is the feedback of this movement on ethical theory itself in order to determine what roles science is now to play within the presuppositions, operations, and methods of ethics as a discipline.

The problem as we see it of whether ethics is a science is changed now in two respects. First, we no longer compare the nature of ethics and the nature of science in the expectation of a single, immutable answer; there is always a temporal and historical reference. Second, to be a science is only the extreme point along a continuum of being more or less scientific—let us speak, though awkwardly, of the degree of ''scientificality''—where physics has furnished traditionally the model for the extreme. But even physics was once largely myth, and even Isaac Newton maintained a continuity with theology in his attempts to extract from alchemy evidence of divine shoring up of the world against processes of degradation. Today the question whether the ideal of physics is profitable for all sciences is actively raised. At any rate, even parts of a single scientific field may vary in the degree of systematic organization. The question therefore is not whether ethics is a science but how scientific ethics has been in various aspects and whether it can become more scientific by cultivating certain kinds of relations and whether it is important that it do so.

The discussion that follows is divided into three parts. The first reconsiders the traditional dichotomies and their present status. The second suggests what ethics would be like if it were more scientific and the advantages of turning it in this direction. The third distinguishes different degrees of scientificality and considers how likely they may be for ethics.

Traditional Dichotomies

Some of the dichotomies that kept science and ethics apart seem to have been quietly passing away, outmoded by scientific progress and the refinement of methods. For example, science as objective versus ethics as subjective was part of the metaphysical partition of matter and mind or spirit. Matter was regarded as regular, quantifiable, and simple enough to be subject to law, whereas spirit was complex and variable, qualitative and not subject to measurement, expressive of man's freedom. The social disciplines, not merely ethics, were disqualified from science. If the social disciplines now are established as moderately scientific, ethics need not be far behind. The psychological and social sciences with the tools of statistics introduced measure into capacities and attitudes, and pretty soon measurement was venturing into all areas of life. About the mid–twentieth century anthropologists tackled values directly (including moralities) in relation to cultural setting and social problems. In ethics itself Francis Hutcheson in the eighteenth century offered an algebra for benevolence as a public benefit, and Jeremy Bentham's felicific calculus could be interpreted to yield partial success for legislative purposes. Contemporary reservations have begun to use the concept of quality of life to replace Bentham's greatest happiness of the greatest number partly because Bentham attempted a stronger measurement than appeared feasible but equally because of concern for the minorities neglected by the "greatest number." In any case, philosophers of science have long realized by this time that the relevant issue is not a metaphysical gulf between quantity and quality. Measurement is an attempt to establish ways of ordering things and properties and events; it has different degrees or strengths and can be done in different ways; indeed attention to the differences within the sciences themselves is required. There remains plenty of room for exploring types of order and for inventiveness in ordering in any field of inquiry.

Other dichotomies also have been blunted. In mid–century analytic ethics there was for a time a great to–do about ethics being practical and science theoretical, and there were attempts to develop a logic of practice distinct from the truth–valued logic. But concern with practice is no obstacle to a theory of practice; after all, engineering and medical sciences are concerned with practice, and ethics may be comparably scientific though practical. If a conception of pure practice as distinct from any theory is offered, doing without any thinking would be reduced to physical motion. Human action is purposive and intentional, and so most practical discourse has cognitive content, just as most theory has a prospective reference to practice.

The history of such dichotomies is instructive. They start off as if they referred to metaphysical distinctions or logical necessities or natural or structural joints of things. As we shall see, however, the moment they are applied to subject matters of this world they act as proposed categories in a tentative classification that are being tried on the material. Usually, when this is done, much more continuity turns up, and the distinctions are seen to be relative ones, usable in some contexts and for some purposes but not in others. Whether we keep them or abandon them depends on how they work out in experience. We would do better then to regard them as programs for research, not absolutely necessary cleavages.

Let us try out such lessons on the two most formidable ones pertinent to our inquiry—the fact–value distinction (and its alternative is-ought distinction) and the means–end distinction. These are the ones most invoked in the separation of science and ethics.

The fact–value dichotomy has been proclaimed as a metaphysical one of ultimately distinct categories, as a linguistic one of the indicative and the imperative, as a methodological one of the descriptive and the prescriptive. But attempts to carry it out by separating off linguistic terms or phenomena have been notoriously unsuccessful. Moral terms such as ''good'' or ''ought'' have nonmoral uses (''That ought to do it'' is predictive and largely factual, though perhaps tinged with a pro-attitude), and descriptive terms can carry moral standards (''Be a man''). And there are numerous terms, such as those indicating practices and roles (''promises,'' ''parent'') from which both ''is'' and ''ought'' statements can be unrolled. The attempt to distinguish moral and nonmoral uses of a term in some general or decisive way has proved equally unsuccessful. It sinks deeper into the context and eventually ceases to be an absolute distinction. As for phenomena, context is again determinative of fact status or value status. That a suit fits is a factual observation, but the fit of the suit can be used as a value criterion of well–made clothing. Similarly to have a given purpose is a definite phenomenon; but the purpose as an objective determines the criteria by which the behavior directed to it is evaluated. I shall not here repeat the long struggles that philosophers have waged in the most technical of terms about these issues. The outcome seems to me to be that fact and value are as relative as theory and observtion, which positivism once sought also to capture in an absolute distinction. Theory in science has observational reference, and observations on no matter how primitive a level have theoretical or interpretive elements. It is also the case that no value is without its theoretical or interpretive elements and no fact without its context of selection and perspective in which values have entered. At this point there is no reason to think they can be unravelled into atomic facts and atomic values so that ordinary judgments are regarded as built up of a combination. It is much more likely that the so–called factual or value character arises from the context of use in different enterprises. Material has a factual character when used in the enterprise of describing, an evaluative character when construed as criteria for evaluating. Any material itself when analyzed can be seen to have embodied value criteria and factual determination in its own construction. As a general category, value indicates the selective aspect that enters into all experience, and knowledge or fact the outcome of experience organized.

In many contexts the distinction is quite useful—for example, the decision situation where it is best to gather all the information required before making the decision. But the gathering of information is not value free ("required" alone would show this); nor is the decision free from further factual encumbrance since it is provisional on the right kind of consequences ensuing. Hence the decision, once made, becomes a fact to be freshly evaluated by its consequences. Again the relative distinction of fact and value does not mean that science and ethics are correspondingly separated. Science may have plenty of values in it and ethics plenty of facts. The moralist can say that the way the world is going is immoral, but his judgment will require many factual supports; and the scientist can say that he does not let the moral judgment enter into his experiments and conclusions. But of course it is a moral commitment to truth that keeps the values out; hence it is a moral exclusion. Contextually relevant distinctions, yes; absolute dichotomy which separates the provinces, no.

The dichotomy of means and ends is perhaps the most vital to our problem. It may be objected that all we can say about scientificality in ethics concerns only the effectiveness of means toward achieving ends, but that when we get to differences in ultimate ends we are up against a blank wall. There is no mode of adjudication, of rational decision, and so of the possibility of scientificality in ethics. Such an argument may be particularly appealing at the present time when whole peoples appear to take opposing sides on ultimate questions—the type of social system, the kind of life to lead—and there is a great deal of talk about choosing a whole style of life, such as the pursuit of inner spiritual peace as against material goods and success. Even the rational pursuit of truth in science has come in for rejection as people turn against the world of technology and its demands.

Two different ways of dealing with this question of means and ends are open to those who do not think of the issue as affecting the possible scientificality of ethics. One is to accept the formulation and deny its impact; the other is to question whether the means–end distinction is more than relative and contextual. Let us look at each.

Suppose we do have the possibility of greater use of science in ethics only with respect to means, within a context of agreement on ultimate ends. How much of ethics is affected as a result? It may be argued that the greater part of ethics is concerned really with structures and practices within ends that are common and unavoidable for human beings. Thomas Hobbes built a whole ethics on the need for peace and security, which he assumed all men sought; and it is quite possible that in the insecurities of today (international as well as national) the state of things is such that its constraints determine practically a whole morality. Moreover, a morality can be built on necessary common means, not only on ends. Even if people's values differ, if peace and the abolition of war are necessary conditions for all value effort, however differently directed, then this means can be the basis for a large part of morality. Great instrumentalities and proximate ends do more of the heavy work of morality than is usually recognized. The emphasis on ultimate disagreement of ends as if it were the central problem of the possibility of a science–oriented ethics no doubt reflected the great social struggles of the twentieth century and the conflict of social systems. But it also was set in intellectual models for ethics. It posed issues as between individuals, on the assumption that statements about groups were to be reduced to statements about individual decisions; and it made the psychological assumption that the affective in a person is quite separate from the cognitive. Both of these are scientific and historical assumptions which may not be warranted. I have suggested elsewhere that we should distinguish between macroethics and microethics on the basis of the kind of problems and so avoid a dogmatic demand for reduction of large problems of mankind to individual will or fiat.[1] Certainly the great contemporary issues of, say, the extent to which our life is to be organized on the foundation of large–scale centralized technology or, to take a quite distinct type of issue, what kind of relations between men and women are morally desirable in our growing consciousness of the permeating role of sexist discrimination and what kind of institutions can support a moral reconstruction, are scarcely to be regarded as individual moral issues, however much individual decision can contribute to them. And the psychological assumption that the cognitive and the affective are utterly distinct is a constitutive scientific component of emotive ethical theories which has little scientific support. For a brief period in twentieth–century ethics, emotive theory tried to make ethics pure expression. It was a passing phase which brought about some new lights, more about language than about morality, but scarcely got rid of the cognitive components in moral utterances. In fact it proceeded from an initial hypothesis that there were none. But there is no reasonable basis for viewing ethics as the effort of a person who has fixed attitudes to try to persuade others to hold them; ethics just as readily can be viewed as the effort of persons who share some values to widen the area of their value agreement by cooperative effort.

The view that the means–end distinction is itself relative and contextual is probably a more profound approach to the issue. It is basic to John Dewey's ethics and expounded by him in various writings that deal with its psychological and social aspects as well as its philosophical analysis.[2] Let me add one point as sufficient here. An examination of how ultimate ends function in human life—or, for that matter, ultimate standards—will show that they are not isolated objects of wish or will or commitment and so cannot be simply accepted or rejected in an atomic fashion. That there can be long–standing disagreements about "ultimates" is not decisive, for there are long–standing disagreements about basics in a science like psychology as well. The point is rather long–range testability in some strong or weak form. Now ultimates in ethics function to organize the whole field of desires and values and commitments and paths of action and so can be themselves evaluated in spite of their phenomenological endlike character by their success in their tasks. In this respect they are like broad scientific theories that organize the domain of knowledge and are refined and altered as they prove satisfactory or unsatisfactory in the long run of experience.[3] So to regard them is to give an even broader scientific character to ethics. It is a matter of scientific study of human life and history to see whether such a view of ultimate ends does not correspond more closely to how moralities have functioned than the individualistic analysis that terminates in ultimate fiats. The character of morality and ethics is itself to be approached in scientific fashion.

Toward a More Scientific Ethics

Contemporary technical moral philosophy has shown great concern in drawing a fine line between doing philosophy and doing science. Under the restrictive view of philosophy that has dominated much of the twentieth century, to do philosophy was to engage in conceptual or linguistic analysis. To do moral philosophy (metaethics) was to analyze the language of morals. Beyond that there lay practical moral judgments (normative ethics), in which the philosopher had no special competence. But anything that savored of description or explanation was doing science. Thus if a moral philosopher invoked a theory of human nature or a psychological account of the affections or of the development of personality in dealing with obligation, or integrated a study of institutional structures in the analysis of moral rules, he risked being charged with doing psychology or sociology rather than ethics.[4] Science had no comparable restrictions. A political scientist could wander freely to gather psychological views of power as a foundation for political theory or deal with the mathematical aspects of decision systems. And it would be obvious nonsense to tell a physicist that he is not doing physics when he analyzes the distinction between force and momentum or works out the theory of dimensions for concepts of mechanics, but rather doing philosophy. The same holds with respect to values: medicine and psychiatry do not cease to be scientific when they adopt a pro–stance to health and work out the consequences of theories of growth and development for the refinement of the concept of health. In sum, there is no partition of analysis and evaluation on the one side as doing philosophy and description and explanation on the other side as doing science. Every discipline involves all four enterprises: it describes its phenomena or initial materials or data; it analyzes its concepts; it explains in causal or other theoretical terms; and it evaluates its aims and constructions. The important distinction is rather a different one: whether the descriptive and explanatory materials play a purely external role or a constitutive (internal) role in ethics itself. For example, if brain electrical conditions for feelings of remorse were discovered, they probably would be external and not add to the understanding of what is going on in the moral field. But a psychological theory of personality development as response to certain strivings in interpersonal relations plays an internal role both in relating moral criteria to underlying objectives and in enabling us to refine criteria of authentic and inauthentic striving.

What would happen to ethics if we opened the doors to a full exploitation of its materials in scientific terms and gave full scope to the descriptive and explanatory as well as the analytic and the evaluative? It surely could be as scientific as, say, political science. Its initial phenomena are the moralities that have existed on the face of the earth. There have been thousands of these, certainly as many as or more than there have been languages. Linguistics could not flourish on merely the introspection of a few users of a few languages. Ethics similarly needs a wide descriptive base. Again it could study its phenomena functionally, just as political science studies the conditions of the rise and forms of governing and states. Political science learns a great deal from studying historical shifts, such as from authoritarian to democratic systems and the role of economic and cultural factors in such processes. So too ethics could pay closer historical attention to great moral changes and the conditions under which they happened—both material and social conditions and the growth of knowledge. Let us sample a few. The discovery of how to preserve food made possible individual accumulation and so intensified moral ideas of individual property. (John Locke points to the invention of money as making accumulation possible.) The discovery of germs as causes of disease displaced an attitude of illness as a moral punishment. (Anthropologists actually have seen this happen in the acculturation of peoples moving into the modern world.) The role of economic changes in the development of an individualistic success ethic replacing an ethics of resignation in one's allotted position is by now an old story in social history. The development of political techniques of voting and election has spread a moral idea of equality, and battery radio communication has given it a revolutionary impetus. The discovery of contraceptive techniques basically affected the relations of men and women in the family and revolutionized general attitudes toward sexual morality. The development of insurance as a social instrument eliminated many moral problems of allocating burdens and so gave a markedly different cast to problems of social justice. The growth of science itself brought a more fallibilistic attitude, almost an experimental approach, toward morality as one option.

Not only the content, structure, and changes of morality thus can be understood in a new light when approached in a spirit of scientific exploration but even the functions and concepts of morality as well. That is, ethical theorizing as philosophical reflection on morality itself becomes more self–

conscious. It is largely relating ethics to psychology and social science that raises the question of the functions of morality—how far moralities have served as an instrument of social control more refined and internalized than legal institutions, how far they have been directed toward muting aggression in society, whether their objective has been to achieve greater social solidarity or to build certain kinds of selves, or whether the picture of the moral has changed in human history, just as the picture of health has changed with the growth of medical knowledge. Analytic refinement too becomes possible when concepts are seen in relation to the contexts which beget and support them. In political science the concept of representation becomes highly refined with changing political forms and techniques of polling and rapid communication. So too in ethics a general concept of the prescriptive can be refined in the light of differences in social situations of command and advice as well as of psychological study of differences in modes of interpersonal influence; and a concept of justice can be attuned to all the investigations of the modes of distribution of gains and burdens inherent in different social structures. Even the most central ethical concepts—good, ought and duty, virtue—can be better understood and refined in the light of the concrete study of strivings and ideals, modes of inner group control, development of character. An excellent current example is the rise of the concept of human rights to a central place on the ethical stage. The very breadth of its use has produced confusion which can be cleared up only by a study of its functioning in terms of contemporary needs and problems.

The consequences of such a scientific approach extend also into normative or value judgments. We see, instead of the sharp break between the factual and evaluative, the continuity that is inherent in the learning process. As we understand better human aims, conditions, and consequences of action and learn what is possible and what is not possible in the human condition, moral reconstruction and ethical reformulation become self–conscious. Such evaluation is not peculiar to ethics; it is part of every discipline. Pure science does it in aiming at a reliable and stable account of the world and in refining its methodological objectives in the light of changing ideas of what stability lies in and similarly in decision among concepts and many of its judgments of adequacy in statistical interpretation and research policy. Engineering, medicine, and agricultural science are all evaluative in their selections and decisions. Medicine would be a strangely truncated discipline if separated from the ideal of health, and the psychiatric decision whether to use a medical concept of health or social concepts of harmonious living (a much debated issue today) is both technical and evaluative. Engineering today has to make decisions between large–scale centralized technologies and medium-dispersed ones, and this too is nonetheless a value decision for being a technical one. In political science the study of social policy and its formation and conditions and techniques is a special part of the science, and the same can be done in ethics. Moreover, just as political decisions may be shaped largely by the use of the methods and techniques elaborated in political science (which include relations to other disciplines), so moral decisions may be shaped increasingly by the use of methods and techniques of analysis and relation to empirical conditions which ethical theory can elaborate. (The rapid rise of such fields as bioethics and technological ethics today shows the need for such an approach in ethics.) Moral decision is thus applied ethics in the same sense that engineering and medicine are applied science. Perhaps in both cases this description is simplistic. What we have rather is that certain crafts or enterprises take on altered shape as they involve in their work the discoveries and developed instrumentation of the several theoretical sciences. As crafts or enterprises they have been directed to certain purposes, and they gather their assistance from the theoretical sciences with these purposes in mind. The purposes of engineering and medicine have been fairly clear. Those of ethics have not been sufficiently explored as we have seen; that is precisely because the question has not been approached in a scientific spirit.

Several different degrees of scientificality have been claimed for ethics in its history, and different strengths are possible. Interestingly the strongest claims for a science of ethics have come from scientists rather than moral philosophers. Usually these are imperialistic measures which reduce ethics to a particular science or integrate it with the scientific findings, the science having undergone a revolutionary development which has made it self-confident. In this way, after Charles Darwin, different patterns of evolution sought to lay down the lines which ethical progress must take or the biological needs it must service. Sociobiology is the most recent field to have such aspirations. On the whole, ethics proves richer than the bare bones thus captured. It is doubtful, however, that it could aspire to be a full-fledged science on its own terms insofar as physics is used as the model. That hardened stereotype insists on strict universality, rigorous deducibility, strong measurement, ample experimentation, an antihistorical attitude, as well as value neutrality. Many fields of science themselves retain their title only by courtesy on these terms, for there is much history in evolutionary biology, astronomy, and geology, not much strict universality in the social sciences, no empirical verification and experiment in mathematics, and definite values in engineering and medicine, etc.[5] It is scarcely worth asking whether ethics ever could approach such a strong degree of scientificality. It might do as well as political science in some respects or economics in others. It is premature to speculate whether,if the view of a science were released from the model of physics and different criteria developed for different kinds of materials, ethics might come to achieve moderately strong scientific status under the revised conditions. It might be the case conceivably that it is still in the position that physics was in the pre–Socratics.

A more plausible claim to scientificality would fasten on the possible use of scientific method in ethics. Of course what this consists in has not the sharpness that it was thought to have in positivistic philosophy. But doubtless a case can be made for the use in ethics of an inductive methodology as utilitarianism conceived it and even for many of its propositions being in fact so certifiable. Even affective indices may be employable, whether they invoke guilt or shame, sense of commitment or of unfairness, though they may lack the present precision of discriminated elements of sense perception as pointer readings. And if experiment in the controlled scientific sense is largely out of reach, there are the lessons of history about alternative institutions and the consequences of social change, and there may be exploratory practice that comes from trying out fresh institutional forms in a period of social change. Again, even with respect to generalization, ethics can move from a rather wholesale notion of moral law to the refinements of logic with respect to types of statements and their truth or adequacy conditions. For example, too often moral discourse does not even distinguish a strict universal purporting to hold for all cases from one that claims to be of weight in all cases but allows of being outweighed. And there are many unexplored, unusual statement forms that broaden the variety of possibilities (e.g., "Never do this, but if you do, do it in such and such a way.") Now while there is no a priori ground against the use of scientific method in ethics, how successful it would be has itself to be judged in experience. It may prove more successful in macroethical then in microethical problems or provide conditions for validation rather than decision. Even in science, scientific method is more regulative than a method of discovery.

A further plausible claim to scientificality lies in using scientific attitudes in ethics—the scientific temper in exploring problems, due consideration for evidence, social cooperation in exploring, due consideration for alternatives, receptivity to accumulation of evidence and the lessons of experience. As compared to the dogmatism and intolerance that have characterized many fields of morality, this has much to recommend it. This should not, however, be interpreted as incompatible with moral firmness or be equated with a morally indifferent relativism.

A still further claim to being scientific is of a quite different sort. It maintains that ethics is becoming increasingly dependent in its presuppositions, assumptions, operations, and equipment on the results and products of the sciences. This is in part the same sense in which urban civilization has become dependent on technological knowledge and processes in its production and consumption and life generally. It is a familiar sense in which a field may be at one point unscientific and at a later point more scientific. For example, criminology both in the understanding of crime and in the detection of crime has become more scientific: as a branch of sociology it has achieved a fuller understanding of the problems that engender criminal action, as well as the conditions of a society that determine what gets categorized as crime; and as an art of detection it has multiplied the products of science and technology that play a part in its operations. (Of course the mere use of scientific paraphernalia is not itself determinative; pseudosciences such as phrenology and racial psychology can use complex apparatus and make intricate calculations.) Perhaps the most refined sense of such dependence lies in the way in which ethical formulations contain variables whose values are furnished by the results of the sciences. For example, traditional formulations of ethics about virtues and egoism are startlingly affected by the knowledge gained in the psychological study of aggression and psychopathy, and historical study has a comparable effect on analysis of the theory of justice. Advances of this sort show that ethics is not an isolated set of beliefs or convictions but a discipline that on both its theoretical and its practical side is capable of increasing organization, is corrigible, and can establish firm relations with the generally growing body of knowledge. It thus becomes more capable of learning in experience and refining itself.

Given the rapidity of technological and social change and the growth of scientific knowledge in all directions, we may conclude that a policy of affiliating ethics with the advance of science is warranted if ethics is to carry out the functions which it has in human life.

Notes

1. See my "Toward an Analytic Method for Dealing with Moral Change," *Journal of Value Inquiry* 12 (Spring 1978): 81–99 (also in my *Exploring Fact and Value, Science, Ideology, and Value*, vol. 2 [New Brunswick, N.J.: Transaction Publishers, 1980], chap. 9).
2. See esp. John Dewey's *Human Nature and Conduct* (New York: Modern Library, 1930), pt. 4.
3. This is spelled out more fully in my *Method in Ethical Theory* (Indianapolis: Bobbs-Merrill Co., 1963), chap. 14.
4. John Rawls (*A Theory of Justice* [Cambridge, Mass.: Harvard University Press, 1971]) marks a definite break with these tendencies, for he deals in a systematic way with normative ethics and carries out analysis—all without stopping for analytic immigration inspection. The resultant structure is too imposing to gainsay its philosophical character.
5. See Max Black, "The Definition of Scientific Method" in *Science and Civilization*, ed. Robert C. Stauffer (Madison: University of Wisconsin Press, 1949), 67–95.

10

Ethical Theory in Twentieth-Century America

In this study, the historical perspective is called on to see whether it casts any light on ethical theory. The philosophy of history suggests many different patterns of possible temporal order—from an eighteenth century intellectual progress to a nineteenth century Hegelian unfolding, or a Spencerian increase in ordered complexity, or, on the other hand, a sheer chance disorder. To the modern scientific temper, there is no alternative to lining up the data and seeing what we find.

In lining up the succession of movements in ethical theory in their temporal emergence on the twentieth-century American scene, it becomes clear that a great part of their dominant emphases can best be understood in relation to the critical sociohistorical problems of their period. If so, historical study is not an extraneous interest but enhances theoretical understanding by bringing out insufficiently noted dimensions.

As the end of the century approaches, American ethical theory—like many other fields—is beginning to speculate about new directions and the task of the next century. Looking forward, however, usually involves looking back for insights from the past. When we ask how ethical theory faced its problems in the twentieth century, the soft spot in the question is to identify *its problems*. It is easy enough to record that moral philosophers debated whether ethical assertions are cognitive or noncognitive, whether morality is relative or absolute, whether any kind of verification for moral judgements is possible and if not, what is the nature of moral decision, whether human beings have rights and what they are and how justified, how ethical theories and moral rules may be applied, what is the relation of fact and value. But there is a kind of scheduling to the questions asked; there are different times in the century when they either slowly grow or suddenly occupy the philosophical horizon. The question may well be raised whether there are not specific sociohistorical problems of a given period that select from the age–old repertoire of themes in ethical theory and give them vital presence. The intellectual tools by which they are addressed are part of the prevailing epistemologies and underlying metaphysical presuppositions of the period. These too may be traced in their succession throughout the century: the conflict of idealism and naturalism in the earlier part, the almost apocalyptic entry of logical positivism in the 1930s, the spread of ordinary language analysis, the modest incursion of phenomenological and existentialist approaches and a revived and strengthened pragmatism.

Our aim here is to tell a story. Whether it is history or fable or a mixture will probably not be clear until into the next century. Its status is rather a methodological hypothesis for understanding what ethical theory has been doing. We look to the sociohistorical conditions, changes, movements, as setting underlying problems; to the epistemologies or methodologies and their metaphysical presuppositions as furnishing intellectual tools and shaping questions within ethical theory; hence to ethical theory as constituting a mode of response directed toward coping with the underlying problems, offering guidance to morality and moral decision.

The drama of ethical theory in twentieth–century America may be written in five acts, followed by an epilogue. It opens in the first third of the century with attempts to fashion a *general theory of value;* though there are opposing answers and interpretations there is agreement on the generality. It is succeeded in the 1930s and early 1940s by intense debate over *emotivism* and *ethical relativism.* Then, beginning in the late 1940s and growing in theoretical strength both in formal ethics and in closely adjoining fields of social and legal philosophy, comes the outburst of a *rights ethic* which overshadows traditional schools. Systematic normative ethics is revived at the beginning of the 1970s, accompanied by a vigorous refurbishing of traditional ethical theories. The last act of the century (although there is still time for surprises) is the almost wildfire spread of *applied ethics* which showed itself in the late 1960s, became widespread in the 1970s, and began to search for its systematic foundations in the 1980s. We are now in the epilogue, where Hegel's comparison to the owl of Minerva taking its flight at the dusk seems appropriate: reflective consideration of the impact of applied ethics and the search for new directions. (Of course the epilogue may be drawn out into an additional act.)

So much for the synopsis or program notes. The account itself has to pinpoint the sociohistorical development, exhibit the philosophical tools, and indicate how they were used. Its reference to names and works is selective sampling from an impressive array of actors, not to speak of the extended chorus, sagely commenting.

Philosophy in the first third of the century is fundamentally concerned with a response to the still recent Darwinian revolution. One wing regards the "naturalizing" of the human being as progress in the growth of knowledge and sees its task as carrying this through for all the works of the spirit—from the intellectual and scientific through the moral and aesthetic and religious. The opposing wing is ready to accept evolution for nature but insists on some mark of spirit that sets it off from the natural world. Its candidate turns out to be a *general concept of value*, traced through knowledge as well as the growth of selfhood and the exercice of will. (cf. Urban, 1909; and the idealist philosophers generally). The naturalizing wing sets off by broadening ethics into the organization of life's *interests* (or natural impulses and drives) and develops into an evolutionary picture of the human scene. R. B. Perry's work best illustrates the development (1909, 1926). In 1913 the American Philosophical Association, planning its annual meeting, invited philosophers to address the concept of value in relation to the nature of things and fundamental standards. Thereafter, value almost replaces the distinctively ethical concept of *good*, while *right* and *obligation* become the distinctive marks of the moral as a species of value.

Dewey promptly answered the Association's invitation, and continued the inquiry for three decades. Among moral philosophers he was most conscious of the social roots of value theory. He saw the rise of industrialism as changing people's mode of life and presenting new problems; he challenged Americans to face these creatively with institutional innovation and intelligent reconstruction. He resisted the fixities (and abstract catalogue of goods) that lurked under the concept of *intrinsic value* and argued for the primacy of *valuation* and *evaluation* as dealing with situations in which habitual patterns failed to provide answers and human decision was required (cf. Dewey, 1939). In his ethical writings (cf. Dewey and Tufts, 1932) he called for utilizing knowledge from all fields of science and history to assist responsible decision. Moreover he did not reduce ethical concepts to an homogenized idea of value, but stressed the variety of contexts and conceptual tools involved in evaluating. Interestingly, a well worked out program for this was first presented in a lecture he gave in France on November 7, 1930 (Dewey, 1984).

The emphasis on evaluation had strong social roots in current developments. With growing industrialization the area of individual choice was broadened both in the greater variety of commodities and in the wider range of individual liberties. Hence selection and comparative evaluation were unavoidable; this required more general standards. In addition, economic theory in its treatment of exchange value (as distinguished from use value, which only provided entry for the commodity into the market) removed commodities from their relation to specific uses and viewed them only as sources of monetary operations; thus economic value itself got a generic character.

Discussion of ethics in the 1930s and 1940s reflected the consequences of the general theory of value. Theoretical questions were asked in generic form, calling for wholesale answers to such inquiries as the cognitive or noncognitive character of ethical judgement, the possibility of verifying ethical statements, absolute or relative standards for morals. What is more, ethical theory was expected to answer such questions on its own, as an isolated discipline independent of knowledge in other fields and relying on its own intellectual resources. This isolation of ethics (regarded as *autonomy*) had been put forward in Britain by G.E. Moore (in his *Principia Ethica*, 1903), and it became influential in America in the 1930s. Moore argued that any definition of *good* (intrinsic value) in descriptive (scientific or metaphysical or religious) terms was a *naturalistic fallacy*; for example, if we identify the good with pleasure, it is always possible to ask meaningfully whether pleasure itself is good, and so we indicate that the idea of the good has a *surplus* meaning beyond pleasure. The effect of this was to make all judgements of intrinsic value ultimately intuitive.

Moore's thesis was reflected in the dominant emphasis on the autonomy of ethical theory for almost four decades in America. But the specific shape that ethical theory took in the 1930s and 1940s was prompted by the spectacular entry of logical positivism, emanating from Vienna and popularized by A.J. Ayer's *Language, Truth and Logic* (1936). In America, Stevenson, building on its sharp division of the analytic (logical and linguistic), the empirical or factual (scientific, verifiable ultimately in sensory terms), and the attitudinal (affective, feeling and emotion), developed the *emotive theory of ethics* (Stevenson, 1944). This interpreted the surplus element in the meaning of value judgements as expressive of emotion and as effort toward persuasion. "X is good" was modelled as "I approve of X; do so thou." A sharp distinction was made between ethical theory *(metaethics)* whose task was analyzing ethical discourse to make its meaning clearer by using logical–linguistic tools, and *normative* or substantive ethics which was not regarded as scientific or even more generally cognitive; moral judgements could thus not be verified, since there was nothing to prove. This resulted from a focus on ultimate disagreement in values. Here analysis ended in the effort to persuade as causal process. Dewey's call for intelligence and knowledge in addressing social problems was regarded as simply attitudinal advocacy of a democratic–rational outlook, hence itself ultimately emotive.

This almost total concentration on ultimate disagreement was paralleled in the social science of the day by the discussion of cultural and ethical relativism (e.g., Ruth Benedict's *Patterns of Culture*, 1934). Ethical relativism remained a widespread topic in American moral philosophy from the 1930s through the 1950s, discussed usually in relation to anthropology (cf. Brandt, 1954; Ladd, 1957; Edel and Edel, 1959). Looking back, it seems clear that these themes in moral philosophy and social science constituted a responsive grappling with the major social problems of the 1930s and early 1940s— conflicts of social outlooks and World War II. The opposition of capitalism and socialism after the Russian revolution of 1917, the rise of fascism in Italy in the 1920s and of nazism in Germany in the early 1930s made the question of how to deal with ultimate disagreements in both theory and practice the vital social issue of the time. People differed on whether a rational decision was possible or whether there could be only nonrational persuasion or actual coercion and war. And even in victory was there a rational justification or only an historical–causal turn?

With the end of the war, however, came gradual changes in the tenor of moral philosophy. Two are particularly marked. One is a methodological shift in ethics, from logical positivism to ordinary language (Oxford) analysis. The other is the emergence of a rights ethics, which begins more in the realm of practice and conquers the realm of theory. Each has its own story.

The first change often went unmarked, obscured by the continuities. Ethical theory was still conceived as metaethics, divorced from the empirical or scientific on the one side and from normative moral judgement of practice on the other. What changed was the mode of analysis. Positivism had seen ordinary language as incorporating the errors of the past and had set its heart on large-scale formal systems, constructed in a logical scientific spirit— prompting the development of deontic logic and the logic of preference. The new method (imported from England) embraced a veneration of ordinary language and its uses, carried in ethics far beyond the emotive. Ordinary language, as J. L. Austin declared, embodied the growth of ages, the collective experience; logical–linguistic analysis of its contexts of use clarified the tangles in which undue abstractions embroiled philosophers. It was a kind of Common Law model in which—reminiscent of Coke and the lawyers in the seventeenth century arguing against the King who wanted simply to decide by exercising his own reason—the philosophers were the specialists by long and arduous cultivation. In America, the ordinary language mode of philosophizing rapidly became popular in ethics and epistemology alike.

Several methodological changes were brought about by this movement. For one thing, it was particularistic: it did not give sweeping theoretical answers, but contextual ones. Thus it did not ask for the meaning of ethical terms like "good," "right," "ought," etc. but probed very specific uses. For example, it did not ask for the meaning of "ought" but for analysis of "I ought," "you ought," "he ought," and usually found them different (e.g., Paul W. Taylor, 1961). In America the analytic movement accordingly undid the work of general theory of value, moving always towards the specific and not to higher levels of generality. Since its answers were pluralistic, ethical terms were not assigned a single function, as emotive theory had fixed on the expressive–persuasive. Ethical terms could carry out a whole variety of functions, as different as prescriptive, advisory, expressive, and performatory; some, however, attempted to make the prescriptive into a generic mark. The distinction between prescribing and describing was strictly maintained (though the overall distinction of fact and value was sometimes scorned as generality) and any attempt to see ethics as descriptive was opposed. Hence for the most part ethics was approached in an activist mood, from the point of view of the agent, not that of the observer or reporter. And throughout, the contexts on which the analysis focused were linguistic contexts; there was no attempt to move into practical contexts, with their many dimensions of the psychological, social, cultural, historical. Indeed for the most part even historical linguistic change was not dealt with, nor the development of technical language. This mode of analysis in ethics remained central for several decades, and in some respects continued as a permanent stratum even after it lost its dominant status.

During this period too, starting shortly after World War II, phenomenology and existentialism seeped into the American scene. Phenomenology stressed direct experience and its meanings. Opposing the behaviorist concern with merely acts, it found no relativism once different situational meanings were grasped (e.g., Duncker, 1939), and it revelled in the wealth of values rather than in rationalistic principles. Existentialism—particularly Sartre's ideas forged under the experience of the French resistance—helped recast ethics from the agent's point of view and enhanced the importance of individual decision and responsibility as against inference from antecedent principles. Again, from a quite different angle on the American scene, decision theory, especially as it began to deal with the complex relation of probabilities and value orderings under conditions of uncertainty and risk, pointed in a similar direction.

Rights theory in ethics had a quite different career. It emerged clearly in America only after the United Nations Universal Declaration of Human Rights. This concept was soon invoked in the successive liberation movements of Blacks, women, handicapped, homosexuals, as well as the general effort to overcome racism and ethnocentrism in favor of universal human dignity. In the Carter presidency of the late 1970s, the concept played its part in international relations to condemn practices of torture and repression, and throughout it was continually invoked in the practical operations of civil rights and civil liberties organizations and such specifically human rights organizations as Amnesty International. The concept of human rights has thus played a practical social role. It did not move into American moral philosophy till it was well launched in practice. It first affected social and legal philosophy, and gradually—in part with the growing interest in legal philosophy among professional philosophers—invaded analytic ethics. During the 1970s and 1980s the human rights concept became a major contender in basic ethical theory: rights laid claim not only to constitute a sizable portion of the content of ethics, but to be either the basic theoretical foundation idea in ethics or, if associated with concepts of the good and well-being, to be independent and not derived from them.

The sociohistorical roots of this remarkable career in twentieth-century America are fairly evident in outline, though require intellectual–historical research for detail. The role of natural rights in seventeenth–century Britain (in the Cromwellian period) and in the American and French revolutions of the eighteenth century is familiar enough. For the greater part of the later nineteenth and early twentieth century, we hear less about rights than about the public good or the general welfare. This seems to be a function of several phenomena: a reaction against the excesses of the French Revolution; during the nineteenth and into the twentieth century, the ascendancy of Utilitarianism in the ethical theory of liberalism, particularly with John Stuart Mill and his influence; then up to World War II, the major use of the concept for conservative defense of property and freedom of contract. The net result was that theories of public welfare became the ethical banners under which reform and social progress were sought. A clear instance in the United States was the battle for the New Deal in the 1930s: the rights concept had appeared most prominently in the conservative Supreme Court decisions striking down social welfare legislation. After World War II the scene changed drastically. The human sufferings of the war, the intolerable injustices of nazism, the promises of better times that had supported desperate populations, all combined to make sharp demands for all people. The probable greatest happiness of the greatest number seemed inadequate; in America it was clearly tied to the general prosperity of the now renascent capitalism of the majority, not to the plight of submerged and repressed minorities. The libertarian movements of the late 1950s and 1960s and the popular resistance to the Vietnam War stirred the youth of the land, and worked its ways into the professional thought of philosophy.

Analytic work on rights theory was further prompted by the outbreak of controversy about the content of rights. While major agreement existed on their extension into social and economic rights as well as their traditional place in civil and political rights—as during the Johnson presidency on the hope of "the great society"—theoretical consideration of the underlying basis of rights had no immediate impact. But with the reawakening of a conservative atmosphere, an intellectual revolt surfaced against the new rights in favor of the more traditional property rights (cf. Nozick, 1974). Disagreement about specific rights made underlying theory more important. A large part of the writing in ethical theory was then devoted to the analysis of rights, different underlying bases, contrast of rights theory with utilitarianism and other theories. This remains a continuing enterprise (e.g., Dworkin, 1977, 1978; Held, 1984; Wellmann, 1982, 1985).

The general character of work in ethical theory changed strikingly in the early 1970s. A large share of this centered around John Rawls' *A Theory of Justice* (1971). Its impact came from several features. In content, it yielded a liberal theory of rights, so extended in its equalitarianism as to be a major object of attack in the conservative reaction. In structure the theory of justice was built on foundations independent of the theory of the good, and so was aligned with the Kantian or deontological wing of ethical theory. In specific theory, however, Rawls revived a *contractarian* approach, with marked Hobbesian overtones—individualistic in its bases, though deriving a social approach through technical analysis of the convergence of individual calculations. The broad scope and multiple theses provoked widespread analysis among both moral philosophers and social scientists. Not the least of its revolutionary effects in moral philosophy was that the book dealt as a whole explicitly with normative or substantive ethics, quietly shunting aside without argument the whole tradition of the isolation of ethical theory that had characterized both logical positivism and ordinary language analysis. It thus in effect closed a chapter in the history of twentieth–century ethics on the American scene. By its stature and its success it gave implicit professional permission for moral philosophers to give greater attention to two traditional occupations: reconstruct more systematically traditional ethical theories, and deal with specific normative judgments, even to the point of making them.

The resurgence of competing large-scale ethical theories became prominent in the 1970s. Critical studies of elements in traditional systems had not, of course, ceased in the interval, though they tended to be piecemeal. Indeed, there were partial analytic experiments in bringing together ideas from different sources, such as rule obedience from the Kantian tradition and calculation of happiness from the Utilitarian (cf. Lyons, 1965). But now, beyond the newer Rawlsian contractarianism we may note in America a much evolved Utilitarianism, a refined Rationalism, and an expanding naturalistic pragmatism.

Utilitarianism coped with an inner split between act and rule utilitarianism. Its subjectivism of pleasure had long been reduced to preferences. What remained was its strong individualism in its foundations and its hope of issuing in a social ethic. The latter, which after all had been a prime objective in Bentham and Mill—to build a firm approach to social policy on individual liberties—was subjected to critical "horror stories" showing how pursuit of the greatest well–being of the greatest number would yield counterintuitive individual frustrations. And yet this showed little more in theory than that it would need supplementation and clearer articulation of the jurisdiction in which individual life aims were legitimate moral criteria. A comprehensive reassessment, with refined psychological criteria, was worked out by Brandt (1979).

A revived Rationalist ethics stayed with a Kantian-like derivation of ratio-nal unavoidable principles. Perhaps the most widespread basic principle, especially prominent after the outrages of the war period, was that of human dignity, the intrinsic worth of the person. A rationalist ethic had the task of providing a foundation for this principle and showing that it would both yield the rights and obligations usually accepted in the existing morality and furnish a way of refining ideas and resolving disputes of the time. For example, Gewirth (1978) begins with the generic features of agency—prospective purposiveness—and sets down the principle that, given universalizability entailed in reason, everyone in claiming freedom and well-being accepts similar rights for others. From this he winds his way to applications in specific domains.

Meanwhile, a sophisticated pragmatism was emerging, found less in cen-tral texts than in a growing utilization throughout ethical theory of the various lessons that a pragmatic-naturalistic philosophy had accumulated through the century. With Dewey, it recognized the importance of social and technologi-cal change as a matrix, and the centrality of the specific problem at any point in providing the criteria for adequacy of solution in moral decision. With C.I. Lewis it could accept not only the empirical character of judgements of value (1946) but the way in which rules of rightness are involved in all thought, whether logical or scientific, and all action, whether prudential or justicial (1955). In firmly distancing itself from positivism in ethics it could reject the isolation of the logical, the empirical, the valuational, and look for the place of scientific knowledge in rendering moral judgements more determinate (cf. Pepper, 1958; Edel, 1955, 1980). In such recognition it revised the dogma of the separation of fact and value that had had a strong hold on both moral philosophy and social science in the twentieth century and incorporated the lesson of the psychology of William James that experience itself is pur-posively selective in both its sensory and conceptual ordering, and the lesson of Peirce's original insight that meaning is practical and experimental. In sum, there was an organized effort to relate theory and practice.

This central effort has been remarkably advanced by the development of ''applied ethics'' which gathered strength for almost two decades and now has an unshakeable place. Casuistry, of course, was an old pursuit; judicial decision was predominantly seen as applied law, and codes of professional ethics a traditional practice. But the rapidity and intensity of the growth of applied ethics was a response to novel situations, many of which were the result of the new technologies. For example, kidney dialysis and organ transplant techniques raised the problem of choice among patients for scarce resources; on a broad front artificial prolongation of life became practical. A greater sensitivity precipitated wide discussion of the treatment of death and the dying patient. Increase in malpractice suits sharpened questions of responsibility. From many directions what had formerly been the narrower field of medical ethics grew into a burgeoning field of *bioethics*, so large as in a short time to produce a specialized encyclopedia (Reich, 1978). The same process went on in many fields. Problems of pollution, responsibility for health in the workplace, conflicts of narrower (e.g., corporate) loyalties with broader social obligations, gave greater urgency to traditional problems of business ethics or legal ethics. Highly visible conflicts—over the morality of the Vietnam War or the issues of Watergate—underscored moral aspects of public policy and political action.

This turn to applied ethics was forced on moral philosophy by the persistent pressure of practical needs. Indeed a large part of the philosophical profession, under the isolationist influence of analytic ethics, had insisted on the aloofness of theory from practice. The moral philosopher, it was argued, had no special expertise in practical decision; at best his/her strength lay in analyzing questions. Nevertheless, all over the country institutes and centers arose dealing with applied ethics and social policy, and publication in the field grew rapidly. The reticence of analytic philosophy had at least this consequence, that answers in practical problems were not expected from philosophers alone—as in older times they had been expected from religious leaders. Exploration of applied ethics became largely a matter for cooperative interdisciplinary action. The paradigm case is perhaps the interdisciplinary committees in hospitals that advise on immediate problems of moral choice, often with life and death in the balance.

Two different trends were discernible in applied ethics. One, looking upon ethical theory as self–sufficient prior to application to practical problems, saw application almost as substituting values for the variables in a formula to get a decision for the case. Textbooks in applied or professional ethics often devoted a first part to different ethical theories and a second to analyses of practical moral problems in the light of the different theories. Presumably the reader would choose a favored theory and derive consequent solutions, or else become appreciative of the importance of theory resolution. The second trend saw application as a much more complex process in which theory itself was put to the test for adequacy and in which theory brought out dimensions of the practical situation and practice furnished lessons for refinement or revision of theory. Such a view of the close and yet complex interrelations of theory and practice raises vital and fresh questions about the nature and functions of ethical theories. It begins to see them less as alternative self–sufficient formulae to dictate practice and more as presenting different perspectives to illuminate problems and multiply the dimensions of inquiry. A further consequence of facing the challenge of applied ethics in the latter way and recognizing the need for interdisciplinary approach to practical moral problems is to show the need for assessing the place of knowledge, especially scientific knowledge, within the very structure and operations of ethical theory.

As these two philosophical issues—the relation of theory and practice and the place of material knowledge within ethical theory—emerged on the agenda of ethical theory, it was not surprising that by the mid-1980s the question of new directions in ethics as a consequence of experience with applied ethics was being consciously raised (e.g. DeMarco and Fox, 1986). At the present time ethical theory stands at a crossroads and has to determine the character of its future work. It is this situation that prompts especially self-consciousness about ethics in the receding century.

The paper was prepared for a special issue of the *Revue française d'Études américaines* (1987) that was devoted to current American philosophy.

References

Brandt, Richard B., *Hopi Ethics* (Chicago: University of Chicago Press, 1954). *A Theory of the Good and the Right* (New York: Oxford University Press, 1979).

De Marco, Joseph P. and Fox, Richard M., *New Directions in Ethics: The Challenge of Applied Ethics* (New York and London: Routledge & Kegan Paul, 1986).

Dewey, John, *Theory of Valuation* (Chicago: University of Chicago Press, 1939.) "Trois facteurs indépendants en matière de morale", 1930. English translation in *John Dewey, The Later Works*, Vol. 5, (Carbondale: Southern Illinois University Press), pp. 279–88 and Appendix 5, 1984.

Dewey, John and Tufts, James H., *Ethics*, revised edition, 1932. (In *John Dewey, The Later Works*, vol. 7). (Carbondale: University of Southern Illinois Press, 1985).

Duncker, Karl, "Ethical Relativity? (An Inquiry into the Psychology of Ethics)," *Mind*, New Series, vol. 48, January 1939.

Dworkin, Ronald, *Taking Rights Seriously* (Cambridge, Mass: Harvard University Press, 1977, 1978).

Edel, Abraham, *Ethical Judgement: The Use of Science in Ethics*, (Glencoe, Ill.; The Free Press, 1955). *Exploring Fact and Value, Science, Ideology, and Value*, vol. II (New Brunswick, USA and London UK: Transaction Publishers, 1980).

Edel, May and Edel, Abraham, *Anthropology and Ethics* (Springfield, Ill.: Charles C. Thomas, 1959; rev. ed.: New Brunswick, N.J.: Transaction Publishers, 1970).

Gewirth, Alan, *Reason and Morality*, (Chicago: University of Chicago Press, 1978).

Held, Virginia, *Rights and Goods: Justifying Social Action* (New York: Free Press, 1984).

Ladd, John, *The Structure of A Moral Code* (Cambridge, Mass.: Harvard University Press, 1957).

Lewis, C.I., *An Analysis of Knowledge and Valuation*, (LaSalle, Ill.: Open Court, 1946). *The Ground and Nature of the Right*, (New York: Columbia University Press, 1955).

Lyons, David, *Forms and Limits of Utilitarianism* (Oxford: Clarendon Press 1965).

Nozick, Robert, *Anarchy, State, and Utopia*, (New York: Basic Books, 1974).

Pepper, Stephen, *The Sources of Value* (Berkeley: University of California Press, 1958).

Perry, Ralph Barton, *The Moral Economy*, (New York: Charles Scribner's Sons, 1909). *General Theory of Value* (New York: Longmans, Green, and Co., 1926.)

Rawls, John, *A Theory of Justice*, (Cambridge Mass.: The Belknap Press of Harvard University Press, 1971.)

Reich, Warren T., editor, *Encyclopedia of Bioethics* (New York: Free Press 1978).

Stevenson, C.L., *Ethics and Language*, (New Haven: Yale University Press 1944).

Taylor, Paul W., *Normative Discourse*, (Englewood Cliffs, N.J.: Prentice Hall, 1961.)

Urban, Wilbur Marshall, *Valuation, Its Nature and Laws*, being an Introduction to the General Theory of Value (New York: Macmillan, 1909).

Wellman, Carl, *Welfare Rights* (Totowa, N.J.: Rowman and Littlefield, 1982). *A Theory of Rights: persons under laws, institutions, and morals*, (Totowa, N.J.: Rowman and Allanheld, 1985)

11

Form: The Philosophic Idea
and Some of Its Problems

This paper, written with artist Jean Francksen, was prepared for a special issue of VIAS (The Journal of the Graduate School of Fine Arts, University of Pennsylvania), 1982. It followed the double track of the development of the idea of form in the history of philosophy, thus exhibiting its thematic content, and the uses of the idea in the various reflections within the arts, particularly painting and architecture. This cooperative approach revealed both the kind of coherence to be found in the concept, and the multiplicity and limits of its aesthetic instrumentality.

Form is one of the most difficult and provocative ideas in the philosophic repertoire. In one sense it is extremely simple; in another, complex beyond comparison. It had a fascinating career in philosophy, where it took its bow, but it has been enriched and entangled during its subcareers in the multitude of arts and sciences and even in the perception, purposive activity, and planning of ordinary life. It is maintained, even when not analyzed, by the human tendency to find order, or to create order, in every human sensing or thinking endeavor. And it is usually given some meaning by the particular context of inquiry or action, even while attempts to give it a general meaning may precipitate intellectual floundering. Features associated with various types of order often cling to *form*, and it is occasionally associated, sometimes disastrously, with dichotomies: material–immaterial, static–dynamic, concrete–abstract, sensory–conceptual, and others. This is because there is a tendency for order to drift away in Platonic fashion from that of which it is the order, and when it grasps this illusory freedom its career usually narrows to that abstraction—for example, the static or the intellectual—of which it has become enamored.

The remarks that follow will attempt to clarify the idea of *form* through examination of the cluster of features that characterized its philosophical genesis in Plato and Aristotle. From this we can untangle a number of issues on which science and art and thought in general have at times taken different paths, and we can try to illustrate what is at stake in these issues from discussions of divergent tendencies in the arts.

Classical Greek Genesis

While the earlier pre–Socratics were looking for a basic matter to which *all that is* might be reduced (water, fire, an indeterminate stuff), the Pythagoreans turned their attention to numbers (and so to abstract ideas) as the key to understanding harmony in music, relations in space, the movement of the heavens, the balance of elements in health, even the nature of justice and the explanation of significant differences in the world and life. From these beginnings, particularly after Socrates had focused on ideas and on how to clarify them in dialectical discussion, Plato fashioned the more general notion of the *eidos*, the idea or form. It is an imposing theory, expressing the convergence of insight in one field after another: linguistics, physics, mathematics, logic, epistemology, metaphysics, psychology, ethics, art. The bulk of language, he saw, consists of terms that are general, and to understand their meaning is to grasp these general ideas. Physical science aims at universals and laws; its explanations give the governing generalities that particular phenomena exemplify. Mathematics, whether in the arithmetical manipulation of numbers or in the deduction of properties of geometrical figures, deals with fixed ideal objects, not with the shifting material things that may suggest them to the mind. Logic provides ideal standards for the mind to derive the implications of what is asserted, and in the search for definitions it looks for the essential as distinct from the accidental. (Form thus provides the essence.) Epistemology, analyzing the nature of knowledge, distinguishes the flux of beliefs from the grasp of the truth; truth is an ideal of the correct and the unchanging. To know what is true is thus to grasp the real (the concern of what is later called metaphysics), and that real is eternal and unchanging, as contrasted with the flux of phenomena all about us. In psychological processes, it is the intellect or reason or thought that grasps the invariant, while the senses present the changing material world. In ethics, we seek rational standards and pursue eternal ideals, which we can use as a basis for criticizing existent ways. In art, both in creation and appreciation, there is a form or idea behind each work, and a grasp of the form guides the hand or mind of the artist and the apprehension of the beholder; beauty itself is the glimmer of the form.

Putting all these principles together, Plato saw forms as the eternal realities at the root of all that is. They are universal, not particular; eternal, not changing; intellectual, not sensible; the objects of knowledge, not of belief. They are immaterial, not material. They are sources of explanation, of meaning, of standards for conduct, of genuine pleasure and of beauty. Much of Plato's philosophical endeavor was directed to systematizing the relations of forms and trying to understand their natures. It is not surprising that in *The School of Athens* Raphael has Plato pointing upward toward a heaven away from the earthly.

Aristotle provides a quite different career for form.[1] Some notion of form is inescapable—Plato's insights into the many disciplines and their structures are not to be gainsaid—but they add up in a different way in Aristotle's philosophy. Aristotle started with a conceptual apparatus in which matter and form are correlative; they refer respectively to the materials and the organization of some situation or product. The distinction is involved in his theory of explanation, the familiar analysis of his four "causes," according to which the factors responsible for anything are: (i) the material cause, the out–of–which the thing is composed, like the bronze out of which the statue is made; (ii) the formal cause, the way the material is organized, an account of which would give its "essence"; (iii) the efficient cause or the moving cause that precipitates the thing's formation, like the advisor for the action, the father for the child, the sculptor for the statue; (iv) the final cause or the for–the–sake–of–which the happening takes place, the end or goal (*telos*) toward which the happening is moving. Aristotle's conception of form absorbs three of these causes—all but the material cause—and the process of absorption shows us the threads in his finished conception.

The final and the formal are assimilated in a teleological view of things and processes. While in the special domain of human affairs, the goal may be projected beyond the form—the statue may be created for a religious setting or for private honor—in the broader domains of nature the final cause is the mature development of the form itself in the specific materials. The acorn grows into an oak tree and its end is to express in its career what it is to be an oak, that is, its form. In general, nature works like the artist; the accounts of craft production and biological process in Aristotle are not far apart. Given the absorption of final within formal, it follows that the functional is contained within the meaning of a thing, and any separation of form and function simply shows that function is taken in too narrow a sense.

A way in which efficient and formal cause are brought together has a startling metaphysical outcome. Aristotle generalizes from such phenomena as adults' generation of children and something's becoming hot by action of something else that is already hot to the proposition that the efficient cause is always some activity *of the same type as that which the mature form manifests*. (The actual is prior to the potential.) This gives a continuity and fixity to the form. New forms do not emerge out of some cosmic or human creation. The form, existent in actual materials, repeats itself into fresh existents (if a house were to grow by nature, says Aristotle, it would do it in the way the architect builds it). On the other hand, there are occasional signs of a form's coming to maturity over an historical period, just as the adult comes to maturity; Aristotle's best example is his discussion of tragedy's achieving its completion in the Athens of the classical period.

Form in Aristotle has thus, while remaining bound to matter, moved from being simply an organization or a structure to being a *culminating design*, achieved or maintained, in a world of continuity and repetition. This is not, however, the end of the Aristotelian conception. At a critical point in his *Metaphysics*, Aristotle carries out a further assimilation: he fuses the concept–set of matter and form with that of potentiality and actualization. Form is the actualizing of the potentialities in the matter, since there is no separate form. (Only in Aristotle's theology does God appear as pure form or pure actuality, but this idea is not used for specific explanations in the world.) Hence form takes on an individual character; the universal is simply an intellectual abstraction of the form. The form of man is, in effect, the life that he leads, in which his specific potentialities are becoming actualized; it is his structured or patterned living. There are, of course, many forms—witness the species of animals—and the relations of individuals living out these forms is full of accidental happenings. The form thus provides the *essential* as contrasted with the accidental or *incidental*. In general, the assimilation of matter–form with potentiality-actualization imparts a dynamic character to form. Not only motion and change but even unchanging existence in which the form is the full actualization gets this dynamic tinge. Things are active—they do not just exist. The marble before us, as an existing statue, is thus a type of actualization, just as much as is its being made into a statue. If we asked the marble statue what it was doing, it could almost reply, in Sartrean fashion, "I am busy at work being a statue."

The Platonic view of form is thus reversed. The form is in the particular, in its organization and function; it is not separate from the material, but is the actualization of that material's potentialities. It is individual, not universal, although it is universalizable. It is grasped in thought, yet this occurs on the basis of sensory experience; such grasp gives us what is essential for each of the many forms we encounter and enables us to see the meaning when we speak of the form, seeing through the maze of incidentals. The eternity of the forms lies in their continued exemplification in the world; there is no evolutionary change in forms; they are what they are. But there can be a shaping of existence to embody a given form, and a coming to maturity in the lives and thought of artists and craftsmen that gives expression to the form.

What, then, are themes that the Aristotelian conception of form articulates that are relevant to the theory of the arts?

The general idea dominating Aristotle's work on form is that form has a guiding role in the arts and in nature. There is always a guiding idea working its way through the processes of art, in both creation and appreciation. This is the distinctive note, over and above commonsensical elements such as the idea of shape and processes of shaping or the descriptive notion of *order*, no matter how numerous the near-synonyms that cluster around that idea (e.g., *pattern, structure, design, composition, organization,* or *relations*).

The guiding idea enables us to distinguish in a particular, whether of science or of art, what is essential and what is incidental. The incidental is what could have been otherwise, the essential is what is fundamental and invariant.

The way in which the form guides processes of nature and art is—since the actual is prior to the potential—a tight governance, just as the program guides the technical process in the functioning of computers or as the genes guide the development and maturation of the organism. To understand human activity and creation we have to find where in experience the form is grasped or locked into place to gain this guiding position.

Under the guidance of form the potentialities of specific materials are actualized or the matter transformed. There is thus a close relation between the opportunities that complex materials provide and the character and meaning of the artistic product.

The form is to be dynamically conceived both on the creative side, in which the materials are being transformed under the guidance of the idea, and on the receptive side, in which the potentialities of experience are being actualized in the apprehension of the form.

There is a rich variety of forms, and these forms are not to be subsumed under some general idea, as if their role were simply to lure us on to some unified goal. Each is its own end, and there is an ultimate pluralism in spite of accidental crossings and cross-purposes. In that sense, the grasping of a form has a final or intrinsic character.

At bottom, form and matter are relative to one another. What is form in one context can be regarded as matter for some other form in some fresh context; and what is matter can be seen as form in some lower–level analysis. They remain intelligible as long as they are inseparable.

Before going to the theory of the arts, let us remind ourselves that such themes, stemming from classical conceptions of form, have not gone unchallenged in the later history of philosophy. For example, Cartesian dualism separates body and mind, the physical and the immaterial, and reopens the doors to an independent realm of ideas and meanings whose nature is not an expression of material potentialities. Again, Aristotelian pluralism is transformed by Hegel into an idealistic monism: the totality is the only real individual, and so the ultimate Idea is the rational pattern of its historical development. (When we grasp that Idea, we see the unfolding that determines what kind of art will have significance at each step—what, as it were, is appropriate to the Spirit of the Age.) Other philosophies tackle not the pluralism, but the fixity and essentialism of the Aristotelian forms. The idea of the creative as something boiling up in the stew of nature and the human spirit, not bound by previous forms or essences but seeing or fashioning new ones, is a conception that builds upon the slow seeping into the modern temper of evolutionary ideas and an open world. Aristotle said that Plato was too impressed by Heraclitus' view that all is in flux and therefore turned away too quickly from the material world to the objects of knowledge. Aristotle himself assumed a more orderly world and could therefore keep his gaze on its well–regulated processes. Darwin, in providing an explanation for the origin of species, put onto the broader metaphysical level a view of the origin and transformation of forms in relation to the conditions of historical existence. In modern times pragmatic philosophies thus abandoned the static view of knowledge that Aristotle retained. Emphasizing change, probabilism, and construction, they opened the world to give form the ebullient career in a changing world that it can now have. This strikes hardest at the Aristotelian (and Platonic) idea of the prior actuality of form and turns attention to artistic creation as a less–than–regulated process in which a new form is being fashioned, and not merely a prior form embodied. Nevertheless, in spite of these historical shifts there is much to be gained from looking at the notion of form in relation to its classical genesis, for many of the features of the original notion have persisted. In what follows we want therefore to ask several questions about the arts.

First, does it make sense to sort out the essential from the incidental?

If the essential is what is tied to the form, then to discern the form in a work of art involves sorting out the essential from the incidental. On the other hand, the attempt to separate essence and accident was developed originally (in Aristotle's philosophy) for science; the form is the governing law, universal and abstract in statement, that enables us to understand and find our way in the richly detailed particular. It enables us—to take a standard example from Aristotle—to realize that having eyes is structural, while their color is an incidental item. It may therefore turn out that the attempt to distinguish essence and accident in art is applying categories of science to art and yielding trivial if not wholly irrelevant results. What do we accomplish if in analyzing a painting we declare the fact of eyes to be essential, and the fact that they are gray–green to be incidental? Suppose, however, the eyes are emerald green. Might this not be significant if the green–eyed person is to be exhibiting intense envy, or if it be a Kelly green and the picture is entitled *Hues of St. Patrick's Day?* Would the green of the eyes then be essential to the guiding idea of the picture? And if so, are there not many ways in which an item in the work could become essential and thus become a guiding idea? For example, the red of the grass in Gauguin's *Jacob and the Angel* might be thought to be essential to that picture because it has an organizing role in the color composition.

Such examples have little to do with the original Aristotelian distinction, since that meant by the essential the invariant and necessary, whereas envy obviously can be conveyed in many different or contingent ways. The examples are thus rather concerned with the differences in the significance of the incidentals in relation to the guiding idea of the work. While the distinction of the essential and the incidental may therefore seem inapplicable to the arts, there are clearly kindred or parallel issues worth exploring. For example, disputes about what is ornament and what is not, or how a theme permeates a construction (such as how a specific religious story or doctrine permeates a cathedral or the myths of Athena give a tight unity to the Parthenon) are of this type.

The interesting issue for art that arises from attempts to distinguish the essential from the incidental is the multiplicity of linkages that are possible between the detailed parts or items of a work and the form as a guiding idea. Now, ideas are more or less general or abstract, while particulars are richly detailed. An item in the particular is linked to the form if it gets its meaning from the guiding idea or somehow enhances the form. This presupposes, however, that we have an assured and articulated knowledge of the form from the outset. It may often be the case that the reverse holds: the testing of different linkages between the form and the detail of the work of art is itself helping us to discern and build up the form. Hence the recognition of linkages is itself the determination of the form. This seems to us the most significant outcome of a distinction between the essential and the incidental. It is also important to note how varied the types of linkage may be—logical, psychological, intellectual, sensory, affective, cultural–historical, and even symbolic (grounded in conventions of the art and its development).

There is a quite different aspect to our present concern that appears when we find the claim that everything in a successful work of art is essential to its being what it is. When Vollard pointed out to Cézanne two tiny spots of uncovered canvas in his portrait, Cézanne replied: "You understand, Monsieur Vollard, if I should put there something haphazard, I should be compelled to do my whole picture over, starting from that place."[2] It is quite conceivable that some works of art are of such a sort, while others are not. If a work is of this sort, then the interesting problem may become its relation to what lies physically beyond the boundaries of the work. This again would require empirical investigation. For example, what is the effect of the frame, if the picture has one? Or of the shade of color on the environing walls, or of the lighting? The history of framing may be of theoretical interest in showing the extent to which frames have secured protective effects for the work of art, have enhanced the form (as in the France of Louis XV and XVI, or in Victorian England), and have successfully isolated the work.

We may conclude that the important problem, if we work with a notion of form as guiding idea, is that of the types of linkage between the form and the detail, and that this is a transactional relation, that it spreads out into many kinds of relations, and that the result is a considerable loosening (in the sense of contextualizing) of the notion of form itself.

The second question we may ask is, How do we construe the relations between form and function?

The classical assimilation of form and function and the basically teleological character of the Greek idea of form yields a tight relationship between form and function, almost as if we were looking at a single phenomenon from different perspectives. On the other hand, in ordinary usage we tend to treat them as separate but as capable of being brought into some sort of congruence. An advertisement for baggage talks casually of "a perfect blend of form and function" as we would talk of blending tobacco or coffee.

To start with a weaker assumption—that form and function are intertwined in many ways—and to let experience determine how far we can go to a tighter unity is probably better. It also has the advantage of turning our attention to the conditions under which stronger relations can be affirmed—whether, for example, it is true as it is so often asserted, that form follows function. Certainly a divergence of form and function cannot rest on the contrast of a richly described form and a single dominant function with the demand that every item in the form be revealed as geared to that function. The contemporary theory of functionalism in social science can at this point come to the aid of a parallel theory in the arts by calling attention to latent functions, hidden functions, and a host of historical functions. These cover everything from social functions of supermarkets, religious functions of baseball, and ideological functions of elections, to the death appeal of the motor car, to sex and power drives. And there are complex historical functions, such as emotional appeals of facial expressions, rooted not only in physiological similarities, but also in survivals of past evolutionary and sociocultural functions. One can only say "and so on."

In such a broader interpretation of the relation, form is redolent of function. An excellent illustration of the proliferation of function and its shaping of form is costume design. Of course there is the basic protective function of clothing, but that is only the beginning, and this function itself is quite different in the case of fur coat, party dress, and medieval armor. If the designer elects to have clothing adapt to the body, then it may be made to enhance body form in the light of existent standards of beauty and of what may be risked with propriety. If, on the other hand, the body is used simply as a support for clothing, then the form of the clothing follows largely from the character of the material, yet there is a crossing of functions. The material can disguise the body, accentuate the body, or intermittently reveal the body when it is in motion, but not when at rest. The permutations are as endless as the styles, but detailed understanding of form leads regularly to detailed specific functions.

The connection of form and function may not be as direct as "form follows function" suggests. For example, the connection may lie in the processes that make the function possible, and here functional meanings may be intertwined with material consequences that in turn provide a route for form. Speculate on the Greek amphora. Its primary function may be to store oil or wine, or the ashes of the dead. The materials used may yield a pleasing combination of earth colors, the colors resulting from chemical effects of the methods of firing. The shape may reflect the ease with which the potter makes a curved vessel. The outer surface now tempts the artist, but of course with scenes relevant to the intended contents: scenes of the household, of battle and of the sad but glorious road to death. Nor is the technique of the scene unaffected by the result to this point: Achilles and Ajax play draughts before us, seated face to face, but their backs are arched in parallel to the curve of the amphora, and the loosely held spear points directly in the line of the handle, almost instructing us where to grasp.[3]

Finally, if we put no constraint on what is to count as a function, a form apparently without a function may carry its function directly within itself. After all, Aristotle defined *praxis* as the doing or action that has an end in itself. So, too, there need be no paradox if the ultimate function of a painting were said to be to provide a visual experience, or of a work of art in general to provide a significant insight. In that case, any war of function and form would culminate in a mutual Aristotelian embrace.

We may also ask if prior existence of a guiding idea is necessary.

Aristotle reiterates that nature works like the artist or craftsman with the actual plan before him. Is it the case, however, that the artist has to work in such a way? Aristotle has allowed that nature makes mistakes (as an artist may), and in the Darwinian world "mistakes" take the shape of incessant mutation, only some of which create the new. It is tempting to ask if a model of this sort, which allows for the novel and the creative and the emerging, with the plan itself transformed in the process, can hold for one or another of the arts.

There are strong metaphysical concerns in this theme. Contemporary philosophy has witnessed a number of revolts against the idea of a fixed nature for man. Historically, it is said, man makes himself. An explanatory model to predict man's path is denied on the ground that any model is a narrowing of perspective to one or another aspect which in its narrowing blots out other perspectives; different models explain more or less, but man is always more than the models. Humans make their own purposes; they do not simply express antecedent purposes. No ideal, too, can wholly capture the human being, since an ideal is itself a thinning of the rich multipotential complex of present existence, which pulls in divergent directions; each ideal clarifies, but no ideal encompasses the whole, for an ideal is directional and not an immaterial reality. Man is always rooted in the thick slice of existence.

How much of this can be found in the arts? In music, of course, the idea of improvisation (as a creative process, not as a makeshift adjustment) is an old one; "Herr Beethoven," a program can announce, "will improvise at the piano." And in the modern world the spontaneous production of the jazz players led the way to today's spontaneity in music and dance. What the planless yields in comparison to the planned still seems to be an unresolved question. It is hard to find unplanned architecture. Will it be improvisation such as that of the Watts Towers? Or is it simply the fact of change in a long-range project, as Gaudi changed the plan of The Expiatory Church of the Holy Family into what will be an imposing Barcelona Cathedral? More likely is the development of the multifunctional, which leaves open varieties of determination and works toward sufficiently small modules to make varieties of form and function possible. Something like that takes place in the prefabrication of parts to allow for variable wholes, but in that case the whole is fixed when its specific plan is made. (Indeed, the totality of the possibilities computable at the outset might be included as part of the plan.) Plans allowing a variety of needs, even changing needs, within a structure that admits of almost casual interior readjustments as those needs arise, offer the possibility of improvisation.

It is also of interest to ask in what sense the product is active or dynamic, and not just a finished object.

Aristotle's assimilation of matter–form to potentiality-actualization gave a dynamic cast to all existence, so that (as suggested above) even being was to be considered a kind of doing. He achieved this through a teleological approach by having form first govern the creation and then maintain the character of the finished work. The dynamism of the modern world has followed a different path, from a mechanistic physics that found the dynamics in an underlying constant movement to a twentieth–century scientific revolution that brought space and time together, all of this accompanied with the growth of a dynamic technology. The world thus comes to be regarded as a collection of events fast or slow, rather than of things; the intellect has even been attacked for its static presentation of phenomena and challenged to develop conceptual tools for encompassing constant change.

What happens when the work of art is sensed as active, and not as a finished object? The turn to the dynamic in art and the works of art cannot be given an oversimplified formulation. There have always been the arts of movement as well as the arts of rest; even the ancients distinguished in classification dance and song and drama from painting and sculpture and architecture. And the medieval folk well knew how the interior of the Gothic cathedral lifted the spirit upward and how the placement of the altar carried the spirit forward; all this was envisaged in the form. The ways in which the dynamic may be embraced in the form are therefore multiple and complex, and their enumeration calls for careful distinction rather than bundling into a single formula.

In perhaps the mildest sense of the dynamic, the form may call for changing uses. The lovely squares of the old European towns today shift in use from markets in the morning, to parking places in the afternoon, to scenes of social gatherings and café life in the evening. The walls of Carcassone, no longer needed for defense, are walks as well as the settings for celebrations and tourist attractions; on July 14 the town itself becomes theater, with fires lighted on the ramparts, just as the canal in Venice on Feast Days can become theater as the people take to barges and gondolas.

In an important sense already suggested, the form may be dynamic in its impact on the observer. Certainly after Kant the perceiver has an active role in the determination of aesthetic effect. We may take this more literally than Kant intended by looking to the effect of the perceiver's activity, just as we may find in Yaacov Agaam's compositions, depicting the multifaceted character of reality, that the resulting picture is different according to the stand of the observer. Again, the guiding idea of a work may well include what it is to evoke in participants and viewers—as simply as when, in Rembrandt's *The Risen Christ at Emmaus*, the ladder in the shadow may be put there to bring to the viewer's mind the background of the crucifixion. In architecture the shaping of space has much to do with an intangible reaction of the people who move in that space. Features of grandeur or cosiness, formality or informality, warmth or coldness, are directly conveyed.

In many respects the most intriguing sense of the dynamic is that in which the guiding idea of a work calls for an internal presentation of motion and change. Films make motion, while Futurism showed motion in a static medium. Of course the problems of the dynamic in painting and architecture in these and doubtless other forms are the special problems of the "static" arts. For the fullest history of the visual dynamic one clearly has to go to the development of photography and the film. Nevertheless, in all art the perspective from which one sees the work as active, not as a finished external object, makes a profound difference insofar as it turns attention to the transactions that are going on with the observing self and the environing culture. This phase was much exploited in the idealist philosophies of art—Croce and Collingwood, for example—that, beginning with their roots in this aspect of Aristotle, ended by locating the work of art itself in consciousness. Collingwood even says that ''The work of art proper is something not seen or heard, but something imagined.''[4] Hence he even denies the distinction between matter and form in a philosophy of art. For Aristotle, however, that distinction is unavoidable, although it remains throughout a relative one.

The final question we should ask is, How are form and matter related?

There are two distinct questions in the relation of form and matter. One is, What is the extent of dependence of form on matter, on its potentials and opportunities as well as on its constraints? This is a familiar topic, particularly with the rapid development of new materials usable in the arts. The second question, which is our present concern, is the correlative character of the two concepts. Aristotle's point was simply that what in one context is regarded as form may in another be regarded as matter, and conversely. He regards earth as matter for marble as form, marble as matter for the statue of Apollo as form, the statue of Apollo as part of the matter for the temple as form; similarly, wood for the house, the house for the city. It is, therefore, the context with its interests and conditions that determines what is to be the *locus* of form, that is, where we are to look for form. Let us illustrate with two cases: one a shift downward on the matter-form axis, the second, a shift upward.

The first is a familiar story, still with us. Impressionism, as is well known, marked a break in the tradition of painting. Instead of forthright presentation of people and things that of course had shapes and colors because things in the world do have shapes and colors, and because the artist working on a two–dimensional canvas has to attend to them, Impressionism shifted the focus to those shapes and, especially, to those colors. They ceased, in a grammatical analogy, to be the adjectives of the objects presented, and made a bid to be the substantives. The pictures presented the tone and color and play of light on surfaces. Where, however, was the locus of the form? The form or guiding idea of Monet's studies of the cathedral at Reims is not the religious vision; it lies in the realization of the subtle play of light at different times of the day. (If we insist that a cathedral is by definition a religious object and look there for the inspiring form, we shall have to invent some Zoroastrian heresy for Monet!) Now while subsequent movements, such as Cubism, weighed geometric structures more heavily, the development through Neo–Impressionism is drawn through the expansion of techniques for the manipulation of color. (It is a suggestive parallel that in philosophy in that period writers on epistemology began to talk of colored surfaces rather than of colored objects, almost as if colored patches, as sense-data, were being peeled from surfaces which themselves had a sensory autonomy from the objects.) Finally, in our own time, there have been attempts to make chromatic structure the central focus of painting.[5] To look for the form in such painting is to look at what the colors do in the mutual sensory interactions.

Our attempt here is not to explore such movements, not to predict their courses or to attempt their aesthetic evaluation. They illustrate strikingly the way in which the locus of form, what is used as the guiding idea in the work, may shift from one level to another. In the older tradition, color and shape were the matter (in the Aristotelian sense) of the painter's art, serving the idea that organized them. In the extreme of the appeal to chromatic structure, the previous matter now is the seat of form.

For an illustration of the upward shift, take the movement from the perspective of the architect to that of the city planner. Ideally, the form that guides the design of the building would be integrated into the form that guides the design of the city. But we know the apprehension that attended the first appearance of a skyscraper on the skyline of London, and the anguish over what should replace Les Halles in Paris. There are the beauties of a city that has chanced to grow well, and there are the horrors of a city that has just happened to grow in an architectural laissez–faire. It would be carrying coals to Newcastle to pursue these topics here. But it is worth noting that there is no easy reconciliation of the levels of form, and we are pressed to relate them instead as matter and form. Edmund Bacon gives an example of five towers in Stockholm's Norrmalm project in which, though there was a general plan in relation to the city area, slight differences between each successive tower resulted in a dissonance, "as in a quartet in which each person is performing slightly off key. It is worse than it would have been if the shapes of the towers had been unrelated, and, of course, worse than if any one of the four designs had been repeated four times.[6] His conclusion is simply that "an organism is all of a piece, and you cannot deal with one part of it, leaving another part out, except at your peril." But of course this simply points to the question of which is the organism, the city or the building. Bacon finally calls for the amalgamation of planning and architecture.[7] This is a challenge rather than something to be done by an act of will. It cannot be left to chance, nor can it always be a matter of fortunate accident, as when, for example, the Roman remains in Split were ample enough so that instead of being relegated to a museum they could continue as an old city in which modern life could build and accommodate itself.

These two brief examples show that the place in which we seek the form is relative to our needs and purposes, values and interests, hopes of experiment and of progress. This is not an arbitrary relativity, for the location of a form is itself a kind of experiment, testing whether such an organization of the materials will prove satisfactory in terms of the underlying needs and interests.

Conclusions

Our first conclusion is more general than one about form itself. It is the need to recognize the relativity of all categories that organize fields of inquiry, craft, construction—a relativity of contexts and conditions and purposes. Let us illustrate this with David Billington's attempt to make a fundamental contrast between structures and machines, and with a response by Mario Salvadori.[8] Billington takes structures to be static and often large–scale, custom–made, designed to last, and unique. Machines, on the other hand, are dynamic, small–scale, mass–produced, not intended to last indefinitely, and universal in the sense of performing a definite function wherever they may be. He suggests that the dike and the locomotive be seen as symbolic of this contrast. Having set down this dichotomy as basic for engineers, he outlines different laws for each, and in the end allies the machine with science and the structure with art.

Now this is a pretty formidable dichotomy. How secure is its categorial contrast? Does it capture two distinct forms? Would it not be possible to think of a structure as itself a machine doing slower or steadier jobs, just as the dike is holding back the constantly beating waves? If so, Billington's contrast concerns chiefly practical methods of construction under different conditions of speed and stability. In responding to Billington, Salvadori quotes Corbusier's *"la maison c'est une machine à habiter."* He calls attention to cases where problems arising in structures are met with machine-like devices; for example, the use of thousands of dampers or dashpots to dampen a building's oscillation; or preventing the outer columns of a building from becoming destructively hot by permanently circulating a liquid. We may add that flying machines serving as temporary hotels and space stations serving as dwellings and factories would likewise straddle the categorical divide. And, it is worth noting, machines that do nothing in the traditional sense can become works of art with a strong kinetic effect, such as Tinguely's machines, whose imprecision of action generates surprise, anticipation, or anxiety while they twitter, creak, and groan.

The illustrations we have considered may suggest that the concepts that organize a field and the modes of organization they dictate hold under limited conditions of materials, purposes, traditions of construction, and ingenuity. Borderline cases may be ignored while the conditions are stable and the clear cases furnish a normal paradigm. But with changed conditions, increased knowledge, new techniques, and more inventiveness come conceptual vagueness and conceptual shifts. Large–scale conceptual alterations become possible.

This conclusion clearly holds for the concept of form itself. It takes different shape as conditions change and knowledge grows, and interests focus more sharply on one or another portion of creative and appreciative processes. Form as guiding idea may be pushed upward Platonically and become more general. Following Aristotle, on the other hand, we see that form may be kept close to the product to become almost the embodied identity of the individual work. In these wanderings, form can come to cover sensory organization, structure, or any of a host of concepts to which the term has been applied in the history of art discourse since its classical genesis. If this is ambiguity, it still may be systematic ambiguity, rendered more precise by attention to focus and level, prompted by conditions and purposes. Form remains a useful notion if we have responsible form–talk. It embodies the search for order in understanding and construction, and delineation of form in a given context under given conditions constitutes a proposal of the order and level of order at which we may significantly aim. But what holds form together is the matter of the context and its potentials and purposeful directions. Form is thus a channel for our discovery of similarities and differences in the flux of things along lines that are humanly and purposively significant. While we continue to use the notion, we should not place too great a burden on it.

Notes

1. For a fuller analysis of the Aristotelian conception, see Abraham Edel, *Aristotle and His Philosophy* (Chapel Hill: University of North Carolina Press, 1982), chaps. 5, 7, 8.
2. Quoted and discussed in Rudolf Arnheim, "Gestalt Psychology and Artistic Form," in *Aspects of Form*, ed. Lancelot Law Whyte (Bloomington and London: Indiana University Press, 1966), 197–98.
3. Such speculations on the amphora are in effect stabs at the complex problem of the relation of technique (perhaps even technology) and art. Compare what Franz Boas says of primitive art: "Nature does not seem to present formal ideals—that is fixed types that are imitated—except when a natural object is used in daily life; when it is handled, perhaps modified, by technical processes. It would seem that only in this way form impresses itself upon the human mind." Franz Boas, *Primitive Art* (Cambridge: Harvard University Press, 1927), 11.
4. R. G. Collingwood, *The Principles of Art* (New York: Oxford University Press, Galaxy Book, 1958), 142.
5. The character of this movement in contemporary painting has been clearly presented in the recent exhibit "Chromatic Structures" at the Philadelphia College of Art, November 5–December 13, 1980.
6. Edmund N. Bacon, *Design of Cities*, revised edition (New York: Penguin Books, 1976), 314. Compare his comments on the tragedy of London (214–215), the ruin of delicate design structures through lack of understanding and lack of protection. Thus neither planlessness nor a simple overall plan will do.
7. Ibid., 319.
8. David P. Billington, "Technology and the Structuring of Cities" in *Small Comforts for Hard Times*, ed. Michael Mooney and Florian Stuber (New York: Columbia University Press, 1977), 182–198; Mario G. Salvadori, "The Aesthetics of Technology: In Response to David P. Billington," ibid., 199–203.

12

Biography among the Disciplines

This study examines how biography, as a branch of literature, has tried to relate itself to science and history in its work. It finds that philosophy, in both metaphysics and epistemology, reacts on these relations: in metaphysics because philosophical changes alter our view of what is a person and so the scope of the life that is being described; and in epistemology because methodological analyses of history and science break open hardened views of their relations. Biography is left with choices rather than a fixed role.

There is a jockeying among the disciplines that strongly reminds us of the relations between national powers. The superpowers are continually aggressive, while the smaller powers draw sharp boundaries and seek alliances.[1] Science, history, and literature are the superpowers. Philosophy has a roving commission and enters into the background everywhere. Particular arts stress independence or else explicit connections: painting tends to the first, architecture to the second. Where does biography stand among the disciplines?

Doubtless biographers differ in the sense of their craft. But the great powers to which they have to frame their relations—explicitly or in practice—are science, history, and literature. Take, for example, what Kennan, looking on biography as a historian, said to the American Academy and Institute of Arts and Letters: "Some of the classic works of history have long been regarded as great literary achievements as well. I think of the Gibbons and the Macaulays, the Parkmans, the Rankes and any number of others who could be mentioned. I think, too, of the great biographers, from Boswell down to our own Leon Edel, because biography is essentially a form of history."[2] Kennan wanted to go beyond the argument that when history and biography are literary it is just that the style of the particular writer has a special felicity though the substance is not the substance of literature. He recognized that truth and factuality have a relevance to history that is less pressing for literary works. His point seems to be that some of the human faculties of mind, primarily imagination, should not be appropriated for literature and banished from history and biography. If he ends with a partition—"the poet, the novelist or the dramaturgist in his own stratosphere of the inspired imagination and the commitment to sheer beauty; the historical crawling earthbound . . ."—he has them go hand in hand on a common task of helping contemporary man see himself.

The partition of literature and science has been standard. For example, C. Vann Woodward takes this for granted, reviewing two books on Henry Adams: "He remained a man of letters and strove to become a man of science. The tensions between allegiances are among the sources of appeal to modern readers."[3] In our own century the wholesale opposition of science and the humanities has been persistent; it is exhibited and lamented in C. P. Snow's account of the "two cultures." They have gone their own way in theory, in practice, in education, and in their hold on the human spirit. Think of the long powerful dogma of the New Criticism that the interpretation of a literary work was to be sought within the work itself, and the resentment it showed to attempts to seek enlightenment from historical and biographical context, or psychological (particularly psychoanalytic) theory.

Philosophy, lurking in the background, has always had some hand in controversy over continuities and discontinuities, in affirming or denying sharp dichotomies. In the late nineteenth and early twentieth century, it made much of the contrast between science dealing with the tangible and the humanities dealing with the intangible; science with the measurable and humanistic disciplines with inner meanings and feelings; science with the mechanistic and the deterministic, the humanistic with freedom and creativity; science with universal laws, history and literature and the study of man with the richness of the particular (the contrast of the "nomothetic" with the "ideographic");[4] science with facts (sensory observation and verifiable truth), humanistic disciplines with values (subjectivity, private expression of feeling). These were all residues of the seventeenth century's hardened dualism of matter and mind, of nature and spirit, and of objectivity and subjectivity. Of late, however, philosophy appears to be reversing itself and attempting to undo the deep chasms it has helped to create. In many different contexts and in many different ways it has attempted to relax, sometimes even to dissolve, the harsh separatisms and to restore the continuities which it had long denied.

Such a reversal is relevant to biography in at least two respects. One is that what happens in philosophy can provide parallels for possible changes in the self-view of other disciplines. The second is a stronger relation: insofar as there is a philosophical background to most disciplines, dealing with their presuppositions about man and the world and methods of inquiry, changes in that background impinge more directly on the ways of the discipline. Biography is, as Leon Edel has formulated it, *writing lives*.[5] It is through the concept of *a life* and *living a life* that changes in presuppositions might affect the biographer's intellectual landscape. Now customarily a life is identified with an individual—with a body whose actions are entered in the biography and a mind or consciousness that manifests intentions, feelings, plans, satisfactions and dissatisfactions. A life is lived within a context of interpersonal and social relations in a background of historical events. The biographer's work is to gather evidence of action and its guiding consciousness; in this he or she is a scrupulous historian, employing historical–scientific methods and criteria. The organization of the data, the patterning of the biography, is an imaginative creation, a literary aspect of the work.

I want to suggest some of the central changes that are taking place as philosophy turns to continuity rather than discontinuity, and to raise questions about parallel or consequent changes that can be found or may be expected in attitudes to biography. Let us first consider the philosophical drifts in general or abstract form, then their implications for the relation and operation of the disciplines, and then some specific consequences for biography.

The philosophical changes have been striking in both metaphysics and epistemology (or methodology). They may be headlined: from the fixed toward the changing; from isolation toward transaction; from a dualism of body and mind toward a naturalism; from an essentialism toward a pragmatism. Some parts of these changes have been centuries in the making; others are relatively recent.

The drift from the fixed to the changing had overlapping paths. The more familiar is the turn from the eternal to the temporal, in all its forms whether of religious or moral concern. It is tied to a scientific outlook and the growth of knowledge about the changing natural world. More subtle, however, is the movement from the primacy of the universal to the primacy of the particular and beyond both. Not only in the ancient (Platonic) tradition, but even for a great part of the history of science, knowledge meant the grasp of unchanging forms or patterns or laws that governed the behavior of particulars. Particulars were themselves understood only as their different properties were capable of universal characterization. In the slow reversal of priorities—starting as early as the medieval debates about "realism" and "nominalism"—the universal became understood as simply the rough similarity of particulars. But then the plot was complicated. Particulars themselves were dissolved into collections of properties, and the prototype of true particularity became the isolated sense-quality—for example, brown–here–now. (This was the bedrock on which positivist philosophies in principle rested the scientific verification of theories.) Eventually, within reach of our century, the analysis of experience itself removed this atomic character. Thus William James in his *The Princi-*

ples of Psychology (1890) made clear the complexity of experience: the deep and wide–ranging *selectivity* that goes into the very happening of experience itself, in perception as well as the framing of concepts and ideas, in the choice of one ordering rather than another in one context rather than another. These processes are all expressive of purpose, and even in their most elemental form are seeking to build an order that will enable us to continue and act, to survive and carry on from moment to moment. It was a direct application to the study of experience of the Darwinian naturalization of the human being. In the end, then, neither the universal nor the particular has a bedrock character. Universals are constancies found in the flux of experience on the basis of discerned or presumed similarities; particulars are fixities (things, substances, qualities) found or constructed as enduring over temporal stretches.

The view of the world as consisting of things and their properties has an isolating effect. We tend to think of individuals and their actions or behaviors by themselves. We learn, however, that no action of anything is without an environment that makes it possible. To take a favorite example of John Dewey's: when I think of myself as breathing I tend to ascribe the phenomenon to myself; but in fact it is a going-on in which the air around us is a coconspirator. Actions are really *transactions* looked at from the point of view of a selected participant. (Dewey was even suspicious of the idea of *interaction* as overaccentuating the separateness of participants.) On such an approach the initial categories for understanding our world are no longer things or individuals and their properties and actions, but situations, contexts, events, processes. (The twentieth century has many "process philosophies" of which Whitehead's was perhaps the most explicit.) Doubtless the discoveries of twentieth–century physics with its ideas of space–time, of fields rather than things, as well as the revelation of more and more minute dynamic entities, precipitated, or at least encourages such modes of thought.

The movement from a dualism of body and mind to a naturalism was a slowly growing one from the time in the seventeenth century when Descartes separated body and mind sharply, making extension the mark of the former and consciousness that of the latter. For a long period the sciences of the two were developed separately, though parallels and interactions were sometimes sought. Naturalism expanded the idea of matter to embrace human beings developing over time out of the processes of the natural world, with successive levels of accomplishment proliferating into the works of the human spirit. It was accelerated by Darwinian evolution which placed on the agenda of philosophical thought the momentous task of "naturalizing" mankind and all its works. Indeed this has been a major dynamic source of philosophical movement for a century, of shifts and conflicts, and of tensions and battles produced in field after field. Today a central task in psychology and social science is still to secure an appropriate integration of human consciousness and human action, of physiology and intentional behavior, of social conditions and individual decision, rather than the maintenance of purely separate accounts.

The transition in methodology from an essentialism to a pragmatism has been equally slow. One thinks of essentialism as an ancient and long abandoned outlook; but its residues are still present today. Its classical form was the view that every kind of substance had its essence or nature and this determined or at least enabled us to understand its typical development, maturation, and normal action. This was, of course, teleological in its Aristotelian and Christian forms. For Aristotle, there were inherent "plans" or designs in things, which were carried out in their careers; in Christian theory God created things according to the divine plan, imparting to each its nature. For Aristotle, scientific inquiry discovered these eternal plans and embodied the results in definitions—for example, of man as a rational animal. In Christian thought the eternal plans could be grasped in part by reason, in part through revelation.

The twentieth–century methodological residues of essentialism are to be found in theories of definition and meaning, and it is here that pragmatism has been making its significant inroads. In the first third of the twentieth century, logic texts still distinguished "real definition" from nominal assignments of proposed uses for a given term, on the assumption that the results of inquiry were in some sense definitive.[6] Reaction against this tended to view all definition as conventional. Pragmatism stressed the tentative, experimental, and instrumental character of concepts and their definitory expression; moreover, since the results were corrigible, constant revision and refinement was an integral part of inquiry. In this the pragmatic approach was incorporating the recognition of change as basic. In its treatment of meaning, its perspective was immediately far–reaching. The meaning of a concept or an idea was not to be found in a finite equivalent expression. It lay rather in the experimental or experiential *consequences* in the use of the idea. But consequences depend on the goings–on of the whole field of inquiry—on contexts and transactions and changes. Essentialism with its fixities of meaning is here clearly abandoned. Meanings grow and are revised with the extension of experience, and they reach out more to the holistic than the isolated part, or at least to contexts that may carry us in inquiry beyond any initially delimited area. What we take to be the meanings and truths at any time, or constituting the body of our knowledge on the basis of funded experience, is thus open to correction, expansion, replacement as experience itself is expanded. Our meanings, our categories, constructions, theories, have this inherently temporal context. We live, think, act, reconstruct our ideas, refashion our institutions, and repattern our provinces of knowledge and action within the operation of this continual process of inquiry.

We may now ask what all these abstract philosophical considerations have to do with the questions about the relation of disciplines asked at the outset. How do they affect the isolation of science and history and literature?

The shift from fixity to change in its several implications affects immediately the sharpness of contrast between science and the humanities, in the latter of which both history and literature are usually assigned their places. The insistence that science and history investigate different realities (universals and particulars) is weakened when lawlike assertions are referred to features in the world (or observations of them) that recur with sufficient frequency, and particulars to properties cohering for an extended temporal period. The difference is thus not in realities but in interest and attention.[7] There is history in the objects of science and varieties of order in the objects of history. As the model of universality projected by physics was enlarged by the historical-evolutionary interests of biology, geology, and eventually astronomy, and as the social sciences grew with weaker (statistical) concepts of law, lines between the scientific and the historical became, in many contexts, harder to draw.

Developments in the discipline of history have themselves contributed to this result, for there have been changing patterns of interest in historical writing. At the outset of our century Santayana, in describing the work of the historian, was reminded of a man looking over a crowd to find his friends. Partly under a more realistic rather than a moralistic philosophy of history, historians extended the scope of their study. Today they look for the story of common people in the seventeenth century, not just the conflict of Cromwell's Puritans with the court party of Charles I. They have begun to study attitudes of women in the past, not just men who presumably "made history." And they no longer worry whether traditional historians call this substituting sociological science for history. Moreover, at every point at which it can help, results and methods of the social sciences are applied, and occasionally even psychological categories, though what is now called "psychohistory" has been the subject of much debate and criticism. And oral history attempts to capture the data of living sources, with whatever checks and corrections theory can offer; it is perhaps not too farfetched to compare this to the physical chemist attempting to describe the data of a particle disintegrating in a minute fraction of a second, with the tools of technology and refined physical theory. The differences are in the tools, not in the pursuit of data that are historical in both cases.

In some respects literature, too, reaches out to both science and history. That literature shares with science and history efforts at describing and understanding the materials with which it deals—human actions and situations and characters and patterns—is of course taken for granted. Indeed, in earlier days of our century it was common to contrast the successful insights of literary works into human beings with the crude and close–to–the–

organism efforts of behavioral psychology, or the vague generalizations of introspective psychology. Only the identification of science as mechanistic in explanation and universal in ambition prevented these achievements of literature from being recognized as scientific in intent, if not in method. Of course there are differences in both method and interest. Take the well–worn illustration: the revelations of Shakespeare's *King Lear* about the plight of old age differ in mode from those of gerontology as a sociological study, though the lessons are not far apart. And the lessons of the ancient Oedipus story are obviously parallel to those of Freudian psychology. Here too, it is interesting to note that American psychologists usually focus on the mother–son relation, while German writers—at least those who grew up under the old strict paternal authority—are prone to focus on the relations of Oedipus and his sons.[8]

Overlapping is manifest too when we look to the borders of literature and history. The events that constitute literary material are the same in kind as those that constitute historical material; the distinction of truth and fantasy does not affect that, though strict historians may regard historical novels and docudramas as barbarian invasions. While an older TV series like *You Were There* could be ignored as history when it featured Walter Cronkite interviewing Julius Caesar about to cross the Rubicon, the more recent claim for deeper truths about historical situations reached by the literary imagination raises more serious problems. It brings into the center the question whether there are not in fact imaginative components in the writing of standard history. Neat issues could be raised about whether a story really falsifies more than a theoretical model of human beings, though perhaps in a different direction. In any case, literature, if we include within it the work of the dramatist and the critic, perhaps even the journalist, is today straining at the categorial leash. The category of *drama*, for example, occasionally moves from the stage to include the audience, and then into the street where a political action or demonstration is "staged." A certain risk attends such passage of metaphor into descriptive category, for it may suggest that all human action is role–playing—a tendency bitterly criticized by Sartre as the core of the inauthentic.

The second of the drifts listed above—from isolation toward transaction—upsets all permanent schemes of self–enclosed or isolated disciplines. If things and their properties are to be seen as goings–on in broader situations and contexts, it is no longer possible to assign fixed disciplinary boundaries antecedent to empirical study of the contexts. Relative isolation may be possible for a given period if what goes on within a domain has no known dependence on what goes on outside it, but with the growth of knowledge there turn out to be very few such domains. What has happened in the philosophy of science is perhaps most impressive because science for so long a period seemed to be a self–sufficient independent inquiry under obligation to nothing beyond its own theory and evidence. For example, the dominant positivism of the middle part of our century made the sharpest of cuts between the logical and the empirical and the affective–valuational. The former two constituted the cognitive, though sharply divided themselves; the latter was the noncognitive. This meant a clear line between science and nonscience. Acceptance of a scientific statement was a purely scientific matter: verification stood on its own, and any resort to historical explanation or social conditions or psychological background to help in assessing a theory was condemned in the sharpest terms as a *genetic fallacy*. Strangely enough, it was precisely work in the history of science—since Kuhn's study of scientific revolutions[9]—that shook the positivist theses, for it showed how much of the broader view of the world and how much of the conditions and problems of a time went into the fashioning of physical ideas. It thus reinforced what the philosophical study of language had argued—that the distinction between the logical–analytic and the empirical–experimental had itself been overdone, and that the isolation of the imaginative and the affective and value aspects had skewed the philosophical perspective.

Underlying this shift was the psychological analysis of experience, whose Jamesian formulation was indicated above. In fact, the positivist view reflected the older faculty psychology in its division of disciplines: philosophy concerned with the logical-linguistic, science with the perceptual, value fields with the affective. But the day of faculty psychologies is gone by, though residues and hangovers are plentiful. The isolation of human capacities in alignment with disciplines proves unwarranted. Doubtless to imagine is not to conceive, nor to feel the same as to think. But there is a purposive content and a cognitive content in feeling, there are cognitive elements and purposive interests in perception, and purposive orientations and perceptual cues in cognition. And as for the grandiose Will, whose blind force has so often been exalted in romantic philosophies, we can trace elements of knowledge, of attention, of interest, as well as of innovation, in its decision. In such terms, the conflict of freedom and determinism, of experience and imagination, of tradition and creation, becomes much subdued.

In general, there has been a loosening of the distinction between science and nonscience, at least in the sense of recognizing the whole complex of common knowledge that lies back of concentration on a specific theory. Some have even inferred from this a continuity that stretches from science to rhetoric. But the recognition of continuity should not preclude the formation of specific standards for the scientific in specific contexts and specific purposes. In any case, the very least that can be learned from these developments is the pervasive role of the imagination in the inner workings of science and history as well as literature, and the constitutive role of the purposive, the value element, as well as the cognitive, in all fields.

This lesson is supported by the third of the philosophical transitions outlined earlier—from a dualism of body and mind to a naturalism. This affects most seriously the partition of science and history as objective disciplines (though different) and literature as concerned with value and subjectivity. The distinction of Fact and Value has been a major support of this partition. At its most extreme, fact is bound to verifiable truth, to sensory observation, to what people who investigate can agree on at least in principle. Value is private, expressive of feeling or its extension to persuade or prescribe to others. Fact is objective, value is subjective. Fact is outer, value is inner. Fact can approximate to the absolute, even if only asymptotically; value is inherently individual and relative.

The idea of neutral objective fact has meaning when contrasted with prejudice and ideology in the context of the conflict of values; it itself becomes ideological when it presumes to refer to a domain without values. One can always manage a distinction between fact and value by shifting contexts, and often a useful distinction, but its relativity to context is not to be forgotten. Thus a "purely scientific proposition" already assumes the values that have enabled us to build up and to hold in isolation paths and methods of inquiry as well as the specific frameworks or models that govern the meaning of the particular proposition. Once we understand the permeating role of selectivity and purposiveness in the very existence of ideas and knowledge—as noted in the previous analysis of experience—then the separation of value from fact falls away.

What has sustained the separation and its consequences in drawing sharp lines among disciplines has been the traditional dualism of body and mind: a physical world of objectivity without any value properties, and a mental world of subjectivity in which values abide. With the growth of a naturalistic outlook, human thinking and feeling become "naturalized," they are activities of the human being in the same world as walking and breathing and talking and planning, as recognizing one's fellows and associating with them. Of course there are multiple conditions and interrelations. But subjectivity and objectivity cease to have separate residence, one in the inner world, the other in the outer. Certainly there are shared experiences and private experiences, shared objects of sensory recognition and knowledge and, at a given time, incommunicable feelings. Philosophical debates about whether we really know one another's mind and anthropological and linguistic debates about whether translatability is possible among cultures and languages should be treated contextually rather than absolutely. For we do find permeable boundaries, growing communication, deeper learnings, and all for specific contexts of interaction and experience. There are no tightly bound realms of objectivity and subjectivity.

Instead, then, of assigning fact to science and history, and value to literature, we have to look for the values that are properly constitutive of the scientific enterprise and the historical enterprise. In a similar way, when we deal with values—say in ethics or aesthetics—we have to determine what scientific results and lessons of history are to constitute the background of knowledge for decision.

The last of our philosophical transitions—from essentialism to pragmatism—parallels on the methodological side the changes already noted, and draws the distinctive lessons of the pragmatic approach. These lessons cut across all the fields, particularly in their treatment of meaning. Perhaps nothing epitomizes the fact that meanings change more clearly than that dictionaries, the guardians of the raw material of literature, now come out in periodic reeditions and readily flaunt the changing meaning of words. Sometimes this is interpreted as a concession that anything goes if it is now habitual; sometimes, however, as a deeper admission that language itself is the creation and constant recreation of a living population of users. But what is distinctive of the pragmatic approach is to sharpen the criteria for the application and revision of terms and concepts in the expectation of change with growing experience.

The primacy of consequences in use occasionally affects the perennial theoretical struggles over meaning in literature and the arts. In the older dualistic views the meaning of a work was certified by the intentions of the creator; the audience could conjecture and offer what evidence the outer world could muster about the inner. But today so-called reception theory has it that the meaning of a work is found in the way the audience receives and takes it. It is not hard to see this—very much like a narrow operationalism or a psychological behaviorism—as a belated extreme reaction against dualism, perhaps in an effort to be scientific, when science itself has moved on to deliberate refinement of conceptual tools. Any relevance that the philosophical changes described may have for biography as a discipline are likely, it was suggested, to come through an altered understanding of a body and its action, of consciousness and its relations, of an individual and individuality, of biographical data and patterning.

When action becomes seen as transaction, when the apparent fixity of the body is itself seen as some degree of stability in process, then the body becomes a body–in–a–field, responsively dependent on properties and systematic organization of the field. In such a mode of systematization, the organism is sometimes compared to a whirlpool within a mass of water, which may retain stability of form even longer than the average human life.

Consciousness is not a self-contained stream governed by inner laws. It is related throughout to the goings-on of the organism and the field, whether to bodily processes, the historical past of the individual, transactions involving others and the social milieu. Attempts in literature to present just the stream of consciousness yield not a solid bed of data but fragments calling for interpretation by relation. Whatever categories will be used for description and whatever methods for determining relations, they will not divide the individual into bodily acts understandable by themselves and consciousness with its own illumination.

The concept of the individual has taken the hardest blows in philosophical changes. Traditionally the individual has been contrasted with the group, the social, the population. The individual is the ultimate unit, whether for description of groups and group action, for understanding and explaining group and social behavior, and for creating institutions (the social contract). A life is therefore strictly the life of an individual, and biography differs from history at least in this respect that it writes individual lives. Now this traditional view, posed in this way, becomes seriously involved in the philosophical disputes about the relation of the individual and the social. Individualism is not without strength; it has been intensified since the seventeenth century. No dogma has become more fixed than that assertions about groups are roundabout assertions about individuals, that groups do not engage in actions, only individuals, that groups do not have purposes, that institutions are only ways of describing individual behavior. To the objection that common language employs all these forms of assertion—that when a king or a president declares war he is not just an individual acting, that the purposes of a corporation may differ from those of its members—the answer usually given is that the group-assertions are reducible to individual-assertions or at least (the methodological individualism of e.g., Karl Popper) that the group assertions are verifiable by assertions about individuals. Of late, however, a greater tolerance has appeared, not only because the intensified individualism has been suspected of ideological leanings, but because group assertions often develop independent modes of research. Animal research often maps the career of a population, not of individual members, and the story of an army is read with ease in terms of groups and subgroups. When we think in processual and transactional terms, to focus in different ways is just a shifting of the lens; it assigns no priorities to one or another perspective, except for specific interests and purposes within a well–defined context. Of course our idea of biography has been that of the individual, but what the biography records is the individual–in–a–group, the individual–under–social–influences, the individual–in–a–mass–of–contingencies. Our individual–centeredness in all these contexts is directed by our awareness that individual action and decision (explicit or drifting) is the turning point in the scene of events, the locus of control or lack of control, life or death, success or failure. Such deep interests are the source of that perspective. But of course other interests produce other ways of looking. It becomes more than metaphor to speak of the life of a family, a nation, even of the life and death of a lake (in our ecologically conscious era), the career of a river, the biography of a star.

Whether in such writing the category of life will undergo change is an open question. Biography would then become a less differentiated part of history, differentiated not in designated subject matter nor particularly in method, but in interest, governed by the profound interest in *individuality*, coupled with the historical interest that makes a career the scene of inquiry. Why is it now that we speak of "historical fiction" but not of "biographical fiction"? Novels depicting careers might properly be seen as possible biographies rather than actual biographies! Both for history and for biography, the continuity of the historical and the literary would be evident.

What are the gains for the biographer in the continuity theses? They can be listed as: broader pastures and experimental openness; clearer self-consciousness of task; closer relation of style and theory; creative responsibilities.

We noted earlier the resistance to biography making use of the insights carried by scientific theories of human action. Sometimes, of course, such use is crude or over–rough or over–devoted, and properly open to criticism even on scientific grounds. These are dangers which perhaps only the skilled biographer can avoid. But on a continuity thesis there can be no principled objections to the biographer looking to any scientific or historical source to enlighten his work. The situation is like that in moral philosophy: the recognition that there are always some theories of how humans operate, and not to look for the best is in effect to preserve without recognition the past forms of knowledge as authoritative. Hence the opening of pastures for relating biographical work is at the same time an invitation to greater experiment.

The clearer consciousness of the fact that interest is what determines the uniqueness in the biographer's task is worth underscoring. It removes a general intellectual error which is a source of divisiveness and isolation. We noted this in talking of facts and values: the tendency to make separate entities out of them, to see them as referring to different subject matters, to insist on different methods of handling them, rather than recognize that we have different tasks or enterprises governed by different purposes or interests. To describe, to analyze, to explain, to evaluate, and so on, are different jobs, not isolated fields. The biographer, freed of dogmatic blinders, can go in any direction of materials and methods that will throw light on his/her interests.

The biographer's choice of form or style thus becomes seen in a different way. It is certainly the feature in the biographer's work that is most distinctive as compared to the presentation of data that is subject to the historian's criteria of adequacy. But it should not be separated off as literary creative imagination, though the imagination is obviously at work in it. Nor should the cut between data and form that guides interpretation be made too absolute. A parallel from science may be helpful. The change in view here is very like that which took place for the relation of data and theory in the philosophy of science. Positivistic and narrow operationalist philosophies made a sharp cut between the theoretical-conceptual and the observational-operational. It was the pragmatist's insistence on the extent of the theoretical that enters into the selection and meaning of the data that blunted the dichotomy of the observational and the theoretical. For example, it was easy to analyze measuring length as simply the reiterated application of a standard ruler, with a few qualifications about temperature and expansion of metal. But when measurement came to deal with a millionth of an inch, there was no missing the permeation of theory into observation. So too—to invoke a familiar example—the understanding of what the governess "sees" in Henry James's *The Turn of the Screw* is dependent on the theoretical account of her state as a person. And such considerations enter even more obviously in selection of areas of data for the biographical accounts. In some respects it would be worth exploring the notion of the biographer, particularly with respect to the form or organization used, as not merely the *writer* of lives but as the *theorist* of lives.

Such a possibility raises the question of creative responsibility. To what extent is the biographer a maker of lives as well as a writer of lives? I am not raising the Platonic question of morality nor the issues of socialist realism— that only the lives of good persons or of socially constructive persons ought to be written. Even in moral terms, respect for all persons (as well as scientific and historical interest) would make any life a worthy candidate for biography; we have begun to see biographies of ordinary men, so designated. The free choice of a subject by a biographer is not only a matter of social freedom, but very like the freedom of scientific inquiry—not to be dictated to, even by the community of professionals. The creative responsibility I am referring to is what the biographer owes to the subject, as well as to others. Leon Edel has raised some of these questions in trying to determine what attitudes are inappropriate, as well as whether items should be muted. Here the responsibilities reckon with attitudes that help or hinder the task performance, and the sensibilities of the living and reputations of the dead. But there is also the possibility of direct social effects. A biographer of a seriously handicapped person will be fashioning social attitudes in an area of social repression. A sculptor once commissioned to do a bust of Carlyle, read some of his works and was repelled by his personality; she asked whether she should abandon the commission. Such problems are not peculiar to biography or literature and art. They hold also for anthropologists thinking they are purely outside observers of a culture. But in some sense they may be affecting members of the culture. Think of the *New Yorker* cartoon of an initiation ceremony in which the old man hands the young boys a copy of Margaret Mead's book on the people as a substitute for the rituals! This would be culture-making with a vengeance. Perhaps too, then, there is a dimension of *making lives* in the task of writing lives. The philosophical changes we have been discussing at least bring such questions into fuller view.

This paper was written for a festschrift for Leon Edel (1988).

Notes

1. As in political annexation there are both legitimate incorporations and dubious ones. The structure of the legitimate is worked out in logical analyses of "reduction" of one system to another: for example, of parts of chemistry to physics. Sometimes these simply express hopes: for example, J. B. Watson in propounding behaviorism looked upon it as only a first step in the eventual reduction of psychological explanation to the terms of protons and electrons. Sometimes claims are made on the basis of similarity of enterprise: for example, Ruth Benedict once defined sociology as simply the anthropology of larger societies.
2. George Kennan, "History, Literature, and the Road to Peterhof," *New York Times Book Review*, 29 June 1986. This was adapted from an address delivered 21 May 1986.
3. *New York Times Book Review*, 6 July 1986, 3.
4. This was part of a more extended attempt; in German philosophy, to isolate the study of man from that of nature—*Geisteswissenschaften* from *Naturwissenschaften*. But when (in the United States particularly) studies of man set themselves up as social sciences emulating the methods of natural science, the same distinction was contracted to History versus Science.
5. Leon Edel, *Writing Lives: Principia Biographica* (New York and London: W.W. Norton & Co., 1984).
6. Once conventionalism became entrenched in the approach to definition, so-called real definitions were viewed simply as discovered laws about the given material. They were accordingly in no way superior to or more revelatory of essence than any other laws established in the given science, and shared all their empirical or theoretical character. To turn one law rather than another into a definition was simply a matter of convenience.
7. To reach this position one had first to get rid of the notion that some things and features of the world possessed necessity while others were just contingent. Hume accomplished this by arguing that all knowledge of the world was matter-of-fact and only probable, while necessity characterized not things but relations of ideas only.
8. Cf. Patrick Mullahy, *Oedipus, Myth and Complex* (New York: Hermitage Press, 1948).
9. Thomas S. Kuhn, *The Structure of Scientific Revolutions*, 2nd ed. enlarged (Chicago: University of Chicago Press, 1970).

13

What Place for Philosophy
in Contemporary Thought?

This study, under the title, "A Missing Dimension in Rorty's Use of Pragmatism", was written for a symposium on Rorty's philosophy, primarily his thesis that epistemology—the driving force of contemporary philosophy—has now become bankrupt, and that philosophy should now be abandoned, not just reformed. Rorty's proposal thus has the same character as the earlier positivism had for metaphysics: it was not bad metaphysics to be replaced by good metaphysics; it was just bad grammar. Rorty finds no marked difference between the discourse of philosophy and that of literary interpretation, and suggests that what succeeds philosophy is simply conversation that is educative.

The critique suggests that both Rorty and the kind of philosophy he is abolishing get into his dilemma because they have missed the detailed connectedness of philosophy itself to the specific state of knowledge of the day, that scientific results (not merely scientific methods), tentative though they are, contribute components which hold strategic positions in the development of the philosophy. Thus philosophic reflection is authentic when it abandons extravagant assumptions of sovereign autonomy. Some illustrations are worked out in detail.

At a meeting of the American Philosophical Association, when Dewey was eighty, William Pepperell Montague praised him for practicalizing intelligence. Dewey replied that this mistook his aim; he wanted to intellectualize practice.[1]

This exchange parallels nicely the criticism I want to offer of Richard Rorty's interpretation of pragmatism. Rorty appeals to Dewey and James, alongside of Heidegger and Wittgenstein, to overcome the tradition, that is, the epistemological tradition since Kant. The enemy consists of the Cartesian immaterial mind, the correspondence theory of truth involving a reality that cannot be directly known so that we are launched on vain searches for privileged representations, a variety of dichotomies ranging from inner and outer to what is science and non-science, subjective and objective, fact and value—all unified in the image of a mirror of nature that has to be looked at from within. With great skill Rorty traces the way in which the epistemology of the past half century has been getting closer along different paths to the limits of this philosophy. Once out of the morass, Rorty calls on us to abandon epistemology totally, not to seek a better epistemology. And because epistemology since Kant is Philosophy—spelled with a capital P—to abandon epistemology is to abandon Philosophy. If we want to do philosophy—spelled with a small p—it will be without the mirror of nature and the dread dichotomies, without substitutes, a thinking in which there are no sharp borders between science and poetry, even more without a specific definition of philosophy that gives it an assigned professional enterprise. We must do as the revolutionary thinkers of the Cartesian period did with respect to theology; they did not try to get better answers to theological questions but asked quite different questions.

The contribution of pragmatism that Rorty chiefly invokes is James's account of truth as what is better in the way of belief. He insists that this is not a theory of truth but simply shelving the question of correspondence. He then becomes a stern guardian of the morals of pragmatism—for example, it must not stray into a metaphysics of pragmatism because that is yielding to the old temptation, nor is there any pragmatic epistemology. In effect, there is no pragmatic philosophy, only a pragmatic overcoming of Philosophy.

Rorty is too learned not to know that anti-philosophy has been one of the great philosophical traditions. He does not, however, appear content simply to add "Against the dichotomies" to Sextus Empiricus' "Against the logicians", physicists, ethicists. Nor again, to add a study of epistemological illusion to Kant's treatment of metaphysics as transcendental illusion. Perhaps our revolutionary period is now greater than any previous one, and revolution can be total instead of partial.

I cannot go into all the points at which I welcome Rorty's attacks and insights, particularly in dealing with the dichotomies. I want to suggest that he has softened the notion of knowledge more than is required to see the continuities of science, philosophy, and poetry, and that pragmatism not only admits of, but actually employs, in its working out, a view of the growth of knowledge *and its impact on philosophical ideas*, which enables us to judge better and worse in philosophy. Hence, instead of looking to overcoming the tradition we had better think in terms of long–range philosophical experiments and criteria for their assessment. In one sense Rorty is himself doing such an assessment for a chapter in epistemology, but not fully enough because he neglects the impact of the growth of knowledge. At times he seems to say that such considerations are simply the history of science, almost in the tone in which the analytic tradition used to dismiss historical questions as philosophically irrelevant. But the history of science as a growing study is an integral part of the growth of knowledge and should itself be expected to have an impact on philosophy. Indeed, history is central in Dewey's notion of genetic method, in dealing with philosophical ideas.

I want to explore this missing dimension in Rorty's treatment of pragmatism not by general argument but along three specific lines: (1) how we would look at Descartes' immaterial mind and the mirror of nature in a different way if we paid attention to the historical context of its development; (2) two brief case studies from Dewey's own development: one on the relation of his method to his own revolutionary theory of psychology, the other on the reconstruction that took place in his previous moral theory because of a change in social science; (3) some consequent suggestions for revision in Rorty's own contrast of the systematic and the edifying in philosophical reflection.

(1) Descartes did not invent the notion of immaterial mind. The soul had of course been used as an explanatory principle before Plato's time; Plato used it to account for even the motion of matter, since matter was presumed dead on its own. Descartes' retreat to mind concerned solely with consciousness was in one sense a scientific advance freeing biology as well as physics for mechanical explanations.[2] Even the growth of the problems of representative realism in Descartes' century is possibly not without its scientific stimulus; Lovejoy thought it a scandal that our epistemology did not reckon with Roemer's discovery that light had a finite velocity.[3] The realization that the object seen had time to change and that vision is a belated report raised problems of correspondence in a way an infinite velocity with instantaneous seeing did not. Aristotle had in fact considered the parallel problem for sound that clearly takes its time, and had suggestions about how the transmitting air mechanism maintained constancy; considered but rejected the possibility that light had a finite velocity and so maintained the instantaneous character of visual contact. Locke was forthright in his attempt to do psychological explanation on Newtonian physical assumptions and very honest in seeing both matter and mind as something–I–know–not–what. What would Rorty, or I for that matter, have done in Locke's time under the impact of those problems and the state of scientific development? Probably we would both have lined up with Hobbes as having a better psychology. For one thing Hobbes sees a permeating purposive strategy in human behavior, and he recognizes the active role of the organism in perception, which Kant later brought out for the mind in more devious fashion. (But even Kant's thinner formulation was progress and doubtless an encouraging factor in the development of pragmatism.)

In the twentieth century it became more difficult to draw a line between the mental and the physical, even within the phenomena of mind—witness the controversies over unconscious thoughts and desires and again, subliminal perception. A contemporary reckoning with the epistemological doctrines Rorty is attacking might do better with current physiological–psychological studies of color vision and with recent devices of medical technology for the sensory handicapped than with searching the doctrines of idealistic holism or various theories of reference for refuting the myth of the given. I am not suggesting that the knowledge with which the philosophical doctrine is to be coordinated is always physical. At a given period in our century, and perhaps even now, there is more knowledge of emotional differentiation in poetry and literature than in the study of gross organic responses. An adequate epistemology requires a coordination of currently available detailed knowledge wherever it can be found. And such an epistemology might include substitutes for outworn categories. For example, some time ago I suggested that the distinction of objective and subjective be replaced by one between qualities whose occurrence requires the presence of my organism, those requiring the presence of some organism, and those (as presumed at least in the period before the earth cooled) requiring the presence of no organism.[4]

Cursory suggestions will not, however, make my point. I turn to Dewey as providing the clearest illustration of the way psychological and social science disciplines may play a formative role in philosophical ideas. Rorty examines unsuccessful attempts to replace philosophy by psychology, but this is not what I am talking about. I am talking about philosophical ideas taking shape under the impact of fresh or growing knowledge.

(2) In recent years there has been a welcome tendency to consider the relation of James's and Dewey's pragmatism to their own psychological theories. After all, James spent a great part of his life doing his *Principles of Psychology* and its effect on Dewey and his psychological revision was revolutionary in his own philosophical thought. Elizabeth Flower's chapters on James and Dewey in Flower and Murphey's *A History of Philosophy in America* are a landmark exploration of this fruitful field of inquiry.[5] If Rorty had dealt with this dimension of pragmatism, its continuities with the philosophical tradition, as correction not as overcoming, would have been more evident. Even more startling, Rorty does not consider the detailed impact of Darwin on Dewey, in spite of Dewey's own detailed exposition of the influence of Darwinism on philosophy.

Darwin is the indispensable background because his evolutionary theory led to naturalizing mind, rejecting the mind–body dualism, and reinterpreting thought as a developed natural phenomenon in the endless struggle of the species to survive and make a home on earth. In Dewey, as in many of the theories thus influenced, brain activity and consciousness in general were taken to arise when a smooth ongoing process is disturbed, and the effort ensues to restore an equilibrium; more properly, since the disturbance betokens a lapse of the previous modes of response and thus generates a problem, to reconstruct the situation and find a new equilibrium. Dewey's "The Reflex Arc Concept in Psychology" (1896)[6] works out this model. He rejects the then-current stimulus–response separation as a residue of the mind–body dualism. Instead of an initial separate stimulus overtaking a passive or quiescent human, followed by a separate central process, and that by a distinct motor response, Dewey calls attention to an integrated feedback process. For example, the motor is already operative in the seeing as the eye turns and focuses, and the content seen is already interpreted through ideas funded in previous experience. Moreover, thought or reflection as conscious experience is already guided by an underlying doubt or hesitation articulated as a problem–situation. So-called psychic elements are thus never self–contained; they embody stimuli that are sought so that acting upon them will resolve the doubt or solve the problem. To be stimulated is thus an active, and not a passive process. Consider the standard example of the baby reaching out to a bright object; no problem arises if it is a glittering toy. The act is thwarted, however, when the next object turns out to be a candle flame. On subsequent occasions there is hesitation on the child's part, which may be resolved if the growing warmth in a slow approach or a flickering of the flame has become an anticipation of the pain that is feared. The hesitation is thus itself an active process of seeking a stimulus to redirect the conduct.

Permanent features in Dewey's epistemology or theory of inquiry, as well as in ethics and politics, reflect this analysis. One is the basic presence of a problematic structure. A second is the active character of inquiry. A third is the reconstructive nature of the process, with the element of novelty or the inventive character of a solution, and the experimental character of its stabilization. A fourth is attentiveness to the temporal process, not as mere sequence, but as a matrix that generates planning through concern with context and conditions and in turn with consequences. A fifth is the integrated, almost organic character of the process.

In this psychological analysis there was no room for any myth of the given. James had already shown the purposive selectivity that went into sensory experience itself, with its formations of likeness and unlikeness. The alternatives that appear in thought for solution and decision are only the tip of the iceberg of selectivity that has entered into our formation of ideas of objects themselves, the tentative classifications and orderings of our established knowledge that has funded our experience. Now at the moment of thought itself, while our funded past experience structures the problem, our imagination at the frontier of the future may design new experimental alternatives to resolve the problem. Here we have a parting of the ways in the theory of knowledge. Most philosophers of science, epistemologists, theorists of induction, are concerned with the elegant organization of the funded capital of experience; hence systems, rules, ordered "nautical tables" to consult, and probabilities to bet with. Dewey is not against such intellectual housekeeping, but he is fearful of its curbing the imagination that faces the existential situation and should be prepared even for the revision of the ordered categories. That is why he is constantly repeating the precariousness of the *rules* and insisting that all orderings be kept as *principles*, that is as aids to analysis of the present situation of decision. In his conception of intelligence, the center of gravity lies in the working use of knowledge in decision, mindful of the complexity and change and contingency that characterize existence.

All these underpinnings of Dewey's theory of knowledge are unrecognized in Rorty's remark about "the vague and uncontroversial notion of intelligence trying to solve problems and provide meaning."[7] Dewey, on the other hand, fully recognizes that his theory of method stems from the impact of the new psychology, and makes this repetitively clear in his innumerable discussions of how we think. Moreover, it is explicit in his deliberate decision to use the notion of intelligence rather than reason. The latter has almost naturally appealed to philosophers since the classical definition of man as a rational animal.[8] The grounds for Dewey's decision are given succinctly in the preliminary outline (1918) of his lectures given in Japan that eventually became *Reconstruction in Philosophy*.[9] He retraces old ground about how experience, which in ancient times meant an accumulation and gradual organization, yielding a practical insight like that of the builder and physician, became, under British sensationalist psychology, a tool for sceptical criticism rather than construction. Reason was for the ancients a faculty of insight into universals, laws, principles; for Kant it was a faculty of organizing chaotic details of experience. But modern psychology, under biological influence, brought out the active and motor factors in experience. Experimental method then emphasized projection and invention rather than accumulation from the past. At this point we have the critical statement: "Reason thus becomes Intelligence—the power of using past experience to shape and transform future experience. It is constructive and creative."[10] Hence the shift from Reason to Intelligence is not simply a verbal shift, nor the discovery of a fresh faculty; it is a philosophic turn to pragmatism, resting on a new psychology.

Now all this sounds very much like epistemology, by whatever name you call it. If we attend to the psychology that underlies the succession of epistemologies in the way the new biology and psychology underlies Dewey's, then there is no reason why only Locke and Descartes and those who continued belatedly to share their physical and psychological presuppositions, or who had forgotten the presuppositions but continued the supported philosophical pattern, should be allowed to monopolize the idea of a theory of knowledge. Rorty says that Aristotle in the *Posterior Analytics* has no epistemology. But if we pay attention to Aristotle's own biological–psychological underpinnings, then the whole of the *Posterior Analytics* is one side of Aristotle's epistemology; the other side is the array of intellectual capacities and virtues, seen systematically in Book VI, of the *Nicomachean Ethics*. For Aristotle, like Plato, treats knowledge and belief in a scheme of capacities and objects, and so the Aristotelian picture of the structure of knowledge is one side of the scheme worked out in great detail. (Rorty seems to me to admit as much in a different context by calling the philosophy of science merely a variant of epistemology.) Now for the theory of how the capacity and the object together achieve a single actualization according to Aristotle, we have to go to the psychological writings and move up the ladder of his analysis of eating, perceiving, and thinking. I have suggested in my recent study of Aristotle that he develops a scheme for eating, adapts it for hearing and seeing, and simply postulates what it requires for thinking.[11] If that analysis is correct, then what has changed in the theory of knowledge from Aristotle to Dewey is the underlying biology and psychology.

I turn now to the second case study from the development of Dewey's thought: how a change in social science affects his moral and social thought. Because of the complexity of the story, I omit here marshalling the evidence and simply present the narrative.[12]

The 1908 *Ethics* of Dewey and Tufts leans heavily on the assumption drawn from anthropology of that period: that the evolution of morality is from the group-customary to the individual-reflective. Reflective thought is an individual matter, and so the historical maturing of morality involves a growth of individualism. Custom is conservative (just as habit in the individual is conservative; customs are group valued habits), a society steered by custom tends to be stationary rather than progressive. A progressive society embodies greater use of intelligence; moreover, its morality becomes differentiated from religion, law, etiquette, etc.

This was the period in which modern man congratulated himself on being the zenith of civilization in all areas. Evolution had gone from promiscuity through polygamy to monogamy; from status to contract; from animism and polytheism to monotheism; from monarchical authority to liberty; from "the cake of custom" to rationality in morals. It was a brief happy interlude of smugness reflecting Spencer's view of evolution as going everywhere from an unorganized homogeneity to organized heterogeneity, and affirming necessary progress. Dewey and Tufts were not smug, and they did not concern themselves with all these specific then contemporary studies, except that Maine's status to contract is occasionally in the background. But they took for granted the general evolutionary picture for morality and they tried to give its historical outline from Hebrews and Greeks on and to see the theoretical consequences of the rise of greater reflection.

A shift in this whole picture came with the emergence of a more scientific anthropology. Franz Boas' *The Mind of Primitive Man* (1911) riddled notions of a uniform primitive mentality distinct from the modern; it asserted a broad similarity of individual capacities in primitive and modern society, differentiated largely by traditional patterns, opportunities, and under different conditions different attentiveness. For the next three decades the Boas school reshaped anthropological knowledge by firsthand field investigations. Dewey was seriously influenced by this growing knowledge. He gave a joint seminar with Boas at Columbia in 1915 and 1916; student notes of his lectures in social ethics and his own syllabi for courses show his concern with these problems. The climax comes with his article on "Anthropology and Ethics" written as a chapter in Ogburn and Goldenweiser's *The Social Sciences and Their Interrelations* (1927). Dewey examines in detail different interpreters of moral evolution, concludes against the isolation of moral conceptions and practices from institutional and intellectual changes, finds no determinate evolutionary pattern whether away from or toward greater individuality, and stresses the need for recognizing a plurality of influences and specific investigations.

A full story of the two decades would trace in detail the way in which this anthropological shift, together with the growth of social psychology (in which Dewey played a more direct part) brought marked step–by–step changes in the several concepts that had been central in the earlier moral philosophy. Individualism was probably the first to crack; Dewey had early already thought of it as itself a social pattern rather than the individual taking his stand against society. More and more it was recognized as a specific historical movement of thought, feeling and practice under specific historical conditions of Western man from the sixteenth to the twentieth century. Dewey's developed analysis of it comes in *Individualism Old and New* (1930). As for contrasting social and individual, he concluded that they are aspects of any moral thought or action and no issue can seriously be posed as individual versus social. His *The Public and Its Problems* (1927) tried to develop fresh categories of public and private to do the concrete work for which social and individual had been misleadingly used. Perhaps the greatest transformation took place in his concepts of custom and habit. Released from constraints of moral evolution theory which compelled it to play the role of opposite to individual reflection, custom had no need to hold together such diverse elements as group cohesion, automatic acceptance, static society. Nor did habit always have to be identified with the drag of the past. Indeed the whole theory of habit was completely altered by the time of *Human Nature and Conduct* (1922), in which social habit not only gives shape to impulse, and itself embodies funded experience, but even intelligence itself is construed in terms of special habits. We have some evidence to show that the reconsideration of custom and habit was not purely an intellectual matter; in the period Dewey spent in China (1919–21) with serious revolutionary changes in the offing, his interest in the role of custom in Chinese thought and practice and Chinese history was an important factor.

By 1932, when the second edition of Dewey and Tufts' *Ethics* was published, the cumulative effect of all these changes was to reconstruct their ethical theory. The detailed changes in the moral philosophy become intelligible in terms of the impact of changes in the social sciences, as well as the influence of social events upon the concepts in terms of which the moral philosophy is fashioned.

Our two case studies of Dewey's development show the role of growing knowledge and its impact on philosophical ideas. That Rorty neglects this dimension explains why he takes pragmatism out of the mainstream of philosophy and sees it as overcoming the tradition. I have no quarrel with Rorty on viewing knowledge broadly and not confining it to purely scientific developments, although these have been most striking. I am puzzled occasionally by Rorty's omission of such impact. For example, he lines up positivism with the epistemological tradition, but nowhere sees its distinctive twentieth century excitement to lie in its response to *Principia Mathematica* and to Einstein's handling of concepts such as simultaneity in his scientific advances. No one who lived through the period of positivism could have missed that.

As long as we can think of knowledge and its growth, and the possibility of judgments of better and worse in respect to it, however anlalyzed, we can retain a notion of the mainstream of philosophical problems. Philosophical analyses that are pluralistic or that insist on a contextual approach are none the less philosophical, though usually less pretentious. Philosophical analyses geared to a world of change, of time and particularity, are not less philosophical than those flaunting eternity and universality. To amend one specific tradition is not to overcome philosophy. But what if the concept of knowledge is itself somehow weakened, so that instead of firmer knowledge we have just continual conversation in a context of social consensus? Something like that is proposed by Rorty's notion of *edification* replacing philosophy. This is our next serious issue, but before that there is some mopping up to do. Is Dewey entitled to have a metaphysics? Rorty says no, and *Experience and Nature* is a bad book. I do not wish here to discuss its merits, but to suggest why we should not deny Dewey the right to try, along the lines that we found continuities in the epistemological enterprise.

An example is better than an argument here to indicate the approach I am taking. James's "will to believe" has often been dismissed as the heart prevailing over the head in the attempt to legitimate religious belief. But if we look at it carefully and take it out of its immediate context, it is an early formulation of the problems of evidence and decision under risk and the role of values in such decision; it is not intended for use where evidence is clear and overwhelming.[13] It is thus an epistemological contribution continuous with the tradition. So too of Dewey's metaphysical attempts. Rorty sees all metaphysics as foundational in the sense of providing antecedently established constraints on all inquiry. I am not sure that the notion of foundation will bear all this weight. In these days in which homes can be established not only on terra firma but on piles in marshland, in earthquake prone land, on floating boats, in airplanes and in space, it surely is clear that the continuity lies in degree of stability that can be achieved against the precarious and the contingent, and that with an eye on specific purposes. The insistence on the unchanging and the eternal is only one extreme, just as if one argued that a home could only be built on earth if the earth were the fixed and unmoving center of the universe. But even Aristotle, who believed that about the earth, was pellucidly clear in stating the problem of "first philosophy." He said that if there is an eternal substance, then its study is first philosophy; but if there is not an eternal substance, then physics (that is, the study of motion) is first philosophy. He was afraid that to deny an eternal substance would land us in Heracliteanism. But there are doubtless different coefficients of Heracliteanism, and Dewey's is a rather uncertain middling one, whose precise value is determined in experience.

The Deweyan metaphysics states all this by making the *stable* and the *precarious* its central categories. This is a distillation of the growth of knowledge about the pervasiveness of change. Such an approach need have no fears about searches for the *formal* or the *structural*, the *phenomenological*, the *grammatical*, the *logical* or *conceptual*—Rorty's list of foundational categories of armchair epistemology.[14] It has only to be very clear that it is not separating the form from the content but treating it functionally: form is simply part of the content, selected for office because of the organizational job it can do, and capable of being recalled and replaced if some other part of the content turns out to do the job better. The same holds for structure. For example, in ethics Dewey thinks that the concepts of the good, the right, and virtue, constitute a permanent structure because existence of desires and ends and the need for evaluating them, the pressure of mutual claims in group life, and the appreciative reactions of people are permanent features of human life. All the dread metaphysical–epistemological categories are experientially based constancies.

Of course we can think of many topics Dewey might have pursued in such a metaphysics. Most of all I wish he had tackled the idea of correspondence or representation in that spirit. He might then have distinguished the contextual uses of that notion: where it is direct comparison of two experiential fields (e.g., looking at a portrait and looking at the subject), where an isomorphism crossing fields (as in cartography), where representation through learned effects, where a symbolic representation, where a justified realism as against a fictional construct (the familiar struggle over atom and gene as compared to gross national product), and so on. A rich topology of representation or correspondence geared to varieties of contexts would have obviated the lament about antecedent a priori assumptions of correspondence. (My complaint here is that Dewey too often sounds like Rorty on this question.) On the other hand, there is one metaphysical topic that Dewey worried about all his life that Rorty fails to appreciate—the theory of interaction. For example, Rorty says "Such phrases as 'qualities of interactions' soothe those who do not see a mind–body problem and provoke those who do."[15] And he thinks Dewey "blew up notions like 'transaction' and 'situation' until they sounded as mysterious as 'prime matter' or 'thing–in–itself'."[16] But from Dewey's earliest (sometimes almost Spencerian) use of the idea of organism and the organic, to deal with a field of investigation, to the widespread use of interaction (for example, his frequent paradigm of the lungs and the air in breathing to prevent our thinking of the individual apart from his environment), to the latest worries with Bentley as to whether "interaction" implied too much the separateness of the entities and "transaction" would be better, he was dealing concretely with how the study of human life should be carried on. The fruits are seen in his analyses of the social environment and in the impact of this in social science and ethics. Perhaps the difficulty is that there was then no vocabulary for expressing the ideas for which we now use the terminology of feedback and the like, developed in relation to our more complex technology. Incidentally, I think Dewey could have made much more refined metaphysical use of his treatment of ideas as instruments than he did. It might have gotten more directly to the heart of traditional struggles to insert concepts as a *tertium quid* between particulars and universals.

(3) It is time to look to the idea of *edification* that Rorty offers in place of the philosophic tradition. Of the contexts in which he discusses it, the most illuminating seems to me that in which he relates his view to Kuhn and Gadamer. With possible oversimplification, it amounts to the following. Kuhn has distinguished normal from abnormal science. In a period of normality there is an unquestioned paradigm, hence it seems reasonable to look for the basic assumptions as truths that underlie inquiries. But in a period of abnormality this is no longer possible; basic assumptions are questioned, we see that they rested on social consensus of belief, and the best we can do is to keep the conversation going. An epistemological period is replaced by a hermeneutical period, a dialectical period. But Rorty seems to go farther here than an evenhanded balance of periods, as one might in social life distinguish a period of stability followed by one of revolution. The period of abnormality

seems to give a deeper understanding. Even if we try to recover stability we see that stability differently. It is always precarious, subject to change, and our best established "truths" will one day meet their comeuppance. So the sense of abnormality becomes our normal way of looking at things. Perhaps, like Santayana, we should now define waking life as controlled dreaming and sanity as controlled madness.

What changes take place in our notion of knowledge? Rorty appears to follow Gadamer in "substituting the notion of *Bildung* (education, self-formation) for that of 'knowledge' as the goal of thinking. To say that we become different people, that we 'remake' ourselves as we read more, talk more, and write more, is simply a dramatic way of saying that the sentences which become true of us by virtue of such activities are often more important to us than the sentences which become true of us when we drink more, earn more, and so on."[17] Our interest becomes less in what is "out there in the world, or in what happened in history, as in what we can get out of nature and history for our own uses. In this attitude, getting the facts right (about atoms and the void, or about the history of Europe) is merely propaedeutic to finding a new and more interesting way of expressing ourselves, and thus of coping with the world." Rorty decides to use "edification" instead of "education" and *Bildung* "to stand for this project of finding new, better, more interesting, more fruitful ways of speaking."[18]

Let me not cavil about such notions as "true of us" or "sentences" (Rorty sometimes appears to be defending a primacy of "propositions" and so beliefs over any other logical constituents) or "more fruitful" to suggest that he has a hidden epistemology of his own. Or even whether replacing knowledge with self–formation is stepping on a slippery slope. It is rather whether *knowledge* should somehow be melted into *self–formation* as the best way of incorporating all the lessons of change and corrigibility and the new vision of the history of science that have overwhelmed the positivist analysis of science and its primacy—in brief, though Rorty would not call it this, the lessons of the primacy of the abnormal period over the normal. And my problem is not the correct approach here but whether Dewey's pragmatism is departing from the promise of pragmatism when he turns out not to have followed a path like Rorty's.

It is not an easy question. Dewey does place the importance of the study of history in its enrichment of the meaning of the present; his overall theory of knowledge is of course instrumental; he does stress, in his moral philosophy, the importance of character and self–formation. On the other hand, his primary picture of conscious experience in the Reflex Arc paper is one of *learning;* his constant picture of education is one of learning; his theory of freedom rests on the human capacity to learn. The very central place of learning in his whole philosophy—even when he is tempted to regard philosophy itself as educational theory—militates against a weakened conception of knowledge. Intelligence is not to be simply practical; practice is to be made intelligent, and what can that mean if not enlightened by the best of knowledge?

There is, indeed, a striking parallel between Rorty's formulation of his problem and Dewey's vacillation about the relation of habit and intelligence. Intelligence is from the beginning aligned with the act of reconstruction. And so intelligence corresponds to Rorty's period of abnormality, while habit corresponds to the stability of the normal period. The business of intelligence is to reconstruct the previous habits—let us call them the prereflective habits. But the reconstruction also issues in the new habits, the postreflective ones. Now in the earlier theory of moral evolution from custom to reflection that we examined, the prereflective and the postreflective habits were not distinguished. So far as I can tell this is because the postreflective are themselves sooner or later to be the prereflective of the next episode of reconstruction. In all this Dewey seems to be like Rorty in giving primacy to the reconstructive, the episode of the abnormal. But this, as we have seen, is not Dewey's eventual view. His mature theory in *Human Nature and Conduct* features habit as the star and even intelligence is a settled group of habits. I can only conclude then that knowledge and the growth of knowledge, in spite of the facts of change and novelty and the mortality of beliefs, have a firm place in Dewey's pragmatism.

Instead of using the knowledge–character of fields outside of the standard sciences to weaken the idea of knowledge as Rorty does, Dewey, while recognizing the breadth of sources for knowledge, tries to bring out the experimental character of these other sources. He does this particularly in the case of history, which he thinks provides the nearest thing we can get to experiment about human affairs. Indeed, he tries to recast the scientific pursuit of the universal in terms of the historical control of repetitive instances. In a burst of philosophical generosity he once says that Plato was correct in maintaining the priority of the forms, since the child does learn to identify objects from the verbal habits of his elders! The general emphasis on the present understanding of ideas by appreciation of consequences simply expresses the reformulation of thought as experimental in its temporal character. Dewey's advocacy of genetic–historical method in philosophy is a complex project, quite as complex as analytic philosophy was in its heyday during recent decades. It deserves much greater philosophical elaboration than Dewey himself gave it. I think it will extend rather than weaken the concept of knowledge and its growth. And if it compels us to fashion more explicit criteria for the success or failure of philosophical experiments over longer periods of time, it will enable us to reinterpret Rorty's critique of epistemology, not as overcoming philosophy, but as a valuable exhibition of the experimental failure of a specific tradition in modern philosophy which has monopolized too much of our philosophical energy.

The symposium was held at the session of the Society for the Advancement of American Philosophy, at the 1983 meetings of the Eastern Division of the American Philosophical Association, in Boston.

Notes

1. Charles Frankel, "John Dewey's Social Philosophy" in *New Studies in the Philosophy of John Dewey*, ed. Steven M. Cahn (Published for the University of Vermont by the University Press of New England, 1977), 5.
2. How far the program of mechanistic explanation can be carried is an empirical matter. A biologist like Lewontin today writes that the Cartesian program was only fully achieved in the midtwentieth century by the discovery of the double helix. Of course the notion of a machine has itself changed from the mechanical to the electrical, and this is relevant to the study of thought and the brain.
3. Although Roemer's discovery is assigned to 1675, after Descartes' death, there appears to be some ambivalence in Descartes about the topic, enough to suggest some impact of the problem.
4. Abraham Edel, *The Theory and Practice of Philosophy* (Harcourt Brace, 1946), pp. 175–77.
5. Elizabeth Flower and Murray Murphey, *A History of Philosophy in America* (Putnam's, 1977; Hackett Publishing Co., 1979), vol. II, chapters 11, 14.
6. John Dewey, *The Early Works* (Southern Illinois University Press), vol. 5, pp. 96-109. The paper first appeared in 1896.
7. Richard Rorty, *Consequences of Pragmatism (Essays 1972–80).* (University of Minnesota Press, 1982) 51.
8. That the same psychological underpinnings that shape Dewey's conception of method are also operative in his moral theory is clear in his repeated grappling with the notion of intrinsic value. It explains why he could never follow the simple path of a Perry or a hedonist who would be content with initial data of desires or feelings and interpret value as the endeavor of liberal maximization; for Dewey the very fact of a desire or a feeling would be a mark of the deeper goings-on, of attempted answers to already contextually structured problems. That is why he insisted so doggedly during a continued span of articles on value over the years that even prizing should not be construed as intrinsic value.
9. *The Journal of Philosophy*, 15, no. 10: 253–58. May 9, 1918.
10. *Ibid.*, 362.
11. Abraham Edel, *Aristotle and His Philosophy* (University of North Carolina Press, 1982) 146 ff. and 162–71.
12. Fuller consideration of this issue and other points discussed in the present paper about the relevance of Dewey's psychological and social theory to his philosophical theory will be found in Abraham Edel and Elizabeth Flower, Introduction to Dewey and Tufts' *Ethics* 1932 edition, Volume 7 of *John Dewey, The Later Works*, ed. Jo Ann Boydston, Southern Illinois University Press. The evidence for this position will be spelled out in full in a later monograph by Edel and Flower on Dewey's two ethics.

13. This interpretation is outlined in Abraham Edel, ''Notes on the Search for a Moral Philosophy in William James'' in *The Philosophy of William James*, ed. Walter Robert Corti (Felix Meiner Verlag, 1976) 255 ff.
14. Richard Rorty, *Philosophy and the Mirror of Nature* (Princeton University Press, 1979) 139.
15. *Consequences of Pragmatism*, 83.
16. *Ibid.*, 84
17. *Philosophy and the Mirror of Nature*, 359.
18. *Ibid.*, 360.

14

The Humanities and the State Councils: Retooling in the 1980s

*This lecture, given as the keynote address to the 1981 National Confer-
ence of State Humanities Councils, in Washington D.C., reflects in
historical and philosophical perspective on the lessons of the ten years
of existence of the program. A central thread is, of course, the fea-
sibility of "outreach," and whether the humanities can really be
"practical", as well as the special role that the humanities may have in
a world of rapid change.*

At a time of crisis such as the present, we have to look to the basic aims of
our program, how they worked out in practice, the rationale for our continued
efforts, and perhaps most of all to see in principle and by example what the
possible contributions of our program are and can be to the ongoing development of American life and its traditions. Part I of this paper therefore deals
with our beginning, our promise, and the context of needs and values to which
the program was addressed. Part II suggests some lines of self-assessment: the
work of the councils, the reaction of the grass roots, the problems of the
humanists. Part III deals with hesitations, external attacks, and inner doubts:
how we may get beyond the recurrent elitist-populist controversy, how to
understand and respond to the fuss over "secular humanism" and the humanities, whether the humanities can really be "practical."

Part 1

First, then, about ourselves. We have had so many projects on oral history
that it should not be difficult to marshall self–consciousness. We are now a
sturdy more–than–ten–year–old. When we were three our parents met in

211

conference, much as we do today, but in as yet unfederated form, and they talked of their hopes and fears. On that occasion, Ronald Berman, then Chairman of the NEH, said of the state councils effort:

> Of all the areas in the public program, in all their variety, responding as they do to many different needs and many different kinds of programs, none, and probably no activity of the Endowment, is as arduous, as fundamental, and perhaps as risky as the task we have asked you to realize. . . .
>
> It is arduous because you are creating an approach to the general public, and doing it in a novel structure and form. It is fundamental, because those who are interested in the humanities must demonstrate that they can do more than profess an article of faith. The state councils, therefore, bear the burden of reintroducing the humanities into American life at the most immediate level—at the level of the individual adult citizen. . . .
>
> It is also risky. Most arduous and fundamental things are: the program may lose its present high quality, it may lose its focus on the humanities, and it may lose its objectivity, and therefore its public acceptance.

And so he called on us to make tough judgments of quality, to keep a clear eye on the centrality of the humanities, to engage in dispassionate discussion.

There is much that we now know about our program and its achievements. Most important, we know that we are grown up, that we have worked out patterns of a relatively independent life so that, whatever the present crisis brings, we will endure. The scope of our work may suffer, and we may have to face certain temptations and resist them if the financial cuts are too great. For example, if we have to depend more on private contributions, it is conceivable that some contributors may want advertising or strings on the kind of projects involved; we will have to make some of those tough judgments of quality.

We do not have to recapitulate today what we all know about the founding of NEH in 1965, the beginning of the state councils in 1970, what our structure became and how it was reshaped in 1976, the prescriptions that ensured our conformity to legal intent and accountability, what different experiments were tried with techniques of organization in many state councils, even what variety of projects by now finds a place in our annals, and what has been our outreach. We are told that there have been 26,000 projects, 10 million active participants, 200 million people reached through print and electronic media, and over 30,000 scholars involved in projects and councils. Such a factual picture is available in the reports of NEH and of our Federation. *Federation Reports* and the work of its Board of Directors are increasingly sophisticated in using comparative experience and in analyzing techniques. (For the latter, see for example the ''First Report of the Federation Study Group on Alternatives,'' in which the advantages and disadvantages of every technique from council-initiated projects to Resource Centers are carefully and subtly weighed.) We may take great satisfaction in our accomplishments, and doubtless this conference will advance fresh lines of effort. But what now concerns us is to clarify our basic thrust, its animating spirit. We know the general charge: to foster public understanding and appreciation of the humanities. But why, to what ends, with what expectations, under what pressures of social or spiritual needs, were governmental resources devoted to such enterprises?

Such an inquiry is usually formulated in terms of needs, problems, values. Concepts of this sort are interconnected: values also satisfy needs and help solve problems; behind needs lie values which make some things necessary; problems are essentially difficulties in satisfying conflicting needs or achieving conflicting values in specific contexts. In practice these are always complexly related. We are constantly surprised by the values that emerge as we deal with needs and problems and the needs that are furthered and the problems that are generated as we pursue known values. Only a conceptual tyranny will insist that we choose between whether the humanities are intrinsically valuable or their pursuit instrumental to allegedly external ends. Whole chapters in the history of philosophy and psychology show how we can be needlessly sidetracked by such dichotomies.

Looking back, then, it is easy to say that after World War II, in a time of rapid economic and technological expansion, when science had already acquired its post–Sputnik momentum and social science was the focus of heavy investment, when higher education was expanding for the first time to include a large proportion of our youth, it was perfectly natural that culture and the arts should have their turn. It did not matter that some saw it as the embellishment of a mature civilization, others as spiritual fuel for progress and a moral sharpening of social direction. After all, did not the great renaissance of ancient Athens come in a century that followed a successful war of defense against external dangers and the establishment of an empire that brought wheat and drachmas and aspiring intellectuals to the port of Piraeus? Joseph Duffey, former Chairman of NEH, looking back fifteen years after its founding, reminds us (*Humanities*, December 1980) that the report of a Commission preceding the founding declared that our "national ethic and morality or the lack of it, the national aesthetic and beauty or lack of it, the national use of our environment and our material accomplishments" depended upon the humanities. And Duffey adds that the argument for the Endowment is essentially a conservative call for the preservation of something of uncontested value.

When we move to the founding of the state councils in 1970, the situation is markedly changed. Now the aspect of problems and pressing needs stands out more clearly, and it becomes even more so as we go on into the seventies. I need scarcely remind you of the revolt of the youth in the sixties, the conflicts over the Vietnam War, the successive liberation movements, the turbulence in the cities, the shock of the Watergate episode. Disillusionment, loss of faith in our institutions, alienation, are the terms so often used to characterize this period. Is it in any way surprising that the initial focus of the state program was on bringing the humanities to the clarification of policy decisions? Where but to the humanities could we have gone at that time? The sciences had long boasted of their neutrality and the social sciences had aped the natural sciences. Of course we were seeking the roots of our American tradition, but how were we to understand that tradition itself? The charge to our program, while thoroughly humanistic, was at the same time thoroughly practical.

We have to look even deeper. It is necessary because we find so often the tendency to dismiss the struggles and disillusionment of the sixties and seventies as if they were brief illnesses in our body politic and our collective mentality, like measles that in the old days a child had to go through and could then forget, or the occasionally disturbing common cold. How often is it said that it is time to get over the ''Vietnam War syndrome.'' But in fact the turmoil of the sixties and seventies is only a small part of the vast changes and problems of our century. We gain a deeper understanding when we look at the last fifty years as a period of practical critique in which traditional institutions and practices, once fixed forms of society, have either been largely abandoned or else so transformed as to be scarcely recognizable. In every case, however, they have left a mass of problems to be faced. Consider the demise of colonialism, once a proud system of empire, and the present problems of the Third World; the practical demise of laissez–faire, whether by state or corporate control, and the problems of a social safety net; the loss of faith in business and in labor, and for that matter, in government and politics. The transformation of standards about sex and the family are almost paradigmatic: it is hard to imagine that only a short time ago divorce was a social disgrace and contraception was illegal; now polls show that 70% of our population, especially those with children under 17, are in favor of sex education in the schools. The succession of liberation movements has uncovered the depths of our discrimination and indifference and shaken faith in our integrity; and yet we now waver between our sense of justice and the cost of remedying our own past practices. We have lost our older confidence in the professions—the doctor, the lawyer, the psychiatrist, the journalist, the teacher—and to handle the resulting problems we tinker with codes of ethics and file malpractice suits. The list is infinitely long, but perhaps the depth of the critique is best shown by the fact that no institution was left standing on which to pivot reconstruction. One might have expected that education and technology would remain as the promise of progress. But higher education itself was a central object of attack in the 1960s; we need not rehearse the charges against it of processing students for the military–industrial complex. And technology was irretrievably associated with the underlying threat of nuclear war, with pollution, and the social sciences with the manipulation of people; the critique of science and technology in the first Club of Rome report in the early 1970s even set a timetable for ultimate disaster.

Disillusionment extended beyond institutions and practices to social philosophies and traditional ideals. This is a more complex story, but one element certainly has been that, as Nietzsche put it long ago, we have looked into the factory where ideals are manufactured. Our media have carried us behind the scenes in the grooming of candidates, the casting of images, and the techniques of Madison Avenue in the making of ideologies. Thus now, when for example George Gilder writes that business investment is carrying out the biblical injunction to cast your bread upon the waters, without a guarantee but only a hope of return, it sounds more like *Mad Magazine* than a serious analysis of economic ideals. Yet a full analysis of our reactions should not stop with the negative critiques alone. New conceptions and alternative ideals were voiced in the process of critique itself: love as against meritocracy; a new sense of personal autonomy and responsibility; a striving for participation and community rather than authority and obedience; and an enlarged conception of human rights.

Whatever the balance of optimism and pessimism, of hope and despair, it is enough to recognize that the America of 1965 and 1970, as indeed the America of the 1980s, was participating in a revolutionary period of history that called and still calls for thorough and pervasive reconstruction. In these respects our century is comparable to the seventeenth century with its revision of science and political forms, and to the late eighteenth century with its industrial, political, and intellectual revolutions. This is the deeper context of the Endowment's state program initiative of 1970—an America challenged and perplexed, yet confident enough still to face its growing problems, and intelligent enough to want the best of traditional thought brought to bear on its needs. How else shall we interpret the statutory mandate in the Endowment's legislative charter that "particular attention" be given to "the relevance of the humanities to the current conditions of national life"? And note too the characterization of the quest: arduous, fundamental, objective, full of risk. It was not a quest for answers, for objectivity means the facing of alternatives. It was a request for clarification and understanding of issues and the values of the American tradition and the human situation. As the Endowment later expressed its assumptions: "The national life is impoverished and the quality of life is endangered by the lack of continuing intercourse between scholars in the humanities and the public on matters of long-term concern." Perhaps too, as the bicentennial came into sight, there was a nostalgia for the way in which culture and philosophy and the growing sciences once played an immediate part in the fashioning of a new policy.

Part 2

We look now at the strengths and weaknesses of our past, in the effort to continue and expand the one and to improve the other. Let us take in turn the operations of: 1) the councils, 2) the grass roots, particularly in generating projects, and 3) the humanists.

1) The state councils got their bearings early. They already had the all-human perspective of national needs. Their urgent focus now was on the states—state consciousness, state geography and demography, state interests, and problems. Rhode Island, taking as much pride in being the smallest state as Texas did in being the largest, analyzed its ethnic population and raised immediate questions of their interrelation. Arizona, similarly mapping its state geographically and ethnically, devoted special attention to its large Native American population. Pennsylvania, finding its projects coming from established urban centers, turned to rural–urban relations and devised special techniques to stimulate and encourage rural areas. Minnesota made regionalism a topic of inquiry. Montana was led to the problem of political power. In one way or another, taking hold wherever projects could really get under way, the councils bit by bit expanded their scope and moved into higher gear.

The councils were quickly faced with a wide range of tasks: to separate projects that would give expression to basic intent from such as would not; to work out criteria of evaluation for projects that were carried through; to learn about the impact of techniques on purposes; to maintain democratic responsibility. In each of these, lessons of experience stand out clearly.

In determining acceptability, the councils had to differentiate projects that merely continued schooling from those that treated policy problems; projects attached to an historical event (such as the Holocaust) that might be merely commemorative from those that were probing lessons for contemporary attitudes; projects that proclaimed the virtues of a particular religion from those that carried human lessons about religion facing the modern world; projects that called for subsidizing works of art or dramatic production from those that dwelt with the impact of art and its criteria. (In this last case, cooperation was eventually worked out with arts councils.)

Criteria of evaluation were sharpened as particular projects were evaluated. Good attendance was not enough; it depended on the way the audience was affected. Audience participation was not enough; it depended on whether the discussion was pointed or just meandering. Even feeling good as a result was not enough; that might come from simply being entertained. And of course just an audience questionnaire was not enough; it depended on what was asked as well as what was answered.

Councils, in considering projects, had to dip into detail for the impact of techniques; the general merit of a proposal was not enough. Take, for example, two projects submitted on the same theme of ethnic discrimination in television. One sorted and presented its material by ethnic groups, and on separate occasions; the other put its data together for comparative analysis. The likelihood was the lesson of the first would be to teach each group separately, that *it* was the object of discrimination; the lesson of the second would pose the common problem of stereotyping and insensitivity to ethnic feeling. We might almost out–McLuhan McLuhan here—not just the medium but the technique shaped the message.

Councils have, on the whole, felt their democratic responsibilities. For the most part they kept full responsibility for decision making as a whole, even though the multiplication of proposals forced some division of labor. They have rarely allowed the administrative apparatus to do such jobs as would limit or predetermine their decisions. They have been careful not to narrow the confines of proposals even when it was the custom to select a state theme, and they responded with cautious experimentation to the changes that were made in 1976 when the policy focus was diminished and greater variety became possible.

On the whole, commentators on the calibre of our state councils have commended the tradition of excellence and devotion. We need not, then, go on with this, sweet as may be the music of congratulations.

2) Perhaps congratulations should go even more to the grass roots from which our projects came. Putting aside the small group that bore the mark of professional grantsmanship, the vast majority came forward with projects and problems of appropriate common concern. And while many were rough–hewn, many were finetuned to the limits of practical decision and to basic values. It is impossible briefly to characterize the scope and variety of the projects. Of course there were innumerable approaches to issues of ethnicity. Of course numerous studies enriched the self–esteem of groups and communities, assisted by historians who taught the techniques of oral history. Of course in the surge of the women's liberation movement all kinds of familial and interpersonal concerns found expression. Let me not continue a recital that properly would require not mere topics but the significance of what was approached, why at that particular time, and what clarification of alternatives was secured. I venture the hypothesis that a collective democratic wisdom was really shown at the grass roots in the perception of what troubles us today. It did not aim necessarily at solutions, but at discovering paths and alternatives, considering arguments and amassing lessons of experience and humanistic insights. Take as an example the large assortment of ethnicity

projects. Think of projects on the reception of different Asian groups at a time when refugees were entering the country and being settled in old and established communities, projects that even in the simplest terms brought different groups living side by side to meet one another, to see the cultural riches on both sides. Think of the lessons of the Holocaust projects at a time when the Ku Klux Klan is attempting to expand by setting interest against interest. Think in general of the many projects that have brought to traditional minorities the sense of their own cultural contribution to the mainstream, the lesson that to have joined American life need not entail an abandonment, that hyphenated Americans are not less integrated Americans, that all Americans, except the American Indians, are essentially newcomers following a promise, with only a difference in time.

The ethnicity projects are also a good example of the way learning could take place over time, not necessarily in solving problems, but in revealing the deeper issues that have to be faced. The earlier ethnicity projects had as their outcome, whether intentional or not, first the enhancement of self-esteem in groups that had been the subject of discrimination or indifference; second, the sense of their positive contribution to American life and culture. The later ones begin to come in sight of the question: Where are we going? It is one thing to add a proud coherence to an ethnic group. But what would you do with a proposal that wanted to investigate ways of restoring an urban ethnic enclave and lamented the fact that the young were moving out into the wide community? I suspect you would think immediately of the cities in which ethnic enclaves do exist and ask whether they are a source of cultural riches or of intergroup conflict. In fact, our ethnic projects are increasingly compelled to face the deeper meaning of an integrated community, once the old and roughshod ideal of wholesale assimilation has been trimmed of its arrogance; we have to face the precise meaning of pluralism and whether it may contain a disintegrating potential. The issue of bilingual education has perhaps brought it to its sharpest focus; whether such a policy is providing an appropriate, even urgent, service during a period in which the student is learning English, and whether teaching history and mathematics in other languages can be used to accelerate the learning of English, or whether the door is rather being opened to the establishment of permanent linguistic enclaves that will thereby be shut off from one another. At that point we have to reckon with the lessons of French Canada and of Belgium. It will not be enough to say, correctly no doubt, that an exploited minority becomes an overreacting minority, and we can remedy this by a fixed policy of equality and freedom. For even with freedom one has to decide which way to go. The United States, which has been moving backwards on questions of language teaching in the schools, has not opted for the happy multilingual solution of small countries like Holland and Denmark. What then lies in the ideal of cultural pluralism that has so often been offered in opposition to an assimilation that submerges the old culture? Or what intermediate ideals may be elaborated?

These are the deeper questions which the most recent of our ethnicity projects may help us ask and face. Indeed, such questioning may be related to the long–standing issue of deliberate communal experimentation in partial isolation. The early history of Mormonism in the United States was such an experiment. Similar experiments have been found among American Indians. For example, the Mesquakie, in the mid-West, disapproving of the competitive–aggressive quality of American life, bought their own land and organized their own community but for the most part remained employed in the larger society. Such social separation may be more frequent in an unstructured way than we think. America is, to speak tritely, a large and varied and complexly differentiated society. We are moving into the area of problems of social and humanistic policy, of where to build bridges and where to cut bridges, and the costs to the people involved.

There are many other fascinating types of projects—concerning business, labor, women, drama, poetry—that could lead us on and on. Let me mention simply two that somehow linger in my mind as showing the creative spirit at the grass roots. A one industry town lost its one industry and found no aid from business or government. What could it do? It could assemble people of experience in business and economics and, in its troubled spirit, humanist scholars to deliberate on its plight. Did that furnish a happy ending? No so far as I know. But it brought greater unity to the community and turned it from despair to collective effort. Santayana's picture of spontaneous prayer well captures the point: we only pray where there is nothing else we can do to alleviate the trouble. Our prayers explain to the deity the detail of our plight and the need for help—despite the belief that God knows everything. In this one-way dialogue, the spirit grows even if the issue is not resolved, and as we clarify our broader purposes we rededicate our efforts.

The second project I have in mind is remarkable in the sheer fact that people thought of doing it. Here is a coal mining town that was long idle and suddenly there is, thanks to the oil crisis, a move toward a new prosperity. Would you expect one to look the gift of prosperity in the mouth? They did. They organized a reflective project, with fine representation of the scientific and philosophic and historical, to see what prosperity coming in this way would mean to their community. Would it be simply a cycle of boom and bust, leaving them with a disintegrated community, a disrupted nature, and an array of fresh problems? How could that be avoided and yet the gift of prosperity accepted? What was worth doing, what not?

3) From the activity of the state councils and the creativity of the grass roots, we turn thirdly to the functioning of the humanists. If in the other two I stress our strengths, here I want to focus on our shortcomings. The record of

project evaluations shows how often a successful humanist presentation stimulates and brings novel elements to discussion. I ask why this does not happen more as a rule than as a gratifying surprise. The answer goes to the heart of the humanities and their mode of operation.

I am not saying that humanists have not done a good job, but that we have made it harder for them to do such a job. For we stereotype them, we want to set them off as a group distinct from any other intellectual group, and we do this by a simplified and wholesale description. For example, if we have a symposium on Three Mile Island, the physicists are there to give us the facts, the economists to present a cost–benefit analysis, and then we call on the assembled humanists, whatever their special discipline, and say, ''Now tell us about the fundamental values involved.'' Or we say, ''We now have the quantitative reckoning; how about the qualitative judgments?'' Or one more: ''Well, folks, that's the picture. Now how do we *feel* about it?''

You recognize the string of dichotomies—fact-value, objective–subjective, quantitative–qualitative, knowledge–feeling (or appreciation)—and could summon up a host of others, by which the humanities have been cut off from other intellectual enterprises and locked into a limiting role. Most of these dichotomies have been challenged as our knowledge grew and our philosophic thought became more refined. They reflected stages in the development of the different disciplines at different periods of human thought. In the seventeenth century the disciplines were still close together; Newton was a natural philosopher. In the eighteenth century, when the social sciences got seriously under way in the economics of Adam Smith, the humanistic disciplines were not set off separately; they all fell under what was called the ''moral sciences.'' Adam Smith's *Wealth of Nations* dealt with economic man and his *Theory of the Moral Sentiments* with moral man; the different human phenomena were self-interest and sympathy, and both could be studied in the picture of human nature, to provide which was the work of psychology. In the nineteenth century, by Darwin's time, physics and biology, as long established sciences, were ranged opposite classics, entrenched as the humanistic and evaluative study of the ideals of life. (Even here Greek had had to struggle against entrenched Latin to be admitted.) T.H. Huxley in the later part of the nineteenth century had to argue for the admission of science into education, and he did it on the claim that science can convey life's ideals as well as classics, apart from being also practical. By the twentieth century, the physical and natural sciences, separately ensconced, became louder in voicing their value neutrality; the social sciences, as they grew, tried to imitate the physical sciences; and the miscellany of disciplines outside both got roughly identified as humanities. All three areas are by this time rich, varied, and complex. I think it should be clear that none of them, whatever the historical reasons for which each has contracted its self–image, really fit the narrowed descriptions imposed upon them. Whatever principle may be suggested as differentiating the sciences and the humanities, we can find sciences and humanities that share it, and sciences and humanities that lack it. A full examination of this situation, with ample illustration, would, I think, make clear that there is continuity in all human inquiry: imagination, values and purposes, formal technicality and measurement and evidence, responsible tracing of relations, general ideas and particular descriptions, and all the rest, belong to all inquiry. There is, of course, division of labor and difference of emphasis in various contexts, but we must not be misled by these into selling short fundamental unities.

Such reflections may help us in correcting what I have suggested to be the chief weakness in program development, namely treating the humanities wholesale. We need to work on the possible contributions of the different disciplines that make up the humanities. This should be done in the formative stage of projects, and attuned more directly to their specific needs. Where there is ethnocentrism, anthropology may enlighten. Where there is dogmatism, comparative religion may be a solvent. Where there is over–intellectualism, poetry can restore the balance of feeling. Where people are lost in detail, drama furnishes a plot or architecture teaches structure. Where words stumble and response becomes inarticulate—where "you know" replaces the comma—literature brings fresh resources. Where we are mired in the present, history liberates us. And since most projects are complex, a selection of a number of the humanities will be most appropriate, but to make a variety of contributions, not just to do the same job.

If this, as I see it, has been our central weakness, it is one that lies wholly within our power to correct. In this respect we are fortunate in its location.

Part 3

We now turn to the debates about the nature of our program, the external attacks upon it, and the inner doubts and hesitations: 1) the view that we are populist but should be elitist; 2) the attack that we are spreading "secular humanism"; 3) the doubt whether we can really be "practical."

1) If any of us thought that the elitist-populist debate concerning our program belonged to the early Carter days, we were disillusioned by the remarks (recently heard on radio) of a professor who was then a leading candidate for the chairmanship of NEH. He said that he would not spend money on populism, that the purpose was not to serve the populace nor the humanists, but the humanities. While he might have popular programs spreading the humanities (like TV presentation of the Adamses), he would not give money to labor unions to explore their past or money to discuss the Carter energy policy, and so forth. In the earlier public debates about popul-

ism, we were charged with bringing a diluted culture to the masses, and it was even contended that culture is intrinsically elitist. In the most practical terms, it was argued, where resources are scarce, they should be apportioned to established centers and known researchers and artists.

The tumult over elitism and populism in connection with our program seems to miss the point. The serious issues of policy in the allocation of resources are not clarified by saying that we have to choose between these alternatives.

Elitism in a democracy sounds innocent enough. It is the natural outcome of meritocracy. You leave an open door and the best will walk through. Such meritocracy pervades all fields. The elite are the achievers, the stars in athletics and acting, in music and book writing, in journalism and politics. Even chess has its innings. But though it sounds innocent, elitism retains the basic aristocratic belief that excellence is limited to the few; the many, marked by incapacity, have little sense of excellence; they long for charismatic leaders and share vicariously in the achievement of their betters. Accordingly, the elitist society directs its resources to the top and elitism thus becomes a self–fulfilling prophesy. Its actual practice curbs opportunity, accepts the manipulation of people, and turns the *de facto* denial of opportunity into the arrogant assumption of inevitable superiority of a few. It becomes too easy then to survey the present scene, as the historian Barbara Tuchman did in an article in *The New York Times Magazine* one Sunday this past year, and deprecate the sleazy in production, the absence of quality in "fast foods and junky clothes and cute greeting cards . . . in endless paperbacks of sex and slaughter, Gothics and westerns" and ask "whether popular appeal will become the governing criterion and gradually submerge all but isolated rocks of quality."

I call this the easy path, because its usual procedure is to give a kaleidoscopic view of lack of quality and jump to an attack on egalitarianism and populism. Influences are not examined: why quality control is ignored in one society and made central in another; the impact of competition for profits on sleaziness; the pressure of advertising, and so on. In fact, a sense of excellence is widespread in many areas: for example, our youth appreciates quality and the discipline that goes into it when they are concerned with sport or with dancing. The issue may then be fields in which it is exercised. Again, it is easy, in assuming basic incapacity, to condemn our educational system and forget that our century is the first in the history of mankind that has attempted to provide education for the mass of people—usually under the burdens of insufficient support, bureaucratic organization, and still dominant elitist attitudes.

The elitist attitude to the populace in matters of culture is a heritage of the past that forecloses experimentation for the future. Cicero once advised a friend never to get a servant from Britain, for they are barbarians, ever incapable of culture. Elitism thus basically sidetracks the democratic faith without giving it the opportunity for a long–range testing—the faith expressed modestly in Jefferson's last letter. He wrote: "the mass of mankind has not been born with saddles on their backs, nor a favored few booted and spurred, ready to ride them legitimately, by the grace of God." (June 24, 1826) In these words he was echoing a long tradition of democratic demand; earlier, in 1685, the Leveller, Richard Rumbold, had said on the scaffold: "I am sure there was no man born marked of God above another; for none comes into the world with a saddle on his back, neither any booted and spurred to ride him."

Such modest rejection of elitism is not equivalent to populism. Populism is the other face of the coin, the extreme reaction of those who are discriminated against to the doctrines of discrimination. It is the "Black is beautiful" stage in the Black liberation movement. One does not argue with populism any more than one argues about standards of beauty with the Black liberation movement, or whether God is female with the women's movement. One removes the discrimination, renews the Voting Rights Act or passes the Equal Rights Amendment. Then we can look realistically to what is possible at what stage of development.

We get nowhere in policy discussion by asking: shall we be elitist or shall we be populist? The realistic problem is to secure a full view of the variety of tasks that a society like ours has to undertake if it is to offer genuine support for and secure the maximum benefit from the pursuit of the humanities. Take as a neutral paradigm for such an analysis the case of science. The first task is to support original scientists in their work. A second is to provide opportunities for people to be attracted to science, to experiment and learn their capacities, especially those whose promise would not be reached in the usual ways. A third task—and this is the center of the storm—is to develop an understanding of science in the adult population generally, so that there will be some acquaintance with and appreciation of its work and ways of operating. We know too well the consequences of neglecting this third task: science is regarded as a kind of magic, TV ads parade the scientist in a white coat as a kind of witch doctor, and science is conceived as another kind of dogmatism.

In the case of the humanities, the first task is obviously the support of research, just as the National Endowment for the Arts supports creative art. The second task, to develop that interest in the humanities out of which future humanistic work will come, is presumably carried out by the schools and colleges and universities, as well as other cultural institutions. The third task—to bring about a widespread sense of the humanities and their relevance to human life—is precisely the work of NEH and our program. Its aim is not just to show the humanities to the people, as works in museums used to be shown and books in libraries were made available. (Now both museums and libraries have moved ahead in the attempt to activate the public.) Its aim is to stimulate the active powers, to involve the public and to bring it into active participation.

The problem for which elitism and populism have served as demagogic counters is that of allocating resources among these three functions. On the one hand it is said that only original work counts and on principle it should have priority, for without it there would be nothing to bring to the adult public. On the other, it is pointed out that without public understanding and appreciation creation would suffer from its isolation and it would lack support. The actual direction of policy is far more complex: it depends on the stage of development of the society, the extent to which other institutions are carrying out the tasks in part, the current needs of the society, and a complex of other factors. We have seen in retrospect (in Part 1) the crisis that generated our program and, if anything, the underlying needs have intensified since that time. Let me cite one startling indication. You have all doubtless studied the report on the state of the humanities issued last year by the special commission set up by the Rockefeller Foundation. Did you not find it astounding that the report called repeatedly on NEH to stimulate educational initiative in the schools to advance the humanities? Why turn to NEH? Does it mean that we have done such a good job for the adults that we are now asked to do a comparable job for the children? When you consider the vast resources of schools and colleges, taken collectively throughout the country, and the meagre total budget of NEH, that such a request should come in our direction must mean something very positive about our work.

2) We now turn to external attacks. They are not merely accusations that projects are propagating "secular humanism," but in some cases involve overt action. Not limited to a particular part of the country, they have come in Maine, Arizona, Louisiana, and doubtless elsewhere. In one place there is a general condemnation of the humanities, in another objection to the discussion of particular topics, in other contexts general attacks on books and schools, in some attempted legislation (the Arkansas legislature passed last March an act which called for teaching creationism as a "scientific alternative" to evolution; it was then challenged successfully in the courts.) In 1980, we are told, 1,200 communities reported pressure for censorship, compared to 300 in 1979. The kind of virulence found may be seen in the Louisiana case, where the idea of a philosopher–in–residence in a hospital was resisted with such intellectual gems as that they would not tolerate an "atheist–communist–existentialist–pragmatist" in the hospital and the charge that it would destroy the religious faith of dying patients. (*Federation Reports* July/August 1981). The literature of assault on secular humanism is, however, much more elaborate than this. An account of the movement in *Newsweek* (July 6, 1981) compares it to the witch hunts of the 1950s. In comparison to the sweep of

these onslaughts, the diatribes on John Dewey and progressive education over the many decades are a model of restraint. The present attacks appear to stretch in their denunciation from the recent "Humanist Manifesto" back to Renaissance humanism (it took early false steps) and even to Thomas Aquinas for reintroducing a humanistic Aristotelianism into Western religion. I quote a further choice item from the *Newsweek* story: "(Anti-humanist) LaHaye excoriates Michelangelo for sculpting a nude David—when the Bible makes it clear in Genesis that, having fallen from grace, man should cover his naked-ness. 'The Renaissance obsession with nude "art forms" ' LaHaye declares, 'was the forerunner of the modern humanist's demand for pornography in the name of freedom'."

There may be an initial hesitation in entering into controversy on matters of religion in our society. This properly reflects our traditional respect for religious beliefs in a society that made religious freedom a basic tenet. Of course, nonbelief is equally protected, while comparative religion is included among the humanities by Congressional listing. In matters of religion and non–religion, we are a pluralistic society.

As to the relation of humanists and religion, it is easy to set the record straight. Since humanists study men's works and interests, there may be different hypotheses about and attitudes toward religion in the outcome of their studies. Some humanists are religious, as were many Renaissance humanists; some are secular. These are not necessarily cut off from one another in contemporary life; for example, a movement like the Ethical Culture Society in the twentieth century is one in which the moral aspect attracts both religious and non–religious humanists. Even among secular humanists there are at least three different views. Some see religion as embodying a dogmatism that stands in the way of human progress; they regard the way the Church treated Galileo in the seventeenth century as the appropriate paradigm for all religious influence. This seems to be the view of the most recent Humanist Manifesto so prominent in the current controversy. A second secularist view, however, sees religion as a sociocultural form through which people have ordered their lives and articulated their values. Of course there has been dogmatism in religion, but there has been dogmatism also in most human institutions—in medicine, psychiatry, economics, even at points in the history of science. Institutions tend to be like that. From this perspective it is more important to know what kind of a God is worshipped than whether one is religious or not. A third secularist view—I have in mind the Marxian—falls somewhere between the other two. The fragmentary quotation that "religion is the opiate of the people" is misleading, for it is often taken to suggest quietistic uses of religion to disarm the oppressed. The full quotation (in Marx's *Toward the Critique of Hegel's Philosophy of Right*) is quite different: "Religious distress is at once the *expression* of real distress and the *protest* against real distress. Religion is the sigh of the oppressed, the heart of a heartless world, just as it is the spirit of an unspiritual situation. It is the opiate of the people.''

Of course such analysis will not stop the attacks. Michael M. Mooney's *The Ministry of Culture* (see Charles Cole's review in *Federation Reports*, March/April 1981) offers the bizarre thesis that the National Federation of State Humanities Councils is a lobby for NEH in its effort to coordinate culture in America and establish the humanities as a secular religion. The argument is apparently having it both ways: secular humanism is irreligious or it is itself a religion, as suits the purposes of a particular contention.

We cannot come to grips with such phenomena without a thorough understanding of what is going on. Let us consider this briefly in two ways: a social analysis of the present context to see what prompts this crude recrudescence, and an historical glance at the intellectual tradition within the philosophy of religion that centers around the response to the growth of secular knowledge.

The historical context of the Moral Majority is the period of revolutionary change in which old ways are broken and adjustment to change is difficult. Over and over again the Moral Majority talks of the breakdown of the family, the drug culture, the increased incidence of crime, pornography, the weakening of responsibility, and so on. Let us frankly recognize that their problems are our problems; not many of the evils by which they are appalled have been undiscussed in our projects throughout the country. What they represent is, however, a far different matter. If their outlook is not the sigh of the oppressed, it is the blind striking out of the depressed. They lack the spirit that has been most characteristic of the American tradition in facing problems—to analyze them and readapt institutions and ways of thought and action to come to grips with them. This is not a liberal prerogative: traditional conservatives too, in clinging to values of the past, at least try to preserve them through a process of reconstructing social life. What we are faced with here, however, is the demand for a wholesale return to an imagined past of blind security.

As for modes of thought, there has always been a regressive approach in the history of religion as well as an approach that reached out to the advance of knowledge. It is clearly seen in the very early question—a very practical one—whether people should run away from plagues, if it is God's will that the plague occur. Or the similar argument that illness is punishment and so should not be treated by doctors; this was countered by the argument that a doctor curing was also God's will. Such arguments are not relics of the past; they are recurring today about genetic engineering as a way of eliminating certain genetic defects, and theologians take opposite sides. The same duality of reaction was found in the rise of science. While Galileo and Copernicus were rejected by the dominant Church of the time, Newtonian science gave an impetus to a religious outlook: God created the world and set up the laws by which it operates; science is thus finding out God's plan in creation. For example, American Puritanism, as seen in the thought of William Ames who was a most influential thinker in seventeenth century Massachusetts, welcomed scientific advance as increased knowledge of God's ways. Both religious and secular scientists continue such a tradition. Immanuel Kant wrote a preface to his scientific treatise, *Universal Natural History and Theory of the Heavens*, in the mid-eighteenth century, explaining why his theory is not deleterious to religion. He was attempting to show, on Newtonian principles, how from the universal diffusion of the primitive matter of all bodies, the evolution of matter to its present form could be explained. This shows the greater, not the lesser glory of God. Many of the nineteenth century formulations of evolutionary theory are in the same spirit. T.H. Huxley, who was an agnostic and in fact coined that term, said (in his Prolegomena to "Evolution and Ethics"): "It is very desirable to remember that evolution is not an explanation of the cosmic process, but merely a generalized statement of the methods and results of that process. And, further, if there is proof that the cosmic process was set going by any agent, then that agent will be the creator of it and of all its products. . . ."

Clearly, science has not been interfering with religion, but attending to its own business. The reverse was not, however, always the case. I recall the classic work of Andrew D. White, *A History of the Warfare of Science with Theology in Christendom* (1895). White, an historian, joined with Ezra Cornell in founding Cornell University as a non–sectarian college. As he says in the Introduction, "It required no great acuteness to see that a system of control which, in selecting a Professor of Mathematics or Language or Rhetoric or Physics or Chemistry, asked first and above all to what sect or even to what wing or branch of a sect he belonged, could hardly do much to advance the moral, religious, or intellectual development of mankind." White was amazed by the storm of opposition to the founding of Cornell along such lines. This roused his interest, for he was himself profoundly religious, and prompted his book. The book traces the battle between dogmatic theology and science in discipline after discipline. It is a massive source book by a professional historian. His conclusion that dogmatic theology is the enemy of science embraces also the view that dogmatic theology is the enemy of religion.

If history is repeating itself after an interval of almost a century, it looks as if it has moved, in the familiar saying, from tragedy to farce. For the situation is now quite different. Science is firmly established in the total character of our life and civilization. It is not threatened by the Moral Majority's dogmatism nor by dogmatism as such, since it has built fallibility and corrigibility into its method. The great threat of theological dogmatism is to religion itself. The Moral Majority, in formulating its case as religion *versus* secular humanism, is attempting to speak for all religion, that is, to identify religion as such with its position. I do not think the vast religious movements of America will allow themselves to be thus outwitted. Religion of our time is not exempt from the ferment of our time.

I do not believe that the humanities are in any serious danger either, provided only that they do not yield to fear. Doubtless you will want to discuss how to meet the current attacks, and what should be done in particular contexts. Obviously publication analyzing the issues is called for. In some cases emphasis might fall, as it does in Yale President A. Bartlett Giamatti's speech to the incoming freshmen recently, on the disastrous effects of the Moral Majority's actions—to stamp out independent thought and inquiry would make a mockery of education. In some cases legal action might be appropriate, as in the American Civil Liberties Union's lawsuit against the Arkansas legislation. And so on. But it would be falling into a trap to try to resolve a particular situation by saying that we are not secular humanists or not humanists of type X but of type Y. Such a mode of defense is equivalent to abandoning the field to the attacking position but claiming personal virtue. If you take an oath that "I am not, nor have I ever been, a secular humanist," you will have surrendered your true ground, that of the American tradition of free inquiry. Scholars in the humanities are committed to a mode of life, and it is a mode that we can proclaim with pride.

3) We turn finally to the problem of the meaning of practicality. In some respects this is most important, for it concerns self–doubt. Attacks from outside have a unifying effect and serve to compel clarification of our purposes. Self–doubt can be much more inhibiting. I have in mind the residual skepticism among many humanists of the practical intent of our program. They feel that by participating in projects they are somehow called upon to produce results. In the now standard examples, they are expected to relate *King Lear* to problems of gerontology, to draw lessons from *Oliver Twist* for day care centers, or about race prejudice from *Othello*. This seems to them to miss the central point of the humanities and to demand of humanists a practical competence which they do not have nor claim to have. These misgivings were recently formulated for the case of applied moral philosophy by Professor Annette Baier of the University of Pittsburgh, writing in the April 1981 issue of *Humanities*. Asking whether professional moral philosophers can be of any practical assistance to business people or to physicians, she decides in effect that they should stick to their unworldly and detached thinking, "that can, over many generations and after much non-theoretical testing, contribute to the quality of our contemplative life, and thus to the quality of our practical decisions." This is what she thinks happened to Locke and Hegel and Mill, and is likely to happen to Rawls. She fears that philosophers, trying to be practical, may engage in rationalizing existent practices or offer half-baked ideas.

I rather think that the experience of moral philosophy has other and different lessons for humanists. They may not be immediately apparent because of what happened in the discipline during the middle third of our century. Moral philosophy, at least in its most popular schools, largely withdrew from normative judgment and set up a Berlin wall between normative thought and the logical analysis of moral discourse. For a period the language of ethics alone became the legitimate subject matter of moral philosophy. Whether it was carried on in the formal language of positivism or the informal language of ordinary discourse, in both cases it became a very technical and very specialized "metaethics." When it looked back to the history of philosophy it focused on parts that helped such an inquiry. Then in the 1970s the pent up normative problems of our world burst upon us. Today moral philosophers are found working in problems of bioethics, technological ethics, legal ethics, business ethics; there are institutes that concentrate on environmental ethics, that deal with population problems and world hunger, and so on and on.

Several important points in this development should be noted. First, the outreach came from the professions, not the philosophers looking for work. It was accentuated in medicine by the new techniques of organ transplant and the like, but it also stemmed from the growth of long time researches. Take an example. A medical professor was doing research on Huntington's chorea. For this he had to gather a population of people who now had the disease and another group in which there was reason to think it was latent. In short, in order to do his research he would have to alarm people who were going along in blissful ignorance, only a few of whom might later get the disease, and with no anticipation of a cure or prediction of incidence. Was it ethical to proceed? He did not have an answer. Whom should he call to clarify and explore the issue? Somehow it reminded him of the kinds of questions his ethics professor had talked about years ago. So he phoned a philosopher.

Second, the appeal was not for answers or assigned imperatives, but for clarification of alternatives and presuppositions, for understanding. Those among you who have had experience of or are acquainted with the numerous humanist–in–residence programs that our councils have sponsored in hospitals, dentistry schools, nursing education, and even in small communities, will bear me out that successes have come not from laying down the line with answers, but from helping clarify problems, unravelling their complexities, and at the same time learning from the cooperation of people in the field. The story of the development of interdisciplinary cooperation on the treatment of human subjects is one of this sort. Take another example: a conference a few years ago between a group of designated humanists and the people in one of the major TV networks who check the suitability of dramas, sitcoms, and the like before they are used. They half hoped that humanists would provide for them a checklist of American values to which they could refer in their work, perhaps even have computerized. Instead, they got a sense of what a full–bodied character and a rich episode would be as developed in great literature with all its conflicts and ambivalences and indeterminacies. They welcomed the cautions against one–dimensionality. And the humanists got a better knowledge of the complexities of a practical decision.

Third, if we look back to the history of philosophy with open eyes and not just as Santayana says of literary history, like a man looking over a crowd to find his friends, it is clear that moral philosophers were constantly dealing with normative questions about the character of institutions and practices—forms of government, property, liberty, family, war, education, and the rest. Aristotle wrote his *Politics* not merely on the structure of ethical concepts; Locke on government, not merely epistemology; Hegel on law, not merely dialectical logic; Mill on liberty and economics, not merely on utilitarian ethical ideas. It was philosophical neglect in the twentieth century, not philosophical history, that gave us the strange idea that philosophy had no practical outreach. Indeed, even if the whole array of present normative ethics had not suddenly blossomed under new problems, the practical side of moral philosophy was always there in the great philosophers.

Fourth, I think a more careful history of moral philosophy—a much underdeveloped field—will show that moral philosophers were generally closer to the firing line in the past than Professor Baier suggests. Aristotle is dealing directly with the class conflicts of his time. Locke is working out a theory of limited government, of property, of the right to revolution, that is, if not tailor–made for the purpose, at least congenial to the bloodless revolution of 1688. Hume states the case against Mercantilism on the verge of the Industrial Revolution. Mill writes his *Representative Government* on the struggle for extension of the franchise and his writings on women and on liberty are directed to what he sees as the necessary reforms of his time. I am not talking of incidents in the lives of these philosophers, of which there are plenty, but of theoretical writings that, in Professor Baier's fine phrase, provide understanding that may (I would rather say *do*) make a difference.

Fifth, there is the question of immediacy. Why insist that philosophers should write for a future that might, after the seeping down of their thought, find it practical? This is exactly the line of argument that scientists used before they got to nuclear energy and recombinant genetics. But historians of technology see the temporal gap between pure science and its uses becoming shorter and shorter. Let me offer a poignant case from moral philosophy. Francis Biddle, having served as Attorney-General in the early 1940s, witnessed with alarm the growth of the loyalty program for federal employees, with its list of subversive organizations. When he saw how it blossomed into a broad witch hunt, he wrote a book, *The Fear of Freedom* (1951), in which he reflected on the phenomena. He recalled the philosophical views of his professor, Josiah Royce, about the nature of loyalty. Royce, in his *The Philosophy of Loyalty* (1911), had argued that loyalty was ultimately to ideals. Biddle decided it was all wrong to ask people to be loyal to the government, that the government was the servant of the people and the master should not be asked to be loyal to the servant. Now, are we to say that Royce's work was detached theory in 1911 and became practical in 1951 in the light of Biddle's experiences in the 1940s? In any case it would have been practical had a project of the D.C. Community Humanities Council presented Royce's ideas for discussion in the early 1940s in relation to the then seething political problem of loyalty. Perhaps the Maine Council is now educating the Biddles of the north in its legislative relations program.

From these considerations I would like to draw two conclusions: one about the meaning of practicality, the other about the returns that practicality brings to the discipline that is concerned with it.

There is a narrow sense of practicality and there is a broad sense. I take it that Professor Baier was protesting against the narrow sense even though she did not do justice to the broad sense. The narrow sense is like the common use of "pragmatic" which equates it with expediency, often opportunism. The broad sense is like the distinctively American philosophy of pragmatism, which saw the purposive character of thought and took an experimental approach to ideas in terms of their consequences in human life, reflection, and action. In the broad sense, Rawls' book *(A Theory of Justice)* was practical, not just because it gave economists something to chew on when it used decision theory in relation to justice, but because it threw down the gauntlet in its fundamental principle of equality. It challenged meritocracy in a country that was struggling with problems of removing discrimination and of affirmative action. For Rawls postulated that everyone was entitled to equal shares except where a less equalitarian principle of distribution brought benefits to the disadvantaged as well; benefits to the greatest number was not enough. For this he was immediately branded by conservative opponents as a "New Equalitarian." The battle over equality and its proper forms is a practical struggle of our time, and ideas that make a difference in it are operating practically. In that sense *King Lear* helps in our understanding of the problems of elders, and *Oliver Twist* sharpens our sense of what is wrong in the relations of adults and children. No narrow further practical application is needed.

Let me illustrate this broad practical sense in the case of humor. It is the last thing we would expect to be practical. But here are a couple of jokes—it is time to throw some into our discussion. One I recall from somewhere in Beard's work (Charles, not James; on American history, not the gourmet life); it is a nineteenth-century joke about a congressional junket and reads something like this: "The train on which the congressmen were travelling was held up by robbers. After relieving the robbers of their watches and their purses, the congressmen went happily on their way.'' Could a practical attitude to the political life have been more pithily conveyed by a treatise on political science? My second example comes from a Sunday column of Russell Baker, attuned to Columbus Day of 1981. He writes in his blithely merry way about Columbus landing in the new world, asking the Indians ''Where am I?'' and then proclaiming that he has discovered America. Baker contrasts this with Julius Caesar landing in Britain, asking the natives about the country, and not claiming discovery but rather seeing it as a nice province to conquer. The practical lesson is biting in spite of its geniality. To celebrate the *discovery* of America is equivalent to saying that the Indians do not count. It is a practical lesson in ethnicity. We can still celebrate Columbus Day, but as a thanksgiving for our opportunities to get here.

This same illustration can make clear our second conclusion, that attention to broad practicality may bring fruitful returns to the discipline on its theoretical side. It has doubtless done that to many participants in our programs. Suppose a historian writes a book examining the evidence whether Columbus or Leif Ericson discovered America. Would not the practical attention we noted change the very formulation of his project? It might even expand it to look for the relations of the newcomers and the natives, and who knows what this would mean for the historical inquiry. A recent review of a book on the history of slavery finds it otherwise excellent but comments on its omission of the experience of the slaves themselves, their feelings and predicament. No historian who had brought his historical learning to our many projects in which such aspects were central would have missed this dimension. Here attentiveness to the practical impact of history would have enriched the discipline itself. This, I think, will happen to the theories of moral philosophy when the vast present extension into practice brings its lessons back to moral theory. Our very conceptions of the nature and tasks of moral theory will be transformed and much theoretical analysis will be required for the reconstruction. I leave it to you in the different humanistic disciplines to decide how far this holds equally for the study of literature when it goes beyond the New Criticism, and brings the reactions of an audience into its historical studies of the great works; for jurisprudence when it goes beyond the skeleton of the legal system to the new impact of law on the lives of people; to linguistics when its criteria of proper usage are shaken by the practice of common dialects; and so on for discipline after discipline. Such inquiries call for an expertise which I do not have, but which collectively you do. Perhaps my example from philosophy can be a useful paradigm.

A final question, particularly for the historians among you. Do you know of any program in the past that ever attempted to move into the whole adult public, to engage its participation, not simply to bring good works to them, and geared to their felt concerns, not merely ours? Has there ever before been such a program sponsored by government? If it is as distinctive as it appears to be, then it is as dramatic as a moonshot. In any case it is an experiment in the relation of democracy and culture that is priceless. For the humanities is a name for the best of the past applied to learning in the present. I do not misjudge the experience of the state councils if I say that the reception has been increasingly one of welcome. Perhaps the lesson of our work could be encapsulated in advice from the surgeon general's office about the humanities:

Warning: the humanities are habitforming, and they are contagious.

15

The Professors and the Grass Roots

Considerable self-criticism took place in the work of the State Councils, and there was a search for new ideas and new techniques in the comparison of experience in different states. At one regional conference a general reconsideration of major policy was suggested, even raising the whole question "Should the Public Policy Focus be Kept?" It had become a matter of controversy, with some claiming that humanists should "do their thing" and not attempt to apply their ideas to practical projects of the sort the State Councils often dealt with. Others argued that a new mode of relation between scholars and public was being worked out.

Questions do not usually arise at random. Even the old caricature question, "How many angels can dance on the point of a needle?" dealt with the serious problem of whether the mind occupies space, and so with the foundations of psychology. Compare the similar question by John Locke, founder of British empirical psychology, whether when he goes from Oxford to London his soul travels with him. And perhaps it is not digressing too far to note that below these questions lies the whole dichotomizing of our world, intensified in the seventeenth century rise of physical science and associated with the dualism of Descartes, into spirit vs. matter, mind vs. body, and eventually the humanistic vs. the scientific. When today we spend a lot of energy trying to make peace between the two cultures, whether in the guise of the humanities vs. the sciences, or the intrinsically worthwhile vs. the practical or utilitarian, it might be sounder to try to get to the root of the whole question by exploring the presuppositions on which their alleged incompatibility rests. But this, fortunately, is not our present problem.

Another preliminary point. Why does our question speak of the focus being *kept*? Clearly there must be an effort, or at least a suggestion that it be dropped. If a bearded man asks, "Should I keep my beard?" he is obviously reaching for an understanding of what his beard has been doing for him. Is it simply saving the labor of shaving? or aligning with the younger generation against the squares, or strengthening a receding chin, or intensifying masculinity under given cultural images, or perpetuating an identity in his family so that his children would protest if he became other than the immediately recognizable dependable father, or what? "Should the public policy focus be kept?" translates into, "What will be lost if the public policy focus is dropped?" and this requires an answer to, "What have we tried to do in installing it?"

The problems generating the question are by now familiar enough in the experience of public committees. In oversimplified formulation, on the one side the humanists ask, "Can't we do our stuff for the public more smoothly and more effectively without it?" On the other side, the grassroots people grappling with a policy issue ask, "Why do we need these abstract academicians to discuss remote matters when we want to get down to what is to be done?" Where there is so much latent bickering, would a divorce be the easiest way?

Let us see first what is not at issue in the situation. It is not at issue that humanists have much to contribute to the consideration of social policy. It is much like the question of getting oil out of shale: are the problems of extraction so difficult that it may not be worth the cost? Again, it is not at issue that the program set up by the NEH is directed to public contribution by the humanists; the question is what kind of public contribution. If the public policy focus is dropped, the grassroots people would not be left running projects under the program by themselves, they would be back where they started—having to operate, as one does in a democracy, through the traditional channels of citizen movements or political movements, to initiate public policy discussion and action. Perhaps there ought to be a government policy of channeling moneys to encourage public policy discussion irrespective of humanists, just as we earmark income tax dollars for political campaigns; but this is not a NEH problem. Finally, it is not at issue that whatever course we take the outcome of NEH projects for the Humanities that we are now concerned with has to be some form of public programs. The question is what kind.

The question whether the present form of public policy focus is worth continuing can be answered in two ways. We can answer that the public policy focus should be dropped, or we can answer that it should be kept, and we should be more creative in trying to overcome the obstacles that have been given rise to the question itself. I want to examine the first answer in some detail, because it is more complex than appears on the surface, and then I want to espouse the second answer with a few—alas too few, but I have hopes for our present discussion—suggestions as to what we can try.

A retreat from the present setup can be of three sorts. It can be a change of tactics with the same objectives; it can be withdrawal to a new line with a change of strategy; or it can be a complete surrender. Let me comment on each.

The tactical change would remove the need for coparticipation of humanists with the grassroots in carrying out projects, but the aim would still be to focus on public policy questions. For example, a roundtable of psychologists, anthropologists, philosophers, theologians, could do a television program on abortion, or professors of social work and value–oriented economists and sociologists could do one on the material conditions of senior citizens, without the participation of either women who have faced the abortion problem or senior citizens who have lived at the margin. These people would be *talked about* rather than *talked to*, and in any case there could be opportunity for them to telephone questions during the program. (I think you will recognize that these are the kind of projects which we have tended to reject in the past.) Perhaps we should call this the *Susskind model*, except that it would be limited to humanists.

The strategic change would substitute a more remote public–interest reference for a public policy focus. Interdisciplinary projects coming from humanists would be screened for their potential interest to a public that has public issues in mind or at heart. This would be very like what goes on in some of the fellowship programs, for example, the one on technology and human values, so that a project in the history of medical concepts is referred to NSF, while one in medical ethics is acceptable. So too, if an historian, a value–oriented political scientist, and a law professor or legal philosopher offered a project on what questions are or are not fit for a constitutional amendment, it might be acceptable since the abortion issue has kindled public interest in it and the answers would be indirectly relevant to public policy attitudes on abortion. Or if a linguist wanted to study vowel shifts in different American localities, he would be referred to NSF's social science division, but if, as Professor Labov has shown, he could make a case for vowel shift as a cohesion phenomenon oriented to developing identifiable social in–groups in localities, it could be admitted as tying in with current problems of ethnic identification and so with obvious policy issues. We might call this the *policy education model* since it functions to provide information and insight that otherwise might be unavailable if humanists did not seek it out.

The complete surrender path requires more argument, since its theoretical foundations get us into the familiar controversy of intrinsic value vs. utility. So let us get the model clear first. We can think of it as the *Endowment for the Arts model*. Humanists have valuable things to offer, just as artists do. If performances of Sophocles' *Antigone* and Anouilh's *Antigone* can be sponsored by the latter, then why not the former sponsor a literature professor's public lecture, TV or radio program, on the Antigone theme in the history of drama? An added appeal, usable in advertising, might hint at the problem of the state, whether the equation of Creon and Laval in the situation of the anti–Nazi resistance, or the problem of civil disobedience to a tyrannical state. But even this gesture to practical questions need not be necessary. Why should a project on African musical instruments have to tie it to continuities in the Black experience, when it might attract public interest on its own? The test here is public interest, enjoyment, and development of sensitive powers of appreciation for things worth-while themselves.

Let me digress on the question of the intrinsic and the useful, for having raised it I cannot be expected to pass it by—no humanist has that strong a will! Now it is true that work in the humanities often prides itself on its lack of utility, and much of it—though far from all—probably does lack utility. In his report of Sept. 1, 1976, Kingman Brewster, president of Yale, who is sympathetic to the problem of the humanities in the present career-oriented educational drift, argued that in some sense the humanists are elitist; they do give a fortunate group an opportunity for indulgence; and there is nothing wrong with that provided all who are able to do so have the opportunity. An analogy he uses points, however, in the utilitarian direction, for it is difficult to avoid broader human utilities; he compares the humanist to one who in a strange country knows the language of that country, and so lives on a different level of sensitivity and awareness. On the whole, I doubt whether the utility demand, in the broad sense in which it includes the opportunity for the public to share in what is worthwhile, can really be wholly shed. It is another of those overenthusiastic dichotomies. I have read somewhere—I think it was Schumacher's *Small is Beautiful*—a report of a Chinese pre–World War II analysis that the cost of a year's education for a university student was equated with the production work of 30 peasants, so that a five–year course would equal 150 peasant years of work. Can this be blithely dismissed without some answer that at least suggests a return? I quoted this to a philosophically minded psychologist friend, and he replied that it signified that the Chinese productive system at that time needed improvement! Perhaps the narrower utility view would try to show that the humanities could help morale toward such an improvement, much as music helps unison in labor, while the wider utility view would argue that a limited part of even low–level productive power should be used to keep open intrinsically worthwhile humanistic activities. There is no conflict between the two arguments. Why then, the partisan of the full surrender might argue, should the National Endowment for the Arts be allowed to appropriate in its public program the intrinsically worth while, whereas the National Endowment for the Humanities should bind itself in its public program to the useful?

I have tried to give the case impartially for all these paths. If now it is time for a jury verdict, my vote is for the status quo, not because it is status quo, but because it has really the most revolutionary perspective. Even to change the tactical approach gives up coparticipation in favor of simply education. There is a loss here—values which it is premature to surrender. It would allow the humanists to perpetuate their familiar isolation—what Elinor Lenz in a recent paper on "The Humanities Go Public" called "an advanced case of privatization" which, she argued perhaps too hastily, leads eventually to "incestuous elitism and intellectual narcissism." She suggests that the NEH public program "with overtones of the lyceum and chatauqua" does bring humanists out of their shell. It is, I think, an experience which many of us in the field have by now either had or seen. We gain a new inner strength when we see the effect the successful relation of the humanities to grassroots concerns and grassroots participation brings about. The fact that it may be unsuccessful in many cases is the problem to be analyzed by us at these meetings; we seek causes and cures. But it is not a ground for sounding a retreat along the whole line.

On the other hand, there is no reason why some place may not be made for some good projects in at least the tactical change and even the strategic change, if they have great intrinsic worth and would have great public interest. But these would be the exceptions; they would not install a new rule of operation with full equality for their type. Dr. Barcroft has recently pointed out (in a meeting with the Pennsylvania Committee) that the insistence in state committee guidelines—all fifty of them—on actual grassroots dialogue with humanists was a prescription of the committees, not a condition of the Foundation. This makes relaxation of the condition allowable, though not necessarily desirable. It encourages a more intensive creative search for alternative modes of public participation, but it should not open the floodgates to a substitution of humanistic education for joint humanist–grassroots participation. I see it as an empirical question. If the door can be opened without yielding to the great temptation to lapse into a slightly revised business as usual, then well and good. If not, let us keep it firmly closed.

Within the limits of the answer I have given to our topical question, let me make two suggestions for tackling the difficulties that begot the question itself. They are in the nature of self–criticism on a general level. One is not to frighten humanists in the program by suggesting that the public policy relation is calling on them to abandon their traditional work. We do not have to run ourselves down in order to take on also something else that is profoundly worthwhile. I think, for example, that Elinor Lenz's argument (in the article I cited earlier) in opening the avenues of public service to humanists is too alarmingly enthusiastic. Perhaps she is bending back the bent stick in the opposite direction in order to straighten it out, but we have to be careful the stick doesn't break. Thus she envisages new public roles for humanists as community consultants, advising school boards and community councils, as academic ambassadors to a larger world. She adds the carrot of self–preservation through new jobs in a diminished market. I think this is insufficient, even though what it points to may happen and be useful. I think back to the physical anthropologist in the depression of the 1930s who replaced the academy with a job dealing with desirable size intervals in the clothing field (perhaps made millions more comfortable); or even the cultural anthropologists in World War II who studied at a distance the cultural food habits of the countries to which the United States would be shipping food packages, and so avoided the mistakes of earlier relief which came with food the people would not eat. I do not recall any feedback from the first shift, though perhaps there was. The second justified itself as more than useful application because it developed methods of dealing with culture at a distance under conditions in which direct contact was ruled out. (A book like Ruth Benedict's *The Chrysanthemum and the Sword* was, if I recall aright, a product of this movement.) Today in my own field of philosophy moral philosophers are moving in droves into medical ethics and legal ethics, but they seem to forget to bring back the theoretical lessons from these shifts and studies. Or again, I wonder what the humanists in literature think of the alarming tendency of which I have heard—to have the textbooks written, not by the authors who furnish the information and the ideas, but by literacy specialists. Presumably, in the coming world the textbook authors will have their own text writers, just as politicians have their own speech writers. Will this tempt the literary humanist as an alternative career, granting only the insistence by the Authors' Guild that the name of the ghost appear on the text? My point is simply that in opening vitally important practical vistas to the humanities, there should be a recognition of the feedback. Quite bluntly, we are not trying to take humanists away from their scholarly work to do something else. We are suggesting that the public experience will enhance their view of their own field and their understanding of the full scope of their work. Theoretical enrichment added to practical importance is the justification, not impoverishment through practicality or substitute fulfillment.

My second suggestion is of a different sort. We have been oversimplifying the humanists as a group by treating them in a bundle or packaging them as "academic humanists." We begin to look for a uniform, like the scientist's white coat or the artist's smock and brush, to signal the "academic humanist." (Was this the strength of Hayakawa's tam–o–shanter?) When humanists are billed that way in a program, they feel uncomfortable and the audience feels uncomfortable. We begin to make up theories about their common contributions and fasten on "values" or "self–consciousness," both of which are of course important. But the different fields have quite varied contributions to make and each can stand on its own. Perhaps we should prepare explicit materials directed to project committees as advice—what different kinds of things a historian could contribute, for what kind of jobs a legal mind is useful or a literary specialty, for what a historian or theorist of the arts, for what a philosopher. These could be worked on by specialists in each field, taking projects from our experiences in the several states to analyze. The results should be specific, full of concrete illustration, not general slogans.

No doubt our discussion will add to these suggestions and dig out the lessons of our common experience. I think it is to their consideration, and in analyzing and correcting our practice, that we should look for answering the question in the title, not—forgive the cliche—engage in throwing out the baby with the bathwater by dropping the public policy focus and the grassroots relation. We are not engaged in an easy task, because in common with many phases of our culture we are trying to overcome traditional cleavages, deep–rooted in the past, such as between thought and action, knowledge and value, science and humanities. Occasionally a Bronowski will break through enough to show us the whole scientific enterprise as a humanistic endeavor and we glimpse the unity of thought, feeling, and action. This is the domain in which I conceive our program to be operating, with deep roots and—in Francis Bacon's conception—no cleavage between experiments of light and experiments of fruit.

This paper was presented at the Northeast Regional Humanities Conference of State Committees, December 3-4, 1976, in Wilmington, Delaware. The topic of the conference was "From Here to Where?" and though it dealt with many aspects of operation of the program, the question about public policy focus was central.

16

The Good Citizen, the Good Person, and the Good Society

This study was prepared for a conference on Citizenship and Education in Modern Society, held at the Mershon Center, The Ohio State University, April 1980. In order to understand the kind of education required by democratic citizenship, it is found necessary to move not only among normative views, but also among factual assumptions concerning humans (psychological and social), philosophical conception of person and role, political theories of the state, and numerous lessons of practice and historical trends. These are not lined up as premises for deduction, but are rather unravelled from an initial position held to a new position developed. The pattern well illustrates, accordingly, the transformation of ideas in one field or with respect to one practical problem, from the growth of knowledge in other disciplines.

The present inquiry has been put as "the requirements, status and nature of the citizen role in modern society," with some consideration of educational implications. This is clearly an interdisciplinary endeavor, drawing on political theory in its focus on the citizen and the state, on moral philosophy in its theory of virtues and the good man, on sociology in its invocation of status and role theory as well as the matrix of society, and on history in pointing to modernity.

In his *Politics*, Aristotle raises the interesting question whether the excellence of a good man and that of a good citizen are identical or different.[1] We are not surprised at his answering that it depends, and that what it depends on is the constitution or structure of the state. In an ideal state they are identical; in a less than ideal state they are not. Furthermore, even in the former, the qualities of the good man are more pertinent to the ruling statesmen, and other qualities relevant to obedience. But he has hesitated in moving to this conclusion, because in the thoroughly ideal form men rule and are ruled in turn.

As often, Aristotle has given us the preliminary dimensions of the problem, and hinted at different lines of answer and what they rest on. The basic categories, at least to our day, are ruling and obedience. The authority of the ruler and the loyalty of the obedience—and the qualities embedded in each—reflect the character of the society. The hesitation comes from not knowing what will happen when a thorough-going democracy comes into being. Aristotle, of course, was not recommending democracy. He saw his contemporary struggles of oligarchy and democracy as basically the conflict of the arrogant rich and the desperate poor, and he recommended the mean of a middle class of good citizens who would hold the balance toward the public good.

By our day there is vast historical experience with the advance of democracy and its problems, with the character of ruling and authority and with the complex issues of obedience and loyalty, with the forms of wealth and its confident arrogance and the impasses of poverty and its despair (to use the features Aristotle singled out), and with the impact of factors—technology is only the most outstanding—that Aristotle could glimpse only in myth. Can we draw clear lessons from this experience, and can we do so not only for the general character of our past but also for the needs of our present?

In this paper I shall explore the thesis that the basic categories in which we have traditionally conceived the requirements of citizenship—*ruling and authority* on the one hand and *obedience and loyalty* on the other—have already cracked, and fresh categories are emerging under the growth of democracy and its equalitarian demands. It looks as though the fresh categories are *participation* on the one side and *responsibility* on the other. Many who look only on the past can see only the twilight of authority and the degeneration of loyalty. Yet even those who look to the future may not yet discern the forms of society and statehood, of leadership and cooperation, in which participation and responsibility can take shape. On the other hand, the dilemmas arising from the change are clearly discernible all around us. The Vietnam War posed the issue of basic citizen disagreement with government policy and the limits of loyalty. The Watergate affair taxed the limits of trust in rulers. The Supreme Court has been struggling with the rights of the media in investigative reporting. Both government and private enterprise are uneasy about what to do with whistle–blowing: is a whistle–blower to be regarded (from without) as a public hero or (as so often from within) viewed with all the opprobrium moral tradition has attached to the informer? We need not continue the list.

Such issues are not marginal cases; they are growing in scope and intensity and lead us often to question the basic assumptions of a profession or a cooperative enterprise.

If we are to assess the requirements of citizenship in our present world, we have to probe deeply into the contributions that the several disciplines can make to our inquiry. The present paper falls into three parts. Our first concern is with specific facets of state and society, virtues and roles, and some historical aspects of the democratic idea; in these we see how the older categories broke down. The second part looks toward the changing character of citizenship under the emerging categories—the state and prospects of participation, rationality and ideology, institution building and reconstruction, individual and community. The third part deals with pivotal virtues required by contemporary citizenship and some of their educational implications.

Part 1
State and Society

If, as Aristotle has it, in a less than ideal state the excellence of a good person and that of a good citizen are not identical, we cannot consider the requirements of the citizen role without reference to the nature of the state. A person might have to be a bad person to be a good citizen in a very bad state. Indeed, the divergences may be even more far–reaching than Aristotle envisages. He takes it for granted that the goodness of the person combined with the goodness of the state yields good citizenship, at least for some. But may it not be the case that the goodness of a state requires the badness of the individual? Take, for example, Mandeville's argument in *The Fable of the Bees* that private vices yield public benefits, that human weaknesses such as the love of luxuries stimulate trade and production, and were a people completely virtuous doing with little, the society would remain at a primitive level.[2] And that scarcely would be a thriving state. Another example: does the goodness of the CIA depend on the readiness of its members to behave at times as a bad person would? Aristotle would say that although they did acts that a bad person would do, they need not do them in the way nor in the spirit that a bad person would. Plato, of course, had argued (in the *Republic*, before embarking on the genesis of the state) that if people did not desire luxuries there would be no need of a state to begin with, people would lead a simple life and society get along with largely informal cooperation.[3] Finally, perhaps the clearest (and most outrageous) instance of the claim to be a good citizen, properly doing evil actions in a bad state, was the defense of obedience presented by the Nazi defendants in the Nuremberg trials.

In the history of modern political theory this problem is complicated by the fact that a good half of the roster of theories of the state describe it in a way that makes its objectives less than good, if not fully evil. In that case citizenship has two strikes against it from the outset. The older liberal theory regarded that state as best which governed least. The Marxian view defined the state as the executive arm of the dominant class, exploiting the mass of the people, but withering away in a socialist world. The anarchist view saw the state as the embodiment of power, which corrupts; it cannot be reformed but has to be abolished. These are not simply past portraits of the state, ancestral theories hung in the gallery of political thought. They are living forces. The older liberalism repeats itself today in the surge of neoconservative libertarian attempts to limit the range of state activities. The Marxian definition remains part of the daily attitudes to "imperialist countries," even while the socialist states in less than a socialist world remain strong and centralized and show no sign of withering away. The anarchist motif, especially during the 1960s, with a phoenix–like vitality encouraged cooperative organization and communal efforts without reliance on the apparatus of the state. In all these cases, if citizenship be taken to be a relation between the individual and the state, the implication is almost that citizenship compels action inimical to the people.

These threats to the integrity of citizenship can be somewhat defused by diminishing the paradoxical elements in the theories. The liberal theory of former times, it could be said, applied to governments in former conditions when life was simpler; perhaps it was easier to be self–sufficient. Nowadays, greater organization of multiple governmental functions is indispensable for the good society, and the so–called evils when they do not issue simply from mistaken policies are part of the price of human advanced civilization—just as accidents are part of the price of an industrial civilization. Effort should go not to abolish industry but to improve its safety; and something similar holds for bureaucracy and governmental callousness and high taxes. (This is the traditional philosophy, if somewhat shopworn, of reform movements.) The Marxian theory, similarly, in distinguishing between exploitative state activity and nonexploitative administration, expects the latter to continue in world socialism. Hence, if organization, with even minimal coerciveness, is required in any complex society, we may think of the theory as directed against exploitative states rather than states as such. As for the anarchist theory, it might be countered with the claim that not all states are bad, that states are conceivable which limit themselves chiefly to what Ivan Illich, in a genial nomenclature, calls convivial institutions, those that serve the public without coercion—post office, telephone and other communication systems, even possibly minimal automatically operative support systems.[4] The increase of such institutions and the diminution of coercive ones becomes increasingly possible when peace and international economic bonds are developed, and this is equivalent to state activity.

Such arguments, whatever their strength, would rescue citizenship from being represented by such activities as going to war, paying taxes, accepting prison systems, acquiescing in bureaucracy and in the games of "politics"— as if these and the qualities of people involved were essential to the nature of good citizenship. No doubt being a citizen has its costs, but what the costs are depends on the kind of society that has the political organization. What citizenship is like may depend on what the state is like, but what the state is like depends on the society that uses political institutions. It is well to recall that even Hegel distinguishes between civil society and the state, whatever the exalted role the latter is given as the synthesis of the society in its historical development. Democratic conceptions of society tend to see the state as a political mechanism for meeting the needs and problems of the society. Hence citizenship, though cast in terms of the state, has the task of seeing through the state to the social requirements and actually developing an appropriate attitude to the political institutions themselves.

That this is not a trivial point but one of the highest importance may be seen by an illustration in which the appropriate attitude of the citizen to government was the pivot for momentous consequences. In his *The Fear of Freedom* (1951), Francis Biddle raises in a very practical way the problem of citizen loyalty to government.[5] He had served as attorney general of the United States shortly before the idea of a list of subversive organizations was introduced, to be used (initially) in judging the loyalty of government employees. The list played a serious part in the growing political hysteria that made guilt by association a sinister feature of the McCarthy period. Reflecting on the current atmosphere and the lessons of experience, Biddle raises the question how it is possible to ask that the citizen be loyal to the government when government is conceived in a democracy to be the servant of the people and not the people to be the servant of government. It is rather government which should be loyal to the people. Recalling Royce's philosophical analysis in his *The Philosophy of Loyalty*,[6] Biddle agrees that ultimate loyalty is to ideals, not to instruments, and in effect that the freedom of the individual in relation to ideals has a vital place in the idea of citizenship. It is hard to see how he could have reached such a conclusion if citizenship had remained bound to the political relation with its traditional intellectual apparatus of ruler and ruled, authority and obedience.

Virtues and Roles

Suppose we were able to specify the requirements of a modern society and the place of the political within it. Could we then go readily from those requirements to the role of the citizen, and from that to the virtues of a good citizen? (The question also remains to compare those to the virtues of a good person.) Certain conceptual minefields lie in the way. Is the identification of virtues an easy matter or are there complexities in ethical theory which stand in the way and which, if not considered, will make our analysis end in superficialities? Is being a citizen a role in the same sense as being a doctor is a role, or is it something more than a role? How does being a person differ from enacting a role, and if it does, are the ideas of being a good person, being a good citizen, being a good doctor, strictly parallel? To answer these questions we have to consider the notions of virtue, role, person.

Virtues

The theory of virtue is one of the most difficult chapters in moral philosophy. And yet the matter seems simple. Why not canvass the virtue clusters that are to be found on the face of history and select those appropriate to contemporary citizenship? There are, for example: the Spartan virtues of courage, tenacity, obedience, loyalty, bluntness, taciturnity, devotion to strength and physical fitness; the traditional Christian virtues of humility, resignation, faith, hope, charity, brotherly and sisterly love, spirituality; the pagan virtues of honor, pride, kinship bonds, friendship, confidence in capacity and power; the Calvinist or puritan virtues or thrift, abstinence, justice, chastity, industriousness, success; the bourgeois virtues of prudence, calculation, accumulation, good management; the liberal virtues of initiative, independence, intellectual confidence, rationality; the nationalist virtues of patriotism, group pride, self–sacrifice; and so on in intricate patterns of self–formation. Does citizenship in today's world call for an intransigent national patriotism or a tolerant cosmopolitan outlook, for a readiness of self–sacrifice or a rational self–regard, for a prompt obedience or a critical spirit? Is our task to analyze carefully the circumstances of social harmony and national well–being, to frame a realistic conception of the national interest, and in its light to weave a virtue–pattern from the available assortment that history has handed down to us?

Unfortunately, the history of moral philosophy suggests that we have to do more than pick a bouquet of virtues. We need a unified moral theory of the good, or at least an in-depth analysis of virtue. This is not a recent discovery, but a recurrent theme. For example, in Plato's *Laches* Socrates riddles the simple view that courage lies in sticking to your post. (It is offered by the general Nicias, who incidentally later lost the Sicilian war for Athens.) Does not the general have to call a retreat on occasion, and will not courage lie then in abandoning your post? It soon appears that some knowledge is always required to differentiate a virtue like courage from sheer obstinacy, a virtue like piety from mere ritual, a virtue like justice from mere rule–following. The Socratic view that all virtue is knowledge, is well known. Equally well known are the difficulties and paradoxes it gives rise to, for it makes a puzzle of knowing one's duty and not doing it. In contrast, Kant regarded virtue not as knowledge but as essentially a conscientiousness in following the path of duty. Since virtue lies in a certain consistency of spirit in respecting the moral law, it cannot be parcelled into separate virtue–traits.

In contemporary thought, psychologists from different schools add to the lesson that the surface catalogue of virtues is misleading. In the 1920s, Hartshorne and May studied honesty in the conduct of children and found that it had no uniform behavioral pattern; what people did depended on the situation, the domain, the interests.[7] This is familiar enough in ordinary experience. People will rip off a corporation or chisel on income tax; yet they would not dream of picking a pocket or not returning a purse that had a name in it. Students will cheat on examinations, but not on one another; some will be ready to help others during examinations, but not necessarily to take help. Some people will tell lies to enhance prestige, but not for direct financial gain; some will lie to spare feelings, but not to exploit. The psychoanalytic literature amply exhibits the different depth meanings of the same surface virtues; for example, Fromm points out that industriousness may be a realistic trait or a keeping busy out of basic anxiety, and love is often found to be an emotional dependence rather than an authentic relatedness.[8] Kohlberg, working in the Piagetan tradition, looks rather to a moral development through stages than a collection of virtues.[9] His currently fashionable schema ends in Kantian principledness as the summit of morality.

We must be careful not to end up in a one-virtue establishment. Whether it be knowledge or conscientiousness or wholeheartedness or principledness, if it is treated as just one virtue it has, in its lone splendor, to face the competition of the other virtues; moreover, such a view reopens the problems which prompted us to go beyond the virtue list to either a more unified picture or a deeper analysis. The historical career of sincerity should teach us that lesson. In the old dogmatic days, no respectable inquisitor would be satisfied if the inquisitee told him truthfully that he had tried as hard as humanly possible to believe the doctrine he was blamed for disbelieving, that he had followed all the prayers and rituals and disputes in a willing spirit, but it had not "taken." Heresy was error taking hold of the person, and the more sincere he was in his heretical belief, the greater proof of inner corruption. Luther's "Here stand I, I cannot otherwise" would then be a confession of corruption, not an affirmation of noble commitment. With the rise of liberalism and the victory of fallibilism in the theory of knowledge and science—and who would question that nowadays?—sincerity became a supreme virtue. There are still many who would echo Voltaire—I despise your belief but I will fight to the death for your right to proclaim it. The Roycean conception of loyalty goes on to analyze all virtue as a form of loyalty to loyalty, which involves strengthening and spreading the occurrence of loyalties. This is an extreme form of a liberal individualism of sincere commitment.

The liberal approach retains a strong hold in a democratic intellectual milieu today. Its merits as contrasted with concepts of heresy are obvious. It is not simply a selection of an attractive virtue, but a sober judgment of how inquiry can best proceed in human affairs and what openness is required to avoid stagnation. In recent times, problems have multiplied with experience of bizarre causes that have won absolute devotion. The obvious case is Nazism. Recent history of what we may call "moralistic terrorism," that is, a commitment to a cause that is even ready to use terrorism as a means to its advancement, intensifies doubts. Sincere commitment still has recognized moral strength, but it no longer has the moral height, much less the moral monopoly, that it seemed to possess in traditional liberalism. Whatever happens in the attempt to overcome the superficiality of a collection-of-virtues approach, it cannot be achieved by installing one virtue as supreme.

Roles

The concept of role is used to analyze aspects of interpersonal relations, to set expectations and (correspondingly) claims and obligations. A person expects a doctor to go about curing him of his ailment, not to experiment on him, nor to be intent primarily on making money. The relevant role, in short, is as a doctor, not a medical researcher nor a business man. Sociologically, institutions have often been analyzed as patterned sets of roles. In psychological development, a role is internalized and role commitment established through the activity of the self in organizing its aims and values in its activities. But selves are originally shaped and developed in the complex process of coming to regard ourselves in the way that others selectively look at us, so that self–expectations and self–steering already incorporate the expectations of others.

In this way of treating interpersonal relations and personal activity, roles become detached, analyzed, and then stand ready—in almost a reified fashion—to be reattached to people, carrying with them all the expectations, claims and obligations that emerged in the analysis. The idea is an old one; for example, the ancient Stoics introduced the notion of an "office," which carried the idea of both a role and a duty, and then proceeded to explore various social offices. (This work had a serious influence on the development of Roman law.) A person's moral problem in a difficult situation was to find his appropriate office in that situation and firmly carry out its obligations.

The role formulation, however, raises two questions: first, whether the obligations of the role are clear enough, and second, whether there is always only one pertinent or primary role for a given situation. On the first question, since roles are identified by tasks and offices, obligations should have an initial clarity, although the detail of application may remain vague. Yet clarity is usually achieved only for the central core of the role; there is always a fringe in which the attachment of the obligation to the role may be uncertain. In the case of the doctor, if he substitutes an experimental treatment with the consent of the patient, is he not still carrying out the medical role, or is he playing two different roles? If a social worker helps organize the poor to secure their welfare rights, is that not conceivably part of his work? (Who defines the roles?) Clarity at the fringes may often be secured at the cost of multiplying roles. In the recent case of the FBI Abscam operation, Attorney General Civiletti attacked those who had leaked the operation and brought notoriety to persons not yet indicted. He suggested that legal penalties might be appropriate for a government worker who did this, since he had presumably taken an oath of confidentiality. Asked whether reporters who published the story were similarly vulnerable, he replied no, for their job was to get the news.

On the second question, the conflict of roles in a moral problem is a familiar dilemma. The jockeying of roles in moral deliberation is in effect looking for the values or obligations that are to be assigned a basic place in the moral economy. A psychoanalyst discovering that a patient is a murderer, or a priest making such a discovery in the confessional, has the problem of weighing the obligations of the medical or priestly role against the obligation of a citizen role. Scientists, bewitched by a fact-value dichotomy which assures a value-free science, have often insisted that when they advocate a social policy they do so as citizens, not as scientists. I have elsewhere suggested[10] that if they embark on such a role differentiation they ought to be more specific about it, and announce—say in recommending the suspension of nuclear energy within a given time–span—that they are doing it x % as scientist, y % as parents, z % as intellectuals, w % as citizens, etc. They would thus make clear both the sources of relevant information which they regard as persuasive and the different value standpoints involved in their commitment. But the crucial point would be the weight given to a particular standpoint. Is a doctor or a scientist or a priest *primarily* that? Or is he or she primarily a human being? In recent literature of the women's liberation movement some make the sex role primary. Or is one primarily one's self, that is, a person or an individual?

These questions raise the problem of the relation of the role to the person: whether being human or being a person should be conceived as a role at all. A similar issue is whether acting as a moral agent is a role performance; this would invite the question whether the moral role should be preferred to the citizen role or the parental role. Dorothy Emmett cites the epitaph on a Scottish tombstone: "Here lies the body of Tammas Jones, who was born a man and died a grocer."[11] We turn then to the consideration of the person. It will help us to determine how far being a citizen should be seen as carrying out a role.

Persons

Plato and Aristotle assume that man as such has a function. Aristotle says: "Have the carpenter, then, and the tanner certain functions or activities, and has man none? Is he born without a function? Or as eye, hand, foot, and in general each of the parts evidently has a function, may one lay it down that man similarly has a function apart from all these?"[12]

If we follow the clue of Greek usage here I think we can resolve our problem. The Greek idea of *virtue* is literally that of excellence or fitness. A knife has sharpness as its virtue—the quality which enables it to perform well in the enterprise of cutting. The idea of virtue therefore stays closer to function and to job or enterprise than the idea of role. The view that man has a function need mean no more than that there are enterprises central to human life by reference to which the standards for character, that is virtues, are to be established. This is why Aristotle's is basically a human-nature ethics; he builds it up from the natural desires and objectives of human striving. Still, he gives it a fixed direction through the content of human nature that he specifies. Taking man to be a *rational* animal, he assigns a contemplative rationality as the supreme end of life, which only a few can fully attain. As we know, others saw the nature of man differently, and different pictures of the human good emerge in the ancient and medieval and even modern teleologies. In the long run, the evolutionary account dislodged the teleological view of human nature, recognized change and some of the patterns of change, opened the way to a clearer realization of the part played by social tradition in determining directions of human striving, and reconstructed the view of reason as an evolutionary instrument in the struggle for survival. In the end it made the tasks of ethics much more complicated than they had been when the good was attached to a presumed fixed direction of human nature.

Logically, it would not matter too much if being a man is regarded as a role, provided that the content of the role were kept wide open, being a role permitted change and development in the content, and room was left for creativity and fresh potentials at almost every point. Such a notion of role would stretch over a human nature that changes, and even the denial that there is a human nature—for example, Sartre's assertion that the individual at every moment is making a free decision though within a framework of the human predicament and basic human problems. But such a conception would make the idea of a role fairly useless in its essential task of analyzing interpersonal relations into strands and establishing the pattern of specific institutions. Given, too, the constant tendency of people to lapse into essentialism and brand people as types, there are good policy reasons for limiting its uses. Let us therefore conclude that we get into too much trouble if we apply the role concept to a human being, a person, or a moral agent.[13]

The important lesson in this brief sketch of the relation of role and person or moral agent is that the concept of role is always limited. Behind any role is presupposed a person who is engaged in many enterprises or who is enacting other roles as well. Hence any obligations assigned on the basis of a single role in a given situation either assume this plurality is not relevant in that situation or else have to reckon with it in reaching a decision. Where there is a conflict of roles, the decision may sometimes invoke an established principle about which has priority, and other things being equal the analysis can stop there. But if the situation is complicated enough and the conflict of roles is serious enough, there is no shortcut: deliberation about the situation becomes recognizably that of a moral agent, and the analysis may have to go so far as to render explicit and invoke a picture of the good life.

Is it then enlightening or confusing to think of being a citizen as enacting a role? If being a doctor is clearly enacting a role and being a person or moral agent is not, then being a citizen appears to have an intermediate position. At one end of its activities it is explicitly role–enacting: a citizen votes, may hold office, has the right of residence in the country without special permission, is entitled to certain protection and benefits, and so on in a whole range of well-recognized and often carefully defined lines of conduct. At the other end, however, being a citizen has the complexity and involves the integrative moral judgment that often requires reference to the good life.

Such an intermediate position is not an unfamiliar phenomenon in moral philosophy. When we are asked whether liberty is a means or an end, we find the categories too restrictive; certainly liberty is a means to a kind of life, but it is more; it is a *constitutive part* of a good life. If we are asked whether virtuous conduct is a means toward happiness, many philosophers become unhappy at a mere means–end construal; virtuous conduct is a constitutive part of happiness. If we are asked whether basic rules of justice are an end or a means to the good life, we are inclined to draw a distinction between rules that are administrative or efficacious in securing the good life and rules that are themselves constituents or structural features of the good life. The usual analogy is between rules that tell us how to win in chess, and rules that define the moves. The distinction between laws enacted by the legislative authorities and provisions of the constitution seems to be of the same sort; the latter express the kind of society that is envisaged as good.

Now if being a citizen were conceived to be a role only at one end but a constitutive part of something at the other, what could that something be? Since we have seen the tie–in of citizenship to the state and through it to the society, we can conclude that being a citizen is a constitutive part of being a member of a community. In the history of political theory this seems to be the sound core of the idealist theory of the state in its battle against contractualist theories. We should not allow the exaggerated attempt to assign real personality to the group or a real will to the community to deny the insight that citizenship is conceptually tied in with some form of community relations of persons. It involves some pattern of interpersonal relations or transactions tied to a view of the good life. And, to that extent, being a citizen resembles more being a person than enacting a role. And whatever the vision of the good life that may guide the community, a basic minimal agreement today would be on respect for all persons, which gives every individual a part in the society and an opportunity to develop and express his or her capacities in the life of the community; and on the development, with advancing knowledge and experiment, of institutions that make this kind of life possible. In general, the good society in the contemporary world is thought of as a democratic society in which wide individual participation is desirable. Such a minimal conception of the good society is not far reaching, but it may do as a start.

Some Historical Aspects of the Democratic Idea

The significant historical thread here is not the vast changes in conditions of life which give shape to our modernity. Our concern is rather the history of the democratic idea and the gradual clarification of layer after layer among its constituent values and ideals. These set the problems in terms of which the character of citizenship is to be determined.

We focus on the disintegration of the categories of ruler and ruled, authority and obedience; in short, we are concerned with roles, virtues, powers and attitudes. In predemocratic times these were sharply etched. We have only to think, in British history, of the doctrine of divine right of kings; Locke spent one of his two treatises, *Of Civil Government*, attacking it. The divine right of kings leaves little room for doubt about what are the appropriate virtues of citizenship, though there could be dispute about whether the royal person should emphasize firmness or mercy or some judicious combination. If we want to see the sharpest break with the aristocratic tradition, though not with the categories of rule and obedience, we should do well to turn back to Hobbes who presents a thoroughly naturalistic theory of sovereignty grounded in his picture of material and human processes. Critical is the basic place he gives to equality. The usual view, engendered by the battle slogans of liberty versus equality in the nineteenth and twentieth centuries, often leaves the impression that equality is a latecomer in the surge of the masses directed to a general levelling and threatening the central liberal ideal of liberty. But Hobbes already gives an important place to equality both in his account of initial conditions and in his listing of the laws of nature. In both cases it is on minimal grounds of maintaining the safety of society, its peace and order— the minimum conditions for any person pursuing his interests on which alone Hobbes is constructing the state and in the recognition of which reason establishes the laws of nature. In the initial conditions, that is the state of nature, Hobbes says that men are equal and no man is so much more powerful than that another could not poison him by guile. Once the enterprise of generating laws of nature is under way, several characteristics of—we may say—good citizenship are specified beginning with the eighth law of nature.[14] The eighth says that no man should "by deed, word, countenance, or gesture, declare hatred, or contempt of another." The breach of this law is labelled *contumely*. This law is justified by the initial equality of men and the fact that all inequality has been introduced by civil law and so rests on consent. Hobbes goes on to argue that if nature made men equal it ought to be acknowledged; or if nature made men unequal, still men think of themselves as equal, and so will not enter into conditions of peace except on equality. (We may recall that Aristotle found the sense of inequality to be the major source of revolutions.) Hobbes accordingly gives us the ninth law of nature as "that every man acknowledge another for his equal by nature." The breach of this is labelled *pride*. Two other laws follow rapidly: the tenth, "that at the entrance into conditions of peace, no man require to reserve to himself any right, which he is not content should be reserved to every one of the rest," and the eleventh, that if a man be trusted to serve as a judge he deal equally between men, a law labelled *equity*.

If such equalitarian principles for the mutual relation of citizens did not immediately provoke a revolutionary overturning of society, it was obviously because the empirical assumptions of the time did not lead them on to far–reaching institutional changes. The history of the next three centuries can be read as the application of the principles in area after area, and liberty, so far from being antithetical to equality, is often simply the name applied to the consolidation of equality in a given area. Intellectual liberty or freedom of thought and inquiry, freedom of conscience, the career open to talent, the right to vote, and the right of revolution, are all equalities of effort and action advanced at times to remove special discriminations and at times to broaden systematically the range of opportunities for individual decision. Milton offers a critique of censorship; Locke a limited defense of religious tolerance; Paine widens it to rule out governmental interference; Jefferson rests freedom of thought on natural rights, while Mill rests it on empirical considerations of long–range utility. Locke defends the right of revolution as the last appeal of the individual to heaven when all other remedial recourse is closed to him; Hobbes, more diffident, allows the individual to be released from political obligation only when the ruler's effective provision of order has utterly broken down, or when the individual has nothing more to lose as when he is being led to the gallows. But Hobbes is a minimalist and does not expect any constructive contribution from the mass of people; his free association for "people" is "tumult."

The almost inexorable march of equality, however, is toward expansion and consolidation of gains. It is a slow march, nevertheless, and even its noblest sentiments are accompanied by harsh reservations. This is clearest in the right to vote. That every man should have a vote is proposed by the Levellers in the mid–seventeenth century when in Cromwell's army they exchange arguments with Ireton and the leadership in the Putney debates. As Colonel Rainborough puts it, "For really I think that the poorest he that is in England has a life to live, as the greatest he." Ireton answers that to give those who do not have a property stake in the kingdom a vote will lead to attempts of the have-nots to take away from the haves. (Compare *The Federalist* on the need to have checks and balances so that the unification of factions should not lead to the largest faction, the propertyless, making inroads on the propertied, the substantial citizens of the country.) The Levellers, of course, are not Diggers; they disavow communism, and even on the vote they do not intend it for women nor indentured servants. Locke, nearly half a century later, ignores the question of extending suffrage. James Mill, in the early nineteenth century, does not care whether a property qualification for the vote is maintained or not; he says it makes little difference since the workers will in any case follow their class masters as a model. His son, John Stuart Mill, knows better; after the Chartists, the beginnings of trade unions, and the *Communist Manifesto*, he wants the broadening of the franchise, the vote for women, and even considers proportional representation. He is thoroughly aware of the class struggle, but believes that if the opposing forces are balanced the liberal thinkers on both sides will sway social policy. On the other hand, the American reformers who meet to plan the abolition of slavery give no thought to (and reject overtures from) women who begin to demand equal rights; and a century has to pass before, at the end of World War I, their right to vote is secured.

Equalitarianism in the twentieth century takes both liberal–reformist and radical shape. For the greater period the ideal of equal opportunity with its meritocratic underpinnings remains dominant. The advances of a social welfare program are largely seen as providing minimal conditions for realistic as against purely formal opportunity. The major cleavage between socialist and nonsocialist has been about the empirical questions of the degree of state control and common property ownership required to ensure opportunity, and about the collateral costs of centralization in controls over individual freedom. After World War II, however, equalitarian theory generates a wider program. Practically, it calls for active redistribution as well as unleashing of production. Theoretically, it challenges meritocracy. A good illustration of the latter is John Rawls's formulation of the principle that equality is only to be departed from in institutional measures that are not merely for the greatest good, but also bring increased benefits to the most disadvantaged; natural gifts are not a moral basis for special reward.[15] It is not surprising that defenders of the older meritocratic position have attacked this approach as a new equalitarianism of results, and see it in its various forms—whether in policies of educational expansion, enhanced economic welfare, or affirmative action—as the unleashing of the predatory in the masses. Casting it as the extreme of equalitarianism, they interpret it as the transition from a sober democracy to ochlocracy—in a spirit not unlike Plato's criticism of democracy as license.

The focus of political theory, in the twentieth century prior to the 1960s and 1970s when the more extreme equalitarianism came to a head, continued to be on the problem of political obligation. The basic categories of authority and obedience were still in the ascendant, but justifications for them became more precarious. Old questions continued, such as whether political obligation to obey rested on contract, purpose, or custom, or some mixture of these elements. Hard–boiled realists, particularly in the self-styled Machiavellian tradition, translated all issue or relation of ruler and ruled into power and charisma. In line with Lasswell's title of his well-known book, *Politics: Who Gets What, When, How*, politics studies influence and the influential, the interactions of the elite and the mass, with the elite getting the available values of deference, income and safety to the greatest extent.[16] There is little place for equalitarianism here. Indeed, ideals of any sort entered into the reckoning largely as bases for power over social groups, as ways of manipulating controls. On the other hand, those dissatisfied with the power emphasis in political science shifted to a focus on political decision and the variety of social decision modes. Others moved back to older ideas of natural rights, or other classical ways (whether ancient philosophical or religious–based) of establishing an explicitly moral basis for political obligation, for legitimate authority (as distinguished from sheer power), and for justified political obedience.

Within the theory of democracy as such, the first half of the century witnessed an internal struggle between those who took it to be government by consent of the governed, and those who wanted to give some operative meaning to the notion of government by the people. The former were generally contractionist in tendency: governing is a specialized business involving knowledge, experience, and constant attention; the most that the public generally can do is have a veto at election time over its rulers, and either reelect or select others depending on its judgment of their performance. Such judgments in some cases will be sophisticated and serious; in most it will be impressionistic and cursory, or the result of political persuasion. Mostly it will be determined by immediate and special interests. The opposing view called for inventive increase of participation by people generally in the operations of government. It was governed less by a romantic "faith in the people" than by a conviction that the public could learn by experience, and only a broad and continually active public interest could support policies of public welfare; otherwise, government would be the preserve not of specialized knowledge of the good, but of special interests of the powerful.

The last two decades in the United States have somewhat put this conflict in the shade, though not as a theoretical conflict. The battle over the Vietnam War and then the Watergate episode roused popular forces. Even without such special events it is likely that the complex problems since World War II, the political changes throughout the world, the expansion of production and technology, the growth of education and the phenomenon of rising expectations for material and cultural progress, would themselves have supported greater endeavors to influence public affairs by larger and larger segments of the public. To all these were added—or perhaps as part of them—the successive liberation movements, equalitarian movements against all forms of discrimination. The ideal of participation, even in such more radical forms as participatory democracy, has taken greater hold. The use of political techniques, such as initiative in California, or nonformal organization such as consumer and ecological movements, are only indications of the experimentation that is now going on in government by the people. Perhaps this should be seen not as government or ruling in the old style so much as a wider phenomenon: the determination of policy has now become a much wider social endeavor breaking the bonds of the narrowly political.

This historical view of the development of the democratic idea suggests that the powerful equalitarian impetus has to be reckoned with. It is either a good tied to respect for all people and their fulfillment, or a necessary ground for any fertile human advances. We have seen this problem reflected in twentieth century theoretical discussions of authority and obedience, of power and influence, and indicated how the pressure of growing complexity and changed conditions of life were on the verge of breaking through these traditional categories. I suggest that these categories of citizenship have now reached a critical point, in the strict scientific sense of that term. The question is no longer who will command and who will obey, who will rule and who be ruled. The character of authority and obedience is being transformed into some kind of broader participation in resolving urgent problems and reconstructing institutions. If this blossoms into a full–fledged categorial replacement, participation and its correlate, responsibility, appear to be the leading candidates. Hence to deal with the character of citizenship as a moral problem is to consider what attitudes, set in what value–orientations, this shift will entail. And to trace the educational implications is to see what changes are required in educational theory and policy in such redirection.

Part 2

If we have correctly analyzed the situation as one in which there is a democratic dissolution of the categories of authority and obedience and a movement toward their replacement by participation and responsibility, under the impact of equalitarianism in the changed conditions of life, then what is the moral warrant of that equalitarianism?

The ultimate warrant would be a whole critique of present life, the failure of the older categories as a structure and the possibilities of the new. It is not a case of jumping on the bandwagon of history and saying equalitarianism is good because it is invincible. Equalitarianism has a possible moral appeal insofar as it seems to actualize the old dream of human brotherhood and sisterhood of people. But it has many a criterion of practicality, enhancement of life, acceptability, comparison with alternative paths, to satisfy before it can be allowed to guide the requirements of citizenship and give free rein to the new categories. The least that could be said for it—and that is a great deal—is that the faith in it has grown to such proportions, with increasing strength, that it has to be given a chance to show what it can do. The signs of the shift are all around us in the scope of the critique of institutions that has permeated our life. In part it represents a judgment that the institutions have not functioned to cope with human problems; in part it is a mistrust of their past uncontrolled authority. This is, of course, a thesis I am proposing about its nature. For an opposing thesis, that the shift represents the sheer breakdown of authority and that in place of obedience there is sheer inner lawlessness, the eclipse of tradition, the release of inner bonds, an emergent narcissistic hedonistic materialism, there are many advocates. A good sample is Robert Nisbet's *Twilight of Authority*; if we wish to consider the tradition from which it issues there is the litany of fears from Edmund Burke to Michael Oakeshott.[17] The dimensions of these contrasting theses will emerge as we tread our way through the several aspects of the problem before us.

The State and Prospects of Participation

I suggest that at the present time we are at a choice point in democracy, in which we can either turn back to elitism or go forward with fuller participation, that the first path will bring chaos and that the second is a better bet for social experiment. This does not mean that differences in social policy will cease to exist; they will instead take the form of different proposals within an equalitarian framework, just as in the general history of democracy a point was reached where all fruitful political theory began to center within the democratic framework rather than in the conflict of antidemocratic with democratic.

About the phenomenon of the breakdown of authority and respect for authority there has been little disagreement—from the spread of revolutions to the milder American phenomenon of a disillusion with politics. What seems to me to be overlooked is the extent of explicit critique. It may be easier, with many academic analyses of the student movements of the 1960s, to dismiss them as irrational outbursts. But they were practical critiques of our institutions, in the sense that they did not merely violate traditional standards but attempted alternative reconstructions. There is a significant moral difference between affirming an institution with its values and obligations, say the family, while violating them on the side, and experimenting with newer forms for which the moral qualities of affiliation and love are claimed. The professions—law, medicine, psychiatry, social work, education, even technology—have been challenged, not only for inhuman violation of their inner standards on the part of their practitioners, but for the shape that the standards themselves have taken. For example, law—particularly in the Watergate episode—was criticized for its amorality, and a strong movement of public legal service emerged. Medicine has been charged, in spite of technical progress, with devoting itself to the well–to–do instead of the health of the public, with a callousness to the human side of medicine, as well as of course with a calculated self–interest. Psychiatry has been charged with building the values of the establishment into its own concept of mental health, social work with doling out palliatives for an unjust system of distribution. We would have expected education to be invoked as an ally for social reform. Instead, people have accused it of coordinating its human raw material for obedience and resignation and not even successfully teaching the elementary skills. The student revolts charged higher education with processing students for the industrial and military purposes of the society, and not doing its job of developing the life of the mind and creative abilities. Perhaps the most devastating critique of technology came from within its citadel, in the extreme form of the first Club of Rome report that almost predicted doomsday with the loss of resources and choking of pollution, if the present technological and economic course were maintained—and this when we might have expected science and technology to be invoked for the development of saving techniques.[18] Nor should we omit the major critique of politics for harnessing all energies for war, for maintaining rather than alleviating the existent oppressions. This issued in the liberation movements, most notably of Blacks and women, and the obvious near insurrectionary movements of the Vietnam War story.

Now significantly in all these events from the point of view of our inquiry, both the resort and the appeal was to a greater participation of people in the affairs of the institution or profession or general reconstruction. For example, the rights of the patient and the doctrine of informed consent and the readiness to charge malpractice, are only part of the attempt to bring the patients as a class into participation in medical affairs. In social work there have been powerful movements to organize the "clientele" and develop community action on welfare rights. In education student rights and student participation in the governance of educational institutions emerged as a serious practical issue, while movements for local control of the schools have taken new forms in urban centers. In science and technology, the old conception of a value–free science has been swept away, and the demand for responsibility and the participation of people in the determination of technological uses has been evident in, for example, the popular movements on questions of ecology and industrial pollution. I note only some highlights; a full study with the techniques of political science would, I think, be overwhelmingly revealing. Nor are these phenomena only critiques stemming from political radicalism. Demands for accountability are very respectable today and issue from the political right as well, for example in urging the accountability of teachers and the accountability of the government for its taxation. Indeed, critique has been impartially directed upon business and labor, on conservatism and socialism and liberalism and Marxism. If I read it right, the movement of critique is a general and sweeping demand for the reconstruction of institutions to meet modern problems, based on the need for wide participation and responsibility rather than authority and obedience.

The responsibility so far considered has been demanded from those who lead in all fields, and the participation is that of specific groups or the public generally. But what about the responsibility of the people themselves? This is the crucial point at which the elitist tradition faults the democratic process. The claim, from Plato to Burke to contemporary laments of the twilight of authority, is that democratic liberty without restraint is license, while the conflict of self–regarding interests can only yield chaos and an incapacity to act. How permeating this fear can be, especially in critical situations, may be illustrated from the fact that a sober and learned conservative–liberal like Walter Lippman wrote a little book in the 1930s, entitled *The Method of Freedom*, in which he toyed with the suggestion that Congress give up its right to propose legislation and retain only the right to vote on legislation proposed by the Executive.[19] This was on the ground that congressional proposals represented diverse and conflicting interests, not general well–being. Now that problem is far from done with. Witness the arguments about Congress in the present period on the question of energy legislation. Note, however, the import of the argument: the claim of dispersive self–interest of groups is not merely being attached to the people, but to the representatives of the people. Can it stop short at the doors of the Executive chambers? The conflicts go on within the Executive, and the history of the Department of Energy in relation to Big Oil is not encouraging as an exemplar of Executive knowledge of the Good versus popular dispersive Will. In short, the problem of the conflict of *Rationality* and *Voluntarism* which underlies the whole tradition of Elitism and Democracy is inescapable at even the present moment. We might phrase the democratic problem of citizenship in a Kantian vein as: how, when the people participate, is a responsible public possible? There is no avoiding what we may technically call the epistemology of citizenship.

Rationality and Ideology

The issues of rationality and voluntarism are well-worn in the conflict over democracy. Aristocracy and elitism insist that politics is a science like medicine; there are some who can *know* what is the public good, and they are the appropriate leaders. As Plato put it in getting this tradition started, they are the ones in whom reason is strong and establishes inner controls over appetite and passion. But of course these were only ideal rulers, and so Aristotle made a move in the direction of democracy: While it would be nice to have such rulers, human beings are too capable of corruption, and even the doctor can be bribed by my enemies to destroy me. Hence let us have a government of laws, not men; the people, precisely because of diverse interests, can be good critics and collectively wiser. In this history of political theory, that move was, however, but a detour to the struggle over who makes the laws. The mainstream of democratic theory, perhaps unwilling to rest its case on the corruption of the wise, appealed to the will of the people. The issue of reason vs. will was fought in gigantic proportions in the late medieval and early modern battle as to whether God's reason or God's will was primary. It looks as if Okham's voluntarism fitted well into the aspirations of the national state in the battle with the papal universalistic control; it therefore scarcely yielded a democratic theory but at most a move away from its opposite. In any case, voluntarist underpinning of democracy carries us to a theory of the will, and so to a psychological question. It is doubtful whether the debate in moral philosophy in our century with its technical formulation, whether moral terms are to be given a cognitive or an emotive (or prescriptive) interpretation, gets far beyond the medieval battle by substituting a linguistic for a theological formulation as a way of begging the psychological questions. The question is what democratic theory in its notion of the will of the people is doing more than rejecting the elitist–aristocratic view of sovereign wisdom. Of course there is the whole history in which democratic liberalism prescribes a mediating process from will to wisdom: for example, Bentham's view of the impact of individual egoism producing collective egoism which is public welfare, Adam Smith's and the economists' faith in self–interest producing, through the market mechanism, the public welfare, and so on. Perhaps only as such defenses wear thin, the conservative attack on the will of the people as a cover for anarchic conflict of interests gains strength again. Or perhaps this reflects simply the intensity of social problems.

In spite of this unresolved conflict, the theory of ideology—the self–conscious critique of theories in relation to specific interests—has made progress. This sociology of knowledge itself has gone in two opposing directions. In one direction it ends with simply the relativistic conflict of theories that have no ulterior rationality. The situation is then simply that there is conflict of social interests and each generates or adopts the theories that serve it best. On the opposite view, the conflict of ideologies is itself grist to the mill of growing self–consciousness, and criteria of the rational accumulate in the process. Granted that there is no philosopher's stone for the instant certification of a social theory, there can be an accumulation of knowledge, methods and techniques in a retail, not a wholesale fashion. The first time a social theory comes swashbuckling on the historical stage it may—to adapt Marx's quip on Napoleon I and III—come as tragedy, the second time as farce. Perhaps this is a bit too hopeful, but at least by the third time people may have learned better. On such a conception of rationality it can in the long run penetrate ideology. Rationality is not a pure method, but embodies the whole careful and cumulative procedure of science and knowledge. It is not pure knowledge versus pure will. The will of the people, properly conceived in the light of our historical experience, need not be chaotic conflict; it can be the results of the learning by experience and collective reflection of the peoples of the world, adding to their knowledge by the lessons of their institutional experience. It is a growing body, and so the concept of rationality is a growing cutting edge.

It will not have escaped the reader that the way indicated in the unnecessarily forced antithesis of objective reason and arbitrary will is precisely the way in which science goes about building up knowledge—the surrender of absolute claims, the long hard process of accumulating experience, the critical questioning of hardened belief, the use of imagination in constructing theory and the constant search for alternatives, the cooperation of many in diverse fields to build a coherent framework. It has taken much longer to project the utility of such procedures in questions of value and morality and social policy. And it will no doubt take much longer to carry these attitudes into practical steps of practices and institutions.

Take, for example, the current use of polling and their publicizing. The questions usually asked are how people, in effect, do or would vote on an issue. The polls are a barometer of instant wish or will; they are not usually an inquiry into people's reasons or arguments for or against. They are repeated at smaller and smaller intervals, in the hope of depicting accurately the swings or locating the tides of opinion or will. They seldom pay attention to their own effect on people generally, that is how they shape public opinion, nor their effect on policy makers who are prompted by fears of bucking tides to pay more attention to "votes" than to the argument about reasons and soundness. In brief, the present tendency of polls is thoroughly voluntaristic. And yet there is no reason in the world why social scientists and responsible media should not develop a polling which is more rationally oriented. We are beginning to question, in the field of educational testing, the effects of the short–answer tests: arbitrariness is installed, a limited view of ability is standardized, and creativity, imagination and a sense of alternatives are thwarted. The same could happen in polling—unless it be that the social scientists and the media really despise the public.

Institution-Building and Reconstruction

Because of the traditional veneration of tradition and the conflicts about paths of social change, we tend to overlook the slow process of practical change and institution–building that takes care of some of our problems. Even where people have been unable to do anything to alleviate their lot they have been inventive in myths to relieve the spirit. But even here techniques and devices play a part; there is no doubt a lesson to be learned from Housman's couplet: "Malt does more than Milton can, to justify God's ways to man." Technological devices are evident enough, but we are less attentive to institutional techniques and devices. Take, for example, the growth of insurance. It had precursors in intricate forms of partnership and patterns of assumed risk that spread the possible losses. (Indeed, such patterns became early grounds for admitting usury). With the mathematical development of statistics it emerged as a powerful social tool. It has collectivized risk–taking and disposed of many of the problems that thwarted the theory of justice concerning distribution of losses and burdens. Sociologists (for example, MacIver) have sometimes distinguished between civilization and culture, stressing the cumulative character of social techniques as defining the former, and the freedom of spirit as the essence of the latter. Certainly a more developed history of such "civilization" would be enlightening. Take property, for example: when we regard it as a constant concept, we overlook the changes in incorporeal forms, corporate development and its techniques, vested rights and tenure rights, collateral effects of pension plans and union contracts, governmental monetary practices, all of which determine the flow of moneys and their distribution. The net result is to alter the concept of property, certainly beyond the recognition of an older landed society. The same point could be made about political institutions, national and international; about economic institutions which are transformed while remaining disguised under the hardened rubric of capitalism and socialism; and about familial institutions, under the acceptance of divorce and contraception and changing child-parent relations.

In general, the direction in social life is from resigned acceptance to intermittent intervention in situations of stress and distress, and from intermittent intervention to the conscious forging of institutional instruments for social progress. The outlook here converges with that of growing rationality.

Individual and Community

In many ways the relation of individual and community is, as suggested earlier, at the heart of the nature of citizenship. Let us pose the problem in its worst light, in the elitist and aristocratic tradition in which the people are taken to act in terms of individual interests and passions without the capacity for developing firm common purposes. It is not enough to show that actual aristocrats and elites do not better; this leads to a universal pessimism. The evidence for such pessimism is by no means weak. Practically every good device or instrument has turned into its opposite. Idealistic revolutions, whether French or American or Russian, have evaporated into politics as usual. Idealistic labor movements have often turned into myopic unions. Promising scientific discoveries have often been converted to profit and war. The liberating promises of education have often ended in alienated students. And the hopes of state action for well–being have led to disillusioned citizens. If we remain on a general level and expect a wholesale cure of our modern malaise, perhaps we are left, as in Nisbet's recent lament, with a call to pull ourselves up by moral-religious bootstraps.[20] If we think rather of the remaking of institutions, with or without the central focus on the state, we rely to some degree on an underlying sense of human nature and its processes which would allow for common purposes. And such a perspective has to come to terms with the view of the individual and the community.

I suggest that historically the moralities of isolated individualism justifying all policies in egoistic terms and the group cohesion that rides roughshod over individual well–being are best regarded as deviations from the moral main-stream. There has always been a strong component of affiliation and mutual aid, with ready cooperation and assistance, with focus on respect for the individual. I do not enter here into the technical questions: whether this component is a late product that emerges when societies become more unified or whether it is inherent in interpersonal relations; whether it is primarily a reaction to existent evils or a positive operation in ordinary life when not distorted by difficult social conditions. But the fact is that there is a present cleavage between individual and community. And this, we can see, has been powerfully promoted by the institutions of the last few centuries in which the competitive and the aggrandizing have been normalized as a mode of life and people driven apart into isolated individualism or have reacted into overriding cohesion. On our view individuality and the capacity to share experience require interpersonal and group cultivation and the sense of community can be expected to be the normal outcome of supporting harmonious institutions. Different moral theories, when they neglect this mainstream cooperative morality, will show, by the way they seek to justify themselves, that they have not looked away from this basic reference point. The isolating egoism attempts to derive, whether by the guiding hand of Providence or the computations of decision theory on a minimax strategy, a viable social ethic. The overriding cohesion theory attempts it by coalescing the general well–being of individuals with the collective policies.

Whatever be the case, it is obvious that we cannot in the modern world be called back to a morality that neglects the individual or leaves the individual on his own; and that the longing for community is a powerful motivation in contemporary morality.

Part 3

Having completed our analysis of the shifts that require a transformation in the character of citizenship today, we can now go directly to the pivotal virtues for contemporary citizenship without the fear that we are simply culling superficial traits assembled without grounding. Our remaining topics concern these virtues and their educational implications.

Pivotal Virtues for Contemporary Citizenship

The virtues of contemporary citizenship are mainly those of equality, responsibility and participation. They have several different aspects; they span both moral attitudes and intellectual qualities, and bear upon both national and international concerns.

The most familiar aspect of respect for persons is overcoming the major discriminations of our time. A contemporary moral citizen takes equalitarianism seriously and supports the achievement of equality for minorities (e.g., Blacks in our country) and submerged majorities (e.g., women). I do not mean that there will not be disagreements among moral citizens about what policies best serve such ends. For example, controversies about bussing and affirmative action and the equal rights amendment are real ones; but there is all the difference in the moral character of citizenship between those who oppose such measures and offer alternatives that move toward the goals and those who oppose such measures and are ready to put off achievement to an indefinite future or oppose them in order not to achieve equality.

A different aspect of equalitarianism is the concern for people throughout the world, not merely those in one's own country. This taps the serious issue of the relation of the national and the global. Every morality has had an implicit concept of what constitutes its moral community analogous to the congregation of a church, i.e., those who belong and who are possible participants. It is a commonplace in moral philosophy, as well as in sociology, that the moral community has grown from the kin and village to the country and beyond, and that since the eighteenth century universalism has moved from a dream to a partial reality. This does not mean that there are no differences in degree of attachment or priorities or special obligations (just as parents owe more to children than to a stranger). It does mean that the well-being of other countries becomes part of the reckoning of national policies. This is not a purely speculative matter, nor purely a matter of sentiment. It is critically practical in a world in which what one country does to land or water or weather or river flow to further its prosperity may mean the dessication or pollution or starvation of a neighboring country; in which the cornering of oil or national resources or their wasting may upset the production or economy of other countries.[21] Interdependence today is too familiar to require recounting. Now as international agenices—whether intergovernmental or nonformal or centralized—arise and are consolidated, the global aspects may be given greater strength and begin to affect the quality of national citizenship. Conceivably people engaged in the international aspects may be moved from guaranteed special status to international citizenship (cf., present dual citizenship even with its ambiguities). Indeed, the desirable universal character of science might even encourage international citizenship of scientists, not unlike priests in medieval times. In any case, the practical problem of contemporary citizenship in this context is to achieve a coherent interrelation of national and global concerns appropriate to the present day dynamic relation of countries in a growingly integrated world. It is a matter of balance in a complexity of considerations and circumstances which cannot be determined by a single rule or simplified principle.

A familiar, and in liberal countries a traditional, mark of good citizenship is strict adherence to the preservation of others' liberties particularly in situations where they differ with majority policies. Though often cast in terms of their rights to their liberties, it is clearly a lesson of the contemporary world: as Mill argued in his *On Liberty* more than a century ago, the losers in repression are the majority since the minority may be correct or partially correct in their views. Certainly in the contemporary changing world there is a need for the free consideration of alternatives. This is not a purely academic matter; we should recall the periods of national hysteria after World War I, again in the McCarthy period, and once again during the Vietnam War. Some today view the last as if it were simply a national spiritual depression which tied our hands thereafter from strong action in international affairs. This obscures the fact that the disagreement about national policy was a profound one in which we suffered through repressing alternative ideas and drove people into near violence.

A further element in a contemporary morality of citizenship is a balanced attitude toward past and future. It may be recalled that the Jeffersonian period revolted against the ties of the past; obligations to the future were not discussed. The world, Jefferson argued, belongs to the living. We can understand why "the dead hand of the past" was unacceptable in a time of revolution. We can also understand why in our own century economically underdeveloped countries have been forced to focus on the future; for their present generations paid the cost of sharp social change, even apart from sufferings of war and battles for freedom. In the industrially advanced countries, too, the problems of utilizing resources and the spectre of overpopulation have focussed attention on the future. Moral philosophers have debated the abstract question of the rights of future generations, but they have also raised the economic question of the percentage of national income that should be devoted to savings and investment for future restoration and replenishment. And strong social movements have grown for preservation and ecological balance. The fact is that such concerns, whether to maintain the best of the past in nature and human life or to plan for a good future, cannot be separated from the critique of the present character of life and its ways, from an evaluation of the extent of waste and recklessness or of wisdom in household and national management.

Such considerations lead to a sense of responsibility as an integral part of citizenship. The sense of responsibility need not be simply general, but can be directed in terms of what we may call the central problems on the agenda of national life. The greatest ones will usually be clear: no one can deny the importance in our time of peace, of avoiding an overpopulation that is a harbinger of starvation, of addressing dangers of pollution, of guarding against the exhaustion of vital resources. Such concerns are basic to all people, whatever the variety of values. Hence whatever other moral disagreement there may be, a specific concern with such problems is a mark of rational contemporary citizenship. To be concerned with such issues, to be ready to engage in cooperative action with respect to them, to be ready for rational sacrifice in meeting them, are therefore present requirements of sober citizenship. The current problem of energy has dramatized this kind of consideration.

Other large issues have not achieved that kind of agreement, but appear critical to different groups of citizens. Some take the conflict of capitalism and socialism to be the problem underlying all others; some formulate the problem politically, rather than economically, and see the issue as democracy against collective dictatorship. In all such questions the responsibility of contemporary citizenship calls minimally for a critical examination, not necessarily adherence to one side or another, nor even acceptance of a particular formulation of the problem. These are individual decisions, but the obligation not to let ideologies take over and close minds is a common one. It is easier to do this in dealing with other's problems than one's own. For example, the concept of the national interest has governed a great deal of policy decision throughout this century, and yet it has tacitly been identified with military strength and the power to have our way, without reckoning the effects on other countries or even the desirability of their autonomy in our national interest. (Controversies about the covert operations of our intelligence agencies sharply raise this question.) The relevant requirement of moral citizenship is, at a minimum, to resist ideological blinders in the use of concepts such as national interest, for they typically block full moral and social consideration.

A consequence of several of the aspects considered is an attitude to change. A rational attitude to change is not, of course, an adulation of change as such. It involves a critique of the need for change and an acceptance of the fact that in modern life change will often be desirable or else inevitable. We may then have to be reconciled to it, although we may work to make its shape more congenial to basic values that endure. Some tendencies have to be checked— for example, that everything technology invents has to be used. (cf, the controversies which occurred over supersonic air transportation and research in recombinant genetics.) This will be a constant issue, as possibilities that now belong in science fiction become technical realities. In brief, citizens may expect harder decisions, closer to basic moral issues, for whole ways of life. It is a far cry from the early part of the century, when the central issue may have been protection or free trade. With the growth of genetic knowledge and technology, we may have to decide on what kind of descendants to have, or whether not to decide at all. In any case, the acceptance of large changes in human life involves a critical as against an all–or–none attitude, and a special tolerance to varied ways of life. The latter will have reverberations in parent–child relations, since the new ways of life will take hold of the new generation more directly.

Most of the points discussed bear on responsibilities. But assigned responsibility without participation (like taxation without representation) invites manipulation or exploitation. Hence the requirement of participation is the very hub of the morality of citizenship today. What differentiates it from older forms, however, is the necessity for an active, inventive attitude, both in criticism and construction. Participation that is simply blind following is no more than obedience, and we have suggested that obedience is giving way as authority has diminished. To sway under charisma is the frequent intermediate posture; charisma often gives the sense of choice. The current need is to complete the passage to fuller participation. We shall see shortly that this has the most serious implications for education.

Finally, a sharpened concept of patriotism and love of country has not lost its place in the roster of qualities of contemporary citizenship. Altered as it is by the individualistic aspects of criticism and inventiveness, by the inter-penetration of the global with the national, infused as it can be by the fuller understanding of the relation of individual and community in a world such as ours is today, love of country still remains a natural human phenomenon, a significant outcome of particularity of setting, association, education, ambi-ent culture. A shaping of these natural impulses under the categories of authority and obedience has in the past provoked the conflict of patriotism versus conviction which led to such condemnatory comments as "Patriotism is the last refuge of a scoundrel" or to different interpretations of "Our country, right or wrong." Decatur's toast to our country in 1816 includes the hope that in her foreign relations she may always be right, before adding "but our country, right or wrong." Carl Schurz, after the century's experience, which includes the growth of imperialism, changes the perspective. His further addition (1899) is: "When right, to be kept right; when wrong, to be put right."[22] In brief, the patriotism that makes a responsibility of participa-tion is quite different from that which insists on thoughtless (though affectio-nate) obedience.

There are no doubt other qualities of citizenship to be traced in a fuller treatment; I think that those stressed above are the ones that emerge most sharply from the conditions and problems of the contemporary world. There is, however, one final point—the recognition of the limits of citizenship. The sense of this issue has haunted the history of political theory in both its religious and its secular forms. Perhaps the clearest formulation within politi-cal theory has been controversy about the right of revolution. It obviously cannot be put into the constitution or the law, for that would be granting the individual legal permission to violate the law. It will, therefore, have to find its place in reflections about the nature of the law. In legal positivist theory, with its identification of law and positive law, there can be an external moral critique of the law or its decisions. In natural law theory, a positive law that violates natural law can be declared not to be law at all, just as a law that goes counter to divine law has no proper legal status. In Hobbes, we saw, the rational purposes that generate law are no longer operative for the individual who is being led to the gallows, and he has no obligation to obey. In Locke, the right to revolution has a dignified centrality (and should it not, for he is justifying the revolution of 1688) as the appeal of people to God when they have exhausted all social appeals against the trampling of their natural rights. The Declaration of Independence follows the same line. Now whether the appeal to revolution be seen as the appeal to genuine citizenship or the transcendence of citizenship by weightier values, is akin to the issue we discussed as to whether citizenship is a constitutive part of the good life or only a limited role. The historical trend of democracy has been to domesticate protest by including it in the rights of citizenship, and therefore to render revolution less necessary. Examples are guaranteeing the rights of protesters to present their case and to organize for democratic change, and extending freedom of conscience to include even individual conscientious objection to military service. One can even read a continuity between revolutionary action and the many ways in which techniques exist in the law for departing from its rules. In an interesting book, *Discretion to Disobey*, (1973), Mortimer R. Kadish and Sanford H. Kadish explore the variety of situations in which (starting with juries) it is acceptable for officials and for individuals to deviate lawfully from the law.[23] Of course to recognize the continuities does not deny the limits. When a union of public workers strikes although it is forbidden to do so, mediation may still continue and the matter be settled, including the withdrawal of in injunction; and something similar may happen in the aftermath of race riots. But organized revolution or in our own day acts of deliberate terrorism are across the line. The great scope that a genuinely democratic society offers for action in disagreement thus enables it to draw the line of citizenship more sharply. Whether it can rule out the occurrence of revolution as a citizenly act depends on causes and content, not on form and method. In the classic revolutions in which a whole new type of society is in the making, those who are in revolt may think of themselves as the citizens of the coming society, rather than of the one that they see as passing.

Some Educational Implications

If we have correctly discerned the requisites of contemporary citizenship in knowledge and inquiry and attitude, then marked changes are overdue in education. They can be indicated briefly in three directions: the broadening of educational opportunities, a basic reorientation in intellectual education, and a rethinking of moral education.

The broadening of educational opportunity simply carries further the movement of the last few decades toward the expansion of secondary and higher education through schooling and outside of schooling. All citizens are to be provided with the knowledge that a contemporary needs. The momentum for expansion already exists in spite of economic difficulties. The crucial question is more likely to lie in the upgrading of quality to the point sufficient to meet the requirements of contemporary citizenship. To take one important example: is the understanding and ability to handle computers requisite for the citizens of the very near future? If so, should mathematical education become as general as we have sought to make reading and writing? Three questions are here involved—the necessity, the ability to manipulate, and the basic understanding. Reading in many places has been a legal requirement for voting. But it is quite possible, as India did, to have voting for different parties by symbols, even simply color differences, and information could be transmitted by sound. In one respect, then, the reading requirement can be relaxed, and has been in some places. If, however, the requirement of citizenship includes careful reckoning with ideas and proposals, it is hardly likely that this can be done in the advanced industrial countries without reading. Even apart from the necessity for reading in the ordinary business of life it has therefore remained as a basic element in the education of citizens. Now this argument about reading has been offered only to prepare us to consider mathematics. Do we need only ordinary arithmetic or more advanced mathematics? It is likely that computers can be so constructed that little understanding is required but only learning the rules of manipulation. Should our instruments of calculation and information storage simply be then the abacus of the new civilization?

Perhaps we can learn a lesson from our experience with statistics. Statistics are quoted in many discussions about public policy, and they are regarded as vital links in the proofs of likely consequences and thus desirable policy. Now it is a commonplace among scholars and scientists that an unenlightened use and acceptance of statistics is most dangerous and can be most misleading. A basic understanding of what is going on in the process is required at least for critical caution. The same point can be made by considering work in psychology or education. Researchers have sometimes mastered the tools of statistical research and used formulae and indices but without understanding the theory of the construction of their tests and the limits within which they are to be interpreted. The results are sometimes sad, and often harmful.

I suggest that from an overall perspective we need a public grounded in a basic education that furnishes understanding and not merely control of the instruments. How this is to be accomplished and how far it can be carried is a problem of detailed and inventive educational research. A cleavage of direction is apparent in educational theory: while some cling to the idea that only a small part of the population can go far in difficult learning, others define the differences among individuals not as capacity and incapacity, but in the time it will take people to learn and the effort and motivation and ingenuity of teaching required. I suggest that the latter is the path that a democracy has to try out in the contemporary world if it aims at an enlightened citizenry, especially as an enlightened citizenry is the requirement of the contemporary world.

The basic reorientation in intellectual education is a more far-reaching matter. It is generally recognized that most of our schooling has taken the form of imparting information and, even where it cultivates insight, of getting the learner to see the point as the teacher and established thought see it. In many respects it is parallel to the situation we have seen in political and social life. Teachers are the authority; students have the task of adequate obedience; the more gifted the students are the more quickly they can be expected to acquire the insights, master the theories, and organize their knowledge as the teachers are conveying it. The shift required in the light of the transition we have discussed from authority and obedience to participation and responsibility has its intellectual counterpart, and it is a drastic one. It is not merely the much desired shift today from deemphasizing fact–gathering (which treats knowledge in the style of the TV quiz shows as knowing and remembering factual items) to a grasp of theory and a cultivation of insight. It goes much farther and wants the student to confront alternatives, develop the habit of looking for and working out alternatives, and cultivate the imaginative and the inventive. This holds for culture as well as science. Ordinarily today this aspect is raised only in graduate work and only for those who are to engage in research. Even here the habit of entering a school of thought and following it out is the method of training. It furnishes depth, but not creativity.

A reorientation has to start at the beginning, not wait for graduate school. In reading, it is not sufficient to ask for *the* meaning, but to investigate different possible meanings. In school assignments it is not sufficient to ask the child to look up something in the encyclopedia and give the correct answer, defined as what the teacher had in mind. Why not send children on simple inquiries for which the teacher openly does not have an answer and awaits the child's construction of the problem? We all know the tests in which children are shown a complex and asked to find a pattern, whether it be a more or less hidden figure in a picture or a formula in a set of numbers or the obvious curve in a graph, or the rule of action in a series of situations. Invariably this test ends with the bright student getting "the correct answer." Why should not the student after getting this be asked to suggest or seek out alternative patterns from the same data or picture or situations? Is it only because such tests could not be automatically scored? Or is it that we are implicitly using a model of obedience to authoritative answers rather than of participation in the processes of advancing knowledge? Once again, the working out of the reorientation in terms of educational techniques is a difficult professional undertaking. But the direction seems to me to be warranted by the conditions of contemporary life, the need for the constant advance of knowledge, the need for deeper appreciation and participation in the understanding and processes of knowledge, and the goal of an enlightened community.

The rethinking of moral education is a more difficult question in its theoretical aspects. Our culture has had a narrow view of the scope of morality, limiting it to individual attitudes in the individual situation and in the treatment of others. It has not seen large problems of social policy as basically moral; thus it has rarely understood the medieval concern with "just price" as a moral problem, or the treatment of usury in ancient and medieval works. We are, however, under the pressure of contemporary problems and large scale contrasts of different societies, as well as the magnitude of evils and the issues of responsibility, beginning to see the larger aspects of morality and the interrelation of the good society and the good person. We are thus coming to see the moral character of institution building and reconstruction. All of this has to be conveyed in education. Insofar as the schools are small communities with ordered relations of persons and institutionalized ways of doing things, they can be a laboratory for moral learning and the character of student participation. A minimal change in the right direction would be to alter the frequent practice of preaching democracy and brotherhood in a functioning atmosphere of authority and punishment. In general, there is no contradiction between cultivating reasoning in moral matters and maintaining an explicit moral order in the way people treat one another and in the distribution of rights and opportunities. Nor is there a contradiction between on the one hand cultivating a place for the individual in criticizing the existent order and justifying proposals for reconstruction, even on the school level, and on the other hand working out cooperative ways of decision that are not simply voluntaristic. Nor is there a contradiction between even special teaching, dealing with moral problems and the recognition that in the deeper sense they can be developed and dealt with in every corner of the curriculum from literature to sport to mathematics. Perhaps the mark of success would be the extent to which students come to see and feel morality as a process of self–making and society–making. This would be a remarkable preparation for citizenship.

Perhaps the primary lesson of our inquiry has been the extent to which apparently simple questions of the character of citizenship under present conditions turn out to have roots and ramifications in basic philosophical ideas, and require for their answers not only philosophical clarification but also the bringing together of inquiries and answers from the whole range of social disciplines. The answers we have suggested are, of course, hypotheses for theoretical inquiry and exploratory practice. The important issue is to decide on basic directions.

Notes

1. Aristotle, *Politics*, Book III, chap. 4.
2. Bernard Mandeville, *The Fable of the Bees: or, Private Vices, Publick Benefits* (New York: Capricorn books, 1962; originally published 1714).
3. Plato, *Republic*, 369–74.
4. Ivan Illich, *Celebration of Awareness* (Garden City, New York: Doubleday and Co., 1970).

5. Francis Biddle, *The Fear of Freedom* (Garden City, New York: Doubleday and Co., 1951). See especially his chapter on The Quality of Loyalty. D.D. Raphael, in his *Problems of Political Philosophy* (London: Macmillan and Co., 1970), contrasts the American legal language in which one speaks of a "citizen of the United States" with the British in which one is a "British subject." The difference lies in the monarchy.

6. Josiah Royce, *The Philosophy of Loyalty* (New York: The Macmillan Co., 1911).

7. H. Hartshorne and M.A. May, *Studies in the Nature of Character* (New York: The Macmillan Co., 1928–30), vol. I: *Studies in Deceit*.

8. Erich Fromm, *Man for Himself: An Inquiry into the Psychology of Ethics* (New York: Rinehart and Co., 1947).

9. *International Encyclopedia of the Social Sciences* (The Macmillan Co. and the Free Press, 1968), s.v. "Moral Development," by Lawrence Kohlberg.

10. Abraham Edel, *Science, Ideology, and Value*, vol. II: *Exploring Fact and Value* (New Brunswick, N.J.: Transaction Publishers, 1980), chap. 11.

11. Dorothy Emmett, *Rules, Roles and Relations* (London, Macmillan and Co., 1966), 154.

12. Aristotle, *Nicomachean Ethics*, Book I, Chap. 7.

13. For a clear statement of this problem, see R.S. Downie, *Roles and Values* (London: Methuen and Co., 1971), 128–34.

14. Thomas Hobbes, *Leviathan* (Oxford: Clarendon Press, 1909; originally published 1651), Part I, chap. 15.

15. John Rawls, *A Theory of Justice* (Cambridge, Mass.: The Belknap Press of Harvard University Press, 1971).

16. Harold D. Lasswell, *Politics: Who Gets What, When, How* (New York: McGraw-Hill Book Co., 1936; Meridian Books, 1958).

17. Robert Nisbet, *The Twilight of Authority* (New York: Oxford University Press, 1975); Edmund Burke, *Reflections on the Revolution in France* (New York: Liberal Arts Press, 1955; originally published 1790); Michael Oakeshott, *Rationalism in Politics* (New York: Basic Books, 1962). For a less dismal outlook, which underscores the need for responsibility, see Clinton Rossiter, "The Democratic Process" in *Goals for Americans, The Report of the President's Commission on National Goals and Chapters Submitted for the Consideration of the Commission*, The American Assembly, Columbia University (Prentice–Hall, Inc.: A Spectrum Book), 61–78. See especially section X on "The Role of the Citizen", 76–7.

18. Donella H. Meadows et al., *The Limits to Growth, A Report for the Club of Rome's Project on the Predicament of Mankind* (New York: Universal Books, 1972).

19. Walter Lippman, *The Method of Freedom* (New York: The Macmillan Co., 1934).

20. Robert Nisbet, "Progress and Providence", *Transaction: Social Science and Modern Society* 17 (November/December 1979): 4.

21. Oscar Schachter, *Sharing the World's Resources* (New York: Columbia University Press, 1977).

22. Schurz said this is an address to an Anti-Imperialistic Conference in Chicago on October 17, 1899.

23. Mortimer R. Kadish and Sanford H. Kadish, *Discretion to Disobey: A Study of Lawful Departures from Legal Rules* (Stanford, California: Stanford University Press, 1973).

17

The Humanities and Public Policy:
A Philosophical Perspective

For more than two years, Columbia University had a project on the humanities and public policy issues. At regular meetings, well–known professors in different fields, from major universities, presented papers on related themes, seen from different angles. It turned out to be my task at the end (May 9, 1975) to act as philosophic critic, in a paper synthesizing the lessons of this accumulation.

The parts in inset refer to papers presented, but the reader will find that they tell their own story and, so far from distracting, add to the development of the theme. The chapter does have a rounded thesis about the relation of the humanities to social thought and public policy, and in this sense serves well to integrate the argument of the present book.

The easy way to enter our topic is through the analytic gate: to reflect on the meaning of "public policy" and of "humanities," and hope that the types of relations encased in the "and" will stand out in bold relief. We must not, however, expect the results to be more than suggestive.

Policies formulate directions for conduct at a moderate level of generality. Too general, they turn into aims; not general enough, they are rules. But these are formal distinctions and do not constrain the content. Any content significant enough to deliberate about can, under some conditions, turn into a policy.

Three general components in policy decision may be distinguished. We have to have aims, purposes or *values*. We need *knowledge*. And we require some account of the situation to which value and knowledge are being applied; let us call this third component the *practical context*. Now the first temptation is to correlate value with humanities, knowledge with science, and practical context with the field that calls upon us for decision. A kind of synthesis of the three would then yield the policy. But this is too neat. For one thing, values are riddled with factual presuppositions and assumptions. For a second, knowledge even in its scientific form has a purposive base and is permeated with selective elements. For a third, the kind of structure to be ascribed to any particular context for action itself involves both knowledge claims and particular purposes. And fourth, decision is only in special cases an intuitive synthesis, just as it is only in special cases a technical computation. Most of the time it is at least a dramatic rehearsal of alternatives and a rough estimate of their consequences.

Now for the "humanities." Fortunately, Congress has given us a good and broad–minded start. The humanities, we are told, include "the study of philosophy, history, literature, language, linguistics, jurisprudence, comparative religion, ethics and archaeology; also the history, theory and criticism of the arts and those aspects of the social sciences concerned with values." In short, not the sciences, not the arts themselves, but a great deal of the rest, and most of it on a reflective level. "Humanities" is thus taken to designate a body of subjects, a way of regarding it often found in academic life.

A second approach to the humanities would be to think in terms of a set of human faculties or functions to be stimulated by such subjects. Just as knowing and reasoning are linked to science, so imagination and feeling and creativity are linked to the humanities. (Insight and understanding hover on the border). A third approach would characterize humanities by the humanistic, no longer a body but a spirit; so freed, there is no field to which it might not be applied. We could envisage a school of humanistic engineering, where physical science was taught in the context of the history of science as an imaginative enterprise (much as Jacob Bronowski saw it); where ideals of technique and practical control were infused with the spirit of Prometheus and the sense of human well–being and the quality of life; and where organizational ideals breathed the air of democracy and community of effort rather than the authoritarian confines of either corporatism or technocracy. And throughout would run the philosophy of history of human beings making themselves, with a full sense of their responsibility for the products. Indeed, it is this sense of "humanities" which often triggers the complaint that much of what passes for the subject matter in humanities can be as narrowly technical as any applied science.

One more preliminary reflection: how practical are the humanities? At once we think of Plato's warning that whoever controls the music of the young controls their character and their fate more surely than they are determined by the laws. And by "music," although he refers to the heroic Dorian mode and the effeminate Lydian mode, he really means the whole range of the humanities, the domain of the Muses. In our time, similar questions are raised, not about the Homeric gods as risky models for youth, but about nursery stories and comic books, riotous music, violence and aggression on TV. All this is too familiar to need discussion here. Yet it is worth noting on a broader social scale that departures in the arts often signal (if they do not control) a restlessness that moves to social change. One thinks of futurism in Italy playing into the hands of fascism and its glorification of strength and antirational spontaneity. Or one thinks of writers like T. E. Hulme in England before World War I and Oswald Spengler in Germany during that war, who traced such connections with a kind of grim joy or pungent gloom. Hulme's criticism in art and the humanities was directed to ferreting out every possible source for glorifying violence and revolt against rationality that could be seen as a forerunner of an antihumanism: the force of Jacob Epstein's sculpture, the retreat from reason to the intuitionism of process in Bergson (Hulme translated the latter's *Introduction to Metaphysics*), even the philosophy of G. E. Moore and Husserl as betokening a break with the subjectivism and relativism of humanist ethics. Hulme was a self-styled reactionary and finally found his violence (and met his death) in World War I. And Spengler too, though he uses a method of riotous analogy, has a sense for the practical relations of arts and modes of thought and feeling. I take from all this no more than the minimal warning that the values to be seen in the humanities at a given period may be foreshadowing, if not actually governing the rising practice of the emerging world.

There is another, quite different sense in which the humanities have shown themselves to be practical: the fancies of one day may be the practical problems of the next. Aristotle, in defending slavery as necessary for the work of the world, says it would come to an end only if spinning took place by itself and the lute played of itself, and perhaps not even then. Today, with automation, the end of exploitation is thus overdue. John Stuart Mill, in arguing for qualitative differences in pleasure, asks the speculative question whether one would choose to be a dissatisfied Socrates or a satisfied pig. Today, lobotomies and psychosurgery, as well as new modes of operant conditioning, make such choices a highly practical matter; less dramatically, in ordinary life, there is always the choice of a tranquilizer to lull the anxieties of facing problems socratically. It is worth noting that the science of tranquilizers— *ataractics*—derives its name from the Greek for lack of disturbance or peace of mind which was the great goal of the ancient Epicureans, much like the "apathy" of the Stoics. Yet there is a great difference—one might almost say a world of value—between tranquility and tranquilizing. I forego what we might do with Schopenhauer's speculative urging that men refrain from procreation to bring to an end the blind restless striving of the Will on earth, now that we can really poison the atmosphere with nuclear energy. . . .

So much for preliminaries. The general subjects of the preceding essays preeminently represent areas of burgeoning policy issues that tap a diversity of central problems, human, global, and contemporary. It is well to keep them before us: Justice and Human Equality, Private Rights and the Public Good, Technology and the Ideal of Human Progress, War and the Social Order, Education and the Good Society. I want to tackle our central problem—what the humanities can do for public policy issues—not by taking each of these in turn but by following a number of theoretical themes that keep weaving their way through these papers, no matter which of the five fields their authors focus upon. Here are the topics I shall deal with:

1. Sibling Rivalry: The Relations of the Humanities with the Psychological and Social Sciences
2. Rationality and Beyond
3. Intimations of a Natural Order
4. The Hold of the Past and the Hope of the Future
5. Symbols, Interpretation and Reality
6. The Study of Values
7. Mine and Thine, or I and Thou?
8. How to Be Practical, though Humanistic

1. Sibling Rivalry: The Relation of the Humanities with the Psychological and Social Sciences

So basic a theme calls for a myth—for surely the intellectual life is entitled to its own myths. Zeus, it is said, seeing the philosophers worried only about questions of physical science, sent Socrates to instill a wider set of questions. But Socrates got so entranced with the phenomenon of asking questions that he never even got to asking all the questions on the list that Zeus had given him. Zeus therefore had Socrates put to death and gave the list to Plato. His instructions were peremptory: Plato was to sow the seeds of the humanities and the social sciences, and he was to write a report—no oral account this time. Plato's report is the *Republic*, which asks all the questions in all their magnificent interrelations. But when Zeus came to read it—or had one of his Ganymede–like scribes do it for him—he found that Plato had become so interested in the questions that he also gave all the answers, and of course such *hubris* brought its own *nemesis*: most of the answers were wrong, though mankind would take millennia to find it out. (In fact, Thrasymachus had tried to steer Plato into social science at the outset, but Plato had violently snubbed him.) Zeus therefore, making the punishment fit the crime, condemned Plato to write another report on the answers, which no one would ever bother reading! This of course was the *Laws*. And ever since then—for every explanatory myth must end with an ''and so''—three things have happened:

the humanities ask the questions and offer only intimations of the answers; the social sciences give the answers but never bother much about the questions; and the foundations insist on written reports but never bother much to read them!

I shall make no attempt here to defend the literal truths built into much of this myth. The *Republic* does ask most of the questions relevant for social policy and does it beautifully, especially in the disorder with which it goes from one field to another, which is the natural way to see all the presuppositions of one's questions. And it does give cursory answers because it begs numerous issues that require a psychological and social science to clarify and furnish evidence. And the sibling rivalry (humanities is the older sibling) has been continuous. Witness the way in which social science long shied away from value problems on the ground that values were unscientific; or the way in which social sciences narrow their path to questions that their tools are capable of dealing with, as if the aim of science were merely to exercise tools; or the way in which departments of psychology and of political science and of sociology have split within recent decades in the United States because one side wanted to hold on to value issues and policy issues, while the other was entranced with behavioral operationism or with simulating human behavior in computerizeable models. Or look at the same phenomenon from the side of the humanities: so anxious are the humanists not to be scientists that they set up rival methods of symbolic analysis and interpretation and grasp every weapon of phenomenology that comes sauntering by as if to say, "Look, we have our own science which is not science, and it's better than my sibling's, and it gives you a real truth, not a spurious one." And if more evidence is needed, look at the way scientists rush to answer humanistic questions in their off moments, or after retirement, or occasionally in a collateral utopia—for example, *Walden II*—as if these really important issues did not require their full scientific concentration.

I say all this not to complain but to suggest a thesis about the relations of the humanities and the psychological and social sciences. They are both cut from the same cloth, and the designs run through them often without a break; we must not mistake historical divisions of labor for metaphysical dichotomies of subject matter or for more than differences of degree in method. Of course, we can manufacture sharply contrasting pictures if every time a scientist uses his imagination we call him a humanist, and every time a humanist looks for evidence we say he is turning scientist. But then *our* dichotomies, not nature's or reality's, will be showing.

I suggest therefore the unity of the human endeavor in these domains, without at the moment presenting it as a structured and analyzed hypothesis. Some considerations along these lines will emerge from the treatment of themes later on. But perhaps a brief case study will clarify what I am driving at.

One of the massive works in psychology and social science at the midpoint of our century was *The Authoritarian Personality* (1950) by Adorno, Frenkel–Brunswik, Levinson, and Sanford. It made broad and extensive studies of the antidemocratic personality, identified initially in the ideology of antisemitism. It sought to establish that there was such a configuration of personality, to identify its marks and degree of generality and typical ideological manifestations, and to correlate its occurrence with familial and institutional patterns. It had all the expertise of scales and tests and statistical correlations. There was, of course, criticism of its foundational ideas and methods, but such criticism is a common phenomenon in controversy over a scientific project that is large–scale in scope, especially where it has broad policy implications for institutional reconstruction; it is not pertinent here to ask how far the criticism was justified.

To the same era belongs Sartre's "Portrait of the Antisemite," which appears in his *Reflections on the Jewish Question* (1947). It asks the same kind of question as the scientific study; that is, it wants to know what is going on in the antisemite. It is anecdotal: for example, it tells about the man who was anti–British and came to life only when someone referred to an Englishman. It has literary references, for example, to the picture of the Jewess in literature. It frames no tables of evidence, but gives conclusions in an impressionistic way: that antisemitism is not an opinion but a passion involving the entire personality; that the antisemite is a man afraid of himself, his freedom, his responsibilities, indeed of everything except the Jews. Ultimately, Sartre interprets antisemitism as a fear of man's fate, as a desire to be a thing—anything but a man. The essay is eloquent, passionate, thoroughly humanistic. Its conclusions are not far from those of the scientific treatise.

I make these comparisons not to argue that a humanist can reach the same results without being scientific. He might, but how would we know he was correct? Nor do I intend to deny a difference in method—whether this be in kind or in degree. Sartre's thesis is not formulated with technical precision, it is not sufficiently refined, and it is intended to lead us in a different direction, to his philosophy of freedom and man's fate. But why should we be so *either–or*? The humanist and the scientist are here doing the same job but pushing in different directions.

It is interesting to note as a historical matter that the scientific study of the authoritarian personality had its origins in value and policy issues. Obviously it was stimulated by the phenomenon of Nazi Germany and the desire to understand what happened to a whole people. Moreover, the roots of its major participants lay in German culture and the experience of the authoritarian family. The Frankfurt school from which Adorno came was fascinated by the phenomena of authority and very early did studies on authority in the family.

This in turn had repercussions in the humanities, as well as the sciences. For example, it is this background which probably explains why Erich Fromm, coming from the same school, focuses on an aspect of the Oedipus myth entirely different from the usual Freudian one: he emphasizes the relation of Oedipus to his sons (as evident in *Oedipus at Colonus* and *Seven Against Thebes*) rather than simply his relation to his mother. The dominating fact is paternal authority. I should not be surprised if in turn the roots of ego psychology, as in Erickson's work, are fed at the same spring.

It may be thought that illustrations from the soft sciences would naturally find the humanities and the sciences close together since depth psychology and personality psychology are sometimes more humanistic than scientific. But the same lessons could be derived from economics, particularly when it is looked at in relation to policy. In his *Proposed Roads to Freedom* (1919), Bertrand Russell suggested that society set up a "vagabond wage," that is, a subsistence minimum which anyone could get if he preferred not to work—for example, if he wished to spend his time on philosophy and poetry. Russell added that enough people would want more than the minimum wage to ensure the production the world required. Half a century later, Milton Friedman proposed his "negative income tax" which would, by income tax rebate, bring every family to subsistence minimum. Russell's view was romantic and humanistic and philosophic; Friedman's is based on hard science. Yet both embody values: the common one of acknowledging some social responsibility for diminishing poverty; the further one on Russell's side of encouraging creativity; the further one on Friedman's side of enhancing liberty by getting rid of state controls in welfare systems and the like. Russell guessed that there would be enough people wanting more to satisfy production needs and that society could afford it. Friedman could give hard figures for manpower in production and for costs. Both were realistic. Russell's impressions of the way his plan would enhance freedom were quite matched by his estimate shortly after of the authoritarian potential of the Russian revolution. Friedman's realism was evident in his blunt remark before a congressional committee (reported in the press) when he was asked whether beneficiaries of a negative income tax should not lose their vote; he replied that if putting one's fingers into the public till meant losing one's vote, businessmen would be the first to lose it.

Actually, the difference between Russell's proposal and Friedman's is accounted for, not by a contrast between humanist and scientist, but by the experience of half a century, the tremendous growth of production, the lessons of both economic waste and human indignity in the workings of the welfare system, and so on. Both show humanistic imagination in making a form of property ("wage" and "income tax rebate") out of the routing of tax funds, and neither loads it with "charity" or even "distributive justice." There is no hard line here between humanist and scientist in their dealings with public policy.

Since these remarks have stressed the community between the sibling disciplines, it is all the more important to note how they diverge when science becomes *technical*—a term, after all, that betokens only the disciplined precision of *technē* or craft. Such divergences can best be seen by dealing with evidence. Imaginative impressionism will no longer do; the responsibility to the real world is as severe as the responsibility to consequences in action.

> Take, for example, the broad question that arose in several papers about whether men at bottom really value conflict and war. In "War and the Clash of Ideas," Adda Bozeman culls materials on war and violence from many different cultures to illustrate her thesis of the natural acceptance of these phenomena throughout history, as compared to the recent emphasis in peace research on conflict control.[1] (I was reminded in this of Santayana's remark that philosophical manipulation of history is like a man looking over a crowd to find his friends.) Now clearly, if the issue called for evidence, we would have to ask whether one could also cull materials on the opposite side; whether all Bozeman's materials concerned men, not women; whether hers came predominantly from preindustrial societies; and so on. Too often, in the humanities, one finds the impressionistically striking rather than the evidential cautions which the sciences have stabilized over a long experience of inquiry.

> A similar question arises in a somewhat different way when Elisabeth Hansot suggests, in her "Reflections on War, Utopias, and Temporary Systems," that peace involves "the absence of certain human capacities or passions which have come to be partially associated with combat." At the very least, we would have to inquire whether this absence held only for certain types of societies such as ours— individualistic societies which set only competitive challenges and not hard communal challenges. The range of evidence is not enough; it involves the analysis of the conditions of the evidential.

> Similarly, William McNeill's comparison of historical empires, "On National Frontiers," from which he seeks to show how great has been the role of polyethnic empires as against the limited role of the principle of national self–determinism, would give only a start to inquiry. We would have to know the conditions under which each occurred and to evaluate the successes and failures (as well as the costs and benefits) with respect to the maintenance of peace; and if interest focused on the future, whether the conditions of the one were likely to pose the problems for action or the conditions of the other.

On this question of evidence the sibling disciplines would cooperate most successfully if rather than jockeying for priority they stressed mutually integrative results. They have been seduced too often by oversharp contrasts between global-synthetic and analytic–statistical, or the various contrasts between portait-painting and generalization that have been argued over in the philosophy of science under such captious captions as "ideographic" and "nomothetic." But to pursue this here would take us too far afield. In any case, they are born together in the problematic field, and they come together in the determination of policy, though they move apart in the intervening processes of methodological differences and technical requirements. Yet even in these intervening processes the similarities may be not without significance.

2.   Rationality and Beyond

There is a class of humanists who take their stand (or rather their comfortable chairs) on sentiment (not sentimentality) as distinct and above rationality. In vain, for them, did William James try to bridge the gap by seeing rationality as itself a sentiment. For them, rationality is on the other side of a great gulf. They would, if they could, revise Emerson's oft-quoted remark about a foolish consistency by calling consistency "rationality" and leaving out the "foolish." it would then read: "*Rationality* is the hobgoblin of little minds." Rationality is practical or rigidly logical; it is useful enough, but utility is the slave of value, and the humanities are the value bosses. I am talking, of course, of the ideal type; for some of our contributors the shoe may pinch a little, but it surely will not fit.

There is always a touch of ideology—usually conservative ideology—about this view. Perhaps we should say of it what Oakeshott says of a conservative philosophy, that if there is a felt need to develop a conservative philosophy, conservatism must be already slipping. So too, a lofty elitist humanism has a certain charm as an expression of truly cultivated spirits, but when it begins to defend itself it is surprising how often we find quotations from the French-monarchist intellectuals still revolting against the revolution, or the picture of culture in T. S. Eliot and a distaste for the masses, or a Bergsonian berating of a static intellect, or a Nietzschean abuse of John Stuart Mill as a blockhead. Still, humanist sentiment must not be condemned by association simply because it attacks rationality. The question rather is: what is wrong with the picture of rationality that cultivated sentiment should shudder at it? It may be simply, as Santayana remarks in a chapter on mechanism, that poets shudder at skeletons and scientists give us the skeletal structure of the universe. Or more likely, there is as much of ideology in concepts of rationality as there is in the attacks upon it. For after all, the history of Western thought resonates loudly with the battles of reason against faith, of science against religion, and all the familiar rest. If sentiment is tied to the aristocracy, reason and science are tied to the bourgeoisie, but our problem is not—or is it?—a question of evaluating the style and quality of life in different social classes.

There is an occasional attempt to treat the issue of reason and beyond as itself a scientific question. Lévy-Bruhl in his *How Natives Think* (1925; French original, 1910) tried to fathom the prelogical mentality that makes its inferences by some feeling of participation, rather than by the law of noncontradiction. But Franz Boas in his *Mind of Primitive Man* (1911) early argued for the logical powers of preliterate peoples; we tend to be misled by differences that are in the assumed premises, not in the processes of thought. Again, in the social sciences, there is the effort to develop interpretation as a distinct category of inquiry, fit for the humanistic; this we shall examine below.

But what of rationality itself and its many portraits? Its minimal sense is of course consistency. A man says, "War is terrible," and the next moment he rhapsodizes, "War is glorious." We confront him with himself and make him say, "War is terrible *and* war is glorious." Then he must look for an out: sometimes terrible, sometimes glorious; terrible in one aspect, glorious in another; glory itself has terror in it; anything but to be led to the brink of the utterance "p and not p." Now take Homer's scene in which Hector says what is to be his farewell to Andromache while holding his young son in his arms. He has just finished saying that he is fighting an unjust war and will continue fighting only to defend his family; the sense of war as senseless is obvious. As he holds up his son, we might have expected him to say, "Let there be peace when this boy grows to manhood." But instead, he prays that the boy's valor may be greater than his father's, and that his mother's heart may rejoice when he brings in the bloody spoils of his slain foe. A contradiction, yes. But contradictories cannot both exist, and here we have a people for whom violence is the source of prestige and status and yet whose violence brings destruction to them in the search for glory. Obviously, the meaning of contradiction has been enlarged. Here it is contradictory objectives, in the sense that there is inner conflict and unavoidable frustration. When Dostoyevski's underground man says that something will yield the greatest happiness but that precisely for that reason he spurns it, is this self-contradiction, or a critique of happiness as the human end, or a rejection of calculation in the good life, or just a clinical symptom?

It would be a long story to trace the path from minima to maxima in the idea of rationality. We could move from conflicting aims to an inner conflict in a system. After all, was not the whole of Marx's *Capital* a theoretical structure to show the underlying conflict in a system of apparent harmony and expression of agreement between buyer and seller (of commodities, including labor), much as two innocent neighbors drilling for oil might not realize that they were tapping the same reservoir? We could follow a different path in which not so much the demand for unity is built into the idea of rationality as the bare notion of utility. Rationality now starts from mere efficiency, the least wasteful use of means for an end. It goes on to include concepts of bureaucratic rationalization (as Max Weber analyzed them), and even often in a disguised way to incorporate the abstract end (power, money) to which the utility is directed. Or, letting people choose their own ends, it develops notions of maximization, scrupulously avoiding, with Pareto's blessing, any interpersonal comparisons. In a more aseptic analysis, limited to the nature of scientific processes, rationality will grow from logical consistency to inductive rationality which incorporates the trend of evidence, and a rational man will be one who follows the evidence.

Clearly then, to reject rationality is to reject the special form of thought and institutional orientation that is elaborated under its broad umbrella. But this does not mean that there is a pure rationality captured by a special pattern. Perhaps ultimately there never has been, and cannot be, a concept of rationality which does not, once it goes beyond logical consistency, embody some view of man, his world, his faculties, his aims, and at least their general requirements. The concept of rationality is therefore a growing one, demanding evaluation at every stage. As we learn the lessons of method in the growth of knowledge, our concept of rationality itself expands. For example, as we come to make fairly reliable predictions over longer stretches of time, a rational person is one who takes the long view, not the short view. As we learn the inner mechanisms of self–deceit, a rational person is one who discounts for his inner distortions. As we come to understand the influence of class and its ideologies, a rational person is one who tries persistently to see things from the other point of view as well, instead of only through any one entrenched perspective. (Is this not the lesson of contemporary liberation movements?) As a global perspective begins to show the confusions and frustrations into which anything less than a global view will get us (at least on some questions such as energy and agriculture and pollution of the ocean and the air), does not rationality begin to embrace a notion of taking a global perspective where a global perspective is essential to answering the problem—even if nationalism has all the strength some of us have attributed to it? Finally, as philosophic wisdom grows and shows us that the kinds of answers we give depend in measure on the kinds of questions we ask, does not rationality begin to embrace a theory of the appropriateness of questions?

Theoretically, there is no reason why the direction of an expanded rationality should not be sensed by humanists with their eyes on values and the imagination sometimes long before scientists who are immersed in present data under a complex establishment or else extrapolating their curves from present dilemmas. Often, however, the scientist and the humanist may be preaching the same lesson in different ways. Take, for example, the great contemporary lesson of the human need for an open system as against a closed total world view. The scientist has long incorporated it in his methods and his probabilism in the face of growing human knowledge. In religion, there has been the shift from a dogmatic assurance about God's will to an existentialist recognition that we act in our own responsibility without a dependable knowledge of what is demanded of us. The emphasis on transcendence in Jaspers, or on self–transcendence in Niebuhr, is on openness. For that matter, when Sartre takes Kierkegaard's analysis of the episode of Abraham and Isaac, he does not see it as illustrating Abraham's depth of faith; rather he wonders why Abraham should not have questioned the command to kill his son as unlike his God, and possibly coming from an imposter. Even Marxism, it should be noted, though often applied in a closed way, contains in its metaphysics the principle of the transformation of quantity into quality, which means the recognition of critical points in historical processes at which new levels of phenomena come into being. (Marx always opposed the structured plans of "utopian socialists.") Although there may be different social stresses in these various views, there seems little difference in the message of contemporary science and contemporary religion and contemporary humanism about the rationality of keeping the system—whatever system—open. The desire for a closed system is, in Dewey's phrase, a quest for certainty. We can sympathize with Santayana's preference for Dante over Shakespeare, because Dante has a total world view whereas Shakespeare only traces the ramifications of fragmentary themes as they generate from his magnificent display of human passions. But we know now that a closed total world view is not a mark of rationality, but its opposite.

Today the concept of rationality needs reassessment in every area of human endeavor. Rationality in law, rationality in ethics, rationality in politics—all call for analysis and evaluation. Was what Watergate revealed the culmination of rationality in politics? When a student says to a professor, "Thank you for your time" instead of "Thank you for your criticism and ideas" (which started, I think, somewhere in the 1950s), is that the culmination of economic rationality in intellectual relations? Is cost–benefit analysis based on the postulate that there is nothing that cannot be overbalanced by some aggregation of other values? With such tasks of inquiry on our collective hands, there is full scope for the humanities and the sciences and practical life to recognize their kinship in the ideal of rationality, rather than to equate it with its historical shortcomings.

3.   Intimations of a Natural Order

In none of these essays is there any loud proclamation of a natural order. This is remarkable, considering how long philosophy and theology and law and economics centered on the concept of nature and the natural and how persistent the tradition of natural law has been. Nevertheless, we are not without some residual intimations that call for exploration. There is a marked propensity for perennialism in the humanities.

Perhaps the notion of a natural order is covered by constant talk of future shock these days. At any rate, the idea of change has grown to tremendous proportions since the nineteenth century. It is still possible, however, to ignore that idea by asking questions about the nature of man and not analyzing the questions. We then get debates between opposing answers. In this fashion we find debates about whether man is naturally aggressive or naturally affiliative, with occasional gimmicks thrown in like territorial imperatives derived from our kinship with animals. Neither side questions the basic concept of a nature or an essence, but we do not notice this because they argue so heatedly as opposites. Even the view of man as plastic has not been cast so much as a denial of a nature as an affirmation of a culturally versatile nature. Again, there are desperate efforts in philosophical anthropology to provide a definition of man. Is he a rational animal, a tool–making animal, a being capable of ideals, a purely historical being, or what else? Perhaps a good answer would be: man is a being who asks the question, "What is man?" and declines to answer it. Why should man not refuse to be defined? "What is man that Thou art mindful of him?" was not a request for a definition but for a ground of divine concern.

In the next section, I shall discuss how the nineteenth century discovery of history and change gradually crept in. Objectively, it was involved in the biological concept of evolution and the different explicit philosophies of history: man came to be regarded as a historical being at the very core—far beyond the eighteenth century notions of indefinite progress toward a fixed ideal. Subjectively, the shift is seen in the emergence of insecurity in men's feelings toward the world. An eighteenth century Hutcheson could rest morality on sentiment because he felt secure that God would not go changing the basic instincts and passions of men. He probably would not have understood a Nietzchean demand that man surpass himself. But already Kierkegaard rejects the socratic maxim of "Know thyself," because presumably there is nothing secure to know. He substitutes, "Choose thyself," and we can be sure that the choosing is done in fear and trembling. In the twentieth century one finds at last talk of man's nature *changing*, and even—in existentialist views—the denial that man has a nature on the ground that a nature is incompatible with man's absolute freedom. Perhaps this is less revolutionary than it sounds since man is said to have a condition, if not a nature, which imposes invariable problems on him (he lives in the world and chooses, works, dies). In the scientifically minded history we find an occasional archaeological vista which prompts a scientist such as V. Gordon Childe to title a book *Man Makes Himself* (1936).

There is one very definite appeal to nature and the natural order in these papers, apart from such residual intimations as allege perennial verities about man's lust for war or suggestions of proper functions for education, and it lies in Roderick Nash's conception of an original and pure Nature.

In "Do Rocks Have Rights?" Nash proposes an environmental ethics that will go beyond human beings to embrace animals, plants, rocks—in short, the whole of our natural world. (The whole view will concern us later.) On the crucial question of the needs and wants of existents, he notes that slaves can speak for themselves, but "what, after all, do rocks want? Are their rights [being] violated by quarrying them for a building or crushing them into pavement or shaping them into statues?" For the time being he compromises on the question, agreeing with Aldo Leopold that "a thing is right when it tends to preserve the integrity, stability, and beauty of the biotic community. It is wrong when it does otherwise."

Now what might justify such a view of rocks? Why should not the statue be a fulfillment of the rock's nature?—Aristotle is often quoted for the view that any stone longs to be a doorstep. Nash's attribution of an essence to rocks is less a Newtonian theory of inertia than a conservative assumption that nothing is to be changed. In his case—that of an environmentalist's battle against corrupting interests in land development and pollution—we must not confuse conservation and conservatism, but neither should we allow one to glide into the other. His mediating idea can only be the concept of a pure unspoiled nature whose restoration is the goal rather than a critical evaluation of competing goods among which the wisest decision is to be made.

If today we have to talk of the natural and the essential, we have to talk of growing essences or changing essences. But the question is not so simple. Why is it the case that though we have the full vista of change in our scientific speculations and give lip service to change when pressed, still in the humanities (and in a great part of the social sciences too) we frame our questions and look for answers in terms of the older appeal to a natural order? Perhaps it is because change in an essence seems spread over a long period of mankind, so that a changing essence is still an essence for a while. And we live in that while. What does it matter that further back our "essence" came into being in an evolutionary process and some day in the future that essence will be different? We know of history, but we live in a present stretch. And so the changes that concern the humanities are the cycles of life and death of our own daily and annual rounds. Is that why Aristotle gave poetry a deeper philosophical status than history; why we respond readily to T. S. Eliot telling us that April is the cruellest month in its contrasts of life and death, its mixing of memory and desire, but feel no palpitation if the historian tells us that the battle of Tours in A.D. 732 ensured a Christian rather than Mohammedan West?

On the other hand, it may be that this luxury of ignoring the matrix of change is running out. Whitehead noted that hitherto great changes were cumulative over many generations, but in the twentieth century they were beginning to come within a single lifetime. Our generation, Margaret Mead has pointed out in her *Culture and Commitment* (1970), is the first to have a generation gap in time, a gap comparable to the culture gap between an immigrant group and its first native born generation in the new land. The strength of her educational ideal—to breed a generation that can bear to be free and make its own decisions about what its life will be like—comes from the fact that it is unavoidable when the rate of change passes beyond a critical point.

If ordinary experience is at last catching up with change and development because the latter are now permeating daily experience, what does this mean for the humanities in their reckoning with the Heraclitean flux?

4.   The Hold of the Past and the Hope of the Future

To include history among the humanities was a stroke of congressional genius. Too often colleges put history in the social sciences. In any case history is just taken for granted. As a discipline it has been around for a very long time; everything has a history, and if you are interested, get a historian to work at it.

If the search for a natural order has indeed abated, there is an explanatory vacuum for filling which history is an obvious candidate. Even more, as a humanistic discipline it may be called on to carry the sense of history into all of human life. I suspect that the first who would have to be convinced of this are the historians themselves. They have been too accustomed to an ancillary role, satisfied by the fact that their assistance was everywhere applicable. Perhaps a philosophical glimpse of the rise of history in the past two centuries would serve some inspirational purpose.

Consider the ahistorical scene under the reign of the Newtonian model. The tendency was to ignore developments and concentrate on universal laws; the physical world had them, the psychological world was getting them, and society would quickly catch up. But about the middle of the eighteenth century there are stirrings, even for the history of the physical world. Kant's work on the theory of the heavens (1755) launched the Kant–Laplace account of the development of the solar system and the formation of the earth. Kant was interested not only in origins, but also in the continuation of change; for example, he has a little paper in which he tried to figure out how much the earth is slowing down under the friction of the tides. Now an earth that came into existence will need a historical account of the origin of life and then of civilization. Once set on this historical track there is no going back. In this vein it seems almost a pity that Kant's tremendous vigor was diverted by the three *Critiques*! He did come back late in his life to the human side in the topic of universal history and the development of freedom and peace.

Hegel's contribution to the sense of history is analytically very rich, and this despite attempts to see him as obscurantist. He adds several explicit features: the search for unity in the life and culture of a people at any historical cross–section (this, already found in Vico earlier, was to beget the idea of cultural patterns in later social science inquiry); the search for *stages* of development in a historical process; the formulation of the historical inquiry in terms of a *world–picture*; and the delineation of a pattern and its elements in each society in terms of what the developing world-pattern requires. All this was then, and is perhaps even now, seen as philosophy of history. But it is much more: it is a set of guides for the sense of history in the description of what is going on.

Darwin's theory of evolution has, of course, been recognized as vital to the growth of a historical sense at least for over the longer time–span, and its impact has reverberated in all fields of thought. In our own day, genetics and the study of mutations produced by radiation (and those engineered in genetic transplant) bring it into the present moment, not merely the long–range future. Hegel might have thought it the cunning of history to have the study of the causes of cancer tied to that of genetic change, as if the gods were using our immediate concern with health to give us an immediate consciousness of long–range unfolding. In the late nineteenth and twentieth centuries the growing consciousness of change and development moved beyond that of the species and into the sense of the individual; this is usually remarked upon in tracing the intellectual antecedents of Freudian psychoanalysis. The minutest scrutiny of the individual's early history (as reflected in his consciousness) became a significant factor in understanding the psyche, in striking contrast to earlier disinterest. Similarly, there is the growth of interest in biography, which presents in its most focused context all the problems of the theory of history.

I do not underestimate the tremendous strength of the antihistorical establishment in the humanities. Its slogans are familiar enough. It brands any interest in the historical context of ideas as a genetic fallacy when one should be busy analyzing the ideas themselves. In literary criticism or in biography it accuses the historically minded of substituting the life for the works. It is ready to tolerate historical study as a side interest so long as it does not pretend to affect the *meaning* of the work; history must limit itself to interesting stories of externals.

We cannot here engage in a battle that is being waged along the whole front of our intellectual life today. Let me simply take an illustration to suggest what I mean by the way in which history affects meaning, whatever be the theory of meaning—and I take the illustration far away from the front of the interpretation of literature and art. In *Sex and Temperament in Three Primitive Societies* (1935), Margaret Mead describes how the Tchambouli males primp and decorate themselves and takes it as evidence of the capacity of males to have the standardized female roles of other societies. I have somewhere seen a critical comment to the effect that decorating had been part of the ritual in preparing for war, but the colonial power had abolished the war, so the preparation went on without the performance! I am not concerned here with the correctness of the criticism, but with the illustration of what plunging an item into its historical context can do for its meaning, how it gives us an altered sense of what is actually going on in the men who are decorating themselves. It is the altered sense of the present that is at stake in historical interpretation, not merely past accumulation or causal suggestion.

Suppose the humanities today were seriously to devote their energies to working out the implications of the shift from essence to history in the various fields of human endeavor. What reorientations in work and attitude would be involved?

Arno Mayer's "The Lower Middle Class as Historical Problem" is an excellent example of the historical sense at work in a present problem. He uses history at full strength and with full complexity, tracing the step–by–step development of the form he is studying: the rise of a first lower middle class, then of a second kind in an altered economic context; the different composition over time; the type of consciousness that accompanied each change; the uses made of this class in different theories; the role played by this class in the onset of war; its central alliances and probable future. (This brief summary scarcely outlines the richness of the paper.) In short, Mayer is not simply using historical data for general social or cultural conclusions; he is attempting to clarify historical process, including of course any general lessons. In this mode, history as humanistic discipline can help the cultivation of the historical sense, giving us the ideational equipment for studying the movement of peoples and the movement of ourselves. (Would a small shopkeeper who read Mayer's paper actually see *himself* as trying to roll back the wheels of history, and pause in his action?) For example, if we pay attention only to the spread of the behavioral phenomena, we are reduced to studying the voting behavior of different groups in different districts, and at best the surface changes. If we approach the subject with the depth of a historical sense, we are directed to the relation of class and subclass aims, behavior, and consciousness. Understanding of action becomes clearer, and predictability acquires a deeper base.

It is not surprising that contemporary thinking about the future finds itself almost immediately involved with methodological questions about the philosophy of history, with the feeling that how one goes about viewing the past, and the present will be vital in formulating questions about the future. A sense of history in its fuller sense begins to focus attention on human beings in the whole developmental process, to see the emergence of specific human problems under specific historical conditions, and to view actions and policies as experiments in the achievement of aims and the solution of problems. This is a fairly new way of looking at man in history. Matured in the historical–

dialectical outlook, it shares the activism which the pragmatic philosophers—particularly James and Dewey—brought to the understanding of human action. It fits precisely the relation of history and policy, as distinguished from simply history and prediction or history as fact and value as ideal norm.

> Louis Henkin's paper, "Privacy and Autonomy under the Constitution," suggests what could happen if a historical sense were given full scope in the theory of law.[2] Henkin distinguishes the concept of private rights from the specific right of privacy. He traces the birth of this right in judicial decision, its ambiguities, the diversity of things swept into the same basket, the finer shades expressed or overlooked. But instead of seeing it as a challenge to the historical sense, he sees the outcome as rather a logical mess. Suppose instead he had traced it as a juristic experiment: how this new concept might help solve in a systematic way problems in our society of electronic eavesdropping, control over one's own body in sex and marriage, safeguarding the individual against intrusive pressures of commercialism, and so on. Could it do things that older concepts of liberty and trespass were failing to accomplish? On such a view, the Supreme Court's action on abortion would be a bold experiment, comparable to its decision on integration in education. The concept of contract once had a similar origin in unifying a variety of legal ideas and institutional procedures, apt for the growth of commerce. Is the concept of privacy likewise on the historic rise, apt for new men and women in a new world? Whatever the correct answer, such a way of asking the question would be quite different. And it would express the changed intellectual attitude in the conjunction of a humanistic history and a humanistic pragmatic epistemology.

Such a shift in orientation does not predetermine the kind of activism that need ensue. There are intervening premises about what is possible, what men need and what they are like, which would have to enter into the demonstration or conjecture, as well as premises about the degree of conscious intervention that is desirable. Activism at its minimum is an interest in the possibilities of control even where modes of actual control may not be available. An activist reads the course of events as if it were an experiment from which he could learn for future planning. Yet strikingly different attitudes are found. On the one hand, for example, there is the outlook of social engineering with its mechanisms set to go and its projects planned to the last detail. On the other, there is the fear of power and manipulation and a faith that people can be trusted to devise and improvise, as in the anarchist reliance on mutual aid and cooperation. At the present time these are broad humanistic attitudes that are far apart—neither has decisively established itself. We work with something in between, or oscillate. Meanwhile, the clarification of both attitudes to people and the desirable patterns of human interrelations constitutes one of the great issues on which the humanities can make their contribution.

5. Symbols, Interpretation and Reality

The history of the social sciences is replete with attempts to deny the continuity of man with the rest of nature. After speculative philosophical arguments based on freedom of the will were thrust aside, the battle shifted within the sciences themselves, taking methodological forms. First a line was drawn between physical–nature science and social science. Then it retreated to a contrast of all science and history. Then, particularly as the social sciences for a while turned rigidly behaviorist, the whole realm of subjectivity was coopted in the fray. Appeals to empathetic understanding as against objective description, to phenomenological method as against causal analysis, are familiar enough, as are the arguments to show that a more liberal version of science than the behaviorist can accommodate the analysis of experience from the agent's point of view. These phenomena in the history of method represent, of course, extreme swings and slow returns. Think how hard E.C. Tolman had to work to reintroduce a respectable notion of purpose in dealing with animals. But the resistance is understandable when we recall the long history of loose teleological explanation in biology.

The most recent attempts to deny the continuity of man with the rest of nature would have the humanities take over a large share of the field, in the name of symbolism and interpretation. They are no longer the old attempts to appeal to *Verstehen* as a distinctive human mode of awareness, though they may still invoke it or draw on its capital.

Perhaps a glance at the problem in anthropology, which has been one of the central battlefields, is helpful. In the older days, when Tylor's all–encompassing definition of culture prevailed, culture consisted of all the habits acquired by man as a member of society. But gradually all sorts of different formulations arose, in both anthropology and sociology. R. M. MacIver's distinction between *civilization* and *culture* put into the former all cumulative techniques, social as well as physical, and left the symbolic for culture. This had, built into the concepts, the contrast of the external and the internal, as well as that of means and ends, natural causation and spiritual value—all pairs correlated. MacIver, in thinking of culture as values, even went on later to think of its symbols as myths. Talcott Parsons distinguished *culture* as symbols, *social structure* as institutions functionally viewed, and *psychology* as impact on individual development. Meanwhile, Ruth Benedict and Margaret Mead continued the integrated and comprehensive descriptive concept of culture which concentrated on the totality of a people's ways, with pattern the discoverable unity. Their interest in personality psychology and education tied in with questions of how cultural pattern became embedded in individuals and later with problems of cultural change. The integrated character of their anthropological method is seen in Benedict's view, as against sharp academic boundaries, that sociology is simply the anthropology of more complex cultures.

When Kroeber and Kluckhohn came to review the concept of culture in their *Culture, A Critical Review of Concepts and Definitions* (1952), they found it too multiple to do more than list and describe. They did not probe far into underlying theoretical presuppositions about inner and outer, or about values as ends and means, and how the picture of culture varied correspondingly.

The situation was even more complicated by the rise of phenomenology in the psychological and social sciences. A bold counterattack against the neglect of direct experience and meaning in behavioristic science, it made good its claim that one should look at the field of awareness and describe it fully and analytically without interrupting with physical conditions and psychological reactions. This is the operative meaning of the famous Husserlian *epochē*, the bracketing of the natural world. But after elaborating some useful techniques and scoring many a useful hit, phenomenology fell into the temptation to become a school. It stalled on removing the brackets and seeking phenomenological–physical and phenomenological–psychological relations, and it turned every question, particularly about humans, into a phenomenological question.

We cannot go further here into the controversies of schools. I am merely suggesting that when a social scientist attempts to isolate the cultural side of anthropology and set it along the structural–functional, not just as a rough division of labor but as a separate field with its own method—contrasting the interpretation of symbols for the one with the scientific for the other (as Clifford Geertz does in his *Interpretation of Cultures* [1973], developing a semiotic theory of culture)—he is taking on the whole burden of a tangled century's conflicts on method. And when in the humanities one talks generally of symbols and their interpretation as a distinctive humanistic task, one assumes also this dubious inheritance. For the crux of the matter is how symbols themselves are to be dealt with in interpretation, and this simply reopens the old issues. Can symbols really be explored as self-enclosed, ending in a self-sufficient state of conscious feeling and awareness, capturing an inner essence removed from the outer natural or social domain? Or does the very exploration of a symbolic web rest on all sorts of presuppositions about the context of its employment? These, if spelled out, would subvert the distinction between inner and outer, and underscore the integrated character of knowledge; and this would open the door to the cooperation rather than the partition of methods.

Man is born and bred in symbols. But language is a system of symbols, and religion is a system of symbols, and science is a system of symbols. A semiotic discipline has great importance, but it cannot be captured for any one distinctive method. To ask how differently nouns and prepositions function in language, or the cross and the flag in religion and nationalism, or different scientific concepts in different sciences, and to make transdiscipline comparisons is as fascinating as it is important. But can it bear the weight of a diremption between scientific objectivity and humanistic subjectivity?

There is considerable proclivity to this subjectivism in literary approaches. For example, in "On Privacy and Community," Emile Capouya looks at the right of privacy not in terms of judicial decision but with a sensitive appreciation of what goes on in the human being whose privacy is being violated. Offenses of searches and seizures are "insults to the soul." Privacy itself is regarded as "communion with our fellow beings when we are not physically in their presence." In a similar vein, Benjamin DeMott in his "Equality and Fraternity" asserts that a fabric of feeling is basic to institutions and ideas. Indeed, he goes so far as to say that equality and justice bemuse us because they are concerned with arrangements whereas fraternity and charity involve subjectivity. Since any system rests really on a grain of feeling, he argues that equality properly is an attitude of feeling—that of respect—or else nothing.

To locate the reality in this fashion in inner consciousness as against social arrangements is strongly reminiscent of the way in which Clement of Alexandria reinterpreted Jesus' call on the rich man to give up his worldly goods if he would be saved. Says Clement: it does not mean actually to give up the wealth, but only the spiritual attachment to wealth. That will suffice for salvation.

The alternative view for the analysis of symbols—as talking of the same world as science does but in a different way—can be illustrated from George Santayana's naturalistic treatment of the relation of myth, science, and religion, in his *Life of Reason* (1905). Myth is a kind of poetry. When it intervenes in human affairs to order life, it is religion; when it supervenes on human life, giving expression to our fantasy, it is poetry. When it is stripped to its fighting weight and valued only for what it points to, it is science. To think of Apollo driving his chariot daily through the sky is a myth, an ingredient of poetry. To pray to the sun at stated intervals in organizing our life is religion. To see the sun as rising and moving through the sky is common or everyday belief, still holding a residue of metaphor. To plot the curve of the relative positions of sun and earth is science. Again, to describe heaven and hell is not a celestial geographic science but a myth symbolizing the moral truth that present action has fundamental importance and should be viewed under the guise of eternity.

In many respects Roderick Nash's paper on environmental ethics can be seen as a glorious symbolic myth in Santayana's sense. It condemns the ethical cut-offs which limit membership in the moral community to humans and projects our kinship with all of being—including land, air, water, rocks. Its map of the rise through time from environment to life to mankind and on finally to family and self (narrowing at every step) and then upward in reverse on the march of ethical expansion from self all the way to environment, fits easily into an old tradition of the alienation of the individual self from the world and its long return. It is of the same order as Plotinus' story of the history of emergence from the primal One and the endeavor of the lone soul to be reunited to its source. As a myth it would not have to argue whether rocks have life or whether they can be as eloquent as babies.

The story simply tells a moral truth of our neglect of our natural environment. It projects a set of human attitudes to our cosmos and its contents. Comparative studies of such world views are by now familiar in the anthropological field.

What of the analysis of a specific symbol? Does the symbol operate to yield an affective insight, or does it break open paths that are amenable to reflection and science and policy as well as to clarified consciousness?

In his "Structures and Machines: The Two Sides of Technology," the article summarized in the first section of his essay on "The Structuring of Cities," David Billington offers us a symbolic contrast for understanding technology: the dyke and the "fast-moving, smoke–belching, harshly shrieking" locomotive machine. It is a striking comparison and Billington spells it out as signifying two aspects of technology: the static permanent structure and the dynamic machine. This becomes for him the basic dichotomy of the engineering field: he outlines different laws for each side, sharpens the contrast (static–dynamic, permanent-changing, individually produced as against mass-produced, and so on) and tries to correct the American overemphasis on the machine. By thinking of structures as works of art, he says, we could conscript in principle the humanistic tradition for awakening the appreciation of structures.

Note then what the symbolic contrast does: it reinforces an opposition of categories by the striking difference of the image. And yet, there are other ways of looking at the dichotomy of structure and machine. Why should not a structure be seen as a machine doing slower or steadier jobs? (The dyke is holding back the constantly beating waves.) Mario Salvadori, in his "Response to Billington," is even ready to use a machine cooling system to maintain the proper temperature of the structural components, a crossing of categories which would horrify a strict structural engineer! Perhaps the differences are not categorical, but only matters of degree of motion or stability. It is clear that the insistence on the separate categories rests in part on different practical principles in construction. But other common features could equally be selected; pragmatically different features are selected in the light of different purposes. Further, Salvadori sees all engineering as essentially defying nature, while others may see it as artistically using nature. One might even suggest that we should work toward the older tradition that did not distinguish art from technology.

The lesson of this inquiry is that the symbol selects features of the existential context and accentuates them. It elaborates them and gives them an identity. A network of similarities and metaphorical transfers carries a set of implicit inferences steeped in feeling. But the content is in effect an hypothesis about the way of analyzing, categorizing, determining relevance, and assigning values for the material under scrutiny. The symbol is poised to move in many directions. It opens, it does not close, inquiry. And interpreting a symbol consists in following some of the many lines laid open.

Perhaps the most direct theoretical confrontation about the character of consciousness is found in the papers of Bozeman and Mayer, in dealing with war. Bozeman thinks consciousness gives the reality in itself so that to have people's thoughts about war gives the realities that perpetuate the phenomenon of war. Mayer, however, sees consciousness as a phenomenal surface to be explained. It is not without effect, but it reflects more basic processes in the real world of which it is only a part. His study of the ideas and values of the lower middle class and of the conditions under which their rigidity swings the balance of forces toward war (referred to above) illustrates both the effects of consciousness and its relation to fundamental processes.

Symbols move humans deeply and set much going. But unless we are ready to dissolve all reality into acts of consciousness, it is better to recall the age–old distinction between the dreams that divide men and the waking life that bring them into a common life. We are today in a period of awakening in which we realize how far we have been locked in one–sided perspectives. A humanistic sense of the plurality of outlooks and the multiplicity of perspectives can help prepare us for constructing a common reality.

6.   The Study of Values

Value has a wide reach and voracious appetite. It is used on both descriptive and normative levels as well as in explanatory contexts. It has served many functions in theoretical controversy and found its way into humanities and social science alike. It is grammatically dexterous: a verb in one context; it is a noun in another; as a noun it may indicate a process of evaluation (just as *price* sums up a market relation) or sink back into substantival inertia, almost as if one were to say: "These are my jewels, those are my values." So versatile a conceptual fellow runs close second to *being* or *is* in ambiguity, systematic or otherwise. My impression is that historically, it was a favorite in Germany and Scotland and America but long ostracized in England, where a fine sense of linguistic differentiation wanted every fine shade to be expressed by different terms in different contexts.

In ethics, *value* may denote a person's likings and dislikings, his criteria for evaluating these (what is good and worthwhile), an objective property of events, a person's obligations (what he ought to do), and his generalized standards (ideals and norms). In aesthetics it bundles beauty with all the other aesthetic attitudes or qualities or sentiments (quite literally spanning the sublime to the ridiculous). Religious values may cover both attitudes to the divine (such as awe or love) and virtues (charity, forgiveness). In economics where it early made its home, it first covered use–value and exchange–value, and then became almost synonymous with the latter. In sociology and psychology it fluctuated between a descriptive notion of a person's interests and preferences and a normative notion of his grounds or criteria in judging these. (Whichever way it went, the term *norm* took up the other way.) More recently, in social science, my impression is that the critical component in the use of the term has been winning over the preferential component. In metaphysical conflicts, the notion of value on the one hand became the standard–bearer for what distinguished spirit from nature (all consciousness is selective–valuational); on the other hand, it became the common feature of all life (animals as well as humans) out of which by differentiation and functional specialization the higher values could be seen to develop. It thus served both antinaturalistic purposes in some and naturalistic purposes in others.

For a long time values belonged to the humanities and philosophy, not to the sciences. Science avoided value judgments. The psychological and social sciences studied human behavior, not human values which were taken to be inner and subjective. But by the midtwentieth century it became clear that man's selective–valuational behavior was a fertile field for scientific study. One of the most fascinating large-scale efforts in this direction was shepherded by Clyde Kluckhohn at Harvard, whose special genius it was to remain humanistic when he was being scientific and not to lose his scientific bent when he was being a humanist. The Harvard Values Studies concerned five cultures in the Southwest of the United States (Navaho, Zuni, Spanish-American, Texan–American, Mormon) and engaged in comparative exploration of values in different areas of life. For example, they included analysis of value themes and value trends in religion, law, attitudes to property and acquisition, music, family, readjustment of veterans to native life, self–orientations, physiological reactions, and of general value–orientations to nature, time, and fellow–men. Similar studies were meanwhile going on under Robert Redfield and Milton Singer at Chicago, into the comparative values of large cultural traditions (Chinese, Indian, Mohammedan, et cetera), while at the University of Pennsylvania Irving Hallowell investigated more particularly self-orientations in the building up of a viable personality in different cultures. All these studies were at the frontier of what had been a dispersed approach to values from many different perspectives—for example, historical studies of changing social ethics in R. H. Tawney and Max Weber on the rise of the Protestant ethic. What the large-scale social science plunge into the field accomplished was to focus the need for comprehensive value study by all available methods and to stimulate greater systematization.

It is perhaps against this systematic treatment that considerable sentiment in the humanities is gathered. Values are regarded as inner, individual, personal. They are the core of subjective reality, what a man stands for, lives by, and dies for. That such a perspective of the individual's phenomenological exploration (though only one of different possible patterns) need not be in conflict with social roots, historical development and social role, is one of the first lessons of wide value study. The comparative projects had no methodological bias. They sought light in every way possible. Observational reports were only one path, linguistic analyses and symbolic analyses were welcomed, experiential reports (for example, in comparative Rorschach studies) were included as a matter of course, aesthetic reactions had their place. It is surprising how dogmas of method tend to evaporate when there is a generous yield of results by all, which turn out to fit well together.

To illustrate the breadth of approach needed in dealing with important cultural values, let us consider *equality*, which was the subject of several of our papers.

The papers by Robert Nisbet, Herbert Gans, Benjamin DeMott, and William Vickrey deal specifically with the costs and humanistic impact of the ideals of equality and justice. (The way DeMott pits an inner attitude of respect against outer institutional arrangements for equality has been touched above.) In "Justice, Equality, and the Economic System," Vickrey seriously canvasses the economic techniques for reducing inequality and finds that some are available and ingenuity would provide others which could be used without seriously impairing economic processes and initiative as they operate in our system. He does not consider basic revisions in the system itself if it fails to yield a greater equality. He finds the ideal of justice fairly useless and likely to lead to perverse results; but this came after examining Rawls's theory, and Vickrey's turning to utilitarianism may be construed as a demand for a utilitarian theory of justice instead. An interesting critique of the concept of justice is his remark that since it is so often defined in terms of existent expectations, it tends to be an essentially conservative concept.

The full–blast attack on contemporary concepts of equality comes from Nisbet in his "Costs of Equality." Here he attacks the New Equalitarians as wanting *equality of results* and therefore revolutionary redistribution of income, property, power, status. He is particularly vehement against Rawls, whom he interprets as demanding equality of results, apparently because Rawls assumes differences have to be justified, and that justification has to show how the lot of the most disadvantaged would be improved. Nisbet canvasses especially the cultural costs of the demand for equality in terms of the untrammeled opening for envy, the attacks on status and prestige, the weakening of the family, and so on. (DeMott, in one of his well–turned phrases, also says that refusal of deference diminishes respect for respect.) Surprisingly, while Nisbet's argument would seem to lead to a defense of meritocracy, he does not approve of the attack on inequality in the name of moral worth or merit, but follows Hayek in allowing reward to go to those who succeed simply as such.

Herbert Gans, branded by Nisbet as one of the New Equalitarian triumvirate, responds to Nisbet's paper in his "Costs of Inequality." He contends that to want greater equality is not to insist on complete equality of results; that the costs of such reform are less than Nisbet envisages; that inequality is breaking up families and greater equality would mean greater familial stability; that Nisbet's account of the costs of equality fails to include the gains; that the costs of continued inequality are vastly greater. He tends to ascribe the differences between his position and Nisbet's to a disagreement on means rather than a broad philosophical conflict.

Actually, what we are now witnessing is a broader and more revolutionary moral movement than this interchange suggests. Conceptions of the good life are being questioned for their overemphasis on competitive success and conceptions of justice for their overemphasis on meritocracy. The historical development—liberty, then political equality, then demands first for a career open to talent and after that for social equality in the removal of discriminations, then demands for wider positive means (such as education and higher education) to open doors of greater opportunity—would if extrapolated yield a complete meritocracy. But this is precisely what is being questioned, not in the sense of rolling back the whole development, but in a new ethical insight of the worth of persons. No doubt its basis includes the fact that the means of production no longer require the exploitation of a part of the population, and the fact that the spread of some competences under universal education and the automation of industry remove large areas from the need for unusual skills. But the impact is primarily ethical—the sense of a new community of people with an all-human morality and a concept of individuality that stresses the diversity of capacities of living beings rather than selecting a few for elitist grandeur. We cannot here enter into the exploration of these new moral trends—this is one of the areas in which the humanities could be most fruitful—but nothing is to be gained by assimilating them to the nineteenth-century battles between liberty and equality or relying on the clichés of the older mistrust of the masses.

> In addition, arguments and proposals, even well–intentioned, will miss the point if they assume as presuppositions the very premises that are being challenged. For example, in "Some Questions in General Education Today," Steven Marcus takes for granted that competitive excellence is a basic aim. Similarly, in her "Some Inconsistent Educational Aims," Onora O'Neill seems to take education to aim in part at a success requiring preeminence rather than excellence. It is no longer possible to argue from such premises as unchallengeable features of contemporary life.

What is more significant is that contemporary antiequalitarian arguments continue to be formulated in terms of the individualist tradition. But the new equalitarianism is not bound to such formulations nor even to the individualist character of the utilitarian concept of the greatest happiness. It does not have to reckon and sum individual benefits or even think in Rawlsian contractual terms. It can formulate directly common goals of a quality of life for the community. In such an approach the dichotomy between public and private itself requires reassessment. Such a vast reformulation cannot be reached by looking into inner feeling alone, for this consciousness is likely to reflect the developed individualist tradition. It has to be grasped by a full sociohistorical study of the development of ideals and conditions.

7.   Mine and Thine, or I and Thou?

If a society does not always get the categories it deserves, it at least gets the ones it cultivates. Our social tradition has worked hard for the last few centuries to reach the point where the only alternatives to stand out are private or public, self or society, me or the rest. This is, of course, the familiar intensified voluntaristic individualism that permeates our economics, our political theory, our ethics. Instead of norms of an economy that will support the good life of a community, we reckon how individual interests may be maximized without affecting entrenched holdings. Instead of systems of organization based on the common participation of a free people, we have the polarization of autonomous individual and threatening state. Instead of the virtues of a common good life, we have virtue bisected into self–regarding and other–regarding, and so the task of ethics becomes one of balancing egoism and altruism.

All of this is usually attributed by the economic historians to the type of economy developed by the bourgeoisie in the rise of commerce and industry out of feudalism, on an individualist pattern. It is attributed by sociological historians to the breakdown of intermediate groupings between the state and the individual as well as to the specific phenomena of urbanization. It is attributed by metaphysicians to the exaggeration of extreme aspects: Bradley thunders against the vicious abstraction of the pure individual and the pure social, and looks to status and its duties (now respectably scientific as role theory) for an expression of the operative totality; Maritain finds both individual and state to be heresies, yielding voluntaristic pursuit of the material on the one side and totalitarian Rousseauesque common wills on the other, and he calls for recognition of the person as a God–oriented being. It is attributed by Marxists to the dominant bourgeoisie who needed individualism to break through the older restrictive economic and social patterns, and who perpetuate it as an ideology to ensure their own exploitation.

I have no doubt that most of these accounts are more or less correct, and I will not pursue here how the variety of conceptualization can be integrated with the variety of social processes. Certainly the family of dichotomies that goes under the contrast between individual and social or private and public has not always been with us. In Aristotle's ethics the private means simply the share in the good life, the fitting roles and tasks that the individual should have in virtue of what he is like and able to do. When Aristotle discusses whether a man should love himself, his answer is that it depends on what he is like: a good man has something worth loving, a bad man has not. Nietzsche, who had a keen sense of the ethical character of intellectual categories and their historical careers, records the remarkable success story of self-interest: it starts as an outcast from morality (selfishness, self-aggrandisement), becomes a respectable member—in fact, a good half—of the team of self–regarding and other-regarding virtues, and ends up as dominant in ethical theory on the Benthamite summit. Bentham's utilitarianism, in fact, shows us the full face of our problem. It is not even a question of private or public since the idea of community is a fiction; there are only individuals, only a reckoning of the sums of individual interests. The social ideal is the greatest happiness of the greatest number, not the structure of a common good life. Perhaps this is why we still find political philosophers, even of opposite persuasions, when faced with "liberty, equality, fraternity" gladly elaborating upon liberty, quarrelling about equality, but very suspicious of fraternity, as if it smacked of totalitarianism. . . .

The fact is that the real content of private vs. public has not been individual vs. group, but me vs. the rest. Only a specialist in the humanities—particularly in mythology—could do justice to the history of attempted reconciliations of mine and thine. There are unseen providential hands working to adjust the actions of individuals so that self–interest pursued reasonably will yield general welfare and conversely to guarantee that pursuing the general welfare is a good investment with high dividends; or again, there is Spencer's optimistic notion that evolution will take care of the integration of egoism and altruism. There are also, of course, realistic attempts to analyze how interests affecting us all generate self-conscious and organized publics—for example, Dewey's *The Public and Its Problems* (1927).

The basic issue of private and public takes two forms. One is the concept of individual rights *vis–à–vis* the public good. The second is a system of private individual property as against collective or social property.

> Charles Frankel penetrates to the heart of the first. In his "Private Rights and the Public Good," Frankel notes our common belief that there are some rights which no government ought to infringe short of an emergency and some not even then. Then he distinguishes the line between public and private from that between what affects others and what affects oneself alone, and recognizes it as a construction. But a construction must be governed by ends, and so we are not surprised that after listing a set of values underlying a system of private rights he decides that these values in the system themselves "define some considerable portion of the public good as it should be understood in a liberal society." Hence the weighing is not of private against public, but "of different social values against one another and their constant readjustment"—in the light of a complex ideal of civilized life.

> Hannah Arendt's "Response to Charles Frankel" similarly breaks through the limited dichotomy of private and public, but in a different way: she sees many of our rights as themselves public not private because, like service on a jury or peaceful assembly, their object is a common one. Arendt relentlessly categorizes in terms of the content, not the legal form or the subject whose right it is. Thus when she pits private against public it is quite literally in the sense of privacy or being left alone in an activity; and she rejects talk of reconciling individual interests and the common good because of the "urgency of individual interests." Actually, her reconciliation would lie in the same individual sharing in the common as well as having the private—being a citizen in the ancient sense as well as urgently individual.

> Both Frankel and Arendt are thus dissatisfied with the intense individualism in which our tradition has culminated. Through one or another different construction they would turn back toward a public good.

The importance of such constructional tasks and the practical impact of our categorial selection is seen in every debate on public policy. Even in the papers on equality, there is the tendency to think of everybody having as much as anybody else rather than in terms of a common life with full participation.

An exception to this narrowed vista is Paul Freund's essay, "Equality, Race, and Preferential Treatment," wherein he calls for the preferential consideration of blacks. He bases his argument firmly on the need for the whole community to bring into participation a minority that was so excluded as to have no stake in the common life, its processes, and its benefits. It contrasts strongly with the interpretation of compensatory justice that Herbert Deane criticizes in his "Justice— Compensatory and Distributive," for that interpretation limits its focus to the conflict of individual claims. Deane's analysis is particularly interesting in two philosophical respects. One is the recognition of the importance of the rubric selected; for example, he wants no–fault insurance also removed from the category of compensatory justice and treated under some different rubric. The other is the clear pragmatic appeal in the selection of categories to those that will help solve the problems at issue rather than engender greater dissent and conflict.

Once a system of private rights (or for that matter a system of public goods) is viewed as a conceptual instrument, an overall conception of a good life is implicit—or the quality of life in a community, or some other higher order, ends in terms of which a choice is made about which conceptual instrument to use. Thus the United Nations went in for lists of human rights, not a utilitarianism of global welfare. Traditionally, the United States has operated chiefly with individual rights, supplemented by general welfare. Philosophers will recognize this as the perennial conflict of the right and the good, or duty and interest, or justice and welfare. But if the solutions I find in the several papers noted point a fruitful direction, we would do better to invoke a political model for analyzing the relation of private rights and public goods. There is a *separation of powers* in the realm of ideas too, analogous to that in our government, and with all the jockeying and contextual emphases that we find in political life. Thus there will be times when reckoning should be cast in terms of welfare, times when in terms of individual rights, but when to do which is a judgment of how best to further the idea of a kind of human life. It is precisely the working out of such an ideal, in close relation to what is going on in the world, that the humanities are asked to contribute.

If we turn back to that world, we find that the type of individualism dealt with above is cracking, not only from the pressure of large–scale organization, but from the growth of communal forms and intermediate groupings. Demands are increasingly being made in the name of groups—unions, blacks, ethnic groups, consumers, not to speak of experimental communes—so that confrontations with economic or governmental power are not just those of the private against the public. It is surprising that political and legal science has done so little with group rights in a rights–culture, when even Richard Price and Tom Paine could speak of the rights of a people to cashier its government, which is obviously not an individual right. In any case, we are obviously in the midst of a social revolution, guided by the movement to community of effort, if not yet focused on community of end. This is one front on the moral revolution I referred to in the last section.

> In Rosemary Park's "The Disestablished Humanities" and Robert Hanning's response, "A View from the Ivory Tower," there is an exchange on whether our cultural institutions beyond the academy can help give us a sense of community which was symbolized by the Parthenon in ancient Athens. Park suggests perhaps, Hanning says no since there is no sense of civic piety involved. Perhaps the secular moral equivalent of the sacred today would be the kind of self in which the communal is integrated within the self rather than confronting it from without—a view of the religious that John Dewey advocated in his *A Common Faith* (1934). Its achievement not only presupposes different social institutions but would be seriously complicated in our time since the City has long given way to the Nation and anticipatory strands of the global community are making inroads on the Nation.

Space and time do not permit me to enter here into the second major problem of private vs. public—the present status of private property. In the not-so-old days, it was discussed in terms of individualist free enterprise vs. socialism. But the plurality of types of economic–political organization now defy these broad categories, though there are no doubt different forms of private and collective control of production and distribution for mankind to choose among. The underlying reality is that property has changed its forms rapidly in the twentieth century due to the rise of corporations and now multinational corporations and the recent rise of quasi property rights through social institutions of redistribution. Hence most of the arguments about the absolute rights of private property are meaningless today (though those concerning near–absolute power are not), and even social defenses of private property are reduced, as in effect Nisbet's attack on equalitarianism was, to threatening us with dire consequences to family and culture if we curb free enterprise. Obviously the study of the rationale of private property today requires the joint effort of three intellectual groups: first, anthropologists and economists to see what is really going on in global society as a whole; humanists to penetrate the folklore and to articulate human aspirations for a good life; and philosophers to devise new constructs for reformulating the issues realistically.

A brief word on I and Thou. This contrast to mine and thine comes (obviously) from Martin Buber's effort to focus on interpersonal relations as a distinct category. Intrasubjective feelings and institutional structures are, in his view, distracting escapes from the authentically interpersonal. Of course his own thought involves a religious background and a quasi–anarchist small–group political philosophy. But its tremendous influence came from the presentation of an alternative to the highly individualistic and the external total structures. Like George Herbert Mead's emphasis on interpersonal relations in the growth of selfhood, it helped break the monopoly of individual and group–social on the feelings of men. It restored on the intellectual level the plurality of categories of human relations (referred to as intermediate groupings above) that had been destroyed in the growth of individualism.

Finally, it should be stated (if it is not already clear) that this brief account is not directed against the social ideal of individuality and the development of individual powers: the task is rather, as Dewey stated it, to rescue it from the older individualism.

8. How To Be Practical, though Humanistic

The humanities have gloried in the absence of practicality. Philosophy bakes no bread. But the philosopher, the poet, and the painter must still eat. And so endowment is necessary though no return other than their self–justifying work is to be expected.

On the other hand, there comes a time in the tangled affairs of men when even to ask a question is to make a significant practical contribution.

> Lionel Tiger said, at one of the conferences on education, that if good ideas may be slow to have effects, bad ideas get macro-development rapidly. Yet Bertrand Russell once argued that if stupidity has such serious effects in human life, there is no reason why intelligence cannot have equally serious effects.

Once, many years ago, I was to give a lecture in an Institute of Humanistic Studies for Executives, organized at the University of Pennsylvania for the Bell Telephone Company. I read the explanatory materials circulated by the administrators: junior executives, it was explained, have to solve problems, and this they can learn by apprenticeship on the job; but senior executives have to discover problems or think them up, and this requires a liberal education. (I do not know where the writer of this circular is now, but I hope he is employed by the National Endowment for the Humanities!)

Let me balance this with another story. Even more years ago, I attended a meeting on adult education for workers, presided over by Harry Carman, the well–known Columbia historian. After almost two hours of discussion, a union official representing one of the garment unions rose, pointed to her associate, and said solemnly, "What have we decided that will justify my having taken Mr. Shapiro out of the shop for two hours?" I must confess that since then, Mr. Shapiro's plight has been on my philosophical conscience (especially when a paper gets too long). In any case, I suspect that the truth about the practicality of the humanities lies somewhere between Ma Bell and Mr. Shapiro. But let us track it down, if possible.

Take, for example, the writing of utopias. It used to be a classic exercise in the humanities. Why has it gone out of fashion? I suppose one hypothesis would be that sensitive thinkers are pessimistic. In the time of the French Encyclopedists, there could be excitement with the view that man is a machine because it meant he could recondition himself and was not bound by original sin. But now we seem to be too disillusioned by the machine to write utopias about it. And so we have had instead our *Brave New World* and our *1984*.

Still, as James Clifford pointed out in the discussion of Elisabeth Hansot's paper, "Reflections on War, Utopias, and Temporary Systems," the eighteenth century also had its anti–utopian writings in Swift and Johnson. Hansot suggests that instead of literary utopias we have now the short–term quasi utopias of meetings, conferences, and commissions!

Perhaps there is a different explanation. Just as in science the time-span between invention and utilization has diminished remarkably, so in social affairs the movement of events overtakes too rapidly the stretch of the utopian imagination. Compare the modern organization of science with what Bacon envisaged in the *New Atlantis*. Even practical programs, such as Marx's list of next steps to be achieved (at the end of the *Communist Manifesto*), are long ago commonplaces in capitalist societies. Thus today instead of utopias we have the broad social programs of actually organizing philosophical–political movements. Why construct a utopia when one can advocate a reform or initiate a revolution? In such a perspective, utopias belong to the stage when possibilities of control have come into sight, when the will turns in a given direction, but the objective is not clarified sufficiently and the means have still to be discovered. Now what happens at an earlier stage, when there are no possibilities of control, and what will happen later, when the limits of control are still uncertain?

Viewed in the perspective of the growth of control in human life, the humanities have always had practical tasks. At the outer limit, where nothing could be done, they furnished attitudes of resignation or reconciliation or even the heroic stance, attuning emotion to face unavoidable suffering.

The ancient Stoics generalized this function as a moral philosophy—controlling our impressions of things in the interest of peace of mind, since we could not ultimately control the things themselves. Greek tragedy, in Aristotle's analysis, served the cathartic functions. The Book of Job is dealing with the extremes at the outer limits; only a modern like Archibald MacLeish could introduce the light touch (in his *J.B.*) of a momentary suspicion on God's part that maybe Job was forgiving Him!

But where control over human responses and human action is possible, even from ancient times, we see how eagerly and speedily the humanities move into the job of articulating attitudes relevant to policy.

It is not just a question of the social import of the histories and the theater—e.g., Thucydides possibly hoping to influence the Greeks by showing the corrupting character of class struggle, or Aristophanes and Euripides writing peace plays. Plato, as usual, shows it most clearly: physics is just a "likely story" and there seems little hope of controlling nature, but the *Republic* is a program for the total control of human nature. And the whole history of humanistic political theory embodies similar aspirations.

The insight conveyed in the great humanistic works, whether in myth or analysis, is the stabilization of an outlook that is always verging on action—where opportunities arise. In this sense, nothing is more practical than understanding. There is thus a continuity in the practicality of the humanities from points of minimal control to points of substantial control in human life. It is not simply a shift from inner to outer, and the development continues in the same way when science begins to bring the natural world into the scope of human powers. The myths of Daedalus in ancient times or the voyage to the moon in a Cyrano de Bergerac shift to the sketches of Leonardo and eventually to the airplane and the moon–shot; it is a progression from fantasy to hope, to aspiration, to plan, to achievement. This is not a discarding of the humanistic and its moral context: the landing on the moon had many of the aspects of theatrical spectacle and even of morality play. . . .

The practical responsibility of the humanities has always therefore been for the moral organization and the quality of human life. The dichotomy of a self–enclosed imagination responsible only to the quality of its fantasy and a self–enclosed science responsible only to its inner development has been an intellectual episode of a very short period in the Western world. No doubt its analysis reveals that it rested on its own myths of preestablished harmony or inevitable progress or the like. The contemporary quest for the policy implications of the humanities is part of the wider effort to restore the older integration of knowledge and value and practice in the new situation of the vastly extended base of possible human control.

How close a basic humanistic question can come to the actual problems of practical decision on life and death is strikingly shown in Daniel Callahan's "Biomedical Progress and the Limits of Human Health." We are used to the perennial question whether life is worth living. It surfaces in ethical inquiries about the nature of happiness and debates over pleasure and pain, in the continuous struggle between optimism and pessimism, in the Christian attitude to despair as the greatest of sins, even in psychological and psychiatric studies of suicide. Perhaps we are tempted to dismiss it as one of the questions we shall always have with us, and so relegate it to our spare time for philosophical reflection or poetic sentiment. Samuel Butler dismissed it with the quip that it was a question for an embryo, not an adult. I wonder whether he realized that so far from dismissing it he was giving it a practical platform to stand on. Callahan's account of the progress of biomedical knowledge and technique translates implicitly from whether life is worth living to what is a life worth living, and explicitly from the latter to *what is a life worth saving*. He notes the paradox that what began as an attempt to remedy limited birth defects has by its unintended consequences raised the question of evaluating the kind of life that survival makes possible, with the result that fewer defective children may now be saved than before. Interestingly too he explores the way in which an overperfectionist definition of health functions evaluatively to open up unrealistic demands in assuming a "right to health." His vigorous attack on individualism and its consequences in hindering greater equalization of health care may perhaps be seen as a demand for more organized planning, but it has to be planning closely tied to basic answers to basic value questions. In short, the problem of using technical knowledge and technical means is fast compelling humanistic answers to humanistic questions—on pain of practical blundering.

Willard Gaylin's "The Technology of Life and Death" carries similar lessons and shows even more strikingly that categories of interpretation are critical in assessing a line of policy. Recent redefinitions of "death" make it morally acceptable to pull the plug on apparatus that continues vital functions. But suppose that instead of pulling the plug we instituted a bioemporium of "neomorts" and kept it going for use in medical training, transplants, experimenting and testing, harvesting medically essential bioproducts. A cost–benefit analysis might justify our doing so. Assuming our moral revulsion to these technologically possible procedures, Gaylin asks whether we would attribute our revulsion to the residue of habit, fear, and ignorance, and thereby risk our tenuous civility and human decency and erase the distinction between man and matter. In effect, he is posing a confrontation of the humanistic and the materialistic view of man. Yet surely this confrontation with its dire moral consequences does not follow merely from the incorporation of man wholly within the system of nature. It follows rather from identifying technological advance with an exploitative social attitude in which the cost–benefit analysis has not asked such vital questions as whether the individual consents to participate in the new institution. Simply to look at what goes on in the bioemporium does not tell its own story, for each item has its precursor in acts on the moral side of the ledger. Repeated blood contributions, sacrifice of an organ for another's dire need, submitting to medical experimentation for human benefit, willing one's body for medical research—all these are moral acts beyond the call of duty and some even approximate heroism. If to participate in the emporium were an act of autonomous decision made during one's lifetime, would not the acts of the emporium become allied with heroic categories rather than callous exploitation? Given a guarantee of no feeling, they might occasion less moral revulsion than the mutilations of war, traditionally accepted as moral sacrifices on behalf of country. Gaylin's account seems to make a metaphysical confrontation inevitable, while what is really required is a refined moral analysis and a refined moral sensitivity.

If we turn now to the future, the question of the extent and limits of control itself becomes central, and the new dangers and the new crises have tended to focus inquiry on mere survival. But the perennial question has not ceased to be the quality and moral organization of the life that is possible. Let us sample the two areas in which these essays face directly problems of policy for the future as enlightened by the humanities. One is education, where the practicality seems to lie in the strangely limited question of the fate of the humanities themselves. The other is technology and the attitudes it involves toward the prospects of mankind in the present world.

On the face of it, the central problems of education appear to be how to achieve established humanistic aims in an altered social and material milieu. But such a formulation is likely to ignore the real issues about aims that are in debate in the contemporary world. For this reason, inquiry has always to be critically focused on possible presuppositions in an analysis.

> For example, at one of the conferences John Silber, arguing against the slackening of standards, said that music schools are not troubled by the egalitarian thrust since one either plays the violin or one does not. But behind this apparent certitude lies the assumption that the present *function* of the music school is not to be questioned. For example, depending on the context, one might raise the question whether there ought not to be music schools where anyone could acquire some appreciation of the practice of music to the extent of his abilities; they would not thus be training places for only the highest performing excellence. Some colleges have the requirement of some practice in an art in connection with their required art course. It will be recalled that Aristotle in the *Politics* asks how much musical performance is required in education and answers it should be enough to give one a critical appreciation of performance. Contemporary aestheticians have often stressed the point that our appreciation tends to be that of the consumer reacting to surface features, rather than of one who understands the problems of creating and reacts to the total character of the art work. All these aspects of the problem can be made clear by a humanistic view of the issues. Of course there are questions of cost and type of institution for such purposes; but it is not unreasonable to hope that a community which builds resources for general gymnastic and athletic training might do so for general musical and cultural development.

Since the humanities have their primary home in the university, any consideration of their place becomes tied into the controversies over what the university is up to and where it should go in the contemporary world. Several different aspects have to be disentangled; for there are external pressures on the universities and there are sharp cultural and social changes, as well as internal conflicts about educational aims.

> George Pierson's "The University and American Society" pinpoints the outside pressures by analyzing the different historical strata of American society whose demands at different times shaped the university. Since his ideal is the liberal and independent university (primarily sheltering teachers and scholars) with a humanistic emphasis, his standpoint is that of the humanities defining the university of their vision and seeking to control the flux of pressures sufficiently to maintain the desirable independence, for example by multiplying and diversifying sources of support. His confidence is breathtaking. It is almost as if he were saying that we humanists know what we want, let us work for it and maintain our ideal, let those who press for other aims and momentary relevance build their own institutions for these purposes, but the academy is ours.

> Wm. Theodore de Bary, responding in "The University, Society, and the Critical Temper," does not believe we can "make a virtue of irrelevance." His eye is on the actual problems with students and the social milieu that actual universities are

having: "There is a very close relationship between our learning or knowing function and what people around us are doing. We can ignore the implications of this, at our own peril." Looking at the American university in relation to its middle–class origins and seeing its unique character on a worldwide scene, he wonders whether the essential critical attitude directed to accepted institutions and values can avoid self–destruction for the universities without a deeper humanism.

Steven Marcus, in "Some Questions in General Education Today," studies with historical sensitivity both the inner conflict of science and the humanities and the relation of the humanities to middle–class culture. Tracing the interchange between T. H. Huxley and Matthew Arnold and the modern variants on Arnold's view of liberal education as the cultivation of the self, he concludes that "with the newly emerging context of the university as part of the system of production, the role of liberal or humanistic education becomes increasingly problematic." And the decline of liberal arts is entwined with the decomposition of bourgeois culture. In his concluding practical proposals Marcus analyzes the historical role of the high schools and suggests the university should consciously undertake reparative functions. He proposes several types of basic humanistic courses.

The net effect of such consideration is more a challenge than an unavoidable conclusion. There remains even at worst the possibility that a humanistic culture could attempt to humanize the professions and vocations. As suggested at the outset, a humanistic science would see itself as a great expression of the human imagination in a context of basic human purposes. And even very practical vocations could be carried on with an eye on fundamental values, as is seen in the current ferment in such fields as medicine, nursing, social work. The humanities hold back from facing the challenge, in part because they understand that it is the whole character of our society and culture that is involved, and this makes the task too gigantic for them alone.

This seems to me to be the source of the underlying sadness in Marcus' view. It also gives us a different way of looking at Onora O'Neill's keen analysis, in "Some Inconsistent Educational Aims," of the incompatibility of happiness and success as educational objectives. Happiness, she points out, involves fullfilling a reasonable proportion of a person's desires while success involves not merely excellence in the chosen pursuit but preeminence or outdoing others. Hence success for all students as an aim is fostering ambitions sure to be disappointed. This is in effect much more than an exhibition of inconsistency. It is a critique, though in abstract terms, of a competitive culture whose economic institutions are unable to carry out what the ideology promises to its people.

In part also the humanities hold back from facing the contemporary challenge because they carry the heavy weight of their own traditional elitism. Rather than seeing them as the last gasp of bourgeois culture, a more hopeful view of the humanities would maintain that elitism is not of their essence but only a historical residue. After all, American thought has not been without its ideal of a rich democratic culture, expressed for example in Walt Whitman's

Democratic Vistas, and the ideal of a higher education open to all the people has made considerable strides though too often negated in the very act of its expansion by a lack of faith in the capacities of the mass of human beings.

> Rosemary Park's "The Disestablished Humanities" comes closest to a democratic vista for the humanities for several reasons. She is dealing with the humanities outside of the academy and precisely because they are there widely scattered, she is compelled to take an all–society perspective. Her focus is accordingly on educational *functions* not particular institutions. While the university often looks to itself as an institution and thus may limit its sights to what it can do for itself in the circumstances, Park's perspective would ask what it could do educationally through all and any institutions in the society. Again, Park relates what gets done and what is desirable to basic changes in the character of life and knowledge: for example, the fact that one used to be able to get the knowledge needed for a lifetime in the early years, but now it takes a whole lifetime; as well as the rapidity of growth and the extent of novelty in knowledge itself. There is also the greater flexibility and freedom in the extra-academic institutions. (Paul Goodman once pointed out that one does not have to present academic credentials to take a book out of the library nor be examined on it when he returns it.) Finally, Park evaluates progress in all corners of the society—in the expansion of book publishing, of college extension work, even of the quality of commercials on TV.

> Robert Hanning's response, "A View from the Ivory Tower," is much more pessimistic, perhaps in part because he catches the impact of the current depression on the extra–academic cultural institutions. His lesson is their general vulnerability to manipulations of the profit motive and its vicissitudes in our society, and he hopes for more from the relation of the academy to the nonacademic cultural institutions.

Humanists certainly have ample ground to fear what happens to their fields when they are commercialized—in research grants as well as in television. But this is a problem of our whole life, affecting the sciences as well as the humanities. There is no answer but vigorous struggle, carried into the full arena of our culture, rather than a retreat behind a dubious Maginot line drawn within the university. There is ample room within for working at the reconciliation of the "two cultures" of science and the humanities, and there is ample room without for humanistic critique and creative development of a democratic culture.

On the question of attitudes to the prospects of mankind, the core lies obviously in technology and the changes it has brought. How intimately questions of value, attitude, and prediction of development are interwoven is clear from the influence that Ellul's *Technological Society* has had in evaluations of technology. It conveys the same mood for technological reckoning that Spengler's *Decline of the West* conveyed in its day for Western civilization. It is more philosophical in its scope than recent doomsday charts emanating from the Club of Rome, for the necessity it preaches concerns the decline of our values not merely our ability to achieve them. Ellul pictures technique becoming omnivoracious, bringing everything into line with large-scale technology and its corporatism, exalting the rationality of the means and enslaving ends. In the interpenetration of means and ends, we come eventually to hold only those debased ends that the machine allows, and so we are gladly enslaved for we get the material goods to which we then limit our desires. Ellul's position is, I think, open to criticism both on the conceptual side and the empirical side as well as for the neglect of alternatives all along the way. It is not so strong as to be faced only by a faith that mankind will not tolerate the outcome. We obviously cannot pursue the critique here. I raise it only to show how important is the humanistic task of a reckoning with technology and its works, and contributing to attitude and policy in facing the future.

In "Living with Scarcity," Roger Shinn seems to me to tap profoundly the problems involved for the humanities here. Considering the larger problems to be permanent not temporary crises, he sees that large–scale reorientations of under-standing, attitude, and policy are required. His sober probe of attitudes to scarcity and the ways of dealing with it could serve as a model of what humanistic learning can do to clarify alternative policies and their grounds. I am tempted to suggest one extension—that the different alternatives be set in their concrete historical contexts. After all, scarcity in preindustrial and prescientific societies has a different charac-ter from that found in industrial and postindustrial society although the situations (and the attitudes) may be analogous. So too, given solutions, like slavery or war, which impose the belt–tightening on a part of society or on one society instead of another, are quite different in ancient slave systems or empires, and in modern class relations within countries and between developed and undeveloped countries. In part, these points are made in Shinn's treatment of justice. In general, he calls for a more realistic attitude than simply oscillation between an excessive confidence in technology and an excessive resignation. (The extremes are symbolized by Prom-etheus and Atlas.) Similarly, while the dynamic factors in social change are some kinds of compulsion, rather than moral reasons, the ethical does make some differences. The situation does not dictate of itself, but in its interaction with commitments, loyalties, and values.

The practical effect of a humanistic analysis may be as immediate today as the effect of scientific generalization. A good example is the meteoric rise of the ethics of *triage* in recent times. This, and variant "life–boat" ethics, see the inevitability of growing scarcity and argue that resources should be apportioned to those countries likely to make the best use of them. Slowly developing countries hitherto unsuccessful in controlling population growth would, if assisted, grow still more populous and more needy. They would bring all closer to doomsday. The slowly developing countries would thus be abandoned to mass starvation.

Such a speculation has the character of an antiutopia. Problems have been raised about its assumptions, particularly that it holds institutional forms constant in its extrapolations, and therefore does not face the totality of issues which a really great crisis of global proportions requires. And there have been scientific objections too, that it has underestimated resources that are still available. But even if it is purely a speculative scenario, envisaging a possibility, it operates to distract us from our problems and responsibilities. It is not, however, pure speculation. It competes for national policy. Its effect on some of the world's poorest countries might very well be immediately disastrous. Not only do scenarios of the future today have practical import, but even the formulation of questions and judgment of priorities in facing questions also have critical effects.

There is a rising scale in the guidance of social action which seems to vary with the degree of complexity and flux in the human field. In stable, relatively simple situations with constant values, we guide ourselves by rules. Increase the complexity and change, and we use not rules but broad principles and standards of evaluation. A further increase, and we appeal to methods. Still further, and our methods may not be enough; we appeal to virtues: face the problems courageously, carefully, deliberately, considering all relevant factors. Still further, even virtues do not help us, for the courageous man may be blundering in the dark. Then we ask for at least a general attitude to life as a whole; then we talk of authenticity and deciding for all mankind. As a last step, in the greatest of complexities and transformations, we can hope for nothing but wisdom. Perhaps the contributions of the humanities to public policy are to be found in what they can bring from their heritage and their continued exercise in the cultivation of wisdom. But wisdom is not a separate light shining from outside. It is rather a full sense of how, in the historical present, knowledge and value and the practical situation operate in their constant interaction, and what our directive values require in knowledge and for action.

REFERENCES

1. Originally presented at one of the conferences on War and the Social Order, Adda Bozeman's "War and the Clash of Ideas" has appeared in *Orbis* 20 (April 1976): 61–102.
2. Originally presented at one of the conferences on Private Rights and the Public Good, Louis Henkin's "Privacy and Autonomy under the Constitution" has appeared in the *Columbia Law Review* 74 (1974): 1410–33.

Index

Adams, Henry, 182
Agency, of groups, 27–28
Analytic method. Modes of: Socratic, 61;
   positivist, 61–64; pragmatic, 62–63;
   ordinary language, 64; judging
   correctness of an analysis, 83–84,
   94–99; ordinary language mode in
   educational philosophy as
   subordinating educational experience,
   86–88; ignoring sociohistorical
   dimension, 89–91; presupposes a
   psychology of human action, 91;
   requires broader inventory of linguistic
   variety and change, 92–94; value and
   policy aspects, 100–103
Anthropology: and ethics, xx; contribution
   of mapping moralities, chap. 7; to
   understanding ethical theories, chap. 8;
   culture-at-a-distance studies, xviii; as
   discipline, xiv
Antigone: Sophocles' and Anouilh's
   compared, 237–38
Aquinas, Thomas, 225
Archimedes, 6
Arendt, Hannah, 304
Aristotle, 3, 38, 75, 79, 136; on form,
   167–70; on causes, 167–68; relevance
   to theory of art, 168–69, 173, 174,
   175–76; contrast with Plato, 178; 185,
   201, 204, 230; on the good man and
   the good citizen, 243–45; 252, 262,
   274, 279, 290, 303, 308, 311
Arnold, Matthew, 37, 48, 312
Arrow, Kenneth, 28
Augustine, 7
Austin, John, 55, 61, 69
Austin, J.L., 83, 103, 118, 125, 157
Authority; as basic category of citizenship,
   244; dissolution of, 257–58;
   replacement by participation, 259;
   authoritarian personality studied,
   282–83

Autonomy, contrasted with isolationism:
   isolationist tendency, vii; departmental,
   vii; boundaries, vii; connections, vii
Ayer, A.J., 156

Babbitt, Irving, 34, 52
Bacon, Edmund, 177, 179
Bacon, Francis, 308
Baier, Annette, on applied ethics, 228–29,
   230, 231
Baker, Russell, 232
Bateson, Gregory, 93
Benedict, Ruth, 49, 116, 125, 156, 194,
   240, 295
Bentham, Jeremy, 65, 66, 143, 262
Bentley, A.F., 43, 205
Berg, Ivar, vii
Bergson, Henri, 279, 285
Berman, Ronald, 212
Biddle, Francis, 230–31, 247, 275
Billington, David, 178, 179, 298
Biography, xiii, chap. 12; dependence on
   concept of a life, 183; and history,
   181; and science, 182; changing
   concept of a life, 191–93
Biomedical progress, resulting problem,
   309–310
Boas, Franz, 49, 179, 202, 286
Bork, Robert, 55
Boswell, James, 181
Bozeman, Adda, 28, 284, 315
Bradbrook, Muriel, 4
Bradley, F.H., 303
Brewster, Kingsman, 238
Bronowski, Jacob, 241, 278
Buber, Martin, 30, 93, 104, 306–07
Burke, Edmund, 27, 35, 259, 261, 275
Butler, Samuel, 309

Callahan, Daniel, 309–10
Carlyle, Thomas, 193
Carman, Harry, 307